THE IMPACT OF A SENSE OF
BELONGING IN COLLEGE

THE IMPACT OF A SENSE OF BELONGING IN COLLEGE

Implications for Student Persistence,

Retention, and Success

Edited by Erin M. Bentrim and

Gavin W. Henning

Foreword by Kristen A. Renn

STERLING, VIRGINIA

Published by Stylus Publishing, LLC.
22883 Quicksilver Drive
Sterling, Virginia 20166-2019

Library of Congress Cataloging-in-Publication Data

Names: Bentrim, Erin M, editor. | Henning, Gavin, editor.
Title: The impact of a sense of belonging in college : implications for student persistence,
   retention, and success / edited by Erin M. Bentrim and Gavin W. Henning.
Description: First Edition. | Sterling, Virginia : Stylus Publishing, LLC, [2022]
   | Includes bibliographical references and index. | Summary: "Over the last 10
   years, colleges and universities have started grappling with the notion that
   their approaches to maintaining and increasing student retention, persistence,
   and graduation rates were no longer working. As focus shifted to uncovering
   barriers to student success while concurrently recognizing student success
   as more than solely academic factors, the term "student sense of belonging"
   gained traction in both academic and co-curricular settings. The editors
   brought this book into being to serve as a single point of reference in an
   emerging and promising field of study"-- Provided by publisher.
Identifiers: LCCN 2022030284 (print) | LCCN 2022030285 (ebook) | ISBN
   9781642672619 (Paperback : acid-free paper) | ISBN 9781642672602 (Cloth
   : acid-free paper) | ISBN 9781642672626 (library networkable e-edition) |
   ISBN 9781642672633 (consumer e-edition)
Subjects: LCSH: College students--United States--Psychology. | College facilities-
   -Psychological aspects. | Belonging (Social psychology) | Place attachment.
Classification: LCC LA229 .I468 2022 (print) | LCC LA229 (ebook) | DDC
   378.1/980973--dc23/eng/20220706
LC record available at https://lccn.loc.gov/2022030284
LC ebook record available at https://lccn.loc.gov/2022030285

13-digit ISBN: 978-1-64267-260-2 (cloth)
13-digit ISBN: 978-1-64267-261-9 (paperback)
13-digit ISBN: 978-1-64267-262-6 (library networkable e-edition)
13-digit ISBN: 978-1-64267-263-3 (consumer e-edition)

Printed in the United States of America

All first editions printed on acid-free paper
that meets the American National Standards Institute
Z39-48 Standard.

Bulk Purchases

Quantity discounts are available for use in workshops and for
staff development.

Call 1-800-232-0223

First Edition, 2022

CONTENTS

PART ONE: THEORIES AND FOUNDATIONS

PART TWO: SENSE OF BELONGING ACROSS STUDENT POPULATIONS

LIST OF FIGURES

LIST OF TABLES

FOREWORD

For a long time, I've been a cautious skeptic about all the excitement surrounding the idea of *sense of belonging*. I've wondered if it is another well intentioned, buzzy concept that promises to be the silver bullet to "solve" student success. Is sense of belonging something that sounds like a good idea—after all, what campus curmudgeon could rant against people feeling like they belong—but lacks empirical evidence to support its reputation for promoting academic, social, personal, learning, and developmental outcomes? The book you are about to read has converted me from cautious skeptic to (still cautious, I admit) proponent of applying sense of belonging research to higher education practice. The authors here take seriously the questions I have had about how to define and measure sense of belonging and its impact on student experiences and outcomes.

Tracing the intellectual history of sense of belonging in higher education research and practice, it is clear that it entered an arena already full of familiar terms of *involvement, engagement, high-impact practices,* and *campus climate.* One of the appealing qualities of these terms is that they use commonsense language to succinctly convey sometimes abstract concepts. They describe how students interact with and experience postsecondary environments. One of their downsides, however, is that the terms are so familiar and straightforward sounding that they are picked up quickly in the field and take on lives of their own outside the small communities of researchers who are trying to define, extend, measure, and describe them. Untangling the terms has become its own subfield of higher education research (see Terrell Strayhorn's chapter 2 in this book, as well as Lisa Wolf-Wendel, Kelly Ward, and Jillian Kinzie's classic 2009 article on this topic). By clearly articulating the theoretical evolution of the term sense of belonging for higher education, Annemarie Vaccaro and Barbara Newman (chapter one in this book) make a clear explanation of what it is and is not. These two chapters together, if read by every student affairs professional aiming to increase sense of belonging on their campus, will go a long way in redirecting the field into more theory-informed practice.

The remaining chapters of the book make a clear and compelling research-based case for understanding and amplifying student sense of belonging and its role in outcomes that higher education professionals value, including but not limited to student persistence. They show that sometimes a buzzy idea is more than superficial. In this case they show that a coherent body of research like the one presented in this book supports the versatility and depth of sense of belonging in relation to campus environments, student experiences, and the interactions between them.

It was this body of research that nudged me away from cautious skepticism about the hold sense of belonging has taken on the imagination of student affairs and student success professionals. But it has left me with some questions that are worth considering when undertaking research and practice utilizing sense of belonging as a starting point. Something the field seems to have learned from picking up on ideas like involvement, engagement, and grit/resilience is that those ideas start with individuals, not the environments we in higher education construct. They become easy ways to shift responsibility from institutions to students: this student should be more involved, that one opted out of high impact practices, that other one lacks resilience. To be fair, some scholars long ago made a shift from focusing only on student involvement as first described by Astin (1984) to "involving colleges" (Kuh, 1991), drawing attention to the ways that some campus environments promoted behaviors and attitudes related to positive student involvement. Even so, higher education has retained a bias in the direction of welcoming "college-ready students" rather than transforming into an ecosystem of "student-ready colleges" (McNair et al., 2016).

Sense of belonging is rooted in the individual experience, but like campus climate the concept shifts attention and responsibility in the direction of institutions and institutional culture. It starts as a research and practice perspective by looking at student-environment interactions and their effects on the student. It is both a describable and measurable end in itself—the extent to which individual students from different backgrounds feel a sense of belonging and a factor in the complex interactions that influence learning, development, persistence, well-being, and a host of other outcomes of intense interest to educators, students, and other stakeholders. The chapters in this book clarify both of these processes: how sense of belonging is influenced and how it influences other outcomes.

Reading theoretical and empirical writing about sense of belonging, where it comes from, and how it operates in student experiences raises another question for me: What are we in higher education doing to make our institutions and systems worth belonging to? Even after shifting our focus from individual student responsibility for success to institutional responsibility for cultivating sense of belonging, I wonder if in my enthusiasm for, and actions directed toward, getting students to feel like they belong I am ignoring key questions related to "belonging to *what?*" and "at what cost?"

Am I asking students to invest so much of their own spirit and resources in my organization that they convince themselves that they belong, because to do otherwise would raise cognitive dissonance? Am I inadvertently putting them through hardships that act like watered-down hazing rituals, which coming out the other side of they feel the sense of belonging of survivors? Do I want them to belong to the ideal higher education of my imagination, or am I willing if our ideals differ to give up my fondly held visions to transform into theirs? Certainly I want students to feel like they belong, but not if that means they are silencing internal voices that ask, "Couldn't higher education be even more, even better, more inclusive, less violent?"

I pose these final questions as a companion to the important writing on sense of belonging that you will read in this book. Many authors here are considering these and related questions, even as they explain and study how sense of belonging develops and works for students in higher education. These questions are the source of my "still cautious" stance as a proponent for sense of belonging studies and action in higher education. They keep me honest in my embrace of this way of thinking about our collective work, and inspire me to work toward increasing students' sense of belonging while also challenging higher education to be a place worthy of belonging to.

—Kristen A. Renn
Michigan State University

References

Astin, A. W. (1984). Student involvement: A developmental theory for higher education. *Journal of College Student Personnel, 25*(4), 297–308.

Kuh, G. (1991). *Involving colleges: Successful approaches to fostering student learning and development outside the classroom.* Jossey-Bass.

McNair, T. B., Albertine, S., Cooper, M. A., McDonald, N., & Major, Jr., T. (2016). *Becoming a student-ready college: A new culture of leadership for student success.* John Wiley & Sons.

Wolf-Wendel, L., Ward, K., & Kinzie, J. L. (2009). A tangled web of terms: The overlap and unique contribution of involvement, engagement, and integration to understanding college student success. *Journal of College Student Development, 50*(4), 407–428. https://doi.org/10.1353/csd.0.0077

Student success in postsecondary institutions is determined and measured primarily by academic preparation (i.e., matriculation) and adequate grade point averages (i.e., graduation). However, by using a singular, academic focus on the tools (academic advising, tutoring centers, study skills workshops, etc.) needed to achieve academic success as a way of getting students to the graduation stage, institutions overlook the more complex issues students as people and the environment of the campus community experience beyond the classroom. Furthermore, it is an inherently deficit-minded approach to student success, as the focus is on what students are lacking that limits their academic success.

Over the past 10 years, colleges and universities have started grappling with the notion that historical approaches to maintaining and increasing student retention, persistence, and graduation rates were increasingly ineffectual. As conversations shifted to uncovering barriers to student success while concurrently recognizing student success as more than solely academic factors, we observed on our own campuses that the term *student sense of belonging* seemed to have gained traction in both academic and cocurricular settings. What we also noticed in these conversations around a sense of belonging was the lack of a consistent definition or an overarching theoretical approach as well as the struggle to connect disparate research. While sound research regarding the impact of a college student's sense of belonging is indeed available, it is strewn across the literature. A compendium of research, applications, and approaches to sense of belonging did not exist. It is our vision that this book will serve as a single point of reference in an emerging and promising field of study. We are pleased to bring together researchers and authors of consequence who are well versed in the field of college students and sense of belonging into one volume. We hope you find this book to be a valuable tool.

PART ONE

THEORIES AND FOUNDATIONS

THEORETICAL FOUNDATIONS FOR SENSE OF BELONGING IN COLLEGE

Annemarie Vaccaro and Barbara Newman

In this chapter, we take a theoretical approach to the development of belonging. We begin by synthesizing a decade of our own grounded theory research. Our work points to key influences that shape student belonging, including the campus environment; relationships with peers and educators; involvement opportunities; and academic success, including mastery of the student role. In the second half of the chapter, we honor the work of prior scholars who have theorized belonging. We begin by examining the roots of belonging, including the notion that belonging is a fundamental universal motivation. Then, we provide a very brief overview of evolutionary theory, social cognitive neuroscience, and psychosocial development. Combined, these historical perspectives offer valuable insight into why belonging is, and has been, such an essential aspect of the life experiences for all human beings—including college students.

Our Theoretical Work on College Student Belonging

As teachers and scholars committed to fostering the holistic development of all college students, we are interested in the processes by which students define and develop a *sense of belonging*. Empirical research points to the benefits of belonging, including academic motivation, success, and persistence (Freeman et al., 2007; Hausmann et al., 2007; Hoffman et al., 2002; Strayhorn, 2012, 2019). We contend that only by understanding the process of belonging development can educators design curricula, programs, services, and policies to better facilitate this development in students. As such, we embarked on a multiyear qualitative study to better understand the development of belonging among diverse college students. Students who participated in our research spoke of belonging at academic, interpersonal, environmental, and cocurricular levels. Our analysis led to an overarching theoretical model of belonging for privileged and minoritized students (Vaccaro & Newman, 2016) as well as in-depth explorations of belonging for particular social identity groups, including lesbian, gay, bisexual, and pansexual students (Vaccaro & Newman, 2017); first-generation women of color students (Vaccaro, Marcotte et al., 2019; Vaccaro, Swanson et al., 2019); and students with disabilities (Vaccaro et al., 2015).

Through intensive interviews with more than 50 undergraduate students, we found that there were both similarities and differences in the ways that students from privileged and minoritized social identity groups defined and developed a sense of belonging. All students noted how three key factors influenced a sense of belonging: the campus environment, involvement in curricular and extracurricular activities, and relationships with peers and educators. We use italicized text throughout this chapter to highlight these common themes. Through ongoing research, we learned that college students from social identity groups who experienced historic and pervasive deficit stereotypes about lack of academic ability or capabilities (e.g., students with disabilities, students of color, first-generation students) added another key element—academic success and/or mastery of the student role. Our work, along with the scholarly precedent (noted later in the chapter), led us to the following theoretical conclusions:

Belonging as a developmental process is rooted in basic human needs to be safe and respected and to comfortably fit in as our authentic selves. As students move into and through college, they develop a sense of belonging as they navigate welcoming and unwelcoming campus environments, engage in involvement in curricular and extracurricular activities, develop relationships with peers and faculty, and achieve academic success and mastery of the student role. Belonging is inherently tied to our social identities and the nuanced forms of oppression experienced, and resisted by, students from minoritized social identity groups. Therefore, the strategies to foster belonging must be equally as nuanced to address both systems of oppression embedded in the environment and biases enacted via relationships by members of the campus community. Although many of our participants fostered belonging via involvement in organizations where they could be their authentic selves, we contend that institutions must not rely solely on student involvement to foster belonging. Instead, campuses must take a comprehensive and holistic approach to fostering belonging for diverse college students.

Figure 1.1 represents the results from our first and overarching grounded theory (Vaccaro & Newman, 2016). That model highlights three elements that all participants described as salient to their process of developing a sense of belonging in college: environment, involvement, and relationships. Figure 1.1 includes four sets of paired circles to highlight the overlapping, as well as nuanced ways that students from minoritized and privileged social identity groups experienced the campus environment, involvement, and relationships, and in turn made meaning of and developed a sense of belonging.

Figure 1.1. Model of belonging for privileged and minoritized students.

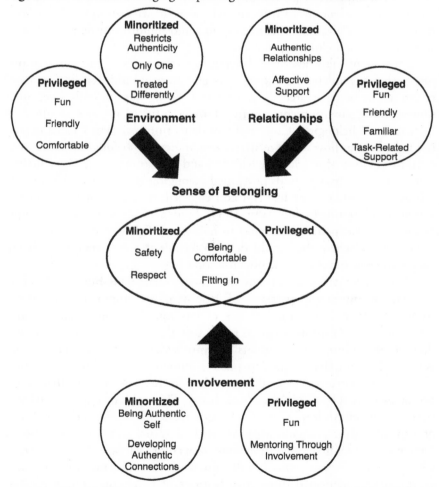

Vaccaro, A., & Newman, B. M. (2016). The development of a sense of belonging for privileged and minoritized students: An emerging model. *Journal of College Student Development, 57*(8), 925–942. Reprinted with permission.

For instance, being *comfortable* and *fitting in* were terms used by all participants to define *belonging*. However, students from minoritized groups also added notions of safety and respect as essential elements to their descriptions of the concepts of belonging.

Students from privileged and minoritized groups talked about the importance of social relationships to the development of belonging. Those with privileged identities developed belonging if they felt a sense of familiarity with peers who were also fun and friendly. In essence, they could develop belonging via surface-level relationships where they garnered task-related support (e.g., homework help) from fun and friendly peers. Conversely, students from minoritized social identity groups talked about the necessity of gleaning affective support and building authentic relationships to develop belonging.

All students also described differences in the types of campus environments that engendered belonging. Students from minoritized backgrounds talked about being treated differently and feeling like the only one. Such unwelcoming environments restricted their authenticity and diminished their sense of belonging. Conversely, students from privileged social identities talked about how it was relatively easy to develop belonging because the campus environment felt fun, friendly, and comfortable. Finally, students from privileged backgrounds developed belonging via involvement in campus activities where they had fun and engaged in actions that engendered feelings of mattering (Schlossberg, 1984). Students from minoritized groups, however, only experienced a boost to belonging if they found involvement opportunities where they could develop meaningful connections by being their authentic selves in those organizations.

The model offers an overarching theory that helps higher educators understand important patterns of belonging development for college students. These contrasting images of environments, involvement, and relationships did capture the lived realities of all our participants. That said, dichotomous grouping of students into minoritized or privileged categories is somewhat simplistic. Students possess numerous intersecting identities. As such, we continued to analyze our data to uncover nuances that could not be explained by a single, unified theory. Through our ongoing analytic process, we delved deeply into the unique ways that various social identity groups, including students with minoritized sexual identities (Vaccaro & Newman, 2017), first-generation women of color (Vaccaro, Marcotte et al., 2019; Vaccaro, Swanson et al., 2019), and students with disabilities (Vaccaro et al., 2015), identified distinctive features of belonging. The following sections build on Figure 1.1 and offer additional theoretic insight into the belonging experiences of diverse college students.

Belonging for Students With Disabilities

Students with disabilities noted a host of unique influences on their development of collegiate belonging (see Figure 1.2). Three interconnected and mutually constituting factors contributed to a sense of belonging for college students with disabilities. The first theme, social relationships, mirrors those described in Figure 1.1. However, the other two factors are specifically relevant to college students with disabilities who often face stereotypes implying that they will not be successful in college. As such, an important part of belonging is students' ability to master the role of successful college student. Students felt like they belonged in the campus environment when they fit in with their classmates. Mastery of the student role included not only earning good grades, but also "'feeling like a college student' by blending in with peers, being viewed as a legitimate student, and gaining recognition for academic success" (Vaccaro et al., 2015, p. 679). Finally, students with disabilities specifically noted that their sense of belonging was intricately tied to their ability to self-advocate inside and outside the classroom (e.g., involvement). See Vaccaro et al. (2015) for a comprehensive discussion of this theoretical model.

Figure 1.2. Theoretical model of belonging for college students with disabilities.

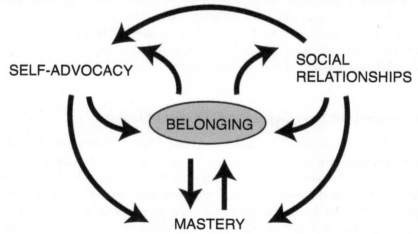

Vaccaro, A., Daly-Cano, M., & Newman, B. M. (2015). A sense of belonging among college students with disabilities: An emergent theoretical model. *Journal of College Student Development, 56*(7), 670–686. Reprinted with permission.

Belonging for Lesbian, Gay, Bisexual and Pansexual (LGBP) Students

As we delved deeply into the experiences of lesbian, gay, bisexual, and pansexual (LGBP) study participants, we uncovered additional theoretical insights related to LGBP belonging. Specifically, we noted four theoretical propositions that summarize the complex relationship LGBP students had with the key categories of belonging (environment, relationships, involvement), as described in Figure 1.1. Our LGBP participants explained how campus messaging about the inclusion of students with minoritized sexual and/or gender identities (MIoSG; Vaccaro et al., 2015)—often via websites, marketing materials, and safe zone signs on campus—was critical to their perceptions of how well they fit into the campus environment. In terms of relationships, LGBP students expressed varying types of belonging: university, group, and friendship—leading us to acknowledge that viewing belonging through a university-wide lens does not sufficiently capture the complicated realities of LGBP students. LGBP students also found casual friendships to be insufficient to the development of belonging. To develop belonging, students needed authentic relationships with peers and groups (often via club involvement), which requires a certain level of comfort with sexual identity, outness, and time to develop. Finally, as their sexual identities evolve, students' perspectives on, and needs for, relationships via group belonging and involvement changed. This has implications for relationships and group involvement in campus organizations (e.g., pride organizations, LGBTQ centers); students described fluctuations in their needs and desires to participate in such involvement opportunities that evolved as their social identities and other campus relationships evolved. In sum, this work offers several theoretical propositions that explicate how perspectives on, and needs for, belonging change over time. As such, we urge educators not to view belonging as a fixed and unchanging developmental milestone.

Belonging for First-Generation Women of Color

Our data also pointed to new understandings of belonging for first-generation women of color (Vaccaro, Marcotte et al., 2019; Vaccaro, Swanson et al., 2019). Powerful narratives from these participants helped us see how women developed a sense of belonging as they transitioned from high school to the college environment. Although their parents had not attended college, their family members possessed valuable insight and imparted much insight (i.e., funds of knowledge; Kiyama & Rios-Aguilar, 2018) about effectively navigating new campus environments. First-generation women of color described how their sense of belonging was diminished when their hopes and expectations for a diverse campus learning environment—as promised in university marketing materials—went unfulfilled. Women of color hoped for a racially diverse environment where their cultural heritage would be valued and diversity dialogues would be the norm. When they encountered a campus environment where they were "the only" woman of color in classes and where they felt excluded by White peers, it was difficult to develop authentic relationships and, in turn, a sense of belonging.

First-generation women of color also described the challenge of developing authentic relationships with White peers who lacked cultural competency, or who failed to express a desire to be more inclusive. Constant interactions with peers who were explicitly and/or implicitly exclusionary contributed to the already unwelcoming predominantly White campus environment. In the face of these challenges, first-generation women of color joined student organizations and programs designed for minoritized populations (e.g., campus cultural organizations, multicultural groups, diversity centers). Such involvement opportunities contributed to the development of a positive sense of belonging. First-generation students encountered, and resisted, deficit assumptions about their academic capabilities. As such, they noted that keeping an academic focus, being a serious student, and earning good grades fostered their sense of belonging. In essence, their sense of belonging relied on academic success and mastery of the student role.

In sum, our research offers theoretical insights into the development of the sense of belonging for college students. The developmental process of fostering belonging is interwoven with the social identity development of diverse college students and is influenced by the campus environment, relationships, and involvement opportunities as well as a need to master the student role and achieve academic success. Our work offers useful insight into the development of belonging, but it is certainly not the only theoretical perspective readers should be familiar with. In the remainder of this chapter, we explore historical scholarship that points to conceptual and theoretical roots of our modern-day understandings of belonging.

Belonging: Theoretical History and Roots

Although this volume focuses on college student belonging, we thought readers should have a sense of the history and roots of this important theoretical concept. In this section, we summarize literature pointing to belonging as a basic human need.

A Basic Human Need

Oft-cited belonging scholarship from higher education (Strayhorn, 2012, 2019) and psychology (Baumeister & Leary, 1995) argue that the need to belong is a basic motivation, common to all humans. They acknowledge prior theoretical works that identify the importance of close, interpersonal relationships for development, health, and psychosocial well-being.

In his model of motivation, Murray (1938) identified affiliation as a major drive. People with a strong need for affiliation require warm interpersonal relationships and approval from those with whom they have regular contact. McClelland (1961) extended this idea, arguing that three universal needs—the need for power, the need for achievement, and the need for affiliation—are present across cultures. However, individuals learn through socialization and cultural contexts to prioritize their needs so that one of these motives dominates the others in shaping behavior. The drive for *affiliation* was defined as a person's need to feel a sense of involvement and belonging within a social group (McClelland, 1961).

Maslow (1968) theorized that there is a continuing motivational press toward growth. His famous model presents motivation as a pyramid with more essential survival needs at the bottom, including the satisfaction of physiological needs of hunger, thirst, and sleep, and the motivation for self-actualization at the top. Love and belongingness needs include friendship, intimate relationships, family and kinship ties, and chosen group belonging is located on the third step of the pyramid, above safety and security needs, and below needs for self-esteem, confidence, and achievement motives. Maslow suggested that one can only address higher levels of motivation once lower, and more essential needs, have been satisfied. According to this view, the need to experience and satisfy belonging is a prerequisite for personal esteem and the full expression of self-actualization.

Many empirical studies with college students reference Strayhorn's (2012, 2019) theory of belonging, which uses Maslow's work as a foundation. Initially proposed in 2012, the revised model (Strayhorn, 2019) situates college student belonging within an adaptation of Maslow's pyramid-shaped hierarchy. In Strayhorn's (2019) book, the pyramid is flanked on either side by one vertical arrow reflecting baseline status and the other basic functions. The arrows begin at the pyramid base (psychological needs) and point upward toward self-actualization. A student's "fullest potential" and a school's "educational mission" are aligned with the top of the pyramid (Strayhorn, 2019, p. 41). Strayhorn (2019) also contends that there are seven core elements of a sense of belonging:

- Sense of belonging is a basic human need.
- Sense of belonging is a fundamental motive, sufficient to drive human behavior.
- Sense of belonging takes on heightened importance in (a) certain contexts . . . [and] (b) at certain times.

- Sense of belonging is related to, and seemingly a consequence of, mattering.
- Social identities intersect and affect college students' sense of belonging.
- Sense of belonging engenders other positive outcomes.
- Sense of belonging must be satisfied on a continual basis and likely changes as circumstances, conditions and contexts change. (pp. 29–40)

In Strayhorn's (2019) book, these elements and visual model are revisited in subsequent chapters that report findings of empirical studies with a variety of student populations. These independent studies offer a glimpse into the ways students in those studies made meaning of belonging.

Bowlby's (1969/1982, 1988) work on attachment is not a theory of motivation per se, but a conceptualization of the basic processes through which enduring emotional ties are formed. His work focuses on the organized pattern of infant signals and caregiver responses that lead to a protective, trusting relationship. Infants form an attachment to their responsive caregiver, resulting in an internal mental representation of the other, and expectations that distress will be relieved and comfort provided. This attachment representation is carried forward as a basis for the establishment of close friendships in childhood and adolescence, romantic relationships in adolescence and adulthood, and parenting relationships as adults engage in the care of their own children (Schneider et al., 2001; Shaver & Mikulincer, 2011). One interpretation of the need to belong is that it is an expression of the early and profound desire to be integrated into protective relationships that will offer security, care, and affection—especially under conditions of threat or distress. This view of belonging highlights the importance of each person's history of close, meaningful relationships. Educators must take into account that college students come to the new collegiate setting with prior expectations and experiences about whether, and how, they have felt valued and safe within the context of interpersonal relationships.

In contrast to these aforementioned theories, Baumeister and Leary (1995) proposed a more detailed consideration of what constitutes the universal need for belonging, including hypotheses about criteria necessary for satisfying that need:

> Satisfying this drive involves two criteria: First, there is a need for frequent, affectively pleasant interactions with a few other people; and second, these interactions must take place in the context of a temporally stable and enduring framework of affective concern for each other's welfare. (p. 497)

Baumeister and Leary (1995) also stated that belonging, as a universal human need, drives individuals to behave in ways that remove obstacles or creatively seek substitutes for belonging. Through their writing, Baumeister and Leary (1995) further contend that belonging is associated with happiness and a sense of well-being, whereas diminished belonging is associated with anxiety, depression, and other forms of emotional distress. It is no wonder that Baumeister and Leary are often cited by higher education scholars studying collegiate belonging.

Additional Theoretical Perspectives on Belonging

In line with the view that the need to belong is a fundamental universal motivation, we examine three sources of explanation: evolutionary theory, social cognitive neuroscience, and psychosocial development. In this short chapter, we cannot offer a comprehensive review of these theories. Instead, we offer readers a glimpse into an array of multidisciplinary theoretical perspectives to contextualize contemporary understandings of belonging.

Evolutionary Theory and the Need to Belong

Evolutionary theory harkens back to a time when human ancestors lived in small nomadic groups, traveling from place to place to find sources of food and trying to protect themselves from the dangers of predatory animals, weather, illness, and other humans. Because of their relatively long period of dependence, infants' survival required being well integrated and cared for by adults. Thus, infancy and families are coadapted: Infants require the support of a group of others, and families are organized to care for infants in order to ensure their survival. The human mind, carried forward over thousands of generations, is organized to monitor social connections and to detect inadequate social bonds as a source of threat to survival. Thus, evolutionary theory requires an appreciation for the deeply implanted aspect of human nature to strive to establish and maintain a sense of group belonging, and to experience emotions associated with loneliness when social connections are inadequate.

Experiences of loneliness, social exclusion, and social rejection are associated with observable consequences, including sleep disturbances, longer time for wound healing, difficulty with communication, and emotional guardedness, that disrupt efforts to form new relationships (Baumeister et al., 2007; Cacioppo & Cacioppo, 2012). Baumeister and Leary (1995) argued that when relationships that satisfy the need to belong are disrupted, a person will strive to replace those relationships. However, not all meaningful relationships are readily substituted (e.g., long-term friendships or loving bonds with a life partner). Experiences associated with social exclusion or perceived social rejection may impede efforts to establish meaningful replacements by creating a new sense of cautiousness in anticipation of future rejection.

Evolutionary theory also introduces ideas about the adaptive value of being a member of a group that have special relevance for adolescents and young adults (Caporael & Baron, 1997; Gibbons, 2018; Hauser, 2006, Seligman, 2011). Whereas the metaphor of survival of the fittest suggests traits that benefit individuals, evolutionary theory considers the skills of communication, cooperation, and sociability as traits that may have advanced the species as a whole (Seligman, 2011). According to an evolutionary view, morality, especially altruism and care for others, as well as fairness and reciprocity in social interactions, help to sustain families and bind members of groups together. Early human groups that were able to create a moral code that rewarded and increased behaviors beneficial to the group (and that punished or reduced selfishness) would have been more successful in attracting new members and fighting off competing groups. Thus, morality is thought to have co-evolved with the formation of larger human communities in which individuals are tied together beyond the basis of immediate kinship. As part of this process, rites, rituals, and institutions have emerged that link emotions, motor behaviors, and states of consciousness of large groups of people such that they are more attuned to one another than to members of out-groups and more willing to share resources, behave in a caring way, and exhibit loyalty to others in their group (Hauser, 2006).

In sum, the evolutionary emphasis is on the benefit of moral emotions for the protection and preservation of the group. They operate to build and strengthen communal bonds, creating a framework for how people should treat others, how they expect others to treat them, and how they should function in a larger social group. They all have implications for the creation of a sense of group belonging and its ability to endure across time and settings.

Social Cognitive Neuroscience and the Need to Belong

With advances in technology, social cognitive neuroscience has begun to explore how the human brain and related hormonal systems function to be attuned to social information, monitor social connections, detect cues for trustworthiness and threat, and assess when social connections are adequate. The neuroscience of attachment, the neuroscience of adolescent sensitivity to social rewards, and the neuroscience of social rejection are explored to illustrate the functional ties between neural functioning and the sense of belonging.

The Neuroscience of Attachment

As Coan (2008) suggested, the whole brain can be considered as an attachment system that uses its hearing, vision, touch, smell, movement areas, memory, affect regulation, and stress/threat responses to form an integrated internal working model of the object of attachment. Numerous features of the neuroscience of social cognition help to account for the rapid and universal capacity for humans to form social ties and establish a sense of belonging.

In the first months of life, efforts that a caregiver makes to comfort, soothe, and respond to infant distress shape the neural pathways associated with memory of care, instigate cues for the release of hormones, and build an embodied set of expectations about the nature of this social contact (Schore, 2013; Vatička & Vuilleumier, 2012). Basic, largely automatic emotional assessments and related responses are gradually modulated and interpreted by voluntary cognitive control processes. Early experiences of sensitive care shape neural pathways that provide a basis for subsequent expectations of comfort and reassurance in meaningful social groups, and in turn may influence human needs for belonging.

Adolescent Sensitivity to Rewards

Adolescents are especially sensitive to rewards (Galván, 2013; Paus, 2009). The reward circuitry of the brain is responsible for producing dopamine, a neurotransmitter that is released during pleasurable experiences; it encourages actions toward anticipated rewarding or pleasurable experiences. This circuitry is more active among adolescents than among children or adults (Telzer, 2016). Social cognitive neuroscience research suggests that adolescents are increasingly attuned to interpersonal and social cues such as facial expressions, hand gestures, and body movements that convey approval or disapproval. Adolescents' emotional reactions are especially intense as the brain processes information relevant to social evaluation (Somerville, 2013). The adaptive value of reading social cues, especially for detecting threat and for assessing potential friendship and romantic relationships, makes the increased sensitivity to complex social expressions all the more relevant to the development of social competence and the establishment of group belonging in early adolescence (Garcia & Scherf, 2015). Whereas some teens may find that risky behaviors are accompanied by the dopamine rush, others find this same surge of reward-related glow from contributing in meaningful ways to the well-being of their families, friends, or communities (Telzer, 2016). Regardless of whether the peer culture is prosocial or antisocial, peer group belonging can contribute to the stimulation of this reward circuitry.

The Neuroscience of Social Rejection

Evolutionary theory points to the essential survival need to maintain social ties. Thus, when examining motivations to sustain the sense of belonging, it is important to consider how the brain processes threats of social rejection or social isolation. Neuroimaging research has shown that there is overlapping neural circuitry that processes physical pain and the distress associated with social rejection or exclusion (Eisenberger & Lieberman, 2004). Physical pain is typically assessed along two related but separate dimensions: the intensity of the pain and the distress or suffering experienced by the person who is in pain (Price, 2000). Several areas of the brain are activated when a person experiences physical pain. One that plays a large role in the affective experience of suffering is the dorsal anterior cingulate cortex (dACC), "a large structure on the medial wall of the frontal lobe" (Eisenberger, 2011, p. 55). Under experimental conditions, this same area of the brain has been found to be activated when a person experiences social exclusion (Eisenberger et al., 2003). People who report more feelings of social rejection in their daily lives also show greater pain-related activity in this neural region under experimental conditions of social rejection (Eisenberger et al., 2007).

The evidence from social cognitive neuroscience informs our appreciation for the processes that support the search for a sense of belonging, as adolescents and young adults in particular, transition to college. Students are sensitive to cues that signal acceptance or rejection; they may experience salient feelings of pleasure as they encounter satisfying social acceptance and distress in the face of social isolation or rejection. Whereas evolutionary theory suggests ancestral origins for the human need to experience belonging, neuroscience provides insights into how that need is embedded and activated in contemporary mental activity.

Psychosocial Development and the Need to Belong

Psychosocial theory explains changes in self-understanding, social relationships, and one's relationship to society as a product of interactions among biological, psychological, and societal systems (Erikson, 1950/1993). From the psychosocial perspective, development results from the continuous interaction of an individual and their social environments. At each period of life, people attempt to master a unique group of psychological tasks that are essential for social adaptation within their society. Psychosocial theories highlight major themes that arise as individuals strive to form, and preserve, meaningful social ties within the context of their social world while creating and preserving a sense of an authentic self. Each life stage brings a normative crisis, a tension between one's competencies at the beginning of the stage and the new demands of society. A positive resolution of each crisis provides new social abilities that enhance a person's capacity to adapt successfully in the succeeding stages. A negative resolution of a crisis typically results in defensiveness, rigidity, or withdrawal, which decreases a person's ability to adapt successfully in succeeding stages.

Throughout life, tensions arise between desires for individuality and for connection. Certain cultures emphasize connection over individuality, whereas others put individuality ahead of connection. However, all societies and cultures have strategies to address both aspects of the ego: the I as agent, originator, and executive of one's individual thoughts and actions, and the we as agent, originator, and executive of collective, cooperative enterprises that preserve and further the survival of the group (Triandis, 1990). During early adolescence, one confronts a new psychosocial conflict, group identity versus alienation, in which pressures to ally oneself with specific groups and find ways of functioning comfortably as a member of a group are major preoccupations (Newman & Newman, 2001). In early adolescence, young people form an integrated set of ideas about the norms, expectations, and status hierarchy of the salient groups in their social world. They build these representations from reference groups, the groups of which they are members or in which they aspire to hold membership (Gurin & Markus, 1988). Adolescents experience a search for membership—an internal questioning about the groups of which they are most naturally a part. They ask themselves, "Who am I, and with whom do I belong?" Although membership in a peer group may be the most pressing concern, questions about other group identifications also arise.

Four processes contribute to the formation of group identity (Newman & Newman, 2001, 2018). First, adolescents begin to recognize the distinguishing features of the social groups in their environment. Second, they have a history of repeated interactions with one or more groups. They may participate in formalized initiation rituals or informal activities that bind them to the group. Third, group identity takes shape as adolescents experience deepening emotional ties to other members of the group and a sense of loyalty to the group. Group identity is typically associated with a willingness to view members of their own group more favorably than outsiders (Mullen et al., 1992). Finally, adolescents recognize the place or status of their group within the larger social landscape of their school and community. They recognize how their group is viewed by others, and they form views of how valued or important their group is in comparison to others. Positive judgments about a group can foster a strong commitment to the group identity. Conversely, being a target of discrimination or social rejection can also strengthen one's personal pride in being a part of a marginalized group (Williams & Thornton, 1998).

In the process of seeking group affiliation, adolescents are confronted by the fit—or lack of fit—between their personal needs and the norms and values of relevant social groups in the environment. In a positive resolution of the conflict of group identity versus alienation, adolescents discover one or more groups that provide them with a sense of group belonging, meet their social needs, and allow them to express their social selves. In a negative resolution of the conflict, adolescents experience a sense of social estrangement, inadequate social support, or a lack of meaningful connections to valued groups.

The psychosocial perspective suggests that students' past experiences of group identity serve as a filter as they strive to experience a sense of belonging in the college environment. As our own theoretical models (Vaccaro & Newman, 2016, 2017; Vaccaro et al., 2015; Vaccaro, Marcotte et al., 2019; Vaccaro, Swanson et al., 2019) suggest, this process unfolds differently for students with diverse social identities depending on the messages they encounter about the fit, or lack of fit, between their needs and values, perception of environmental cues, interpersonal relationships, and opportunities for meaningful involvement in campus life.

Conclusion

In this chapter, we introduced readers to a variety of theoretical perspectives on belonging. We began the chapter by sharing our own theoretical understandings about belonging for college students. We contend that the developmental process of belonging is interwoven with the social identity development of diverse college students. Moreover, belonging is influenced by the campus environment, relationships, and involvement opportunities as well as a need to master the student role and achieve academic success. Our work contributes to a growing body of literature about belonging. As such, part of this chapter is dedicated to scholarship, from multiple disciplines, that contributes to conceptual and theoretical roots of our modern-day understandings of belonging. Taken together, these theoretical works provide a complex foundation for educational efforts to foster belonging in diverse college students.

References

Baumeister, R. F., Brewer, L. E., Tice, D. M., & Twenge, J. M. (2007). Thwarting the need to belong: Understanding the interpersonal and inner effects of social exclusion. *Social and Personality Psychology Compass, 1*(1), 506–520. https://doi .org/10.1111/j.1751-9004.2007.00020.x

Baumeister, R. F., & Leary, M. R. (1995). The need to belong: Desire for interpersonal attachments as a fundamental human motivation. *Psychological Bulletin*, *117*(3), 497–529. https://doi.org/10.1037/0033-2909.117.3.497

Bowlby, J. (1982). *Attachment*. Basic Books. (Original work published 1969)

Bowlby, J. (1988). *A secure base: Parent-child attachment and healthy human development*. Basic Books.

Cacioppo, J. T., & Cacioppo, S. (2012). The phenotype of loneliness. *European Journal of Developmental Psychology*, *9*(4), 446–452. https://doi.org/10.1080/17 405629.2012.690510

Caporael, L. R., & Baron, R. M. (1997). Groups as the mind's natural environment. In J. Simpson & D. Kenrick (Eds.), *Evolutionary social psychology* (pp. 317–342). Erlbaum.

Coan, J. (2008). Toward a neuroscience of attachment. In J. Cassidy & P. R. Shaver (Eds.), *Handbook of attachment: Theory, research, and clinical applications* (pp. 241–268). Guilford.

Eisenberger, N. (2011). The neural basis of social pain: Findings and implications. In G. MacDonald & L. A. Jensen-Campbell (Eds.), *Social pain: Neuropsychological and health implications of loss and exclusion* (pp. 53–78). American Psychological Association. https://doi.org/10.1037/12351-002

Eisenberger, N. I., Gable, S. L., & Lieberman, M. D. (2007). Functional magnetic resonance imaging responses relate to differences in real-world social experience. *Emotion*, *7*(4), 745–754. https://doi.org/10.1037/1528-3542.7.4.745

Eisenberger, N., & Lieberman, M. D. (2004). Why rejection hurts: A common neural alarm system for physical and social pain. *Trends in Cognitive Sciences*, *8*(7), 294–300. https://doi.org/10.1016/j.tics.2004.05.010

Eisenberger, N., Lieberman, M. D., & Williams, K. D. (2003). Does rejection hurt? An fMRI study of social exclusion. *Science*, *302*(5643), 290–292. https://doi.org/10.1126/science.1089134

Erikson, E. H. (1993). *Childhood and society* (2nd ed.). Norton. (Original work published 1950)

Freeman, T. M., Anderman, L. H., & Jensen, J. M. (2007). Sense of belonging in college freshmen at the classroom and campus levels. *Journal of Experimental Education*, *75*(3), 203–220. https://doi.org/10.3200/JEXE.75.3.203-220

Galván, A. (2013). The teenage brain: Sensitivity to rewards. *Current Directions in Psychological Science*, *22*(2), 100–105. https://doi.org/10.1177/0963721413480859

Garcia, N. V., & Scherf, K. S. (2015). Emerging sensitivity to socially complex expressions: A unique role for adolescence? *Child Development Perspectives*, *9*(2), 84–90. https://doi.org/10.1111/cdep.12114

Gibbons, A. (2018). Complex behavior arose at the dawn of humans. *Science*, *359*(3681), 1200–1201. https://doi.org/10.1126/science.359.6381.1200

Gurin, P., & Markus, H. (1988). Group identity: The psychological mechanisms of durable salience. *Revue Internationale de Psychologie Sociale*, *1*, 257–274.

Hauser, M. (2006). *Moral minds: How nature designed our university sense of right and wrong*. HarperCollins.

Hausmann, L. R. M., Schofield, J. W., & Woods, R. L. (2007). Sense of belonging as a predictor of intentions to persist among African American and White first-year college students. *Research in Higher Education, 48*, 803–839. https://doi .org/10.1007/s11162-007-9052-9

Hoffman, M., Richmond, J., Morrow, J., & Salomone, K. (2002). Investigating "sense of belonging" in first-year college students. *Journal of College Student Retention, 4*(3), 227–256. https://doi.org/10.2190/DRYC-CXQ9-JQ8V-HT4V

Kiyama, J. M., & Rios-Aguilar, C. (Eds.). (2018). *Funds of knowledge in higher education: Honoring students' cultural experiences and resources as strengths*. Routledge.

Maslow, A. H. (1968). *Toward a psychology of being* (2nd ed.). Van Nostrand.

McClelland, D. C. (1961). *The achieving society*. Van Nostrand.

Mullen, B., Brown, R., & Smith, C. (1992). In-group bias as a function of salience, relevance, and status: An integration. *European Journal of Social Psychology, 22*(2), 103–122. https://doi.org/10.1002/ejsp.2420220202

Murray, H. A. (1938). *Explorations in personality*. Oxford University Press.

Newman, B. M. & Newman, P. R. (2018). *Development through life: A psychosocial approach* (13th ed.). Cengage Learning.

Newman, B. M., & Newman, P. R. (2001). Group identity and alienation: Giving the we its due. *Journal of Youth and Adolescence, 30*(5), 515–538. https://doi .org/10.1023/A:1010480003929

Paus, T. (2009). Brain development. In R. M. Lerner & L. Steinberg (Eds.), *Handbook of adolescent psychology, Vol. 1. Individual bases of adolescent development* (3rd ed., pp. 95–115). Wiley.

Price, D. D. (2000). Psychological and neural mechanisms of the affective dimension of pain. *Science, 288*(5472), 1769–1772. https://doi.org/10.1126/science .288.5472.1769

Schlossberg, N. K. (1984). *Counseling adults in transition*. Springer.

Schneider, B. H., Atkinson, L., & Tardif, C. (2001). Child–parent attachment and children's peer relations: A quantitative review. *Developmental Psychology, 37*(1), 86–100. https://doi.org/10.1037/0012-1649.37.1.86

Schore, A. N. (2013). Bowlby's "environment of evolutionary adaptedness": Recent studies on the interpersonal neurobiology of attachment and emotional development. In D. Narvaez, J. Panksepp, A. N. Schore, & T. R. Gleason (Eds.), *Evolution, early experience and human development: From research to practice and policy* (pp. 31–67). Oxford University Press.

Seligman, M. E. P. (2011). *Flourish: A visionary new understanding of happiness and well-being*. The Free Press/Simon & Schuster.

Shaver, P. R., & Mikulincer, M. (2011). An attachment-theory framework for conceptualizing interpersonal behavior. In L. M. Horowitz & S. Strack (Eds.), *Handbook of interpersonal psychology: Theory, research, assessment, and therapeutic interventions* (pp. 17–35). Wiley.

Somerville, L. H. (2013). Teenage brain: Sensitivity to social evaluation. *Current Directions in Psychological Science, 22*(2), 122–127. https://doi.org/10.1177/0963721413476512

Strayhorn, T. (2012). *College students' sense of belonging: A key to educational success for all students.* Routledge.

Strayhorn, T. (2019). *College students' sense of belonging: A key to educational success for all students* (2nd ed.) Routledge.

Telzer, E. H. (2016). Dopaminergic reward sensitivity can promote adolescent health: A new perspective on the mechanism of ventral striatum activation. *Developmental Cognitive Neuroscience, 17,* 57–67. https://doi.org/10.1016/j.dcn.2015.10.010

Triandis, H. C. (1990). Cross cultural studies of individualism and collectivism. In J. J. Berman (Ed.), *Nebraska symposium on motivation, cross-cultural perspectives* (pp. 41–133). University of Nebraska Press.

Vaccaro, A., Daly-Cano, M., & Newman, B. (2015). A sense of belonging among college students with disabilities: An emergent theoretical model. *Journal of College Student Development, 56*(7), 670–686. https://doi.org/10.1353/csd.20150072

Vaccaro, A., Marcotte, M. A., Swanson, H. & Newman, B. M. (2019). Using familial funds of knowledge to transition and develop a sense of belonging: Reflections from first-generation college women of color. *Journal of the First-Year Experience and Students in Transition, 31*(2), 29–44. doi.org/10.15763/issn.2642-2387.2019.5.2.32-65

Vaccaro, A., & Newman, B. M. (2016). The development of a sense of belonging for privileged and minoritized students: An emerging model. *Journal of College Student Development, 57*(8), 925–942. https://doi.org/10.1353/csd.2016.0091

Vaccaro, A., & Newman, B. M. (2017). Belonging through the eyes of first-year LGBPQ students: A multi-layered analysis. *Journal of Student Affairs Research and Practice, 54*(2), 137–149. https://doi.org/10.1080/19496591.2016.1211533

Vaccaro, A., Russell, E. I., & Koob, R. M. (2015). Students with minoritized identities of sexuality and gender in campus contexts: An emergent model. In D-L Stewart, Renn, K. A., & Brazelton, G. B. (Eds.), *LGBTQ Students in Higher Education* (New Directions for Student Services, no. 152, pp. 25–39). Jossey-Bass. https://doi.org/10.1002/ss.20143

Vaccaro, A., Swanson, H., Marcotte, M. A., & Newman, B. M. (2019). Insights into the sense of belonging from women of color: Interconnections of cultural competence, expectations, structural diversity, and counterspaces. *Journal Committed to Social Change on Race and Ethnicity (JCSCORE), 5*(2). https://doi.org/10.15763/issn.2642-2387.2019.5.2.32-65

Vatička, P., & Vuilleumier, P. (2012). Neuroscience of human social interactions and adult attachment style. *Frontiers in Human Neuroscience, 6*(212). https://doi.org/10.3389/fnhum.2012.00212

Williams, T. K., & Thornton, M. C. (1998). Social construction of ethnicity versus personal experience: The case of Afro-Amerasians. *Journal of Comparative Family Studies, 29*(2), 255–267. https://doi.org/10.3138/jcfs.29.2.255

2

UNRAVELING THE RELATIONSHIP AMONG ENGAGEMENT, INVOLVEMENT, AND SENSE OF BELONGING

Terrell L. Strayhorn

Several years ago, I delivered a keynote address at the annual meeting of a major student affairs professional association that boasted over 10,000 members. The conference theme was focused on the all-important work of student affairs professionals—employed across a variety of functional areas such as advising, financial aid, student activities, and athletics—who dedicate their time and energy every day to helping college students succeed. While over 21 million students are enrolled in colleges and universities in the United States, we, as a field, have known for some time that roughly 50% of students who enter college complete their degree within 6 years of initial entry. Some students take longer, while upward of 40% drop out or leave higher education altogether (U.S. Department of Education, 2019).

There are a variety of reasons students may not succeed in college, primarily lack of social support. Contrary to popular belief, *all students* need help or assistance of one kind or another. It has been repeatedly demonstrated that social support is an important factor in students' adjustment to the academic and social demands of college. For example, Tinto (1993) posited that student decisions about whether to stay in or leave college depended on the extent to which they benefited from frequent and meaningful supportive interactions with faculty and staff in the various domains of campus life. Evidence accumulated over decades points to the crucial role that social support plays in college student success, especially instrumental, informational, and emotional assistance provided by faculty and campus personnel such as student affairs professionals (Fosnacht et al., 2017; Strayhorn, 2008b).

Within the social support literature, scholars differentiate between the structural and functional aspects of social support (Kawachi & Berkman, 2001), as well as how it operates at the institutional and individual levels (Means & Pyne, 2017). Structural support refers to the presence and quantity of social relationships, whereas functional support refers to their perceived quality and purpose (Hefner & Eisenberg, 2009). Colleges and universities that employ an adequate number of academic advisors, counselors, campus ministers, or financial aid specialists to help their student population represent good examples of structural support. When student affairs professionals working in those offices meet with students regularly, respond efficiently to phone calls and email messages, provide accurate and timely information, or go beyond the call of duty, the mere presence of structural support transforms into functional care.

In similar fashion, prior research has shown that socially supportive systems operate at both the institutional (i.e., university, department, classroom) and individual levels in higher education. Prior studies have shown that it is essential for students to form positive, meaningful relationships with others, such as with faculty and staff, during their college careers (individual) (Ribera et al., 2017; Strayhorn, 2008b). Yet other scholars posit that institutions have a responsibility—an imperative—to formulate programs and policies that facilitate positive, supportive relationships between faculty/staff and students (Hausmann et al., 2007; Hurtado & Carter, 1997; Kuh, 2003). Both perspectives are correct. Students benefit significantly from establishing positive, supportive interpersonal relationships with their advisors, counselors, and instructors. But we have known for quite some time that, without institutional intervention, like intrusive advising, less than one third of college students meet directly with their advisor for academic guidance (Schwebel et al., 2008). Given such evidence-based knowledge, I believe postsecondary institutions have an "equity imperative" to formulate new or revise existing policies and programs in ways that ensure all students, regardless of their social class, race/ethnicity, sexuality, ability, major, or ZIP code, get access to the social support necessary for college success. The research base is clear—providing social support to students is a key to educational success, far too important to be left to chance.

There are other factors related to social support that have been consistently linked to college student success, namely engagement, involvement, and, more recently, sense of belonging. Some writers suggest that "these terms are in many ways distinct," while others use them interchangeably (Wolf-Wendel et al., 2009, p. 407). As I have stated elsewhere, "I tend to agree . . . that there are important nuances to the definitions of these terms, although it's not my purpose to 'split hairs' over each and every distinction between them" (Strayhorn, 2019, p. 143). Rather, my purpose is to synthesize otherwise separate streams of literature to offer operational definitions for each concept, vivid examples from student affairs practice, and theoretical observations that reveal linkages among these ideas while also reducing, if not removing, any ambiguity or confusion that currently exists. This is the gap addressed by the present discussion.

Purpose of Chapter

The purpose of this chapter is to explore the independent meaning and significance of these three concepts—engagement, involvement, sense of belonging—and to provide some clarity to the distinctive elements and interrelationships among them. To be sure, there are obvious and undeniable parallels between and among these concepts. That has been affirmed by several authoritative texts and seminal pieces (Strayhorn, 2019; Walton & Brady, 2017; Wolf-Wendel et al., 2009). However, in my opinion, much of the "conceptual confusion" or "construct conflation" is the result of diminishing details, thinning texture, and fading facts about each that get transmitted over time from one study to the next, one theorist to their successor, one generation to another.

Because each is built on the abstract, multidimensional notion of social support (and its derivatives), the ideas of engagement, involvement, and sense of belonging are subject to significant fuzzy thinking; "definition creep," as I like to call it, referring to a gradual or incremental shift in understanding beyond something's original scope; and, perhaps even, misinterpretation. Interpretation is subjective and, no matter how rigorous our scientific methods, it is generally a messy, imprecise process that relies heavily on limited human experience(s), bounded imaginative vision, and one-dimensional words or phrases to capture (and reflect) the complexity of multidimensional phenomena. What we gain in simplicity, we give up in specificity—as clarity increases, complexity decreases. It is no wonder that present-day descriptions of concepts like engagement, involvement, and sense of belonging represent "a tangled web of terms," sounding like synonyms, not correlates (Wolf-Wendel et al., 2009, p. 407). This chapter attempts to untangle them, laying them bare for student affairs professionals' effective use.

Engagement Matters

A substantial evidence base supports the notion that student engagement matters in higher education. *Engagement* is defined as "the time and energy that students devote to educationally purposeful activities and the extent to which the institution gets students to participate in activities that lead to student success" (Kezar & Kinzie, 2006, p. 150). Countless derivatives of this definition exist, some better than others (Kuh, 2003; Kuh et al., 2003). Despite divergent definitions, the weight of empirical studies consistently shows that student engagement positively affects college student learning and development, across both sexes and all races, institutional types, and campus racial compositions (Bridges et al., 2008; Carini et al., 2005; Wood & Ireland, 2014).

Recent scholarship reveals two dimensions of engagement (Gasiewski et al., 2012). *Behavioral engagement* refers to what students do—that is, one's investment of time, energy, and resources to college-related activities and experiences. *Emotional engagement*, however, refers to perceived positive and negative affective responses to college experiences. And a third dimension has been referenced in some reports referring to the psychic and intellectual resources directed to comprehend complex concepts or acquire difficult skills: *cognitive engagement*. All have been linked to college success generally, and greater appreciation of diversity, enhanced self-esteem, or clarified values specifically (Bowman, 2012; Bridges et al., 2008; Garvey et al., 2018).

If I left it there, engagement would be analogous to Astin's (1984) involvement theory, and my interrogation of the concept would be incomplete at best. Engagement distinguishes itself from involvement in a number of ways, such as identifying and prioritizing certain collegiate conditions purported to produce the learning and development outcomes that college educators desire for students. Those conditions are delineated in Kuh et al.'s (2003) five benchmarks framework: academic challenge, active and collaborative learning, student–faculty interactions, enriching educational experiences, and supportive campus environment. By creating such conditions, institutions assume their responsibility for promoting engagement and student success by producing systems that drive students to be involved in academic and social activities that help them grow.

Engagement—that is, what students and institutions do—has both proximal and distal effects. Survey and quasi-experimental studies demonstrate that engagement is positively linked to critical thinking, retention, and persistence to degree, accounting for potentially confounding differences like academic readiness and demographics (Kinzie & Kuh, 2017). Engagement also seems to have a compensatory effect for some students, especially historically underrepresented minorities (URMs) who sometimes have the least in terms of supportive resources (Greene et al., 2008; Griffin & McIntosh, 2015).

Engaging colleges acknowledge the role they play in promoting student success (Kuh et al., 1991). They strive to create the conditions under which college students thrive. They listen to and assess the unique needs of their students rather than talking about the latest fads or trending "best practices," which may work for *some* at one campus but none at another. The engagement scholarship, popularized by George Kuh, is based on the involvement literature. The next section turns to that bin of knowledge.

Involvement Matters

Simply put, student involvement in college matters (Astin, 1984). Involvement refers to the "amount of physical and psychological energy that the [college] student devotes to the academic experience" (Astin, 1984, p. 297). In his original formulation of the concept, Astin clearly expressed a behavioral orientation to emphasizing *what students do* rather than *how* they think or feel. Although some researchers falsely claim involvement as merely a psychological state, Astin (1999) rightly clarified: "It is not so much what the individual thinks or feels, but what the individual does, how he or she behaves, that defines and identifies involvement" (p. 519). In this way, proxies for involvement include vigilance, effort, time on task, and action, to name a few.

The existing involvement literature offers insight into Astin's (1999) five basic postulates. They range from notions that involvement requires the investment of physical and psychological energies in various experiences to notions that the effectiveness of any educational policy or practice is directly proportional to its capacity to increase involvement. An expansive body of research has amassed, documenting that college student involvement positively affects civic responsibility (Astin & Sax, 1998), critical thinking (Flowers, 2004), racial identity (Harper & Quaye, 2007), and character development (Strayhorn, 2008a).

Involvement, a frequency-based behavioral measure, encompasses the energy expended on and time invested in goal-oriented tasks. In other words, there's an "input–output" equivalency formula when it comes to involvement. "The extent to which students can achieve particular development goals is a direct function of the time and effort they devote to the activities designed to produce [such] gains" (Astin, 1999, p. 522). Consider, for instance, a Black undergraduate woman majoring in engineering at a large, public predominantly White institution (PWI) in the Midwestern region of the country. In an advising session, she shares that she feels "out of place . . . isolated and different" from other students in the department. Suffering under the weight of isolation, she acknowledges that she's "the only Black person in most classes." Worried but supportive, her advisor suggests that she gets involved in the National Society of Black Engineers (NSBE) chapter on campus. Part of what justifies the efficacy of this prescription is that NSBE and groups like it were designed to improve the retention and academic adjustment of Black and other minority engineers in academia and industry. So, it is not that involvement in *anything* produces everything; involvement presupposes a level of intentionality that aligns investments with desired outcomes.

In fact, it seems important to note that the benefits of involvement are not always positive or in the expected direction. For instance, a crucial ingredient of Astin's (1999) theory of involvement is the belief that "the psychic and physical time and energy of students are finite" (p. 523), with definite limits. Time and energy invested in outside commitments like work, family, friends, and play reduces the time and energy available to devote to educational programs. As another example, students who are deeply involved academically may be more satisfied with college life but report fewer meaningful friendships with other students as they forgo hanging out in campus clubs and organizations to study quietly in isolation. Again, prevailing theories hypothesize that campus involvement helps college students forge supportive relationships with peers, faculty, staff, and student affairs professionals who serve as a foundation for sense of belonging. The next section further explores this concept and frames sense of belonging as related to, but conceptually different from, engagement and involvement.

Sense of Belonging Matters

Sense of belonging is a basic human need (Maslow, 1962), dependent on frequent and meaningful interpersonal social connections for fulfillment. The need to belong is as basic as air, water, food, and sleep. Everybody wants to belong, and it takes on heightened importance in college contexts where individuals are vulnerable to feeling alone, isolated, or being judged by others (Strayhorn, 2019). Definitions vary, but generally college students' sense of belonging refers to "an individual's sense of identification or positioning in relation to a group or to the college community, which may yield an affective response" (Tovar & Simon, 2010, p. 200).

In general, sense of belonging characterizes a person's perceived belief of indispensability within a system (Anant, 1966). Applied to higher education, it reflects the social support that students perceive on campus and refers to a feeling of connectedness, that one is important to others, and one matters (Jacoby & Garland, 2004–2005). Whereas *engaged* colleges devote effort to using effective educational practices like peer mentoring, intrusive advising, living-learning communities, or intergroup dialogues (*engagement*) and *involved* students invest time and energy toward such activities (*involvement*), it's when students perceive the presence and helpfulness of such services as supportive that they *feel* a sense of belonging.

Not all college students experience sense of belonging the same way. For example, in a relatively recent analysis of nationally representative survey data, researchers found that first-generation and URM first-year students report lower sense of belonging than their peers at 4-year colleges. Furthermore, belonging varies by institutional and student characteristics like sex, institutional selectivity, self-efficacy, and expenditures (Gopalan & Brady, 2020). Sense of belonging may be particularly important or "take on heightened importance" for some students who perceive themselves as marginal to campus life (Strayhorn, 2019, p. 28). For instance, Black and Latinx students are "less likely to feel part of the campus community if they perceive racial tension or have experienced discrimination" (Hurtado & Carter, 1997, p. 337).

It is important to note that *academic* sense of belonging presupposes that classrooms and other learning contexts (e.g., laboratories) are perceived by students as important places—or settings—where they desire to be accepted, connected, and feel a sense of membership (Freeman et al., 2007). It was Tinto (1997) who noted the primacy of the college classroom and acknowledged its centrality to educational activity in colleges and universities. College classrooms can be intimidating, scary places for students, such as for adult learners who return after years out of school. They can be chaotic, disorderly, and triggering for military veterans utilizing federal education benefits like the GI Bill to reenter the workforce after coming home from combat. A steady line of inquiry shows that classroom instructors can foster students' sense of belonging by personalizing instruction (e.g., learning students' names), imposing structure on studies, adopting a student-centered teaching style, and accelerating community through group work (Goodenow, 1993; Strayhorn, 2019).

Students with a sense of belonging in academic settings feel socially connected, supported, and respected by others, including peers, faculty/teachers, and administrators. They trust their teachers and peers generally and, consequently, feel a sense of fit at school. They are not worried about being treated like a stereotype or "less than" and, thus, are confident that they are seen (*visible*), cared about, and a person of worth who adds value to the academic learning space, albeit a classroom, laboratory, department, or university (Strayhorn, 2019, 2020b).

Students who are confident that they belong academically are able to engage more fully in teaching and learning, which links belonging to engagement. For instance, such students are open to critical feedback. They take advantage of learning opportunities and have generally positive attitudes toward college life. In short, reams of research have shown that if students feel like they belong, they excel, thrive, and persist through college (York & Fernandez, 2018), even in international countries like Tobago and Trinidad (Niehaus et al., 2019). If students do not feel like they belong, they may transfer or simply drop out (Hausmann et al., 2007).

Although sense of belonging can be achieved in academic contexts, it also holds importance in social spheres of college life (Bollen & Hoyle, 1990). Indeed, students who feel a strong sense of belonging in college have fewer behavior problems and less absenteeism and feel motivated to devote the time and energy necessary to complete academic tasks (Nuñez, 2009; Ribera et al., 2017; Strayhorn, 2019). But they also build important, new relationships with others, including peers, faculty, staff, and student affairs professionals. In fact, these relationships serve as the foundation for students' sense of belonging. This has led scholars to conclude that "personal adjustment and integration into the social fabric of campus life plays a role at least as important as academic factors in student retention" (Gerdes & Mallinckrodt, 1994, p. 286).

Student affairs professionals play a role in facilitating college students' sense of belonging. For instance, an academic advisor can nurture a students' sense of belonging in their major by providing accurate, timely information about degree requirements, decoding unwritten rules, and anticipating a student's problems and pitfalls using predictive analytics and other tools. First-year seminar directors, summer bridge staff, activities coordinators, and wellness coaches can boost students' sense of belonging by helping first-year students adjust to college, normalizing feelings like loneliness and homesickness, while also encouraging them to know that such feelings pass with time and active *involvement* in campus life (Cheryan & Bodenhausen, 2000; Strayhorn, 2020a; Walton & Cohen, 2011).

"Critical" Considerations

Before bringing this chapter's discussion to end, I want to highlight several "critical" considerations. By critical, I do not mean to suggest the level of importance attached to these points, although I believe they are significant in advancing our collective understanding of engagement, involvement, and particularly sense of belonging. "Critical" is also not used to express negative, adverse, or condemnatory judgment on prior scholars or past scholarship that has reduced differences between these terms to mere semantics. Rather, by "critical," I invoke sentiments from critical race theory and intersectionality to contest existing ways of talking about these concepts. It is important to cast a critical gaze to issues of equity, identity, and power (Collins, 2000).

Transforming present understandings of engagement, involvement, and sense of belonging involves reevaluating current definitions and terms attached to certain campus activities and practices that aim to privilege them above other options. For instance, the weight of published work steadily suggests the importance of college students' engagement in what is known as *high-impact practices* (HIPs): time-intensive academic pursuits that provide structured opportunities for meaningful interactions with faculty and peers in course-related or academic-enriching activities like first-year seminars, study-abroad programs, and writing-intensive courses (Garvey et al., 2018; Gipson & Mitchell, 2017). While undeniably effective in their ability to catalyze cognitive dissonance, which in turn facilitates learning, not all students are able to participate in these HIPs equitably; neither do these HIPs affect all students equally. Studying abroad, for instance, often requires students (or their families) to have sufficient disposable income to spend thousands of dollars beyond tuition and fees for a student to travel, live, and study overseas. Estimates indicate that less than 10% of all Black, Indigenous, people of color (BIPOC) participate in study-abroad programs annually (Gipson & Mitchell, 2017; Jessup-Anger, 2008). So, while studying abroad might be a HIP for more affluent students, other potent experiences, such as learning a foreign language/culture, joining a gospel choir, leading a grassroots racial justice movement, or participating actively in a minority male initiative, deserve explicit mention and empirical exploration (Strayhorn, 2011).

Advancing what is presently known about these concepts also requires changing ingrained ways of thinking and questioning basic assumptions and terminology. For example, Tinto's (1993) integrationalist model of college student departure framed attrition (or, conversely, retention) as a longitudinal process of personal commitments shaping students' academic and social integration in campus life. The term *integration*, in this case, refers to the extent to which students have attitudes and beliefs in common with the dominant groups, norms, and values on campus (Wolf-Wendel et al., 2009). However, integration also has an offensive, racist history with racialized groups in the United States, especially Black Americans, who were expected to "integrate" or assimilate into White society by surrendering their own cultural preferences, tastes, freedoms, institutions, and traditions. They were forced to adopt the attitudes and beliefs of dominant culture, which are acknowledged, celebrated, and circulated as "the norm," the standard, and the rule in White social institutions like schools and colleges. Consequently, integration elevated White culture while reducing and relegating Black and other nonmajority cultures as deficient, inadequate, and abnormal. A critically conscious perspective on engagement, involvement, and sense of belonging recognizes this problematic history and deliberately challenges the use of such terms, replacing them with words like *collaborate, connect, join,* or *participate,* if not *forced exclusion* and *inclusion,* to name a few.

Higher education literature has shown time and time again that students of color, especially BIPOC, can encounter hostile, unwelcoming, and/or unsupportive campus climates at PWIs. "Overt and subtle forms of exclusion in college can hinder [students'] development of a sense of belonging to university communities" (Nuñez, 2009, p. 46). Marginalizing experiences such as isolation, discrimination, and exposure to negative stereotyping negatively affect social adjustment for BIPOC, especially those attending PWIs. Thus, promoting engagement, encouraging involvement, and nurturing belonging for students at such institutions requires paying attention to the campus's climate barometer, checking implicit biases, and enforcing policies and practices that prohibit discrimination and systematic exclusion, to name a few.

Conclusion

The purpose of this chapter was to explore the independent meaning and significance of three concepts—engagement, involvement, and sense of belonging—whose etymological evolution in the higher education literature has led to fuzzy understandings, conceptual confusion, and overlapping ambiguities that hinder the translation and use of information from different studies. Insights shared herein provide some clarity to the distinctive elements and interrelationships among them. I offer these thoughts not only to avoid conflicting these terms as advised by our colleagues (Wolf-Wendel et al., 2009) but also to highlight the impact of belonging in college so that we can maximize its use in college contexts. Without greater conceptual clarity, our efforts result in costly campus initiatives that are burdensome to students demanding more *involvement,* disconnected from institution's strategic objectives (*engagement*), organizationally inappropriate, and, thus, wildly unsuccessful. Conflicting conceptual and philosophical views have other real-life practical consequences. They lead to power struggles in the boardroom or, nowadays, "the Zoom room," over how to help students best, where to direct limited resources, and even when to address sizable inequities, all of which reduce the usefulness of the literature base. Clarifying the terms gives us power to put theory to practice, words to work.

References

Anant, S. S. (1966). The need to belong. *Canada's Mental Health, 14*, 21–27.

Astin, A. W. (1984). Student involvement: A developmental theory for higher education. *Journal of College Student Personnel, 25*, 297–308.

Astin, A. W. (1999). Student involvement: A developmental theory for higher education. *Journal of College Student Development, 40*(5), 518–529. https://www.middlesex.mass.edu/ace/downloads/astininv.pdf

Astin, A. W., & Sax, L. J. (1998). How undergraduates are affected by service participation. *Journal of College Student Development, 39*(3), 251–263. https://digitalcommons.unomaha.edu/cgi/viewcontent.cgi?article=1012&context=slceh ighered

Bollen, K. A., & Hoyle, R. H. (1990). Perceived cohesion: A conceptual and empirical examination. *Social Forces, 69*, 479–504. https://doi.org/10.1093/sf/69.2.479

Bowman, N. A. (2012). Promoting sustained engagement with diversity: The reciprocal relationships between informal and formal college diversity experiences. *Review of Higher Education, 36*, 1–24. https://doi.org/10.1353/rhe.2012.0057

Bridges, B. K., Kinzie, J., Nelson Laird, T. F., & Kuh, G. D. (2008). Student engagement and student success at historically Black and Hispanic serving institutions. In M. Gasman, B. Baez, & C. S. V. Turner (Eds.), *Understanding minority-serving institutions* (pp. 217–236). State University of New York Press.

Carini, R. M., Kuh, G. D., & Klein, S. P. (2005). Student engagement and student learning: Testing the linkages. *Research in Higher Education, 47*(1), 1–32. https://doi.org/10.1007/s11162-005-8150-9

Cheryan, S., & Bodenhausen, G. (2000). When positive stereotypes threaten intellectual performance: The psychological hazards of "model minority" status. *Psychological Science, 11*, 399–402. https://doi.org/10.1111/1467-9280.00277

Flowers, L. A. (2004). Examining the effects of student involvement on African American college student development. *Journal of College Student Development, 45*, 633–654. https://doi.org/10.1353/csd.2004.0067

Fosnacht, K., McCormick, A. C., Nailos, J. N., & Ribera, A. K. (2017). Frequency of first-year student interactions with advisors. *NACADA Journal, 37*(1), 74–86. https://doi.org/10.12930/nacada-15-048

Freeman, T. M., Anderman, L. H., & Jensen, J. M. (2007). Sense of belonging in college freshmen at the classroom and campus levels. *The Journal of Experimental Education, 75*(3), 203–220. https://doi.org/10.3200/jexe.75.3.203-220

Garvey, J. C., BrckaLorenz, A., Latopolski, K., & Hurtado, S. (2018). High-impact practices and student-faculty interactions for students across sexual orientations. *Journal of College Student Development, 59*, 210–226. https://doi.org/10.1353/csd.2018.0018

Gasiewski, J. A., Eagan, K., Garcia, G. A., Hurtado, S., & Chang, M. J. (2012). From gatekeeping to engagement: A multicontextual, mixed method study of student academic engagement in introductory STEM courses. *Research in Higher Education, 53*, 229–261. https://doi.org/10.1007/s11162-011-9247-y

Gerdes, H., & Mallinckrodt, B. (1994). Emotional, social, and academic adjustment to college students: A longitudinal study of retention. *Journal of Counseling and Development, 72,* 281–288. https://doi.org/10.1002/j.1556-6676.1994.tb00935.x

Gipson, J., & Mitchell, D. M., Jr. (2017). How high-impact practices influence academic achievement for African American college students. *Journal Committed to Social Change on Race and Ethnicity, 3*(2), 124–144. https://doi.org/10.15763/issn.2642-2387.2017.3.2.123-144

Goodenow, C. (1993). Classroom belonging among early adolescent students: Relationships to motivation and achievement. *Journal of Early Adolescence, 13,* 21–43. https://doi.org/10.1177/0272431693013001002

Gopalan, M., & Brady, S. T. (2020). College students' sense of belonging: A national perspective. *Educational Researcher, 49*(2), 134–137. https://doi.org/10.3102/0013189x19897622

Greene, T. G., Marti, C. N., & McClenney, K. (2008). The effort-outcome gap: Differences for African American and Hispanic community college students in student engagement and academic achievement. *The Journal of Higher Education, 79*(5), 513–539. https://doi.org/10.1080/00221546.2008.11772115

Griffin, K. A., & McIntosh, K. L. (2015). Finding a fit: Understanding Black immigrant students' engagement in campus activities. *Journal of College Student Development, 56*(3), 243–260. https://doi.org/10.1353/csd.2015.0025

Harper, S. R., & Quaye, S. J. (2007). Student organizations as venues for Black identity expression and development among African American male student leaders. *Journal of College Student Development, 48*(2), 127–144. https://doi.org/10.1353/csd.2007.0012

Hausmann, L. R. M., Schofield, J. W., & Woods, R. L. (2007). Sense of belonging as a predictor of intentions to persist among African American and White first-year college students. *Research in Higher Education, 48*(7), 803–839. https://doi.org/10.1007/s11162-009-9137-8

Hefner, J., & Eisenberg, D. (2009). Social support and mental health among college students. *American Journal of Orthopsychiatry, 79*(4), 491–499. https://doi.org/10.1037/a0016918

Hill Collins, P. (2000). *Black feminist thought: Knowledge, consciousness, and the politics of empowerment* (2nd ed.). Routledge.

Hurtado, S., & Carter, D. F. (1997). Effects of college transition and perceptions of campus racial climate on Latino college students' sense of belonging. *Sociology of Education, 70*(4), 324–345. https://doi.org/10.2307/2673270

Jacoby, B., & Garland, J. (2004–2005). Strategies for enhancing commuter student success. *Journal of College Student Retention: Research, Theory, & Practice, 6*(1), 61–79.

Jessup-Anger, J. E. (2008). Gender observations and study abroad: How students reconcile cross-cultural differences related to gender. *Journal of College Student Development, 49*(4), 360–373. https://doi.org/10.1353/csd.0.0015

Kawachi, I., & Berkman, L. F. (2001). Social ties and mental health. *Journal of Urban Health: Bulletin of the New York Academy of Medicine, 78,* 458–467. https://doi.org/10.1093/jurban/78.3.458

Kezar, A. J., & Kinzie, J. L. (2006). Examining the ways institutions create student engagement: The role of mission. *Journal of College Student Development, 47*(2), 149–172. https://doi.org/10.1353/csd.2006.0018

Kinzie, J., & Kuh, G. D. (2017). Reframing student success in college: Advancing know-what and know-how. *Change, 49*(3), 19–27. https://doi.org/10.1080/000 91383.2017.1321429

Kuh, G. D. (2003). What we're learning about student engagement from NSSE. *Change, 35*(2), 24–32. https://doi.org/10.1080/00091380309604090

Kuh, G. D., Palmer, M., & Kish, K. (2003). The value of educationally purposeful out-of-class experiences. In T. L. Skipper & R. Argo (Eds.), *Involvement in campus activities and retention of first-year college students* (pp. 19–34). University of South Carolina, National Resource Center for the First-Year Experience and Students in Transition.

Kuh, G. D., Schuh, J. H., Whitt, E., Andreas, R. E., Lyons, J. W., Strange, C. C., Krehbiel, L. E., & MacKay, K. A. (1991). *Involving colleges: Successful approaches to fostering student learning and development outside the classroom.* Jossey-Bass.

Maslow, A. H. (1962). *Toward a psychology of being.* Van Nostrand.

Means, D. R., & Pyne, K. B. (2017). Finding my way: Perceptions of institutional support and belonging in low-income, first-generation, first-year college students. *Journal of College Student Development, 58,* 907–924. https://doi.org/10.1353/ csd.2017.0071

Niehaus, E., Williams, L., Zobac, S., Young, M., & Fullerton, A. (2019). Exploring predictors of sense of belonging in Trinidad and Tobago. *Journal of College Student Development, 60*(5), 577–594. https://doi.org/10.1353/csd.2019.0057

Nuñez, A. M. (2009). A critical paradox? Predictors of Latino students' sense of belonging in college. *Journal of Diversity in Higher Education, 2*(1), 46–61. https://doi.org/10.1037/a0014099

Ribera, A. K., Miller, A. L., & Dumford, A. D. (2017). Sense of peer belonging and institutional acceptance in the first year: The role of high-impact practices. *Journal of College Student Development, 58*(4), 545–563. https://doi.org/10.1353/ csd.2017.0042

Schwebel, D. C., Walburn, N. C., Jacobsen, S. H., Jerrolds, K. L., & Klyce, K. (2008). Efficacy of intrusively advising first-year students via frequent reminders for advising appointments. *NACADA Journal, 28*(2), 28–32. https://doi .org/10.12930/0271-9517-28.2.28

Strayhorn, T. L. (2008a). How college students' engagement affects personal and social learning outcomes. *Journal of College & Character, 10*(2), 1–16. https://doi .org/10.2202/1940-1639.1071

Strayhorn, T. L. (2008b). The role of supportive relationships in facilitating African American males' success in college. *NASPA Journal, 45*(1), 26–48. https://doi .org/10.2202/1949-6605.1906

Strayhorn, T. L. (2011). Singing in a foreign fand: An exploratory study of gospel choir participation among African American undergraduates at a predominantly White institution. *Journal of College Student Development, 52*(2), 137–153. https://doi.org/10.1353/csd.2011.0030

Strayhorn, T. L. (2019). *College students' sense of belonging: A key to educational success for all students* (2nd ed.). Routledge.

Strayhorn, T. L. (2020a). Measuring the relation between sense of belonging, campus leadership, and academic achievement for African American students at historically Black colleges and universities (HBCUs): A "gender equity" analysis. *Journal of Minority Achievement, Creativity, & Leadership, 1*(1), 94–118. https://doi.org/10.5325/minoachicrealead.1.1.0094

Strayhorn, T. L. (2020b). Sense of belonging predicts persistence intentions among diverse dental education students: A multi-institutional investigation. *Journal of Dental Education, 84*(10), 1136–1142. https://doi.org/10.1002/jdd.12243

Tinto, V. (1993). *Leaving college: Rethinking the causes and cures of student attrition* (2nd ed.). University of Chicago Press.

Tinto, V. (1997). Classroom as communities: Exploring the educational character of student persistence. *Journal of Higher Education, 68*(6), 599–623. https://doi.org/10.1080/00221546.1997.11779003

Tovar, E., & Simon, M. A. (2010). Factorial structure and invariance analysis of the Sense of Belonging Scales. *Measurement and Evaluation in Counseling and Development, 43*, 199–217. https://doi.org/10.1177/0748175610384811

U. S. Department of Education. (2019). *The condition of education 2018.* U.S. Government Printing Office. https://doi.org/NCES 2000-062

Walton, G. M., & Brady, S. T. (2017). The many questions of belonging. In A. J. Elliott, C. S. Dweck, & D. S. Yeager (Eds.), *Handbook of competence and motivation: Theory and application* (2nd ed., pp. 272–293). Guilford.

Walton, G. M., & Cohen, G. L. (2011). A brief social-belonging intervention improves academic and health outcomes of minority students. *Science, 331*(6023), 1447–1451. https://doi.org/10.1126/science.1198364

Wolf-Wendel, L., Ward, K., & Kinzie, J. L. (2009). A tangled web of terms: The overlap and unique contribution of involvement, engagement, and integration to understanding college student success. *Journal of College Student Development, 50*(4), 407–428. https://doi.org/10.1353/csd.0.0077

Wood, J. L., & Ireland, S. M. (2014). Supporting Black male community college success: Determinants of faculty-student engagement. *Community College Journal of Research & Practice, 38*(2–3), 154–165. https://doi.org/10.1080/10668926.2014.851957

York, T. T., & Fernandez, F. (2018). The positive effects of service-learning on transfer students' sense of belonging: A multi-institutional analysis. *Journal of College Student Development, 59*(5), 579–597. https://doi.org/10.1353/csd.2018.0054

3

REVIEWING, THEORIZING, AND LOOKING AHEAD

The Relationship Between College Students' Sense of Belonging and Persistence

Bert Ellison and John M. Braxton

Despite the growing consensus outlined in this text that college students' sense of belonging correlates with positive outcomes such as persistence, extant models of college student persistence do not incorporate clearly defined constructs of belonging. The works of Astin (1975), Tinto (1993), and Braxton et al. (2014) regularly function as starting points for a variety of empirical studies, yet none of their traditional models incorporate a construct of belonging. Instead, scholarship on the topic often deploys sense of belonging as the dependent variable, an outcome of the research. However, the goal of attending college is not to belong; the goal of attending college is to graduate (though we hope that belonging occurs along the way). And to graduate, students must persist from one semester to the next. If that is the case, then models of college student persistence should reflect the reality that belonging occurs (or not) during undergraduate enrollment and that the end result is whether a student persists. Thus, sense of belonging should be a variable within the longitudinal process of college student persistence, and student persistence should be the dependent variable.

It is the goal of this chapter to introduce sense of belonging as a formal variable of inquiry in theories of student persistence. Such a task involves connecting the historic development of college students' sense of belonging to a working definition of the concept, reviewing relevant literature, hypothesizing the role of college students' sense of belonging in current theories of persistence, and looking ahead to subsequent research opportunities.

Sense of Belonging: Toward a Working Definition

This section highlights key contributions from psychology and sociology that inform a working definition of college students' sense of belonging.

Psychological Roots

The term *sense of belonging*, as it relates to college students, draws on fundamental psychological literature. For instance, in Maslow's (1954) hierarchy of needs, the related concept of belongingness is the first psychological need to be met after other basic needs. For Maslow (1943), belongingness is a reciprocal phenomenon that involves both giving and receiving belonging. It is because of such mutuality that the concept of belonging is perceptional in nature; someone might report a *sense* of belonging based on degree of mutuality.

The concept gained further social psychological clarity within the field of health care (Hagerty et al., 1992). Early health-care research ultimately coalesced into the following formalized definition of sense of belonging: "the experience of personal involvement in a system or environment so that persons feel themselves to be an integral part of that system or environment" (Hagerty et al., 1992, p. 173). This work informed the Sense of Belonging Instrument (SOBI), made up of two distinct scales: the SOBI-P (psychological state) and SOBI-A (antecedents; Hagerty & Patusky, 1995). The authors tested this instrument in three distinct samples, one of which consisted of community college students. They found that the two distinct scales were moderately correlated, thus implying that they did "indeed measure different but related concepts within a broader theoretical domain" of the SOBI (Hagerty & Patusky, 1995, p. 12).

It is important that these two concepts are different but related because they acknowledge the conceptual development of sense of belonging as both a psychological and sociological phenomenon. Whereas the SOBI-P reflects respondents' personal perceptions of fit and valued involvement in a group, the SOBI-A reflects the variety of experiences that respondents have had—in relation to others—that impact the degree to which they develop sense of belonging in a new context. Hagerty and Patusky (1995) noted in their study that more attention is needed on precursors to sense of belonging. And indeed, that is exactly what has happened in the years since their landmark study.

Sociological Branches

Belonging research increasingly incorporated a more sociological perspective as subsequent measures of belonging were tested, specifically in higher education contexts (Freeman et al., 2007; Hurtado & Carter, 1997). Hurtado and Carter (1997) elaborated on Bollen and Hoyle's (1990) position that sense of belonging is inherently perceptional in nature, meaning that students' perceptions of their own belonging are more meaningful than any objective operationalization of the concept. This notion that sense of belonging is primarily a subjective phenomenon, filtered through students' own multifaceted experiences, is now a commonplace stance in the field (Goodenow, 1993; Strayhorn, 2012).

Sense of belonging has always been a multidimensional concept. Hurtado and Carter's (1997) foundational work addressed three dimensions of college students' sense of belonging: academic experiences on campus, social experiences on campus, and students' responsibilities at home. Even so, the dependent variable of *what* one belongs to has evolved considerably over time. Early scholarship focused on student's belonging to the university community as the unit of analysis, without much differentiation between various contexts within the university (Hoffman et al., 2002; Hurtado & Carter, 1997; Maestas et al., 2007). More recent scholarship has continued an exploration of sense of belonging to the university specifically (Shook & Clay, 2012), but has also focused on the contextual nature of belonging as students might report belonging to discrete aspects of their university experience. For instance, Freeman et al., (2007) reported that belonging occurs at the campus level as well as the classroom level, while other research highlights the ways in which residence halls might impact students' sense of belonging (Johnson et al., 2007). As such, various spheres of belonging exist to which students might belong.

Other scholarship focuses on *who* belongs. Examples include scholarship that addresses the unique educational experiences of international students (Terrazas-Carrillo et al., 2017), first-generation students (Gibbons et al., 2016; Stebleton et al., 2014), and students who identify as racial and ethnic minorities (Gummadam et al., 2016; Mallett et al., 2011; Meeuwisse et al., 2010). This research is a natural extension of the aforementioned fact that belonging is a perspectival concept.

Here, it is worth emphasizing that the question of *who* belongs encapsulates the full range of students' identities. Intersectionality is key to understanding how sense of belonging operates among various student groups, as impediments to belonging can manifest differently based on identity and intersectionality (Murdock-Perriera et al., 2019).

A Working Definition

What follows is an attempt to extract a definition from the formulations of this section that appropriately addresses how diverse groups of students develop a sense of belonging to a wide variety of contexts. We offer this definition as an open concept, not a final word. With this caveat in mind, for the purposes of discussing the connection between sense of belonging, retention, persistence, and student success, *college students' sense of belonging* refers to the myriad ways that students perceive their importance as cocontributors to various campus contexts, a perception that in turn is impacted by background characteristics and institutional factors and results in positive outcomes as defined by students themselves. In light of this definition, we now turn to a review of relevant literature on the topic.

Background: Antecedents, Experiences, and Outcomes of Sense of Belonging

Using the aforementioned definition as a reference point, Astin's (1991) I-E-O model offers a helpful framing tool: One might envision belonging as a function of inputs (e.g., background characteristics) and environment (e.g., institutional factors) that results in outputs (e.g., positive outcomes as defined by students). This section covers an overview of Astin's I-E-O model, including some theoretical underpinnings, then utilizes his framework to organize relevant literature on college students' sense of belonging into three camps: inputs (or antecedents), environment (or experiences), and outputs (or outcomes).

Astin's I-E-O Model and Theoretical Underpinnings

Astin's (1991) I-E-O model suggests that inputs influence environment, which influences outputs and, additionally, inputs influence outputs directly. For Astin (1993),

> *Inputs* refers to the characteristics of the student at the time of entry to the institution; *environment* refers to the various programs, policies, faculty, peers, and educational experiences to which the student is exposed; and *outcomes* refers to the student's characteristics *after* exposure to the environment. (p. 7, emphasis in original)

In light of this, we consider sense of belonging to be an output, while also generating outputs of its own. In other words, inputs influence environment, which influences outputs, and, additionally, inputs influence outputs directly, with the update being that belonging is an output in its own right even as it produces outputs of its own. Thus, for the purposes of this chapter, Astin's (1991) I-E-O model refers specifically to relevant *inputs* to belonging (e.g., student characteristics), *environments* of belonging (e.g., campus experiences), and *outputs* of belonging (e.g., outcomes of belonging).

The prioritization of sense of belonging in this way is justified on a theoretical level for two main reasons, both hinging on the assumption that sense of belonging is a mutual phenomenon, as illustrated in its conceptual underpinnings in psychological literature. First, college student life is fundamentally group-oriented. When discussing the role of universities in French society during his time, Durkheim (1976) called for the creation of more opportunities for students to affiliate with groups during their time as students, based on similar interests, in the hopes that in doing so students would develop a sense of group identification to sustain them in their studies and even beyond graduation: "The community of tastes and sentiments . . . create among the members of these small circles bonds which endure beyond student life" (p. 384). Sense of belonging develops as a result of students with shared characteristics engaging in collaborative experiences. And, as Durkheim (1976) noted, this results in positive outcomes.

Second, students are constantly being exposed to new contexts, people, and experiences in a way that is unlikely to occur later in life. According to Baumeister and Leary (1995), humans need and seek out strong, positive relational bonds with other humans. These bonds might vary in length and intensity, but not in importance. This is especially true in a collegiate setting, where students are constantly exposed to new opportunities to develop sense of belonging. Sense of belonging takes on what Strayhorn (2012) dubbed "heightened importance" (p. 20), as contexts for belonging development are numerous and shifting. Students have the opportunity to develop deep relationships with peers and faculty as well as shallower (but no less important) relationships.

Inputs to Sense of Belonging

Inputs to sense of belonging include student characteristics such as socioeconomic status (SES), first-generation status, and racial and ethnic minority background.

SES and Social Class

The fact that students from working-class families experience college differently than students from higher SES levels is well documented in the scholarly literature (Goldrick-Rab, 2006, 2016; Jury et al., 2017; Ostrove & Long, 2007; Walpole, 2003). This literature suggests that students from relatively lower SES or working-class families often experience lower levels of belonging than their peers from higher SES families. In a selective liberal arts college setting, students' class background was a statistically significant variable of belonging; this claim held true both for objective measures of class (i.e., family income, parental education level) and subjective measures of class (i.e., self-reports; Ostrove & Long, 2007). Furthermore, low sense of belonging in college can impact students long after graduation, as exemplified by a retrospective study of women at a private institution (Ostrove, 2003).

The connection between SES and belonging is consistent even in a more generalizable sample. In a longitudinal study of over 4,800 students at 209 4-year colleges and universities, Walpole (2003) found that students from relatively low-SES backgrounds often have to work more and therefore study less than their higher SES peers which, in turn, also means that they were not as involved on campus and reported lower GPAs. Of note, this discrepancy in collegiate experience between students from lower versus higher SES levels continued even after graduation; her study drew on data gathered 9 years after commencement and showed that low-SES students still did not have the same social and economic capital as their high-SES peers, even if they had relatively higher levels of capital than their low-SES peers who did not attend college. Additionally, data from a national longitudinal sample showed that students from relatively lower SES backgrounds are more likely than peers from higher SES backgrounds to take time off or drop out during their higher education journeys (Goldrick-Rab, 2006).

First-Generation College Students

First-generation college students experience lower levels of belonging than their continuing-generation peers (Stebleton et al., 2014). This is at least partially due to the fact that first-generation students have been shown to work more hours and be less involved in cocurricular activities than their peers (Pascarella et al., 2004). First-generation students experience unique barriers in the adjustment to college and the navigation of campus resources, specifically related to meeting academic expectations, balancing family obligations, and knowing where to find support on campus (Gibbons et al., 2016). First-generation college students are often worried about financing their college educations, and this fact is a statistically significant predictor of first- to second-year retention (Pratt et al., 2017). All this coalesces into the reality that first-generation students are more likely to struggle with academics, with making friends, and more generally with acclimating to the campus environment (Pratt et al., 2017).

Racial and Ethnic Background

Racial and ethnic minority students are susceptible to lower levels of belonging as compared to their White peers, and this is especially true at predominantly White institutions (PWIs; Johnson et al., 2007). Murphy and Zirkel (2015) revealed that belonging—both anticipated and experienced—is important for all students in an academic setting; even so, they showed that belonging is lower for students from underrepresented racial and ethnic groups as compared to their White peers, and these lower levels of belonging correlate with poorer academic outcomes. Other research has shown that a targeted intervention designed to normalize collegiate hardships serves to increase belonging and academic outcomes for minority students (Walton et al., 2017; Walton & Cohen, 2007).

Environments of Sense of Belonging

Environments of sense of belonging include campus experiences regarding peers, faculty, cocurricular engagement, and campus climate.

Campus Experiences Regarding Peers

Discrete subsets of the student population thrive when engaged in certain types of peer-to-peer relationships. For instance, participation in racially diverse friendship groups has positive outcomes for minority students but not for White students (Antonio, 2004). At an urban PWI, minority students with randomly assigned interracial roommates report higher levels of belonging and higher GPAs after the first year than minority students with same-race roommates, even as majority students with minority roommates report no impact on belonging (Shook & Clay, 2012). Overall, first-year students who perceive that their residence hall peers are tolerant and supportive report higher levels of belonging (Johnson et al., 2007). Peer interactions regarding academics are also important mechanisms for belonging. For instance, the act of talking about academic challenges and triumphs with others correlates with increased academic self-efficacy (Altermatt, 2016). Likewise, students who engage with peer mentors report higher levels of belonging to campus than their nonmentored peers (Yomtov et al., 2017).

Campus Experiences Regarding Faculty

In a study of students' sense of belonging in the classroom setting, the researchers found that faculty encouragement of student participation and interaction is a positive correlate with belonging (Freeman et al., 2007). Furthermore, students experienced higher levels of belonging when professors were compassionate and took the time to interact individually with students (Hoffman et al., 2002). Positive interactions with faculty are particularly important to the fostering of belonging for minority students as compared to majority students (Meeuwisse et al., 2010). Mentorship provides one particularly important form of students' interactions with faculty. Mentorship exists in relationships that are defined by intent and involvement between a relative newcomer to the community and a longer-tenured community member (Mertz, 2006). A mentorship relationship might be comprised of individual relationships between faculty and students, exemplified by academic advising. It also might include a more group-based model in which mentoring communities develop among members in both formal and informal ways (Parks, 2011). Regardless of the form of mentorship, literature suggests that engagement mentorship provides students with opportunities to belong.

Campus Experiences Regarding Cocurricular Engagement
The positive correlation between students' cocurricular involvement and academic and social outcomes is well documented (Asher & Weeks, 2012; Astin, 1975; Bergen-Cico & Viscomi, 2012; Fincher, 2015). Engaging in community service via participation in a formal club, organization, or academic department correlates with increased sense of belonging. However, students who find community service opportunities via their own initiative report lower levels of belonging (Soria et al., 2012). Hence, the organizing structure of involvement is important to how students experience college. Indeed, involvement with any clubs, organizations, activities, and leadership roles correlates with belonging (Asher & Weeks, 2012). This literature suggests that students benefit when universities provide opportunities for engagement.

Campus Experiences Regarding Campus Climate
Students' perceptions of a negative racial campus climate correlate with lower levels of belonging for all students, especially at PWIs (Locks et al., 2008). Perceptions of negative racial campus climate stem in large part from discrepancies between a university's stated values related to diversity and the lived experiences of marginalized students (Linley, 2018). Hurtado and Carter (1997) found that Latino students' negative perceptions of a hostile racial campus climate impact belonging even in the 3rd year of study. At a PWI, minority students' psychological sense of community (similar to campus-level belonging) was a statistically significant product of perceptions of campus racial climate (Berryhill & Bee, 2007).

Outputs of Sense of Belonging

Minority students who undergo an intervention designed to increase feelings of social belonging report stronger health and well-being and go to the doctor less than their peers in a control group, even 3 years after that intervention takes place (Walton & Cohen, 2011). This same observation period showed that an intervention that normalized adversity results in African American students' increased GPAs and halved the minority achievement gap. Furthermore, this change occurred "outside conscious awareness" in that respondents could only vaguely recall the details of the intervention in which they participated years earlier (Walton & Cohen, 2011, p. 1450).

Other positive outcomes of a strong sense of belonging for college students include academic achievement, retention, and persistence (Hausmann et al., 2007), and this is especially true for students from underrepresented populations (Maestas et al., 2007). Correspondingly, a lack of belonging in a higher education context correlates with a variety of negative outcomes. Lack of belonging impedes academic performance (Walton & Cohen, 2007) and influences students' decisions to stay enrolled in college (Milem & Berger, 1997).

In Sum

This literature outlines findings that are "strong and consistent: Students who experience acceptance are more highly motivated and engaged in learning and more committed to school" (Osterman, 2000, p. 359). A strong sense of belonging is integral to college student flourishing and, conversely, lack of belonging correlates with negative outcomes. Since persistence and dropout are common indicators of student success, a key extension of this cumulative view is that the concept of belonging is ripe for incorporation into theories of student persistence. As such, in the subsequent section of this chapter, we incorporate the concept of belonging into two extant theories of college student persistence.

We do so because extant models of college student persistence do not incorporate clearly defined constructs of belonging. The works of Astin (1975), Braxton et al. (2014), and Tinto (1993) regularly function as starting points for a variety of studies in the field, and none of their traditional models incorporate a construct of belonging. Instead, researchers have deployed a variety of related but distinct constructs. For example, Tinto (1993) deployed language related to "integration" in his work, even as others have critiqued him for assimilationist terminology that alienates students (Hurtado & Carter, 1997; Tierney, 1999).

Sense of Belonging: Its Role in Current Theories of Student Retention

As stated, the concept of belonging stands ready for incorporation into theories of student persistence given that extant models of college student persistence currently fail to incorporate clearly defined constructs of belonging into their formulations. In this section, we incorporate the concept of belonging into two different extant theories of college student persistence. In doing so, we use a modification of the process of theory elaboration. Theory elaboration entails the use of concepts derived from other theoretical perspectives to explain the focal phenomenon (Thornberry, 1989). Rather than taking a concept derived from another theoretical perspective, we take the concept of sense of belonging and the associated empirical findings to revise the two focal theories of college student persistence.

The theory of student persistence in commuter colleges and universities and the revised theory of student persistence in residential colleges and universities constitute the two theories we will use in our efforts to incorporate a sense of belonging into extant theories of college student persistence. Braxton et al. (2004) first posited these theories in their volume *Student Understanding and Reducing College Departure*, and subsequent empirical testing of these theories was reported in *Rethinking College Student Retention* (Braxton et al., 2014). Empirical support exists for both theories (Braxton et al., 2014).

The need for different theories to account for student persistence in residential colleges and universities and in commuter colleges and universities stem from two differentiating dimensions between these two types of institutions of higher education: the characteristics of their social communities and the role of the external environment (Braxton et al., 2014). In contrast to residential institutions, commuter colleges and universities lack well-defined and structured social communities for students to establish membership (Braxton et al., 2004). Moreover, the external environments in commuter colleges and universities play a defining role in the college experience for their students that substantially differ from the role of the external environment for students at residential institutions (Braxton & Hirschy, 2005). To elaborate, commuter institutions enroll a wide variety of students such as traditionally aged students who live at home with their parents, older students, students with family obligations, working students, and part-time and full-time students (Bean & Metzner, 1985; Stewart & Rue, 1983). Moreover, while attending college, many adult students also have other day-to-day commitments and obligations, such as family and work responsibilities (Tinto, 1993). Such obligations shape the daily activities of commuter students (Webb, 1990) as well as their collegiate experiences.

We first describe the placement of a sense of belonging into the formulations of the theory of student persistence in commuter colleges and universities and then present these formulations.

The Theory of Student Persistence in Commuter Colleges and Universities

This theory regards student persistence as a longitudinal process with six primary dimensions that seek to account for the persistence of commuter students: entry characteristics, the external environment, the campus environment (e.g. organizational characteristics such as commitment of the institution to student welfare), student academic and intellectual development, subsequent institutional commitment, and student persistence in the college or university (Braxton et al., 2004, 2014). Because of space limitations for this chapter, we confine our descriptions of the formulations of this theory to those concepts that pertain to our placement of a sense of belonging into this theory. Nevertheless, Figure 3.1 graphically portrays the relationships among these six dimensions and the placement of a sense of belonging within the context of the pertinent concepts. We refer readers to Braxton et al. (2014) for a complete description of this theory.

We posit that two empirically supported concepts of the theory of student persistence in commuter colleges and universities function as antecedents to two forms of a sense of belonging: (a) commitment of the institution to student welfare, and (b) academic and intellectual development. An *institutionally anchored sense of belonging* and *sense of belonging anchored in shared purpose* constitute these two forms of a sense of belonging. The positing of two forms of belonging stands consistent with the perspective that belonging is a multidimensional concept (Hurtado & Carter, 1997).

Organizational characteristics, such as commitment of the institution to student welfare, constitute an important aspect of the campus environment. Commitment of the institution to student welfare consists of several dimensions. The first, and primary, dimension takes the form of an abiding concern for the growth and development of its students expressed by a given college or university. Other important dimensions include the high value the institution places on its students, treating each student with respect as an individual, and the equitable treatment of students (Braxton & Hirschy, 2005; Braxton et al., 2004, 2014). Commitment of the institution to student welfare also functions as an antecedent to academic and intellectual development (Braxton et al., 2014). Empirical backing for this relationship between the commitment of the institution to student welfare and academic and intellectual development exists (Braxton et al., 2014).

We posit herein that commitment of the institution to student welfare works as an antecedent to an *institutionally anchored sense of belonging*. An institutionally anchored sense of belonging reflects a student's feeling that they themselves are a valued part or member of their college or university. They hold such a feeling because they perceive that their college or university demonstrates a commitment to the welfare of its students through the observable actions of the administration, faculty, or staff of their college or university (Braxton et al., 2014). An institutionally anchored sense of belonging resonates with the view of Shook and Clay (2012) that a sense of belonging also exists at the level of the university. It further resonates with research showing that students' positive relationships with faculty engender sense of belonging (Freeman et al., 2007; Hoffman et al., 2002; Meeuwisse et al., 2010; Tovar & Simon, 2010).

We also posit that the concept of academic and intellectual development operates as an antecedent to a *sense of belonging anchored in shared purpose*. Academic and intellectual development represents a core value of the undergraduate experience (Lattuca & Stark, 2009). Students who perceive that they have grown in their academic and intellectual development come to regard themselves as holding educational values similar to those espoused by their college or university. In turn, they also come to view themselves as being an integral part of the purposes of college attendance. Put differently, they regard themselves as holding a sense of belonging anchored in shared purpose. Like an institutionally anchored sense of belonging, this form of a sense of belonging echoes the perspective of Shook and Clay (2012) that a sense of belonging transpires at the level of the university as well as with Freeman et al.'s (2007) contention that a sense of belonging takes place at the level of the classroom. Subsequent affirmation of our position stems from research showing the positive associations between participation in learning communities, first-year seminars, and summer bridge programs with sense of belonging (Hoffman et al., 2002; Strayhorn, 2011).

Thus, we place commitment of the institution to student welfare as an antecedent to an institutionally anchored sense of belonging and academic and intellectual development as an antecedent to sense of belonging anchored in shared purpose within the context of the formulations of the theory of college student persistence in commuter colleges and universities, as depicted in Figure 3.1.

To further elaborate on these formulations, student perceptions of their academic and intellectual development also act as an antecedent to subsequent institutional commitment. The greater the degree of academic and intellectual development perceived by a student, the greater their degree of subsequent commitment to their commuter college or university (Braxton et al., 2014). Empirical support for this anticipated relationship also exists (Braxton et al., 2014). By extension, we also contend that the greater the students' institutionally anchored sense of belonging and the greater their

Figure 3.1. Theory of student persistence in commuter colleges and universities with sense of belonging constructs.

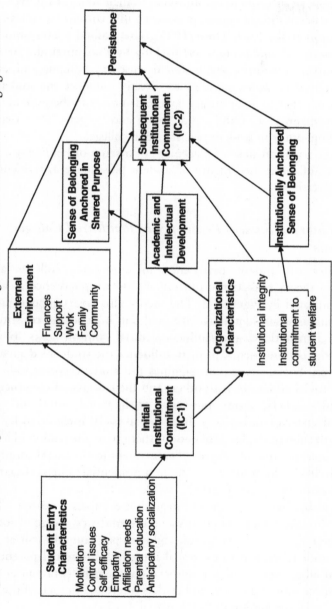

Adapted from Braxton et al. (2014).

sense of belonging anchored in shared purpose, the greater their degree of subsequent commitment to their college or university. In turn, the greater the student's degree of subsequent commitment to their college or university, the greater the student's likelihood of persistence in a commuter college or university (Braxton et al., 2014; Tinto, 1975). This posited relationship, as illustrated in Figure 3.1, holds empirical backing by Braxton et al. (2014). Moreover, a student's institutionally anchored sense of belonging and *sense of belonging anchored in shared purpose* also directly influence the student's likelihood of persistence in a commuter college or university because of the findings of Hausmann et al. (2007) and Milem and Berger (1997) that a sense of belonging results in student persistence in college.

We turn our attention next to placement of a sense of belonging into the formulations of the revised theory of student persistence in residential colleges and universities.

The Revised Theory of Student Persistence in Residential Colleges and Universities

Like the theory of student persistence in commuter colleges and universities, this theory depicts the process of student persistence as longitudinal, as indicated by Figure 3.2. The theory also posits gender, race/ethnicity, parental education, and average grades in high school constitute student entry characteristics that influence initial commitments to the institution. Initial commitments, in turn, influence the student's degree of social integration. Social integration signifies the student's perception of their degree of social affiliation with others and their degree of congruence with the attitudes, beliefs, norms, and values of the social communities of a college or university (Tinto, 1975). Increases in social integration led to greater degrees of subsequent levels of commitment to an institution (Tinto, 1975). The greater the student's degree of subsequent institutional commitment, the more likely the student persists in a residential college (Braxton et al., 2004; Braxton et al., 2014; Tinto, 1975).

As indicated by Figure 3.2, social integration occupies a central place in this theory with six antecedents that shape the student's degree of social integration. These six antecedents include ability to pay, commitment of the institution to student welfare, institutional integrity, communal potential, proactive social adjustment, and psychosocial engagement (Braxton et al., 2014). Given space limitations, we refer readers interested in each of the six antecedents to social integration to Braxton et al. (2014).

As indicated by Figure 3.2, we revise this theory by positing that social integration functions as an antecedent to a *peer-anchored sense of belonging*.[1]

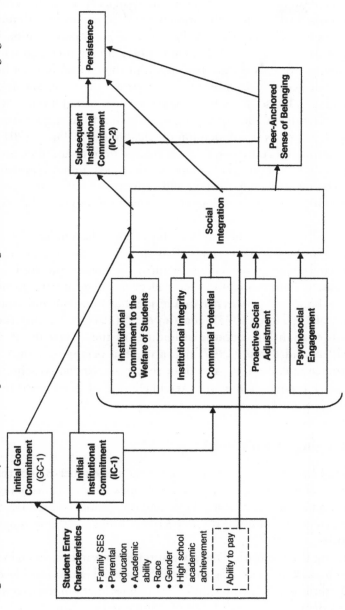

Figure 3.2. Revised theory for student departure in residential colleges and universities with sense of belonging constructs.

Adapted from Braxton et al. (2014).

Social integration denotes the student's perception of their degree of social affiliation with others and their degree of congruency with the attitudes, beliefs, norms, and values of the social communities of a college or university (Tinto, 1975). Because their social affiliation with others emanates with their social interactions with peers (Milem & Berger, 1997) and participation in extracurricular activities (Christie & Dinham, 1991), a peer-anchored sense of belonging results from a student's perception of their social integration. The greater their degree of social integration, the greater their peer-anchored sense of belonging. This sense of belonging resonates with Hurtado and Carter's (1997) view that a sense of belonging emanates from social experiences on campus, as well as the contention of Chambliss and Takacs (2014) that the most meaningful college experiences emerge from their interactions with specific people. Other points of connection include findings suggesting that students who report having tolerant and supportive peers in their residence halls have higher levels of belonging relative to their peers (Johnson et al., 2007).

By extension, we also contend that the greater the student's *peer-anchored sense of belonging*, the greater their degree of subsequent commitment to their college or university. In turn, the greater the student's degree of subsequent commitment to their college or university, the greater the student's likelihood of persistence in a residential college or university (Braxton et al., 2014; Tinto, 1975). Braxton et al. (2014) offer empirical support for this relationship. Because of findings of the Hausmann et al. (2007) and Milem and Berger (1997) that a sense of belonging results in student persistence in college, we also posit that a peer-anchored sense of belonging directly influences the student's likelihood of persistence in a residential college or university.

Sense of Belonging: What's Next?

Clearly, empirical tests of the two theories of college student persistence that incorporate forms of belonging into their formulations stand as a critical next step. We recommend that commuter colleges and universities and residential colleges and universities comprise the respective settings for the testing of these two theories.

In conducting these empirical tests, we also urge researchers to include students with characteristics such as family SES, parental educational level, and racial and ethnic group membership. Research reviewed in this chapter suggests that students vary in their levels of belonging based on these characteristics. To elaborate, students from lower SES background experience lower levels of belonging than their counterparts from higher SES families (Goldrick-Rab, 2006, 2016; Jury et al., 2017; Ostrove & Long, 2007; Walpole, 2003). Moreover, first-generation students (Stebleton et al., 2014) and students from underrepresented racial and minority groups experience lower levels of belonging (Murphy & Zirkel, 2015).

In addition to these recommendations for research, the next step pertains to the specific measurements of sense of belonging in general and our three forms of belonging in particular. For example, what are the implications of different forms of measurement? Asher and Weeks (2013) shed important light on the importance of using appropriate metrics to measure sense of belonging. They reviewed existing measurement practices and note multiple instances of scales that contain "diverse and confounding item content that overlaps with the hypothesized causes of each type of experience" (Asher & Weeks, 2013, p. 284). In short, conceptual overlap exists between factors impacting sense of belonging and retention, and straightforward measurements of sense of belonging function to delineate clearly specific aspects of sense of belonging versus retention.

Conclusion

Scholars and practitioners understand not only the value of a college degree but also the importance of all the things that happen between matriculation and graduation. As reviewed in this chapter, the scholarly community is amassing a great deal of research, which concludes that fostering a sense of belonging for today's college students should be one of those key things that happen during undergraduate enrollment. It is our hope that this chapter contributes to the formalization of the relationship between college students' sense of belonging and persistence.

Note

1. The literature raises the issue of whether belonging is an antecedent or outcome of social integration. Asher and Weeks (2013) write that social integration is a "cause of belongingness" (p. 284). They make this claim in their introduction, almost as a passing comment, thus highlighting how commonplace it is to assume directionality from belongingness to social integration. We concur with Asher and Weeks by viewing social integration as an antecedent of sense of belonging.

References

Altermatt, E. R. (2016). Academic support from peers as a predictor of academic self-efficacy among college students. *Journal of College Student Retention: Research, Theory & Practice, 21*(1), 1–17. http://dx.doi.org/10.1177/1521025116686588

Antonio, A. L. (2004). The influence of friendship groups on intellectual self-confidence and educational aspirations in college. *The Journal of Higher Education, 75*(4), 446–471. http://dx.doi.org/10.1353/jhe.2004.0019

Asher, S. R., & Weeks, M. S. (2012). *Social relationships, academic engagement, and well-being in college: Findings from the Duke Social Relationships Project.* Duke University. https://sites.duke.edu/dsrp/files/2012/10/Duke-Social-Relationships-Project-Report.pdf

Asher, S. R., & Weeks, M. S. (2013). Loneliness and belongingness in the college years. In R. J. Coplan & J. C. Bowker (Eds.), *The handbook of solitude: Psychological perspectives on social isolation, social withdrawal, and being alone* (pp. 283–301). Wiley. http://dx.doi.org/10.1002/9781118427378.ch16

Astin, A. W. (1975). *Preventing students from dropping out.* Jossey-Bass.

Astin, A. W. (1991). *Assessment for excellence: The philosophy and practice of assessment and evaluation in higher education.* American Council on Education & Macmillan.

Astin, A. W. (1993). *What matters in college?: Four critical years revisited.* Jossey-Bass.

Baumeister, R. F., & Leary, M. R. (1995). The need to belong: Desire for interpersonal attachments as a fundamental human motivation. *Psychological Bulletin, 117*(3), 497–529. http://dx.doi.org/10.1037/0033-2909.117.3.497

Bean, J. P., & Metzner, B. S. (1985). A conceptual model of nontraditional student attrition. *Review of Educational Research, 55*, 485–540. https://doi.org/10.3102%2F00346543055004485

Bergen-Cico, D., & Viscomi, J. (2012). Exploring the association between campus co-curricular involvement and academic achievement. *Journal of College Student Retention: Research, Theory & Practice, 14*(3), 329–343. http://dx.doi.org/10.2190/CS.14.3.c

Berryhill, J. C., & Bee, E. K. (2007). Ethnically diverse college students' psychological sense of community: Do their perceptions of campus racial climate influence it? *College Student Affairs Journal, 27*(1), 76–93. https://www.proquest.com/scholarly-journals/ethnically-diverse-college-students-psychological/docview/224819185/se-2

Bollen, K. A., & Hoyle, R. H. (1990). Perceived cohesion: A conceptual and empirical examination. *Social Forces, 69*(2), 479–504. http://dx.doi.org/10.2307/2579670

Braxton, J. M., Doyle, W. R., Hartley, H. V., III, Hirschy, A. S., Jones, W. A., & McLendon, M. K. (2014). *Rethinking college student retention.* Jossey-Bass.

Braxton, J. M., & Hirschy, A. S. (2005). Theoretical developments in college student departure. In A. Seidman (Ed.), *College student retention: Formula for student success* (pp. 61–87). Praeger.

Braxton, J. M., Hirschy, A. S., & McClendon, S. A. (2004). Understanding and reducing college student departure. *ASHE-ERIC Higher Education Report, 30*(3), 1–128.

Chambliss, D. F., & Takacs, C. G. (2014). *How college works.* Harvard University Press.

Christie, N. G., & Dinham, S. M. (1991). Institutional and external influences on social integration in the freshman year. *Journal of Higher Education, 62,* 412–436. https://doi.org/10.2307/1982003

Durkheim, É. (1976). The role of universities in the social education of the country. *Minerva, 14*(3), 380–388.

Fincher, J. (2015). *Powerful pathways across race: Sense of belonging in discriminatory collegiate environments* (Publication No. AAI3627635) [Doctoral dissertation, University of Maryland]. ProQuest.

Freeman, T. M., Anderman, L.H., & Jensen, J. M. (2007). Sense of belonging in college freshmen at the classroom and campus levels. *The Journal of Experimental Education, 75*(3), 203–220. http://dx.doi.org/10.3200/JEXE.75.3.203-220

Gibbons, M. M., Rhinehart, A., & Hardin, E. (2016). How first-generation college students adjust to college. *Journal of College Student Retention: Research, Theory & Practice, 20*(4), 488–510. http://dx.doi.org/10.1177/1521025116682035

Goldrick-Rab, S. (2006). Following their every move: An investigation of social-class differences in college pathways. *Sociology of Education, 79*(1), 67–79. http://dx.doi.org/10.1177/003804070607900104

Goldrick-Rab, S. (2016). *Paying the price: College costs, financial aid, and the betrayal of the American dream.* University of Chicago Press.

Goodenow, C. (1993). Classroom belonging among early adolescent students: Relationships to motivation and achievement. *The Journal of Early Adolescence, 13*(1), 21–43. http://dx.doi.org/10.1177/0272431693013001002

Gummadam, P., Pittman, L. D., & Ioffe, M. (2016). School belonging, ethnic identity, and psychological adjustment among ethnic minority college students. *The Journal of Experimental Education, 84*(2), 289–306. http://dx.doi.org/10.1080/00220973.2015.1048844

Hagerty, B. M. K., Lynch-Sauer, J., Patusky, K. L., Bouwsema, M., & Collier, P. (1992). Sense of belonging: A vital mental health concept. *Archives of Psychiatric Nursing, 6*(3), 172–77. http://dx.doi.org/10.1016/0883-9417(92)90028-H

Hagerty, B. M. K., & Patusky, K. (1995). Developing a measure of sense of belonging. *Nursing Research, 44*(1), 9–13. http://dx.doi.org/10.1097/00006199-199501000-00003

Hausmann, L. R. M., Schofield, J. W., & Woods, R. L. (2007). Sense of belonging as a predictor of intentions to persist among African American and White first-year college students. *Research in Higher Education, 48*(7), 803–839. http://dx.doi.org/10.1007/s11162-007-9052-9

Hoffman, M., Richmond, J., Morrow, J., & Salomone, K. (2002). Investigating "sense of belonging" in first-year college students. *Journal of College Student Retention: Research, Theory & Practice, 4*(3), 227–256. http://dx.doi.org/10.2190/DRYC-CXQ9-JQ8V-HT4V

Hurtado, S., & Carter, D. F. (1997). Effects of college transition and perceptions of the campus racial climate on Latino college students' sense of belonging. *Sociology of Education, 70,* 324–345. http://dx.doi.org/10.2307/2673270

Johnson, D. R., Soldner, M., Leonard, J. B., Alvarez, P., Inkelas, K. K., Rowan-Kenyon, H. T., & Longerbeam, S. D. (2007). Examining sense of belonging among first-year undergraduates from different racial/ethnic groups. *Journal of College Student Development, 48*(5), 525–542. http://dx.doi.org/10.1353/csd.2007.0054

Jury, M., Smeding, A., Stephens, N. M., Nelson, J. E., Aelenei, C., & Darnon, C. (2017). The experiences of low-SES students in higher education: Psychological barriers to success and interventions to reduce social-class inequality. *Journal of Social Issues, 73*(1), 23–41. http://dx.doi.org/10.1111/josi.12202

Lattuca, L. R., & Stark, J. S. (2009). *Shaping the college curriculum: Academic plans in context* (2nd ed.). Jossey-Bass.

Linley, J. L. (2018). Racism here, racism there, racism everywhere: The racial realities of minoritized peer socialization agents at a historically White institution. *Journal of College Student Development, 59*(1), 21–36. http://dx.doi.org/10.1353/csd.2018.0002

Locks, A. M., Hurtado, S., Bowman, N. A., & Oseguera, L. (2008). Extending notions of campus climate and diversity to students' transition to college. *The Review of Higher Education, 31*(3), 257–285. http://dx.doi.org/10.1353/rhe.2008.0011

Maestas, R., Vaquera, G. S., & Zehr, L. M. (2007). Factors impacting sense of belonging at a Hispanic-serving institution. *Journal of Hispanic Higher Education, 6*(3), 237–256. http://dx.doi.org/10.1177/1538192707302801

Mallett, R. K., Mello, Z. R., Wagner, D. E., Worrell, F., Burrow, R. N., & Andretta, J. R. (2011). Do I belong? It depends on when you ask. *Cultural Diversity and Ethnic Minority Psychology, 17*(4), 432–436. http://dx.doi.org/10.1037/a0025455

Maslow, A. H. (1943). A theory of human motivation. *Psychological Review, 50*(4), 370. https://psycnet.apa.org/doi/10.1037/h0054346

Maslow, A. H. (1954). *Motivation and personality*. Harpers.

Meeuwisse, M., Severiens, S. E., & Born, M. P. (2010). Learning environment, interaction, sense of belonging and study success in ethnically diverse student groups. *Research in Higher Education, 51*(6), 528–545. http://dx.doi.org/10.1007/s11162-010-9168-1

Mertz, N. T. (2006). What's a mentor, anyway? *Educational Administration Quarterly, 40*(4), 541–560. http://dx.doi.org/10.1177/0013161X04267110

Milem, J. F., & Berger, J. B. (1997). A modified model of college student persistence: Exploring the relationship between Astin's theory of involvement and Tinto's theory of student departure. *Journal of College Student Development, 38*(4), 387–400. https://psycnet.apa.org/record/1997-06050-002

Murdock-Perriera, L. A., Boucher, K. L., Carter, E. R., & Murphy, M. C. (2019). Places of belonging: Person- and place-focused interventions to support belonging in college. In M. B. Paulsen & L. W. Perna (Eds.), *Higher education: Handbook of theory and research* (pp. 291–323). Springer.

Murphy, M., & Zirkel, S. (2015). Race and belonging in school: How anticipated and experienced belonging affect choice, persistence, and performance. *Teachers College Record, 117*(12), 1–40. http://dx.doi.org/10.1177/016146811511701204

Osterman, K. F. (2000). Students' need for belonging in the school community. *Review of Educational Research, 70*(3), 323–367. http://dx.doi.org/10.2307/1170786

Ostrove, J. M. (2003). Belonging and wanting: Meanings of social class background for women's constructions of their college experiences. *Journal of Social Issues, 59*(4), 771–784. http://dx.doi.org/10.1046/j.0022-4537.2003.00089.x

Ostrove, J. M., & Long, S. M. (2007). Social class and belonging: Implications for college adjustment. *The Review of Higher Education, 30*(4), 363–389. http://dx.doi.org/10.1353/rhe.2007.0028

Parks, S. D. (2011). *Big questions, worthy dreams: Mentoring emerging adults in their search for meaning, purpose, and faith*. Wiley.

Pascarella, E. T., Pierson, C. T., Wolniak, G. C., & Terenzini, P. T. (2004). First-generation college students: Additional evidence on college experiences and outcomes. *The Journal of Higher Education, 75*(3), 249–284. http://dx.doi.org/10.1353/jhe.2004.0016

Pratt, I. S., Harwood, H. B., Cavazos, J. T., & Ditzfeld, C. P. (2017). Should I stay or should I go? Retention in first-generation college students. *Journal of College Student Retention: Research, Theory & Practice, 21*(1), 105–118. http://dx.doi.org/10.1177/1521025117690868

Shook, N. J., & Clay, R. (2012). Interracial roommate relationships: A mechanism for promoting sense of belonging at university and academic performance. *Journal of Experimental Social Psychology, 48*(5), 1168–1172. http://dx.doi.org/10.1016/j.jesp.2012.05.005

Soria, K. M., Troisi, J. N., & Stebleton, M. J. (2012, June 3). Reaching out, connecting within: community service and sense of belonging among college students. *Higher Education in Review.* https://hdl.handle.net/11299/150026

Stebleton, M. J., Soria, K. M., & Huesman, R. L. (2014). First-generation students' sense of belonging, mental health, and use of counseling services at public research universities. *Journal of College Counseling, 17*(1), 6–20. http://dx.doi.org/10.1002/j.2161-1882.2014.00044.x

Stewart, S. S., & Rue, P. (1983). Commuter students: Definition and distribution. In S. S. Stewart (Ed.), *Commuter Students: Enhancing Their Educational Experiences* (New Directions for Student Services, no. 24, pp. 3–8). Jossey-Bass. https://doi.org/10.1002/ss.37119832403

Strayhorn, T. L. (2011). Bridging the pipeline: Increasing underrepresented students' preparation for college through a summer bridge program. *American Behavioral Scientist, 55*(2), 142–159. http://dx.doi.org/10.1177/0002764210381871

Strayhorn, T. L. (2012). *College students' sense of belonging: A key to educational success for all students*. Routledge.

Terrazas-Carrillo, E., Hong, J. Y., McWhirter, P. T., Robbins, R., & Pace, T. M. (2017). Place-making and its impact on international graduate student persistence. *Journal of College Student Retention: Research, Theory & Practice, 19*(1), 59–80. http://dx.doi.org/10.1177/1521025115611403

Thornberry, T. P. (1989). Reflections on the advantages and disadvantages of theoretical Integration. In S. F. Messner, M. D. Krohn, and A. E. Liska (Eds),

Theoretical integration in the study of deviance and crime (pp. 52–60). State University of New York Press.

Tierney, W. G. (1999). Models of minority college-going and retention: Cultural integrity versus cultural suicide. *The Journal of Negro Education, 68*(1), 80–91. http://dx.doi.org/10.2307/2668211

Tinto, V. (1975). Dropout from higher education: A theoretical synthesis of recent research. *Review of Educational Research, 45*(1), 89–125. http://dx.doi .org/10.2307/1170024

Tinto, V. (1993). *Leaving college: Rethinking the causes and cures of student attrition* (2nd ed.). University of Chicago Press.

Tovar, E., & Simon, M. A. (2010). Factorial structure and invariance analysis of the Sense of Belonging Scales. *Measurement and Evaluation in Counseling and Development, 43*(3), 199–217. http://dx.doi.org/10.1177/0748175610384811

Walpole, M. (2003). Socioeconomic status and college: How SES affects college experiences and outcomes. *The Review of Higher Education, 27*(1), 45–73. http:// dx.doi.org/10.1353/rhe.2003.0044

Walton, G. M., & Cohen, G. L. (2007). A question of belonging: Race, social fit, and achievement. *Journal of Personality and Social Psychology, 92*(1), 82–96. http://dx.doi.org/10.1037/0022-3514.92.1.82

Walton, G. M., & Cohen, G. L. (2011). A brief social-belonging intervention improves academic and health outcomes of minority students. *Science, 331*(6023), 1447–1451. https://psycnet.apa.org/doi/10.1126/science.1198364

Walton, G. M., Murphy, M. C., Logel, C., Yeager, D. S., & The College Transition Collaborative. (2017). *The social-belonging intervention: A guide for use and customization.* The College Transition Collaborative. http://collegetransitioncollaborative.org/content/2017/belonging-custom-guide/

Webb, M. W., II. (1990, April 16–20). *Development and testing of a theoretical model for predicting student degree persistence at four-year commuter colleges* [Paper presentation]. American Educational Research Association Annual Meeting, Boston, MA.

Yomtov, D., Plunkett, S. W., Efrat, R., & Marin, A. G. (2017). Can peer mentors improve first-year experiences of university students? *Journal of College Student Retention: Research, Theory & Practice, 19*(1), 25–44. http://dx.doi .org/10.1177/1521025115611398

PART TWO

SENSE OF BELONGING ACROSS STUDENT POPULATIONS

4

FACILITATING A SENSE OF BELONGING FOR STUDENTS WITH MULTIPLE IDENTITIES

Ronald Hallett, Adrianna Kezar, Joseph Kitchen, and Rosemary Perez

Practitioners have long understood the importance of creating a sense of belonging among at-promise students. We strategically employ the term *at-promise* to identify the large group of college students who are traditionally underserved by higher education institutions—including low-income, racially minoritized, and first-generation college students. Often, these students are associated with deficit language, such as *at-risk* or *underperforming*. Shifting language is more than semantics. By considering using *at-promise*, we focus on the potential of students while also recognizing the systemic barriers that often exist.

As the previous chapters in this book illustrate, establishing a sense of belonging is linked to academic, personal, and social outcomes. Sense of belonging is a relational construct that reflects students' subjective sense of connectedness to others in college, feelings of being welcomed, supported, and included at their institution and of fitting into social and academic communities on campus (Hurtado & Carter, 1997; Strayhorn, 2012). The concept is the "sense of personal involvement in a social system so that persons feel themselves to be an indispensable and integral part of the system" (Anant, 1966, p. 21; see also Bollen & Hoyle, 1990). There are behavioral consequences to belongingness, and fostering a sense of belonging is linked to students' college persistence, success, and completion (Hausmann et al., 2009; Hoffman et al., 2002; Hurtado, 2007; Maestas et al., 2007; Strayhorn, 2012). A sense of belonging is important for fostering the success of all students, especially at-promise students (Strayhorn, 2012), with postsecondary institutions bearing responsibility for creating the conditions that foster students' sense of belonging (Hurtado & Carter, 1997; Kitchen & Williams, 2019; Museus et al., 2017). Belonging is affected by factors such as campus climates (Hurtado & Carter, 1997; Johnson, 2012; Johnson et al., 2007), validation from educators (Hurtado et al., 2015), culturally relevant learning environments (Museus et al., 2017), and involvement and engagement in educationally purposeful social and academic experiences in college (Kitchen & Williams, 2019; Museus, 2008; Ribera et al., 2017; Strayhorn, 2012).

Most colleges and universities are designed to support White, male, and middle- to upper-class students. As a result, these students often feel as though they belong on campus while at-promise students may feel excluded or like imposters. We join a group of scholars who argue for intentionally rethinking practices in higher education in order to create the context for how at-promise students feel a sense of belonging. Many researchers and practitioners focus on interventions designed for a specific subgroup of at-promise students. While these approaches can be an important aspect of designing a program on campus where these students belong (e.g., identity-based programs and multicultural centers), they do little to shift the overall culture of postsecondary institutions that exclude students by moving their identities to the margins. Further, these spaces that focus on a singular identity can make it difficult for students who possess multiple marginalized identities to feel a sense of belonging anywhere on campus. In this chapter, we argue for an approach to fostering belonging that considers supporting a diverse group of at-promise students in a way that shifts the culture of the institution to becoming multiple-identity conscious while also affirming identity-centered programming and multicultural centers that provide a supportive role for minoritized students.

Our research illustrates the potential of programs and institutions to create a sense of belonging for a large group of at-promise students with diverse backgrounds, experiences, identities, and goals. We found that *what* program elements (e.g., mentoring, shared courses, first-year seminar) were included in the program was less important than *how* the program was implemented. Instead of focusing on the specific program elements that should be included, this chapter explores the underlying approaches to practice that programs and institutions can incorporate in order to support a sense of belonging for a large group of at-promise students with multiple identities. We share some insights that emerged from our study of a program that supported a large group of at-promise students in a multiple-identity conscious way that fostered a sense of belonging.

Description of Thompson Scholars Learning Community Program

The Thompson Scholars Learning Community (TSLC) is a foundation-supported 2-year comprehensive college transition program at the University of the Nebraska system. The TSLC program is located at three campuses with different profiles—the Kearney campus is relatively smaller and located in a rural portion of the state, the Omaha campus is a metropolitan university serving a large percentage of commuter students, and the Lincoln campus is a land-grant research-oriented university with a national profile as part of the Big Ten Conference. TSLC began in 2008 with the goal of supporting students from low-income backgrounds in the state of Nebraska. Housed in academic affairs, the programs have dedicated staff working with 200–600 first- and second-year students who also receive scholarships that cover, approximately, the cost of tuition and fees. The program includes shared academic courses, proactive advising, peer mentors, and academic, social, and career support (Hallett, Kezar, Kitchen, & Perez, 2020). All the students come from low-income backgrounds (estimated family contribution of $10,000 per year or less); over 60% of the students are first-generation college students, and many identify as racially minoritized (Omaha campus, 66%; Lincoln campus, 36%; Kearney campus, 29%). Although students officially are in the program for 2 years, they continue to receive scholarship support for up to 5 years and can continue to receive support from staff if they need it. Approximately 2,800 TSLC students are supported across the three campuses each year.

We engaged in a 5-year mixed methods study of the TSLC program (Cole et al., 2019; Hallett, Kezar, Kitchen, Perez, & Reason, 2020). The study included longitudinal surveys and interviews with TSLC students as well as case study data collection (e.g., program observations, interviews with instructors and staff, and document analysis). For more information about the program or study, visit https://pullias.usc.edu/tslc/.

Sense of Belonging for Students With Multiple Identities

The size and diversity of the TSLC program requires the leadership and staff to explore ways to ensure that all students felt a sense of belonging. Drawing from our quantitative analysis, we found that students with differing identities (e.g., race, sex, first-generation college status) have experiences in the program that led to a similar sense of belonging. In this section, we explore how the leadership and staff promoted a similar sense of belonging among at-promise students for such a large and diverse group of students while considering their multiple identities and backgrounds. We identified four themes that explain facets of the TSLC approach to facilitating a sense of belonging among a large and diverse group of students: creating validating experiences, being conscious of multiple identities, tailoring support for belonging, and acknowledging a continuum of belonging.

The four themes worked together to create a context where students with different identities could feel a sense of belonging to the same program. Creating *validating experiences* for students within TSLC serves as the superordinate aspect of the program where the staff, instructors, peer mentors, and leadership proactively build trusting relations with students, learn about their multiple identities, and gain information about potential challenges students face and opportunities they could pursue. Within the context of validation, the program staff and leadership are *conscious of multiple identities*—meaning they are aware of and sensitive to the many different identities that students possess without privileging or minimizing any specific identity. Through doing their work using a multiple identity-conscious approach within a validating context, the program staff explore common themes that emerged from students' experiences and make decisions about how to create *tailored support* in order for the program to meet the needs of subgroups of students who may have challenges. At-promise students have validating experiences with staff and instructors who acknowledge and affirm that their multiple identities are welcome and an integral part of the TSLC community, which helps foster a sense of belonging among the wide group of program participants. Finally, the program assumes a *continuum of belonging*, meaning that some students may only have felt a minimal level of connection to the program and find stronger connections in other places on campus. The program staff actively help facilitate belonging in other spaces on campus that may be more conducive for individual students.

This overarching approach to belonging enables the TSLC programs at three very different campuses (i.e., rural, research-oriented, metropolitan) serving a large and diverse (e.g., race, income, first-generation status, immigration background, majors) group of students to create a sense of belonging for all students. In the sections that follow, we provide more detailed explanation and illustration of each theme.

Creating Validating Experiences

One of our key findings was the importance of validating experiences for at-promise students for promoting their success (Hallett, Reason et al., 2020). Validating experiences was an essential aspect of how the programs create a context for belonging. Validation is a strengths-based and proactive process initiated by institutional agents that affirms, supports, and empowers at-promise students in holistic ways that allow them to realize and (re)learn their innate potential for success (Rendón, 1994; Rendón & Muñoz, 2011). Students in the program are referred to as *scholars*, which is more than semantics. The staff, mentors, and instructors use this term to affirm that students belong—both individually and collectively—within the higher education context. The staff and directors consistently express to the students that they believe in their potential as scholars, and their job is to serve as a resource to help students realize their full potential. Each of the program elements involve opportunities to validate students' potential in order to demonstrate that they belong within the program and higher education more broadly.

The program creates validating experiences through program elements that enable them to get to know and support students, including becoming familiar with students' backgrounds, goals, and multiple identities. For example, students meet with staff and instructors about halfway through the semester for the first 2 years as part of the program's proactive advising process (Kitchen et al., 2020). This proactive advising process enables the program staff and instructors to build trusting relationships with students as well as to review students' grades in order to identify potential issues and connect students with resources. The staff members take a validating approach to these midsemester meetings. These meetings could have easily resulted in a deficit perspective where students felt like the staff were checking in because they did not trust the students or thought that the students lacked the ability to be academically successful. Instead, the midsemester meetings are an opportunity to affirm students' potential and to create a space where all students felt like they belonged. These meetings also provide an opportunity for staff to get to know students' multiple identities. As one staff member explained,

> We try hard to let the students know they're important, they're noticed. We know their names. We care about their stories, and again, try to constantly communicate that fact so they don't feel like they're not noticed as they continue to move through the year.

This kind of experience contributes to students feeling like an integral part of the community, and this investment in them from staff creates a sense of personal involvement in the social system that is key to developing a sense of belonging (Anant, 1966; Bollen & Hoyle, 1990; Strayhorn, 2012).

The staff members and peer mentors are expected to know students as individuals. During one mentor training about halfway through the year, a director gave the mentors a quiz about their mentees with questions that included full name, information about family, the mentees' personal and academic experiences the first semester, if the mentees work and how many hours, current major, career goals, any challenges they currently are experiencing, and the mentees' accomplishments. The final question was "Do you really know how they are doing?" If the mentor could not answer any of the questions, they had 1 week to schedule an additional meeting to connect with their mentee. The mentors at this campus also coordinate events for their small groups of five to seven mentees, including game nights, dinner in the residence hall, or other activities that did not cost money. The goal is to create a small space where students and peer mentors could get to know each other, build relationships with one another, and feel connected to a peer who was a part of the program (i.e., a sense of belonging).

Knowing students is essential to creating validating experiences. Getting to know the students also occurs within the first-year seminars taught by the staff members. Although teaching content about how to successfully navigate college is a goal of the seminar, the staff members are also focused on getting to know students and helping them build connections with each other. At two of the campuses, they start out each seminar with "highs/lows" or "happies/crappies" to allow each student the opportunity to express how they were doing that week. This acknowledges and affirms both the personal and academic experiences of students as being valid. Although a student may be nervous to share a personal or academic challenge, they often feel validated when another student affirms that they had a similar challenge. The students could also share resources with each other and build social connections.

While many offices and programs on campus tend to be segmented to address a single identity or issue, the programs recognize, validate, and support students holistically. Instead of waiting for students to experience challenges related to not feeling a sense of belonging, institutional agents assume that they need to proactively build trusting relationships with students in order to identify potential barriers and opportunities related to students' feeling a sense of belonging in the social and academic settings on campus. The assumption is that creating validating experiences is the foundation for all students to feel a sense of belonging within the program and, hopefully, within higher education more broadly.

Being Conscious of Multiple Identities

A key part of validation is taking a proactive approach to student support, and one way the program did this is by proactively building relationships with and getting to know students so that the staff members are aware of the multiple identities the students bring with them into the TSLC and campus community, and so that the staff members could meaningfully validate who students are and affirm that they and their whole selves (multiple identities) belonged in the community. Thus, within the context of validating experiences, the program staff are *conscious of multiple identities* by leveraging the relationships with students to holistically consider students' experiences, identities, and goals as well as societal barriers that exist related to race, class, gender, sexuality, and other social injustices. While not centering a singular identity, a multiple identity-conscious approach allows for all identities to be equally considered and for space to be created for individuals with those identities to belong. The program recognizes that individual students possess more than one identity and that students within the program have different identities that shape their sense of belonging. By being multiple-identity conscious, the programs also demonstrate how *all* students could belong in higher education. As one staff member explained,

> They come from various backgrounds, come from various pressures. Some of them are still very tied to home and helping keep the family going, whether that's financially or other ways they support their family members, that they know they have a voice, that we understand the pressures they're under as students.

In addition to helping individual students feel a sense of belonging, a multiple identity-conscious approach also enables students to learn about and appreciate the identities of others.

Students often discuss how they experience TSLC spaces and interactions differently from other spaces on campus. As one student shared,

> I feel like we do address different race and ethnicity and different issues in every sphere of everything. Like [the program director] is very open about it and all of our advisors and stuff like that. So, I don't think we ignore it; I think we embrace it more than you could do in individual classes that you are not with these people a lot. We embrace differences a lot better here, and I think it's encouraged more.

Even though the program is compositionally diverse, the students discuss it being a "community" and "family" where they belong and could find support. Another student explained, "TSLC acknowledges differences by race, sexual orientation, gender, etc. and validates it has a place in the community, 'empowers it,' but also emphasizes [it] 'about being TSLC.'" The program staff, director, mentors, and instructors consistently send the message that all students belong in the program.

An important aspect of affirming that all identities and backgrounds belong in TSLC involves hiring a compositionally diverse group of staff, mentors, and instructors. In particular, the programs recruit mentors while considering the multiple identities and backgrounds of students, including race; gender; sexuality; majors; career goals; personalities; academic successes; and, connections to rural, suburban, and urban areas. Even if a student did not work directly with a mentor, staff member, or instructor who shared their identities, it still matters to students and their sense that they belong in the program space and community that those identities are represented.

Instructors in the program also create space in their curriculum to recognize the multiple identities of their at-promise students. They are encouraged to do this by program staff, and many took it upon themselves as part of their commitment to helping students see themselves reflected in the curriculum and to feel a part of the class and learning experience. For instance, take two classes in particular—a TSLC speech class and TSLC autobiography writing class—where assignments are embedded in the class that explicitly (a) provide a space for students to learn the mechanics and content of the fields of speech and writing, and (b) to do so in a way that is situated in an exploration of students' multiple identities and who they are as people. This is completed in a classroom setting, and this information is shared with others in the classroom with the intent of helping foster community, connections, and mutual understanding across peer groups. Being able to situate their learning in an exploration of who they are is a validating experience for students. Through this process, many students share they are surprised to learn of identities and experiences they have in common with peers of which they were not previously aware. This realization helps foster a sense of connection and promotes relationship building and a sense of belonging.

The program also explicitly incorporates recurring events and opportunities that highlight not only the importance of diversity, but also of *inclusion* in the community with the idea that everyone has a place in the community and should feel that they belong there—partly in response to the increasing diversity of the program. For instance, one campus hosted a "Diversity Event" for their students to learn about multiple identity groups among students and the importance of ensuring that everyone felt included in the program and connected to the community. The presenter emphasized the importance of not "tokenizing" or singling out individuals for one particular identity, that "we are multiple things all at the same time," and that it is important in the community not to take a unidimensional view of others' identities or else risk alienating others (i.e., the opposite of belonging). She then very explicitly described multiple identities (e.g., undocumented, socioeconomic status, race, sexual orientation, etc.) and discussed the importance of everyone in the TSLC community acknowledging, affirming, accepting, and including these multiple identities in the TSLC space. This example of TSLC programming illustrates the intentional efforts on the program to validate the multiple identities of their at-promise students and to engage students in an open discussion about their role in fostering an inclusive community where everyone feels like they can belong (Rendón, 1994; Strayhorn, 2012).

Being conscious of multiple identities involves looking for strengths and opportunities for students. Since many of the students are unfamiliar with how the higher education system functioned, they benefit from having institutional agents discussing opportunities to belong related to their goals. As one staff member mentioned, "To have someone say, 'You belong here; you're not an impostor, you can make it' and help them get to those pathways, help them see things, like you can be a graduate assistant. You can do this or do that. That's so important."

In addition, multiple identities could be expressed and validated in a singular space—which is particularly important for students who possess multiple identities that are at times in conflict. For example, one student described feeling valued in TSLC as a low-income person with multiple chronic disabilities who was coming into their own bisexual person. Similarly, a trans* woman of color described being supported and affirmed by members of the TLSC community throughout her transition process. In other spaces on campus, these students often feel that they could not express their multiple identities, which undermines their ability to feel a holistic sense of belonging.

Tailoring Supports and Opportunities

Belonging as *tailored* involves stakeholders proactively reflecting in a multiple identity-conscious way to identify ways to tailor support that can create opportunities for traditionally marginalized groups of at-promise students to succeed. A tailored approach requires institutional agents reflecting on their practice and identifying subgroups of students who may require different forms of support (Kezar et al., 2020). It is important to note that this does not mean changing program requirements. Maintaining similar general requirements appears to be an important aspect of a strengths-based approach because students may feel frustrated if some students have requirements waived. Rather, a tailored approach involves creating the scaffolding needed for all students to feel supported in ways that allow them to utilize their innate potential and feel a sense of belonging in higher education.

The TSLC program serves several subgroups of students who benefit from a tailored approach, including those designated as English language learners (ELL), commuter students, first-generation college students, racially minoritized students, and those who experienced trauma. The program staff engage in professional reflection and data analyses to make decisions on whether a tailored approach may be needed. For example, staff found that first-generation college students "carry that imposter feeling all the way through" college. One staff member explained how they worked with these students:

> So for us to continually say you belong here, you can do it, don't quit, don't give up I think is a message that they continue to need to hear. I think, again, trying to always add value to their lives is continuous. Recognizing they are in different places. Success sessions, for instance, they can all go to the same ones, but how they pick and choose depends on where they are at in their journey and what they recognize they want to do next.

By keeping program requirements the same for all students but tailoring how support is offered, the programs avoid a deficit orientation where some students feel like the expectations are lowered because they lack the capacity to achieve success.

Acknowledging a Continuum of Belonging

Finally, belonging as a *continuum* acknowledges that not all students will feel the same level of connection and comfort within any program. While some students may have a strong sense of social, academic, and/or cultural belonging in a program, others may only experience a lower level of connection to a staff member and/or a mentor. By having a space that prioritizes validating experiences that are multiple-identity conscious, the program staff are able to know the students and explore how to assist them in feeling a sense of belonging on campus—even if that belonging is not primarily within the TSLC program.

Some of the students develop strong connections in other spaces on campus. For example, there are students whose primary sense of belonging is in a Greek organization, honors program, academic majors, or an identity center. The program encourages these students to be engaged in these spaces, with TSLC being their secondary support system. These students still meet the minimum requirements that include doing midsemester proactive advising, but the staff members are not as concerned about encouraging the students to do extra things to be connected with the TSLC community. In addition, the staff members do not take offense that the students feel more connected elsewhere. One director acknowledged that different student populations may feel a greater "sense of belonging or affiliation" with other groups on campus, which she fully supports—she just makes sure students know and that "TSLC is still there to support them." In many ways, the program's ultimate goal is to facilitate connections to the campus so that when students transitioned out of the formal program at the end of the second year they will be successful. Having students feel those connections earlier is something they celebrate. In doing so, the students know that the TSLC supports exist if they need them in the future, even if they do not feel a primary sense of belonging to the program.

Some students with multiple identities who are not necessarily well represented in the program do not feel a strong social connection within TSLC. Instead of trying to force these students to feel a strong sense of belonging within TSLC (which might lead students to disengage from the program), the institutional agents leverage proactive, identity-conscious, and tailored approaches to belonging to help these students find additional connections in other places on campus. For example, some of the undocumented Latinx students benefit from developing connections to the multicultural center and undocumented student support services on campus. The programs do not assume all students in a particular subgroup feel the same sense of belonging to the program. Rather, they use the relationships established within the program elements to identify when individual students would benefit from connections outside the program. Staff members consistently nurture relationships with other offices on campus in order to be able to facilitate connections for students. Instead of handing students an email address, the staff member makes an introduction to a specific person.

The program informally assesses where students are on the continuum of belonging and try to develop a sense of belonging that would meet their needs. There are students whose primary sense of belonging on campus centers on their interactions with the staff members. At times, the program staff create volunteer opportunities for these students to stay more connected with the program.

Conclusion

The potential exists for postsecondary institutions to facilitate a sense of belonging for students from different backgrounds who possess multiple identities. By moving away from silos of support that often relegate some identities to the margins, institutions develop structures and policies that create validating experiences and that allow for a multiple identity-conscious approach that allows for tailoring supports on the continuum of belonging for all students.

References

Anant, S. S. (1966). Need to belong. *Canada's Mental Health, 14*(2), 21–27. https://doi.org/10.2466/pr0.1967.20.3c.1137

Bollen, K. A., & Hoyle, R. H. (1990). Perceived cohesion: A conceptual and empirical examination. *Social Forces, 69*(2), 479–504. https://doi.org/10.1093/sf/69.2.479

Cole, D., Kitchen, J. A., & Kezar, A. (2019). Examining a comprehensive college transition program: An account of iterative mixed methods longitudinal survey design. *Research in Higher Education, 60*(3), 392–413. https://doi.org/10.1007/s11162-018-9515-1

Hallett, R. E., Kezar, A., Kitchen, J., & Perez, R. (2020). A typology of college transition and support programs: Situating a 2-year comprehensive college transition program within college access. *American Behavioral Scientist, 64*(3), 230–252. https://doi.org/10.1177/0002764219869410

Hallett, R. E., Kezar, A., Kitchen, J. A., Perez, R. J., & Reason, R. (2020). *Qualitative narrative of methods: Promoting At-Promise Student Success (PASS) project.* Pullias Center for Higher Education. http://doi.org/10.13140/RG.2.2.13814.63046

Hallett, R. E., Reason, R., Toccoli, J., Kitchen, J., & Perez, R. J. (2020). The process of academic validation within a comprehensive college transition program. *American Behavioral Scientist, 64*(3), 253–275. https://doi.org/10.1177%2F0002764219869419

Hausmann, L. R., Ye, F., Schofield, J. W., & Woods, R. L. (2009). Sense of belonging and persistence in White and African American first-year students. *Research in Higher Education, 50*(7), 649–669. https://doi.org/10.1007/s11162-009-9137-8

Hoffman, M., Richmond, J., Morrow, J., & Salomone, K. (2002). Investigating "sense of belonging" in first-year college students. *Journal of College Student Retention: Research, Theory & Practice, 4*(3), 227–256. https://doi.org/10.2190/DRYC-CXQ9-JQ8V-HT4V

Hurtado, S. (2007). The study of college impact. In P. J. Gumport (ed.), *Sociology of higher education: Contributions and their contexts*, (pp. 94–112). Johns Hopkins University Press.

Hurtado, S., Alvarado, A. R., & Guillermo-Wann, C. (2015). Creating inclusive environments: The mediating effect of faculty and staff validation on the relationship of discrimination/bias to students' sense of belonging. *JCSCORE, 1*(1), 59–81. https://doi.org/10.15763/issn.2642-2387.2015.1.1.59-81

Hurtado, S., & Carter, D. F. (1997). Effects of college transition and perceptions of the campus racial climate on Latino college students' sense of belonging. *Sociology of Education, 70*, 324–345. https://doi.org/10.2307/2673270

Johnson, D. (2012). Campus racial climate perceptions and overall sense of belonging among racially diverse women in STEM majors. *Journal of College Student Development, 53*(2), 336–346. https://doi.org/10.1353/csd.2012.0028

Johnson, D., Alvarez, P., Longerbeam, S., Soldner, M., Inkelas, K., Leonard, J., & Rowan-Kenyon, H. (2007). Examining sense of belonging among first-year undergraduates from different racial/ethnic groups. *Journal of College Student Development, 48*(5), 525–542. https://doi.org/10.1353/csd.2007.0054

Kezar, A., Kitchen, J., Estes, H., Hallett, R. E., & Perez, R. (2020). Tailoring programs to best support low-income, first-generation, and racially minoritized college student success. *Journal of College Student Retention.* https://doi.org/10.1177%2F1521025120971580

Kitchen, J., Cole, D., Rivera, G., & Hallett, R. E. (2020). The impact of a college transition program proactive advising intervention on self-efficacy. *Journal of Student Affairs Research and Practice, 58*(1), 29–43. http://doi.org/10.1080/19496591.2020.1717963

Kitchen, J. A., & Williams, M. S. (2019). Thwarting the temptation to leave college: An examination of engagement's impact on college sense of belonging among students of color. *Journal for the Study of Postsecondary and Tertiary Education, 4,* 67–84. https://doi.org/10.28945/4423

Maestas, R., Vaquera, G. S., & Zehr, L. M. (2007). Factors impacting sense of belonging at a Hispanic-serving institution. *Journal of Hispanic Higher Education, 6*(3), 237–256. https://doi.org/10.1177/1538192707302801

Museus, S. D. (2008). The role of ethnic student organizations in fostering African American and Asian American students' cultural adjustment and membership at predominantly White institutions. *Journal of College Student Development, 49*(6), 568–586. https://doi.org/10.1353/csd.0.0039

Museus, S. D., Yi, V., & Saelua, N. (2017). The impact of culturally engaging campus environments on sense of belonging. *The Review of Higher Education, 40*(2), 187–215. https://doi.org/10.1353/rhe.2017.0001

Rendón, L. I. (1994). Validating culturally diverse students: Toward a new model of learning and student development. *Innovative Higher Education, 19*(1), 33–51. https://doi.org/10.1007/BF01191156

Rendón, L. I., & Muñoz, S. M. (2011). Revisiting validation theory: Theoretical foundations, applications, and extensions. *Enrollment Management Journal, 5,* 12–33.

Ribera, A., Miller, A., & Dumford, A. (2017). Sense of peer belonging and institutional acceptance in the first year: The role of high impact practices. *Journal of College Student Development, 58*(4), 545–563. https://doi.org/10.1353/csd.2017.0042

Strayhorn, T. L. (2012). *College students' sense of belonging: A key to educational success for all students.* Routledge. https://doi.org/10.4324/9780203118924

5

HOW AND WHERE DO QUEER- AND TRANS-SPECTRUM COLLEGE STUDENTS EXPERIENCE BELONGING?

A Critical Review of the Literature

Brian C. Gano

Queer- and trans spectrum (LGBTQ+)-identifying college students rightfully belong on their campuses. While this statement seems incontrovertible, the extant literature on LGBTQ+ college students' sense of belonging indicates this is not the case. In this chapter, I will discuss the findings from recent research on LGBTQ+ college students' sense of belonging. In the first sections, I review the ways belonging is conceptualized and defined in the literature. Next, I present findings from recent literature on LGBTQ+ college student belonging as to how and where belonging is experienced. The literature is limited to research that focused on sense of belonging among queer- and trans-spectrum college students, and the review is not exhaustive but includes much of the recent literature that met the criteria. Lastly, I provide recommendations for future research and practice through a critical lens.

The Need to Belong

To better understand how and where LGBTQ+ students and other students experience belonging, it is important to understand how the concept of sense of belonging has been applied in the research. Depending on the field of study, sense of belonging holds different meanings, including the sociological and psychological concepts of belonging. Sociologically, the concept of sense of belonging is to feel part of, fit, or membership within a community (Bollen & Hoyle, 1990; Goodenow, 1993; Hagerty, 1992). Psychologically, the need to belong is a fundamental human motivator, and sense of belonging is the fulfilled need to belong (Baumeister & Leary, 1995). Individuals are motivated to take actions to fulfill the need through deep, meaningful, and consistent interpersonal relationships (Baumeister & Leary, 1995; Maslow, 1943). These relationships go beyond mere affiliation and superficial relationships and must evoke mostly positive affective responses (Baumeister & Leary, 1995). Maslow (1943) placed belonging and love third on the hierarchy of human needs, above safety and below esteem needs. He theorized that to fully meet belonging and higher needs, safety and security needs must first be met. Subsequent researchers questioned if every culture had the same hierarchy of needs (Gambrel & Cianci, 2003). For example, in China, a collectivist culture, esteem needs were eliminated, and belonging needs were lowest on the hierarchy, making the need to belong more essential and a prerequisite to fulfill all other needs (Gambrel & Cianci, 2003). Therefore, it is possible that sense of belonging is more important for some students than others, and that the order in which needs are met differs among student communities.

In the literature on college student sense of belonging, the two concepts of belonging are often conflated. Quantitative instruments typically measure the sociological concept of belonging, such as feeling part of or fit within a community (Budge et al., 2020; Ribera et al., 2017; Strayhorn, 2019). However, in qualitative research, students described sense of belonging in psychological terms as a need to belong, and these needs were fulfilled through meaningful relationships (Holloway-Friesen, 2018; Means & Pyne, 2017; Tachine et al., 2017; Vaccaro & Newman, 2016). LGBTQ+ students in particular have discussed belonging as the fulfilled need to belong and the importance meaningful and authentic relationships have for a developed sense of belonging (Duran, 2019; Gano, 2021; Gonyo, 2016; Strayhorn, 2019; Vaccaro & Newman, 2017). These two concepts of sense of belonging are not mutually exclusive and together may describe the way students experience belonging at their colleges and universities. In this review, I frame many of the findings through the psychological concept because LGBTQ+ students have consistently described sense of belonging as fulfilling a need to belong through close and meaningful relationships (Gano, 2021; Strayhorn, 2019; Vaccaro & Newman, 2017).

LGBTQ+-Inclusive Definitions of Belonging

Definitions of sense of belonging used in the literature have not explicitly included the voices of LBGTQ+ college students (e.g., Bollen & Hoyle, 1990; Goodenow, 1993; Hagerty, 1992; Strayhorn, 2019). When LGBTQ+ voices have been included, students discussed elements of belonging that were absent in the definitions of belonging, including safety (Gano, 2021; Vaccaro & Newman, 2017), the ability to be themselves (Gano, 2021; Vaccaro & Newman, 2017), and having their salient identities validated by others (Duran, 2019; Gano, 2021; Gonyo, 2016).

LGBTQ+ students have associated other feelings and emotions with sense of belonging that echo definitions used in the literature (e.g., mattering, acceptance, fit, community, connectedness; Hagerty, 1992; Strayhorn, 2019). In Vaccaro and Newman's (2017) grounded theory study of first-year lesbian, gay, bisexual, queer, and pansexual (LGBQP) students, participants defined belonging as having a sense of acceptance, community, and safety and being able to be themselves. Gano (2021) found similar findings in a qualitative study involving eight LGBTQ+ students: Belonging evokes positive emotions and feelings and was commonly described as a place where students felt comfortable being themselves and felt accepted, close to others, and safe. In two other qualitative studies, queer students of color associated the concepts of fit, connectedness, and mattering to developing belonging (Duran, 2019; Gonyo, 2016). Additionally, studies indicated that queer students of color found belonging when their racial, ethnic, sexual, and gender identities were accepted, validated, and affirmed by in-group members (Duran, 2019; Gano, 2021).

How LGBTQ+ Students Experience Belonging

How LGBTQ+ students experience belonging is largely dependent on the environment in which they interact (Duran, Dahl, Prieto et al., 2020; Gano, 2021). Also, LGBTQ+ students hold intersecting salient identities that interact with the environment, which influences sense of belonging. It is important to note that a student's identity does not predispose them to a lesser or greater sense of belonging. For example, a Black pansexual student is no less capable of experiencing sense of belonging than a White straight student, but the environment more adversely impacts Black and pansexual students, which leads to less belonging. In the following sections, I discuss the ways environments and identities influence how LGBTQ+ students experience belonging on campus, often in contrast to their straight and cisgender peers.

Campus Environments

LGBTQ+ college students perceive their campuses as more hostile than their straight and cisgender peers (Rankin et al., 2019). LGBTQ+ students report higher rates of microaggressions, verbal harassment, physical abuse, and perceptions of hostile climates related to their sexual or gender identity (Hughes & Hurtado, 2018; Tetreault et al., 2013). How LGBTQ+ students experience their campus environments is directly related to sense of belonging. Results from quantitative studies suggest positive correlations between perceptions of positive campus climates and sense of belonging among LGBTQ+ students of color (Duran, Dahl, Prieto et al., 2020) and among nonbinary students (Budge et al., 2020). Wilson and Liss (2020) found that LGBTQ+ students feel less safe than their heterosexual peers, which was associated with less belonging.

In qualitative studies, LGBTQ+ students have indicated that campus and organizational environments impacted their sense of belonging. Positive environments that led to a developed sense of belonging included feeling safe and supported and being able to express themselves freely (Gano, 2021; Vaccaro & Newman, 2017). LGBTQ+ students also discussed negative and hostile campus environments that led to feeling isolated and disengaging from groups (Duran, 2019; Gano, 2021; Vaccaro & Newman, 2017). In one example, a transgender student discussed feeling isolated in his academic department partly because of being the only LGBTQ+ student in the program and professors not using his name and pronouns (Gano, 2021).

Residence Hall Environments

In residence hall environments, when LBGTQ+ college students felt safe they were able to develop sense of belonging (Gonyo, 2016; Vaccaro & Newman, 2017). Students credited residence life staff with creating a sense of safety by announcing a zero-tolerance policy of anti-LGBTQ behavior (Gonyo, 2016). In a multi-university survey of 169 lesbian, gay, bisexual, and queer (LGBQ) residential college students, experiencing interpersonal and environmental LGBTQ microaggressions were negative predictors of sense of belonging (Blackmon et al., 2020). Among 1,468 lesbian, gay, bisexual, queer, and other sexual minority (LGBQ+) students of color in a national survey on college residential environments, there was a positive correlation between supportive residence hall environment and sense of belonging; however, within the LGBQ+ student population, there was a negative correlation among gay students of color (Duran, Dahl, Prieto et al., 2020). Again, a sense of safety stands out as a crucial factor for LGBTQ+ students for their development of sense of belonging, whether in their residence halls or on the campus.

Salient Identities

Researchers have explored how a student's multiple, intersecting identities (e.g., race, ethnicity, gender, sexuality) influenced their sense of belonging. There are mixed findings on the level of belonging felt between heterosexual and LGBQ students; the authors of one study found a greater sense of belonging among heterosexual students (Duran, Dahl, Stipeck et al., 2020), and other researchers identified no significant difference (Hughes & Hurtado, 2018). Within the LGBTQ+ community, belongingness levels can vary. In one survey of LGBTQ students, bisexual students had higher levels of belonging than their lesbian, gay, and queer peers (BrckaLorenz et al., 2019). Contrastingly, other researchers have suggested bisexual and queer students had a lower sense of belonging than their gay and lesbian peers (Duran, Dahl, Prieto et al., 2020; Duran, Dahl, Stipeck et al., 2020). Among LGBQ students of color, belonging levels for LGBQ Asian students were higher than average, and White students were lower than average (BrckaLorenz et al., 2019). However, authors of another study found no differences among LGBQ students based on race (Duran, Dahl, Prieto et al., 2020). Gender identity may also be an indicator of belonging. In another survey, identifying as trans or genderqueer was negatively correlated to sense of belonging (Duran, Dahl, Stipeck et al., 2020). There is a dearth of literature on other salient identities among LGBTQ+ students, including socioeconomic class, disability, and religion.

Where LGBTQ+ Students Experience Belonging

Sense of belonging can be felt with multiple groups, people, or entities. It is also possible for a student to feel no sense of belonging, although the literature is limited on the lack of sense of belonging among college students (Gano, 2021). Most literature has focused on measuring sense of belonging with a student's college or university (Ribera et al., 2017). Instruments assess if a student feels fit, connected, or a part of the campus community but do not necessarily measure specifically where on- (or off-) campus sense of belonging is felt. Among LGBTQ+ students, the literature suggests belonging is associated with individuals and groups with whom meaningful relationships can be developed (Gano, 2021; Strayhorn, 2019; Vaccaro & Newman, 2017). In the following sections, I discuss findings from the literature on where LGBTQ+ students have indicated they found sense of belonging.

Authentic Relationships

The need to belong is fulfilled through deep, meaningful relationships that evoke positive affective responses (Baumeister & Leary, 1995). Although limited, the qualitative literature on LGBTQ+ students consistently suggests students feel sense of belonging most strongly with individuals or groups of people (Duran, 2019; Gano, 2021; Gonyo, 2016; Strayhorn, 2019; Vaccaro & Newman, 2017). LGBTQ+ students place high importance on authentic relationships, or "fictive kin" (Gano, 2021; Strayhorn, 2019; Vaccaro & Newman, 2017). In a qualitative study of 16 Black gay men, high-quality friendships with whom participants could express their whole identity were associated with belonging on campus (Gonyo, 2016). Gano (2021) found that even when students identify sense of belonging with entities or groups, they describe the deep, meaningful relationships within the entity. Often, a student formed authentic relationships with group members or individuals when they held the same LGBTQ+ or other salient identities as the student (Duran, 2019; Gano, 2021; Gonyo, 2016; Vaccaro & Newman, 2017). LGBTQ+ students have described authentic relationships as ones where they felt they could be their true selves, did not have to censor themselves, and felt validated (Duran, 2019; Gano, 2021; Vaccaro & Newman, 2017).

Academic Belonging

College students have indicated feeling a sense of belonging with majors, departments, and other academic entities (Strayhorn, 2019). Academic factors such as faculty interactions, academic self-efficacy, and involvement in high-impact practices have also been found to contribute to a student's sense of belonging (Freeman et al., 2007; Hausmann et al., 2007; Knekta & McCartney, 2018). The literature on LGBTQ+ students and academic belonging is limited. In a study by Duran, Dahl, Stipek et al. (2020), there was a positive correlation between faculty interaction and sense of belonging for lesbian, gay, and bisexual (LGB) students of color. In qualitative studies, LGBTQ+ students have described how academic-related experiences influenced their belonging (Gano, 2021; Gonyo, 2016). Students associated mastering a subject, achieving academic self-efficacy, and participating in faculty-led research projects as contributing factors to sense of belonging (Gano, 2021; Gonyo, 2016). However, there are mixed findings regarding LGBTQ+ students belonging with academic departments or entities. Gonyo (2016) reported some participants found belonging in their majors, whereas Gano (2021) suggested that most participants indicated no feelings or shallow feelings of belonging to academic departments or their campuses.

LGBTQ+ Clubs and Organizations

Research has shown positive correlations between campus and cocurricular engagement and sense of belonging among LGB college students (Duran, Dahl, Prieto et al., 2020). However, there are mixed findings regarding whether LGBTQ+ students find belonging within LGBTQ+ clubs and resource centers. Some students met their belongingness needs through an LGBTQ+ club and described family-like relationships with club members (Gano, 2021). Other students have said that LGBTQ+ resource centers provided a place to find community, educational resources, and support services (Vaccaro & Newman, 2017). In one study, none of the Black gay men were involved with LGBTQ+ student organizations; however, outreach from those same organizations did contribute to a sense of belonging with the LGBTQ+ student community (Gonyo, 2016). Still, not all LGBTQ+ students have found belonging within LGBTQ+ spaces. In several qualitative studies, students described the spaces as unwelcoming, exclusionary, too political, or not aligning with their values (Duran, 2019; Gano, 2021; Strayhorn, 2019; Vaccaro & Newman, 2017). In Gano's (2021) study, three participants from different campuses described their university's LGBTQ+ club as being cliquey and only being accepting of "that stereotypical flamboyant gay" (p. 94).

A student's race and ethnicity may be a factor in finding belonging within LGBTQ+ spaces. For example, students of color have discussed the challenge to find belonging within LGBTQ+ clubs and organizations, especially if their racial identity was not affirmed (Duran, 2019; Gano, 2021; Strayhorn, 2019). Therefore, students joined queer student of color organizations where their racial and ethnic identities were also affirmed (Duran, 2019). In another study, a Vietnamese, queer, nonbinary student found belonging within the Trans Student Union but not within the LGBTQ+ club primarily because the latter space was "really White" (Gano, 2021, p. 94). In his study, Strayhorn (2019) reported that the majority of the ethnic gay men were involved in ethnic identity organization rather than LGBTQ+ organizations; one participant discussed feeling the need to choose one identity over another and picked his Black identity over his gay identity.

Off-Campus Belonging

If a student's belonging needs are not met on campus, they may seek to fulfill the need off campus. There is scant literature on LGBTQ+ college students fulfilling belongingness needs off campus. However, in Gano's (2021) study, most participants met some of their belongingness needs off campus with three of the participants' active belonging groups being off campus only.

Strayhorn (2019) found that ethnic gay men sought to fulfill their belong-ingness needs off campus at ethnic nightclubs (48%), gay nightclubs (41%), a church (34%), and gay pride events (77%).

Sense-of-Belonging Outcomes for LGBTQ+ Students

Generally, the literature on college student sense of belonging suggests positive relationships between a developed sense of belonging and academic, personal, and health outcomes (Backhaus et al., 2019; Freeman et al., 2007; Wilson et al., 2015; Wilson & Liss, 2020). In the scant literature regarding LGBTQ+ students, findings are limited to emotional and health outcomes. One health concern for LGBTQ+ students is minority stress, the result of dealing with verbal and physical abuse, internalized homophobia, and the stigma of being LGBTQ+; this stress is carried with LGBTQ+ individuals and predisposes them to a higher risk of adverse mental and physical health outcomes (Meyer, 2003). In a survey of 380 nonbinary college students at multiple universities, Budge et al. (2020) found students who had a higher sense of belonging had lower levels of minority stress. In addition, there was a correlation between high minority stress and adverse health outcomes among LGBTQ+ individuals. Backhaus et al. (2019) completed an analysis of a large-scale national health study and discovered a statistically significant negative correlation between sense of belonging and suicide ideation and depression among LGBQ college students. In another survey, a lower sense of belonging among LGBTQ+ students was associated with higher levels of depression, greater anxiety, and less happiness (Wilson & Liss, 2020). The literature on other outcomes (e.g., academic, social) related to sense of belonging among LGBTQ+ students is limited.

Conclusion

Future researchers should consider that the current measures for sense of belonging do not necessarily measure belonging in the way LGBTQ+ students understand the sensation. Sense of belonging for LGBTQ+ students includes the ability to be their whole self and feel safe within the group. Maslow (1943) posited that safety needs must be met before belonging needs could be addressed, but this may not be true for all cultures or communities (Gambrel & Cianci, 2003). With the consistency in qualitative findings among LGBTQ+ students linking safety and belonging (Gano, 2021; Vaccaro & Newman, 2017), is it possible that safety is a corequisite for LGBTQ+ college student sense of belonging? Future researchers should explore the interplay of safety and belonging among queer- and trans-spectrum students.

Next, LGBTQ+ students felt belonging most strongly toward individuals and not necessarily toward their university and described sense of belonging in the psychological terms of fulfilling the need to belong (Gano, 2021; Vaccaro & Newman, 2017). However, quantitative researchers often rely on Likert-type scales that ask about a student's fit with, connection to, or being a part of their campus or university (i.e., the sociological concept), which may not fully represent participants' experiences. To improve construct validity in future studies, researchers should test if existing instruments that measure the sociological concept of sense of belonging are appropriate to be used among LGBTQ+ students.

Furthermore, researchers must understand that not all students have experienced sense of belonging on their campus. In one qualitative study, several participants indicated that they had never experienced sense of belonging before attending college, and others had no sense of belonging toward groups or individuals on campus (Gano, 2021). Several of the participants stated their gender and sexual identities were factors in a lack of belonging. Future researchers should consider that LGBTQ+ students and other students may lack experience with belonging or have no need to find belonging on their campuses.

A critical lens needs to be applied to extant and future research to determine if it applies to all students or only cisgender, straight students. LGBTQ+ students are a community that has been historically subjugated, excluded, and pathologized in the literature (Cuyjet et al., 2016; Hurtado, 2015; Rankin et al., 2019). Researchers must include LGBTQ+ student voices throughout the meaning-making process and in research on college student sense of belonging (Hurtado, 2015). Without their voices, researchers and practitioners cannot be certain that they are measuring appropriate constructs or implementing effective and inclusive policies or programs.

For practitioners, the research indicates that LGBTQ+ students continue to have their belonging thwarted on their campuses because of hostile campus environments. Students have described making attempts to fulfill their belonging needs with individuals or groups on campus, but because of the actions or a perceived negative environment, belonging was thwarted (Duran, 2019; Gano, 2021). When belonging was felt, it was with individuals or in spaces where others affirmed their identities. Positive and pro-LGBTQ+ campus climates are necessary for students to develop sense of belonging. While the goal should be for the entire campus to be accepting, affirming, and inclusive of LGBTQ+ students, practitioners must address issues within already designated LGBTQ+ spaces. LGBTQ+ clubs do not necessarily accept or affirm all members of the LGBTQ+ community, particularly those on the trans spectrum and students of color (Duran, 2019; Gano, 2021; Strayhorn, 2019). University administrators must recognize that sense of belonging is felt most with people, including faculty, staff, and students; programs and policies should be human centered and involve consistent and constant levels of interactions that promote the development of deep, meaningful relationships.

LGBTQ+ students belong on their campuses and should be able to develop sense of belonging with people throughout their campuses. The literature suggests that this statement is more aspirational than reality. Higher education administrators, researchers, faculty, and students must create positive campus environments that support and foster belonging for LGBTQ+ students.

References

Backhaus, I., Lipson, S. K., Fisher, L. B., Kawachi, I., & Pedrelli, P. (2019). Sexual assault, sense of belonging, depression and suicidality among LGBQ and heterosexual college students. *Journal of American College Health*, *69*(4), 404–412. https://doi.org/10.1080/07448481.2019.1679155

Baumeister, R. F., & Leary, M. R. (1995). The need to belong: Desire for interpersonal attachments as a fundamental human motivation. *Psychological Bulletin*, *117*(3), 497–529. https://doi.org/10.1037/0033-2909.117.3.497

Blackmon, Z. R., O'Hara, R. M., & Viars, J. W. (2020). Microaggressions, sense of belonging, and sexual identity in the residential environment. *Journal of College and University Student Housing*, *46*(3), 46–59. https://libres.uncg.edu/ir/uncg/f/Blackmon_uncg_0154D_12610.pdf

Bollen, K. A., & Hoyle, R. H. (1990). Perceived cohesion: A conceptual and empirical examination. *Social Forces*, *69*(2), 479–504. https://doi.org/10.1093/sf/69.2.479

BrckaLorenz, A., Duran, A., Fassett, K., & Palmer, D. (2019). The within-group differences in LGBQ+ college students' belongingness, institutional commitment, and outness. *Journal of Diversity in Higher Education*, *14*(1), 135–146. https://doi.org/10.1037/dhe0000135

Budge, S. L., Domínguez Jr., S., & Goldberg, A. E. (2020). Minority stress in nonbinary students in higher education: The role of campus climate and belongingness. *Psychology of Sexual Orientation and Gender Diversity*, *7*(2), 222–229. https://doi.org/10.1037/sgd0000360

Cuyjet, M. J., Linder, C., Howard-Hamilton, M. F., & Cooper, D. L. (Eds.). (2016). *Multiculturalism on campus: Theory, models, and practices for understanding diversity and creating inclusion* (2nd ed.). Stylus.

Duran, A. (2019). A photovoice phenomenological study exploring campus belonging for queer students of color. *Journal of Student Affairs Research and Practice, 56*(2), 153–167. https://doi.org/10.1080/19496591.2018.1490308

Duran, A., Dahl, L. S., Prieto, K., Hooten, Z., & Mayhew, M. J. (2020). Exposing the intersections in LGBQ+ student of color belongingness: Disrupting hegemonic narratives sustained in college impact work. *Journal of Diversity in Higher Education.* https://doi.org/10.1037/dhe0000222

Duran, A., Dahl, L. S., Stipeck, C., & Mayhew, M. J. (2020). A critical quantitative analysis of students' sense of belonging: Perspectives on race, generation status, and collegiate environments. *Journal of College Student Development, 61*(2), 133–153. https://doi.org/10.1353/csd.2020.0014

Freeman, T. M., Anderman, L. H., & Jensen, J. M. (2007). Sense of belonging in college freshmen at the classroom and campus levels. *The Journal of Experimental Education, 75*(3), 203–220. https://doi.org/10.3200/JEXE.75.3.203-220

Gambrel, P. A., & Cianci, R. (2003). Maslow's hierarchy of needs: Does it apply in a collectivist culture. *Journal of Applied Management and Entrepreneurship, 8*(2), 143–161. https://www.proquest.com/scholarly-journals/maslows-hierarchy-needs-does-apply-collectivist/docview/203916225/se-2?accountid=14606

Gano, B. C. (2021). *The experiences, thoughts, feelings, and emotions LGBTQ+ college students associate with sense of belonging* (Order No. 28419611) [Doctoral dissertation, University of North Carolina Wilmington]. ProQuest.

Gonyo, C. P. (2016). *The sense of belonging of Black gay men at predominantly White institutions of higher education* (Order No. 10152831) [Doctoral dissertation, Michigan State University]. ProQuest.

Goodenow, C. (1993). The psychological sense of school membership among adolescents: Scale development and educational correlates. *Psychology in the Schools, 30*(1), 79–90. https://onlinelibrary.wiley.com/doi/10.1002/1520-6807(199301)30:1%3C79::AID-PITS2310300113%3E3.0.CO;2-X

Hagerty, B. M. (1992). Sense of belonging: A vital mental health concept. *Archives of Psychiatric Nursing, 6*(3), 172–177. https://doi.org/10.1016/0883-9417(92)90028-H

Hausmann, L. R. M., Schofield, J. W., & Woods, R. L. (2007). Sense of belonging as a predictor of intentions to persist among African American and White first-year college students. *Research in Higher Education, 48*(7), 803–839. https://doi.org/10.1007/s11162-007-9052-9

Holloway-Friesen, H. (2018). On the road home: A content analysis of commuters' sense of belonging. *College Student Affairs Journal, 36*(2), 81–96. https://doi.org/10.1353/csj.2018.0017

Hughes, B. E., & Hurtado, S. (2018). Thinking about sexual orientation: College experiences that predict identity salience. *Journal of College Student Development, 59*(3), 309–326. https://doi.org/10.1353/csd.2018.0029

Hurtado, S. (2015). The transformative paradigm: Principles and challenges. In A. M. Martínez-Alemán, B. Pusser, & E. M. Bensimon (Eds.), *Critical approaches to the study of higher education: A practical introduction* (pp. 285–307). Johns Hopkins University Press.

Knekta, E., & McCartney, M. (2018). What can departments do to increase students' retention? A case study of students' sense of belonging and involvement in a biology department. *Journal of College Student Retention: Research, Theory & Practice, 22*(4), 721–742. https://doi.org/10.1177/1521025118788351

Maslow, A. H. (1943). A theory of human motivation. *Psychological Review, 50*(4), 370–396. https://doi.org/10.1037/h0054346

Means, D. R., & Pyne, K. B. (2017). Finding my way: Perceptions of institutional support and belonging in low-income, first-generation, first-year college students. *Journal of College Student Development, 58*(6), 907–924. https://doi.org/10.1353/csd.2017.0071

Meyer, I. H. (2003). Prejudice, social stress, and mental health in lesbian, gay, and bisexual populations: Conceptual issues and research evidence. *Psychological Bulletin, 129*(5), 674–697. https://doi.org/10.1037/0033-2909.129.5.674

Rankin, S., Garvey, J. C., & Duran, A. (2019). A retrospective of LGBT issues on US college campuses: 1990–2020. *International Sociology, 34*(4), 435–454. https://doi.org/10.1177/0268580919851429

Ribera, A. K., Miller, A. L., & Dumford, A. D. (2017). Sense of peer belonging and institutional acceptance in the first year: The role of high-impact practices. *Journal of College Student Development, 58*(4), 545–563. https://doi.org/10.1353/csd.2017.0042

Strayhorn, T. L. (2019). *College students' sense of belonging: A key to educational success for all students* (2nd ed.). Routledge.

Tachine, A. R., Cabrera, N. L., & Yellow Bird, E. (2017). Home away from home: Native American students' sense of belonging during their first year in college. *The Journal of Higher Education, 88*(5), 785–807. https://doi.org/10.1080/00221546.2016.1257322

Tetreault, P. A., Fette, R., Meidlinger, P. C., & Hope, D. (2013). Perceptions of campus climate by sexual minorities. *Journal of Homosexuality, 60*(7), 947–964. https://doi.org/10.1080/00918369.2013.774874

Vaccaro, A., & Newman, B. M. (2016). Development of a sense of belonging for privileged and minoritized students: An emergent model. *Journal of College Student Development, 57*(8), 925–942. https://doi.org/10.1353/csd.2016.0091

Vaccaro, A., & Newman, B. M. (2017). A sense of belonging through the eyes of first-year LGBPQ students. *Journal of Student Affairs Research and Practice, 54*(2), 137–149. https://doi.org/10.1080/19496591.2016.1211533

Wilson, D., Jones, D., Bocell, F., Crawford, J., Kim, M. J., Veilleux, N., Floyd-Smith, T., Bates, R., & Plett, M. (2015). Belonging and academic engagement among undergraduate STEM students: A multi-institutional study. *Research in Higher Education, 56*(7), 750–776. https://doi.org/10.1007/s11162-015-9367-x

Wilson, L. C., & Liss, M. (2020). Safety and belonging as explanations for mental health disparities among sexual minority college students. *Psychology of Sexual Orientation and Gender Diversity, 9*(1), 110–119. https://doi.org/10.1037/sgd0000421

6

CONNECTING GENDER AND BELONGING

An Intersectional Approach

Michael Steven Williams and Ekaete E. Udoh

Analyzing connections between gender and belonging through an intersectional lens presents a unique opportunity. This connection allows higher education scholars and professionals to explore how opportunities for belonging may be compromised by otherwise unseen identity politics and power relations on campus. It also allows us to think about the possibilities for enhancing research and praxis related to our understanding of gender and belonging. This chapter demonstrates how a nuanced understanding of the connections between gender and belonging holds promise for improving college student outcomes. We begin by briefly outlining our conceptualizations of gender and sense of belonging. We then turn our attention to intersectionality and use it as a guide to explore connecting gender and belonging in college. We use Black male initiative (BMIs) programs as an illustrative example to discuss the implications of an intersectional approach to gendered belonging for research, policy, and praxis. Although our discussion centers on the experiences of Black collegians, we see it as a model for critical thinking about the complexity introduced by considering gender, belonging, and intersectionality that could be useful for anyone interested in supporting college student success.

Gender Considerations

Gender and sex are complex concepts that influence college students' lived experiences, whether we acknowledge their complexity or not. Although a discussion of the nuances of differentiating sex and gender (e.g., poststructural theorists like Butler [2006] suggest that sex *and* gender are socially constructed in such a way that they are functionally indistinguishable) is beyond the scope of this chapter, we use the following definitions from the World Health Organization (WHO, 2021) to frame our discussion. *Gender* references "the characteristics of women, men, girls and boys that are socially constructed," including "norms, [behaviors,] and roles associated with being a woman, man, girl or boy" (para. 1). *Sex* refers to "the different biological and physiological characteristics of females, males, and intersex persons, such as chromosomes, hormones, and reproductive organs" (para. 3). *Gender identity* alludes to "a person's deeply felt, internal and individual experience of gender, which may or may not correspond to the person's physiology or designated sex at birth" (para. 3). Beyond gender, sex, and gender identity, notions of sexuality further complicate the normative structures that college students must navigate.

Sense of Belonging

College students' sense of belonging has received increased scholarly interest as a catalyst for desirable student success outcomes, including but not limited to mental health, well-being, engagement, retention, and persistence (e.g., Baumeister & Leary, 1995; Hurtado & Carter, 1997; Maslow, 1943; Strayhorn, 2019). For instance, Baumeister and Leary (1995), in their comprehensive and multidisciplinary literature review on belonging, suggested that belonging has two core features. First, people need frequent positive interactions with significant others. Next, people need to perceive that these relationships are stable and mutual. Thus, while satisfying the need to belong is undoubtedly concerned with group affiliation, we should keep in mind that frequency of interactions and the perceptions of positivity, stability, and mutuality in those interactions are also foundational.

Although there is widespread agreement among scholars that belonging matters for college students, the construct is considered, discussed, and measured differently in studies across the postsecondary educational scholarship. We rely on Strayhorn's (2019) model of college students' sense of belonging for this chapter. Rooted in a social cognitive theoretical perspective, Strayhorn suggested that belonging is a basic human need that influences behavior. Here, belonging refers to a sense of connectedness to essential others in the campus community. Although the need to belong must continually be fulfilled, students who feel valued, respected, and cared for are more likely to learn and grow in the collegiate milieu. While the model focuses on students' experiences, we believe that the core ideas extend to all campus community members (e.g., faculty, administrators, staff).

In his model, Strayhorn pays particular attention to the influence of intersecting social identities, noting that belonging needs may take on heightened importance depending on various demographic and contextual factors. He also notes that while belonging and behavior are linked, those who feel alienated or otherwise rejected in college may seek connection in ways that defy norms and eschew traditional success notions. For example, picture a Black woman collegian at a large historically White university. She could excel in her engineering coursework but still decide to change majors because the lack of same-race peers and professors compromised her sense of belonging. In his 2019 model, Strayhorn attends to (a) the influence of intersectional identities, and (b) the potentially unexpected behavioral responses people may utilize in pursuit of belonging. These factors make it ideal for our discussion.

Intersectionality

While the term *intersectionality* is relatively new in academic parlance— most contemporary scholars associate the term with Kimberlé Crenshaw's (1989, 1991) critical legal scholarship—Black thought leaders have a long tradition of commentary on the complexities of navigating multiple social identities in the distinctive sociopolitical theater of the United States. For example, more than a century ago, Anna Julia Cooper (1892/2017) wrote,

> The colored woman of to-day occupies, one may say, a unique position in this country. . . . She is confronted by both a woman question and a race problem and is yet an unknown or an unacknowledged factor in both."
> (p. 134)

About a decade after Cooper, W.E.B. DuBois (1903/2007) offered,

> He [the American Negro] simply wishes to make it possible for a man to be both a Negro and an American, without being cursed and spit upon by his fellows, without having the doors of Opportunity closed roughly in his face. (p. 9)

In their work, both Cooper and DuBois shared how race, gender, and national origin, among other identities, influence whether and how Black Americans feel like they belong in the United States.

Crenshaw's (1989) influential work *Demarginalizing the Intersection of Race and Sex: A Black Feminist Critique of Antidiscrimination Doctrine, Feminist Theory, and Antiracist Politics*, drew on the Black feminist intellectual tradition to explain the ways Black women—by virtue of the inseparability of their race and gender—find their needs marginalized and voices silenced by White supremacy and patriarchy. Black women interested in belonging, social recognition, advancement, and protection did not find their unique needs addressed by feminist movements that centered the needs of White women or struggles for racial progress that center(ed) the needs of Black men. Although rooted in Black women's experiences, intersectionality has utility and theoretical heft for any examination of power, oppression, and differential experiences rooted in social identities. Crenshaw's (1991) work explicitly introduced three dimensions of intersectionality: (a) structural, (b) political, and (c) representational. *Structural intersectionality* focuses on structural oppressions (e.g., racism, sexism, classism) that influence lived experiences. *Political intersectionality* refers to how unique aspects of a person's social address (e.g., race, class, gender, sexual orientation) can lead to silencing and erasure from political agendas. *Representational intersectionality* refers to how facets of identity (e.g., race, gender, sexual orientation) are connected and used to reinforce cultural stereotypes that often undermine and disempower their targets. The three foci of intersectionality are valuable analytic tools for exploring the micro (i.e., individual) and macro (i.e., systemic) environmental conditions that influence gender and college belonging. The following section demonstrates how intersectionality applies to gendered belonging experiences on campus.

Connecting Gender and Belonging Through Intersectionality

The following section uses BMI programs to illustrate how attention to the three intersectionality dimensions can advance our understanding of gender and belonging in higher education.

BMIs

Facilitating belonging and connection for Black male collegians is a core intention of BMI programs. Supported by the proliferation of research on Black men in postsecondary education and popular political initiatives like Obama's "My Brother's Keeper," these programs are an increasingly popular intervention in higher education. Although they differ in implementation (e.g., Brooms, 2018; Cuyjet, 2006), BMIs facilitate the retention and persistence of Black male collegians through programming that attends to their social, emotional, and academic needs. While these programs are important and well intentioned, we use the three intersectionality dimensions to demonstrate how these programs can undermine and compromise belonging for Black men and women.

BMIs and Structural Intersectionality

Structural intersectionality can be used to understand how various identity-based oppressions converge to shape gendered belonging experiences in higher education. In the case of BMIs, while the programs may appear intersectional (i.e., accounting for race and gender) in nature, they still may not reflect the diversity *within* Black male subgroups in higher education. Black men come to higher education contexts with distinct racial, socioeconomic, religious, and political backgrounds that influence their conceptions of gender and gender identity. If higher education researchers and practitioners are going to understand the belonging needs of their students, they must interrogate how gender intersects with other social identities. Although BMIs are lauded for their contribution to the retention and persistence of Black men in higher education, the field knows relatively little about the experiences of Black men with nonnormative gender identities and sexualities in these programs. The way these programs challenge or reinforce preexisting ideas about appropriate gender presentation (e.g., Black professional men in suits) and behavioral repertoires (e.g., "real" men don't cry) can significantly influence participants.

Carefully considering the design of BMI programs is critical to ensuring they meet the unique belonging needs of the students they serve. For example, patriarchal and heteronormative constructions of Black masculinity could be a hidden form of domination that alienates program participants. This requires researchers and practitioners to ask several questions about the design and implementation of these programs: How are these programs defining race and gender, respectively? Do the curriculum and programming of these initiatives highlight the within-group diversity of Black men? Are issues of gender identity and sexuality explicitly covered? If so, how? Does the program make space for nonnormative identities socially and educationally? Are program administrators, speakers, and guest lecturers diverse? How is that diversity centered? Students that see themselves and their unique needs in educational and social programming are likely to feel a greater sense of belonging from participation.

BMIs and Political Intersectionality

Political intersectionality can help illuminate individuals' belonging struggles with multiple salient marginalized identities, including but not limited to gender. BMIs serve as a useful example because they help higher education professionals think critically about Black women's erasure from political agendas on campus and beyond. Although Black women collegians face similar threats to their belonging (e.g., racism, limited structural diversity) at historically White postsecondary educational institutions, fewer services and supports have been put in place to bolster their retention and persistence to graduation. The proliferation of BMIs without commensurate efforts to develop similar programs for Black women in college offers a clear example of this erasure.

The relative absence of Black women's initiatives and other forms of Black women–focused retention and persistence interventions highlights how the intersection of race and gender is used to disempower and silence Black women implicitly and explicitly. Campuses that focus on Black male success without a similar commitment to Black women send a message, but it is likely not their preferred message. This failure forwards racial justice agendas that center Black men while ignoring Black women—reinforcing the subordination of Black women's needs to those of Black men. How are Black women supposed to feel like they belong on campus when services and supports are tailored to meet Black men's needs but not theirs?

BMIs and Representational Intersectionality

BMIs can also offer insight into the relationship between representational intersectionality and gendered belonging experiences in higher education. The need for BMIs cannot be separated from the larger sociopolitical landscape on campus and beyond. Issues with racism and exclusion in higher education are connected to larger social narratives that position Black men as barbaric, dangerous criminals whose academic ineffectiveness is more about the limits to their intelligence than the institutional and systemic barriers they face. Black women face stereotypes that limit their academic achievement as well. For example, the "strong Black woman" trope and statistics about their educational attainment relative to Black men have been used to deny Black women service and support in scholarship, on campus, and in society.

If higher education wants our students to feel like they belong, we must do more to educate campus community members about their intersectional needs. There are many questions to consider in this vein: What do campus structures (e.g., the availability or unavailability of programs and services) suggest about the importance of belonging for students with different gender identities? Are campus services painting a picture—covertly or overtly—that certain groups are not worthy of belonging support? What would more robust services designed to promote belonging with attention to gender look like? How can our understanding of the various intersectionality forms guide the development and implementation of these programs moving forward?

Conclusion

In this chapter, we detailed how BMIs, uncritically deployed, can detract from belonging rather than promote it when considering the intersectional identities of Black collegians. Our overarching goal is to remind readers that intersectionality and belonging are essentially indivisible when we think about our lives as raced and gendered humans. How people are *allowed* to express themselves (e.g., gender, social identity, activism) and their needs deserves more attention in research, policy, and praxis related to belonging. Depending on the context; race, gender, and their intersections can be taken for granted or violently disciplined. Belonging is similarly context dependent.

Belonging, like most social justice–oriented constructs, is about consistent directed action. *Belonging* is an active word. It is a psychological state that requires maintenance through consistency and intentional effort. However, it is essential to remember that belonging does not function similarly for all human beings. Connecting gender, belonging, and intersectionality reminds us that our social address influences the possibilities and opportunities to belong on campus and in society. Avoiding single-axis studies of belonging is an important step, but merely disaggregating by race and sex—as we demonstrate with our discussion of BMIs—is only the beginning. Future inquiry must continue to explore the causes and consequences of belonging with attention to race, gender, and other intersectional identities.

References

Baumeister, R. F., & Leary, M. R. (1995). The need to belong: Desire for interpersonal attachments as a fundamental human motivation. *Psychological Bulletin, 117*, 497–529. https://doi.org/10.1037/0033-2909.117.3.497

Brooms, D. R. (2018). "Building us up": Supporting Black male college students in a Black Male Initiative program. *Critical Sociology, 44*(1), 141–155. http://doi.org/10.1177/0896920516658940

Butler, J. (2006). *Gender trouble: Feminism and the subversion of identity.* Routledge.

Cooper, A. J. (2017). *A voice from the South.* University of North Carolina at Chapel Hill Library. (Original work published 1892)

Crenshaw, K. (1989). Demarginalizing the intersection of race and sex: Black feminist critique of antidiscrimination doctrine, feminist theory and antiracist politics. *University of Chicago Legal Forum, 1989*(1), 139–168. https://chicagounbound.uchicago.edu/uclf/vol1989/iss1/8

Crenshaw, K. (1991). Mapping the margins: Intersectionality, identity politics, and violence against women of color. *Stanford Law Review, 43*(6), 1241–1300.

Cuyjet, M. J. (2006). *African American men in college.* Jossey-Bass.

Du Bois, W. E. B. (2007). *The souls of Black folk* (B. Edwards, Ed.). Oxford University Press. (Original work published 1903)

Hurtado, S., & Carter, D. F. (1997). Effects of college transition and perceptions of campus racial climate on Latino college students' sense of belonging. *Sociology of Education, 70,* 324–345. https://doi.org/10.2307/2673270

Maslow, A. H. (1943). A theory of human motivation. *Psychological Review, 50*(4), 370–396. https://doi.org/10.1037/h0054346

Strayhorn, T. L. (2019). *College students' sense of belonging: A key to educational success for all students* (2nd ed.). Routledge.

World Health Organization. (2021). *Gender and health.* https://www.who.int/health-topics/gender#tab=tab_1

7

ON THE OUTSIDE LOOKING IN

Reflecting on Native American Students' Sense of Belonging

Mark Alabanza

In this chapter, I discuss how Native American students develop and experience a sense of belonging during their college experiences at a public college in California (PCC) known for its Native American presence. The term *Native American* (or *American Indian*) is used to indicate the Native peoples of the present-day United States, as opposed to *Indigenous*, which is viewed as a more global definition (B. Neddeau, personal communication, January 24, 2021).

I employed Brayboy's (2005) tribal critical race theory (TribalCrit) and its tenets (see Table 7.1) to provide the lens through which I analyzed

TABLE 7.1
The Nine Tenets of TribalCrit

Tenet
1. Colonization is endemic to society.
2. U.S. policies toward Indigenous peoples are rooted in imperialism, White supremacy, and a desire for material gain.
3. Indigenous peoples occupy a liminal space that accounts for both the political and racialized natures of our identities.
4. Indigenous peoples have a desire to obtain and forge tribal sovereignty, tribal autonomy, self-determination, and self-identification.
5. The concepts of culture, knowledge, and power take on new meaning when examined through an Indigenous lens.

Tenet
6. Governmental policies and educational policies toward Indigenous peoples are ultimately linked around the problematic goal of assimilation.
7. Tribal philosophies, beliefs, customs, traditions, and visions for the future are central to understanding the lived realities of Indigenous peoples, but they also illustrate the differences and adaptability among individuals and groups.
8. Stories are not separate from theory; they make up theory and are, therefore, real and legitimate sources of data and ways of being.
9. Theory and practice are connected in deep and explicit ways such that scholars must work toward social change.

Note. Adapted from Brayboy (2005, pp. 429–430).

concepts such as cultural representations, relationships on campus, and psychological resources. Brayboy developed TribalCrit to focus on Native Americans' identities and complex relationships with the federal government. The goal of the study was to provide information that could help lead institutions to provide more culturally affirming and appropriate support for Native American students.

Background

My review of the existing literature included social and historical conditions of Native Americans in education, institutional barriers, the construction of Native American identity, and the use of TribalCrit. I explored the intersections and relationships that served to construct and define Native American students' belonging during college. Furthermore, I explored potential support services for students made possible by examining Native American students' perceptions of higher education and belonging.

Government-Sanctioned Extermination

The federal government's attempt to eradicate or assimilate Native Americans inside and outside the classroom has resulted in continuous challenges for Native American students (Alabanza, 2020). In 1887, the federal government sanctioned the forced redistribution of land from Native Americans through the General Allotment Act of 1887 (also known as the Dawes Act) in an effort to legitimize the erasure of Native Americans (Echohawk, 2013). In addition to displacing Native Americans by reallocating natural resources, the federal government forced the concept of individualism to replace the

Native American culture of community (Carlson, 1981). The mandatory reallocation of land also fractured tribal communities to further assimilate them into the hegemonic culture (Echohawk, 2013). Scattering Native American communities throughout the country made it difficult for tribes to function as self-governing communities. The widespread locations and erasure of Native American tribes reflects the consequences of dispersing the targeted population throughout the United States.

Forced Assimilation Through Education

The United States' educational systems institutionally discriminate against Native American students and seek to assimilate them into the hegemonic, Eurocentric culture (House et al., 2006). Current Native American students may experience a conflict within their cultures due to the history of formal education (Brave Heart et al., 2012; Fischer & Stoddard, 2013). The federal government's early intervention in the instruction of Native Americans (i.e., Indian boarding schools) sanctioned Eurocentric ideals in academic institutions while simultaneously disparaging Native American culture. Colonialism effectively destroyed "Indigenous cultures and communities by taking away the young, breaking their connections to their communities, and producing shattered persons with no strong sense of identity" (Dawson, 2012, p. 88). Forced changes in physical appearance (e.g., cutting their hair) and the erasure of Native American languages and religions embodied the attempts to remove students' Native American identity (Brayboy, 2005; Dawson, 2012). Acknowledging the continued attempts of colonization and assimilation socially and through education offers perspective to educators about Native American students' identity in higher education (House et al., 2006).

Indian boarding schools also served as a foundation for institutional barriers for Native American students. In an attempt to subvert traditional Native American pedagogy, where a holistic approach is used (Cajete, 2010), Indian boarding schools attempted to submerge students in the hegemonic culture through separation and removal from cultural teaching methods and from their families and communities (Keene, 2016). Boarding schools also established a fixed hierarchy, which subjugated Native Americans through overt (e.g., openly disparaging verbally) and subtle (e.g., lowered expectations) discrimination. The hierarchy was designed to remove Native Americans through elimination or assimilation (Deyhle, 1995) and continues today as cultural bias through education (Tachine et al., 2017).

Modern educational institutions' attempts of assimilation also challenge Native American student identity (House et al., 2006). Native American students' identities may be based on culture, academics, social circles, ethnicity, or family (Lundberg, 2014; Waterman & Sands, 2016). Akee and Yassie-Mintz (2011) found that Native American students who maintained connections to their culture (i.e., values, beliefs, languages) also maintained their cultural identity. Similarly, Native American students who retained connections to their culture were able to develop positive ethnic identities and reject campus stereotypes (Fischer & Stoddard, 2013).

Conversely, Native American students who were not able to sustain connections to their family and cultural identity experienced feelings of being unsupported (Flynn et al., 2012). Because Native American students need to have connections to culturally appropriate support in education (Fish et al., 2017; Waterman & Sands, 2016), institutions must understand the challenge Native American students face to sustain their cultural identity in higher education, thereby providing increased support and developing positive psychological resources for those students. If students can form relationships similar to their family or communities, negative influences on belonging can be offset (HeavyRunner & DeCelles, 2002).

TribalCrit

I used TribalCrit and its tenets to view the current educational and institutional support systems from the perspective of Native Americans. Understanding that Native American students must conform to learning based on a different culture (Hare & Pidgeon, 2011), TribalCrit's fifth tenet highlights how hegemonic concepts, such as knowledge and power, shift when viewed from a Native American perspective (Brayboy, 2005). For Native Americans, stories are a culturally appropriate way to teach and pass on knowledge (Tachine et al., 2017). TribalCrit's eighth and ninth tenets focus on the power of stories as components of theory, which is connected to practice and should be used for social change (Brayboy, 2005).

Using TribalCrit also underscored the importance of understanding the complexity of Native American identity and the effects of how barriers are created specifically for Native Americans. These barriers amplify TribalCrit's sixth tenet, which emphasizes the underlying goal of assimilation of educational and governmental policies (Brayboy, 2005). Using TribalCrit as the lens for Native American students' experiences produced opportunities for educational institutions to understand the effects of colonization on that student population and underscored how colonization is an underlying factor for Native American student challenges.

Observations

My study provided a means for students to "acknowledge and resist systemic cultural assimilation while attending college" (Alabanza, 2020, p. 161). From the study, a central finding emerged that focused on a psychological resource for the Native American participants: the unique concept of belonging on campus. Sense of belonging on campus consisted of the students' belonging based on people and based on space.

Sense of Belonging Based on People

Belonging based on people centered on the participants' relationships with other Native Americans on the campus (e.g., faculty, staff, students, community members). These relationships created deep and meaningful connections and supported the formation of the participants' Native American communities on campus. As a result, the participants experienced enhanced connections to the campus and to others. The participants discussed how their experiences were shaped by the relationships with other Native Americans and created their belonging based on people. One of the participants, Felicity (a pseudonym), elaborated on her experience with a Native American admissions counselor:

> She reached out to me and said that she was hosting this small, kind of informal, breakfast meet and greet just a couple hours away from where I lived. Seeing her and seeing that she would make the effort to actually come to where I lived and that she was also a Native woman in this academic setting, I think really had a big impact on me. It really solidified for me that the university was going to be a good choice.

In addition to building community, the Native American staff and faculty offered guidance to help the participants develop their cultural heritage knowledge. One important feature of these relationships was that there was no fear of judgment or repercussions as the participants experienced their cultural heritage. This provided a safe space for the participants. Another participant, Gianna (a pseudonym), described her experience:

> And then through just going to the center and being present in the center, opportunities were thrown at me; they said, "Oh, we have this club, we have the Native American student union on campus and we have a program where you can get a paid job to do retention and recruitment programming for Native Americans." And "Oh, we're meeting with the chancellor about this issue." And there were just things that were being thrown from all the

other various connections. I took advantage of the opportunities because I thought, "This is a huge part of my identity that I've always kind of just shoved away." And then I thought, "Oh, I can do both. I can be in school and in academics and be a transfer student and all of that. And I can be a Native American student and incorporate the two." And that was the first time that really has ever happened.

As evidenced by the experiences with the Native American admissions counselor, the director of the Native American Center, and the faculty who teach Native American courses, the participants found role models who supported them and discovered a distinct way to view themselves in higher education.

Sense of Belonging Based on Space

Sense of belonging based on space focused on how specific locations influenced the students' feelings of connection to the campus. This belonging based on space was created when the students could positively relate to physical and curricular spaces on campus. Physical spaces included the campus' arboretum and Native center. Curricular spaces included academic courses and research.

Exposure to Native American studies served to support the participants' belonging based on space. These courses provided contextual and supportive perspectives of Native Americans in academics and were taught by Native American faculty. Because the curriculum promoted their cultural heritage in a higher education environment, the participants felt more connected and visible and less isolated from the campus through accurate representation and recognition. Acknowledged Native American presence in the formal curriculum underscored a contrast to their K–12, instruction which was full of misconceptions and deficient perspectives. The increased visibility of Native American curriculum at PCC counteracted the invisibility established in the K–12 curriculum (Shotton et al., 2013).

Similarly, connections to physical spaces supported belonging based on space. Once the participants assigned significance to a space, the space became important and meaningful, creating place (Gupta & Ferguson, 1992). The participants agreed that the Native center on the campus served as a focal point for their community building. Acknowledging these feelings, the participants used their agency to attribute meaning to other specific spaces on the campus (i.e., creating community). The spaces became important to the participants based on the significance of their experiences with other Native Americans. The participants constructed places from which they could draw strength to resist institutional bias on the campus. In California, this is especially relevant considering that many of the public colleges and universities reside on the homeland of Native American tribes. Gianna described the feeling of having a place for Native American community:

> I started to realize that it's pretty isolating holding all this knowledge and all these traditions and having the need to be around Native community, that navigating higher education outside of that was just exhausting and isolating. And it was really nice to go back to the center and say, "Oh, well today we talked all about Columbus in my class," and that kind of thing. So it was just somewhere to really be together and we all didn't even have to say, you didn't even have to vocalize like what we needed. We just knew that being together is healing.

The combination of relationships (belonging based on people) and the importance of space (belonging based on space) created "a unique psychosocial resource for Native American college students to help them resist cultural assimilation during their college experience" (Alabanza, 2020, p. 162). A distinct trait of this psychological resource was the reliance on external factors as opposed to remaining internal. Being able to understand this resource helped provide insight into its use as a resource for the students' cultural affirmation.

Relating to Their Own Culture

Enculturation emerged as a salient influence on the participants. Enculturation is a way to understand bicultural efficacy as it allows Native Americans to appreciate their individual relationship with their culture while they navigate the current hegemonic culture (Zimmerman et al., 1996). Bicultural efficacy allows an individual to live "effectively, and in a satisfying manner, within two groups without compromising one's sense of cultural identity" (LaFromboise et al., 1993, p. 404). The concept of enculturation surfaced as a way for the participants to understand how to combine previously separate aspects of their lives, resulting in a shift in perspective of academic life and cultural heritage.

Due to differences in socioeconomic status, family history, and other factors, not all participants came to PCC on the same path or with similar experiences. Although several participants did not have a meaningful connection to their cultural heritage when they arrived on campus, all participants acknowledged feeling part of the Native American community based on their experiences at PCC. The Native American communities the participants developed with other Native Americans provided holistic support and created opportunities to resolve different aspects of their identities, enhancing their belonging on the campus. This feeling of belonging allowed the participants to view their experiences through a culturally affirming lens.

Recommendations

To improve Native American students' sense of belonging, colleges and universities should consider options such as creating spaces for Native American students, raising cultural awareness for non-Native faculty and staff, and revising the curriculum.

Spaces for Native American Students

Space provides an environment where students gather with each other and build community. This space could serve as a central hub for Native American student services (e.g., academic advising, financial aid, counseling), staffed by employees who provide support in a culturally appropriate manner. Including amenities such as a kitchen or library would provide areas of respite for Native American students.

Cultural Awareness and Connection

Training should be offered to non-Native American staff and faculty to understand the historical context of educational institutions (e.g., Indian boarding schools), the cultural context of tribal community, and ways to provide culturally appropriate support and guidance. Additionally, it is imperative to realize the importance of direct contact with students and their families. Creating connections between staff and Native American families could help create a connection between the recruiter and the community. Having the campus reach out to the local tribe(s) could help facilitate this dialogue and training.

Having Native American staff and faculty serve as mentors can teach students how to address and overcome institutional bias and provide new perspectives for students, resulting in increased feelings for belonging on campus. In many cases, having Native American staff and faculty who have successfully navigated higher education mentor Native American students can be another way to provide culturally appropriate support. These faculty and staff could provide emotional and social support, serving as role models in and out of the classroom.

Transformative Curriculum

As noted, the participants felt their cultural heritage was distorted or erased from the curriculum prior to attending PCC. Revising courses to address and correct misrepresentations would promote a more comprehensive understanding of Native Americans in history while simultaneously removing an institutional barrier for Native Americans. Revision processes could include inviting Native American faculty to provide contextual perspective where Native American voices (or narratives) had previously been ignored. Furthermore, this would provide learning opportunities for non–Native American faculty to better understand how to support Native American students in their courses.

Conclusion

This chapter provides some social and historical context of Native American students in higher education. There is no one-size-fits-all model when working with Native American students (similar to other underrepresented student populations), and cultural bias can influence Native American students' belonging (Tachine et al., 2017). It is imperative for practitioners to understand the social and cultural nuances that must be acknowledged and applied to better support this student population.

References

Akee, R. Q., & Yassie-Mintz, T. (2011). "Counting experience" among the least counted: The role of cultural and community engagement on educational outcomes for American Indian, Alaska Native, and Native Hawaiian students. *American Indian Culture and Research Journal, 35*(3), 119–150. https://doi.org/7953/aicr.35.3.c4xu43p5160m2jtn

Alabanza, M. V. (2020). *Inequities, support, and success: Influences on Native American students' sense of belonging.* California State University, Stanislaus. https://scholarworks.calstate.edu/concern/theses/n296x033r?locale=en

Brave Heart, M. Y. H., Elkins, J., Tafoya, G., Bird, D., & Salvador, M. (2012). Wicasa Was'aka: Restoring the traditional strength of American Indian boys and men. *American Journal of Public Health, 102*(22), 177–183. https://doi.org/10.2105/AJPH.2011.300511

Brayboy, B. (2005). Toward a tribal critical race theory in education. *Urban Review, 37*(5), 425–446. https://doi.org/10.1007/s11256-005-0018-y

Cajete, G. A. (2010). Contemporary Indigenous education: A nature-centered American Indian philosophy for a 21st-century world. *Futures, 42*(10), 1126–1132. https://doi.org/10.1016/j.futures.2010.08.013

Carlson, L. A. (1981). *Indians, bureaucrats, and land: The Dawes Act and the decline of Indian farming.* Greenwood.

Dawson, A. S. (2012). Histories and memories of the Indian boarding schools in Mexico, Canada, and the United States. *Latin American Perspectives, 39*(5), 80–99. https://doi.org/10.1177/0094582X12447274

Deyhle, D. (1995). Navajo youth and Anglo racism: Cultural integrity and resistance. *Harvard Educational Review*, *65*(3), 403–445. https://doi.org/10.17763/haer.65.3.156624q12053470n

Echohawk, J. E. (2013). Understanding tribal sovereignty: The Native American Rights Fund. *Expedition*, *55*(3), 18–23.

Fischer, S., & Stoddard, C. (2013). The academic achievement of American Indians. *Economics of Education Review*, *36*, 135–152. https://doi.org/10.1016/j.econedurev.2013.05.005

Fish, J., Livingston, J. A., VanZile-Tamsen, C., & Patterson Silver Wolf (Adelv unegv Waya), D. A. (2017). Victimization and substance use among Native American college students. *Journal of College Student Development*, *58*(3), 413–431. https://doi.org/10.1353/csd.2017.0031

Flynn, S. V., Duncan, K., & Jorgensen, M. F. (2012). An emergent phenomenon of American Indian postsecondary transition and retention. *Journal of Counseling & Development*, *90*(4), 437–449. https://doi.org/10.1002/j.1556-6676.2012.00055.x

Gupta, A., & Ferguson, J. (1992). Beyond "culture": Space, identity, and the politics of difference. *Cultural Anthropology*, *7*(1), 6–23. https://doi.org/10.1525/can.1992.7.1.02a00020

Hare, J., & Pidgeon, M. (2011). The way of the warrior: Indigenous youth navigating the challenges of schooling. *Canadian Journal of Education*, *34*(2), 93–111.

HeavyRunner, I., & DeCelles, R. (2002). Family education model: Meeting the student retention challenge. *Journal of American Indian Education*, *4*(2), 29–37. http://pieducators.com/sites/default/files/Student-Retention.pdf

House, L. E., Stiffman, A. R., Brown, E., & Bailey, B. A. (2006). Unraveling cultural threads: A qualitative study of culture and ethnic identity among urban Southwestern American Indian youth parents and elders. *Journal of Child and Family Studies*, *15*(4), 393–407. https://doi.org/10.1007/s10826-006-9038-9

Keene, A. J. (2016). College pride, Native pride: A portrait of a culturally grounded precollege access program for American Indian, Alaska Native, and Native Hawaiian students. *Harvard Educational Review*, *86*(1), 72–97. https://doi.org/10.17763/0017-8055.86.1.72

LaFromboise, T., Coleman, H. L. K., & Gerton, J. (1993). Psychological impact of biculturalism: Evidence and theory. *Psychological Bulletin*, *114*(3), 395–412. https://doi.org/10.1037/0033-2909.114.3.395

Lundberg, C. A. (2014). Institutional support and interpersonal climate as predictors of learning for Native American students. *Journal of College Student Development*, *55*(3), 263–277. https://doi.org/10.1353/csd.2014.0027

Shotton, H. J., Lowe, S. C., & Waterman, S. J. (Eds.). (2013). *Beyond the asterisk: Understanding Native students in higher education*. Stylus.

Tachine, A. R., Cabrera, N. L., & Yellow Bird, E. (2017). Home away from home: Native American students' sense of belonging during their first year in college. *The Journal of Higher Education*, *88*(5), 785–807. https://doi.org/10.1080/00221546.2016.1257322

Waterman, S. J., & Sands, T. L. (2016). A pathway to college success: Reverse transfer as a means to move forward among the Haudenosaunee (Iroquois). *Journal of
American Indian Education, 55*(2), 51–74. https://doi.org/10.5749/jamerindieduc
.55.2.0051

Zimmerman, M. A., Ramirez-Valles, J., Washienko, K. M., Walter, B., & Dyer, S.
(1996). The development of a measure of enculturation for Native American
youth. *American Journal of Community Psychology, 24*(2), 295–310. https://doi
.org/10.1007/BF02510403

8

ASIAN AMERICAN STUDENTS AND SENSE OF BELONGING

Cassie Kao

Research on Asian American students in higher education has been lacking, partly because many funding organizations do not recognize Asian Americans as an underrepresented racial and/or ethnic minority—which means funds are not necessarily allocated for research on this population (Museus & Chang, 2009). This lack of funding and research is problematic because Asian Americans are one of the fastest growing populations in the United States. To provide some context to this socially constructed category, Asian Americans are quite diverse, with over 50 ethnic groups, over 100 languages, and numerous religious groups (Lee & Kumashiro, 2005). Additionally, Asian Americans can be considered a cultural group, an immigrant group, and an ethnic minority group (Yoshikawa et al., 2016), which may impact individual experiences in the United States, especially as some Asian Americans are multigenerational Americans, some are from immigrant families, some are refugees, some are mixed race, and some are adopted by non-Asian American parents (Lee & Kumashiro, 2005). These experiences influence academic preparation and result in a variation of academic achievement (Reeves & Bennet, 2004; Zhou & Lee, 2017).

Variation of Academic Achievement

In higher education, because East Asians (e.g., Chinese, Japanese, Korean) make up about 20% of first-year students at Ivy League schools (Zhou & Lee, 2017) and are overrepresented in STEM-related fields (Hui & Lent, 2018), they are considered more academically successful. Unfortunately, Asian

Americans are seen as one high-achieving group, and the needs of many Asian American subgroups are obscured because of the diversity of the subgroups. Southeast Asians (e.g., Cambodian, Laotian, Vietnamese) significantly lag behind East Asians and South Asians (e.g., Bangladeshi, Indian, Pakastani; Maramba & Palmer, 2014; Pak et al., 2014; Palmer & Maramba, 2015). Southeast Asians are more likely to attend community college after high school and are less likely to obtain a degree than South Asians or East Asians (Pak et al., 2014). While this information highlights some of the inequities among Asian American subgroups, it is important to note research on Asian subgroups has been limited. Because of the dearth of research on disaggregated Asian American students, the majority of this chapter will be based on aggregated research.

Sense of Belonging

Connections have been made between student involvement and student engagement with student success (Harper & Quaye, 2009; Kuh, 2001; Quaye & Harper, 2015); however, there are inconsistencies when considering Asian American students specifically. There seems to be a disconnect between student engagement and student success for Asian Americans (Kao, 2018a). Kao (2018a) found Asian American students were largely not as engaged when compared to their peers based on the 2015 administration of the National Survey of Student Engagement; degree attainment seemed to have an inverse relationship with student engagement for Asian Americans. If student engagement is not the reason for Asian American students to succeed in school, then there must be another factor related to their success, such as sense of belonging.

Sense of belonging has been defined as "the extent to which students feel personally accepted, respected, included, and supported by others in the school social environment" (Goodenow, 1993, p. 80). The term has also been defined as "students' perceived social support on campus, a feeling or sensation of connectedness, the experience of mattering or feeling cared about, accepted, respected, valued by, and important to the group (e.g., campus community) or others on campus (e.g., faculty, peers)" (Strayhorn, 2012, p. 3). This support is foundational to how a person identifies with a group and how that person ultimately behaves because a person's perceived cohesion or their tendency to "stick" to a group "encompasses an individual's sense of belonging to a particular group" (Bollen & Hoyle, 1990, p. 482). Especially for students of color, having a sense of belonging is critically important to their success (Strayhorn, 2012)—academically and socially.

How well students integrate to the academic environment is closely associated with the level of the sense of belonging they experience on campus (Hausmann et al., 2007). Lundberg and Schreiner (2004) found the "quality of relationships with faculty was the only variable that significantly predicted learning for all racial/ethnic groups" (p. 555), which furthers a sense of belonging. This finding is significant as Asian American students are more likely than their peers to interact and work with faculty (Kao, 2018a). Additionally, Hurtado and Carter (1997) found that when students talked about course content with other students outside the classroom they had a higher sense of belonging. For Asian American students, they are more likely than their peers to ask another student to help them understand course materials, more likely to explain course material to one or more students, more likely to prepare for exams by discussing or working through course material with other students, and more likely to work with other students on course projects or assignments (Kao, 2018a).

Socially (i.e., outside the classroom), students who have strong cultural ties and positive perceptions of their identities are more likely to experience a higher sense of belonging level (Lee & Davis, 2000). Museus and Maramba (2011) found Filipino American students who kept ties to their cultural heritage increased their sense of belonging and were able to adjust better than those who did not. Li (2018) suggested a strong cultural orientation helped Asian American students feel like they belonged at a predominantly White institution. Lim (2015) found there was a "significant positive relationship between high participation in socio-cultural discussions and high perception of sense of belonging" (p. 120) when she studied perceived campus climate among three Asian subpopulations (Chinese American, Filipino American, Asian Indian).

Shared Cultural Values

Kim et al. (1999) developed an instrument they named the Asian Values Scale and identified six shared cultural values among Asian Americans: (a) collectivism, (b) conformity to norm, (c) emotional self-control, (d) family recognition through achievement, (e) filial piety, and (f) humility. Kim et al. (2001) further found these six cultural values were similar among Chinese Americans, Japanese Americans, Korean Americans, and Filipino Americans. These cultural values are highly influenced by philosophies in Confucianism and Buddhism (Chuang & Wang, 2018; Kim et al., 2001) and held in high regard (Chuang, 2011). As a result, these shared cultural values provide commonality (Kim & Park, 2015) and, in turn, sense of belonging (Yeh &

Huang, 1996). However, similar to other areas of study on Asian Americans, more research with disaggregated data is necessary before assuming all Asian American ethnicities share the same cultural values (Kim et al., 2001). Nevertheless, researchers have found sense of belonging for Asian Americans is largely influenced by relationships (Hom, 2015; Yeh & Huang, 1996) and connections with their cultural heritage (Museus et al., 2017; Museus & Maramba, 2011).

The connection of Asian Americans to shared culture is crucial because "Asian American students who feel marginalized from both their own ethnic culture and the majority culture are least able to adjust to college" (Lee & Davis, 2000, p. 113). This belonging is more than just finding a place to belong on a college campus, but finding a belonging within a group (Cheng, 2004; Lee & Davis, 2000). The experience of being ostracized not only prevents students from being able to adjust to college (Cheng, 2004), but it also negatively impacts their perception, their participation, and their sense of belonging (Gin, 2019; Li, 2018; Samura, 2016). In fact, this marginalization affects the perception one has of the campus climate in which they find themselves, which significantly correlates with their sense of belonging (Li, 2018; Wells & Horn, 2015). As Lim (2015) stated, "The individual experience within racism is what drives a discriminatory climate which contributes to a lower sense of belonging" (p. 126). Because Asian American students have been marginalized (Lee & Davis, 2000), it is not surprising they have reported being least satisfied with their institutions compared to their peers (Museus et al., 2008). Students who feel invisible on their campuses question whether they belong at the institutions (Kao, 2018b). This perception is not just in a physical sense, but also in a virtual sense through social media. Gin (2019) suggested that "the racialized climate of social media also negatively contributes to the ways Asian Americans perceive they are welcomed, respected, valued, and matter" (p. 16). Thankfully, there are opportunities for students to feel connected to a community on campus (Hom, 2015).

While Kao (2018a) found Asian American students were less likely to interact with peers from diverse backgrounds, Johnson et al. (2007) found Asian American students are more likely than their peers to participate in ethnic and cultural clubs that celebrate their ethnic identities. This involvement in ethnic organizations is important because students are able to feel validated on their campuses through these groups (Museus, 2008). When a student joins a student organization related to their ethnic or racial identity, they are more likely to boost their sense of belonging (Li, 2018; Samura, 2016). This membership is one way students can stay connected with others who are culturally similar to themselves (Museus & Quaye, 2009). Students with ties to their cultural heritage experience have an easier adjustment and find belonging on their campus (Museus et al., 2017), partly because of shared cultural values (Hom, 2015; Li, 2018).

As a result, it is important for institutions to determine what cultural communities are relevant on their individual campuses and encourage students to engage with these cultural identities in a meaningful way (Museus et al., 2017). Institutions that provide students the opportunity to be involved in student governance and campus-wide programming help them to participate and use aspects of the campus environment to contribute to their sense of belonging (Slaten et al., 2016).

Conclusion

It is obvious additional research is needed on disaggregated Asian American students in higher education because Asian Americans are generally viewed only as one group. Furthermore, it is important that future studies focus on how cultural values and generation status impact these students and their academic success. In the meantime, this chapter has highlighted factors inside and outside the classroom that may contribute to a student feeling like they belong at an institution (e.g., engaging with other students regarding course content, having positive interactions with faculty, having strong cultural ties and positive perceptions of their identities).

Sense of belonging refers to the extent a student feels included, accepted, valued, and supported on their campus. While there are many Asian American subgroups, researchers have found cultural values (i.e., collectivism, conforming to norms, emotional self-control, family recognition through achievement, filial piety, and humility) are shared among at least four Asian subgroups (Kim et al., 1999, 2001). These shared cultural values are important because students are able to find a sense of belonging by engaging with others from similar cultural identities. When they have an increased sense of belonging, they are able to more easily adjust to their campus and in turn achieve academic success.

References

Bollen, K. A., & Hoyle, R. H. (1990). Perceived cohesion: A conceptual and empirical examination. *Social Forces, 69*(2), 479–504. https://doi.org/10.2307/2579670

Cheng, D. X. (2004). Students' sense of campus community: What it means and what to do about it. *NASPA Journal, 41*(2), 216–232. https://doi.org/10.22021949-6605.1331

Chuang, S. (2011). The relationship between cultural values and learning preference: The impact of acculturation experiences upon East Asians. *International Journal of Training and Development, 16*(1), 1–22. https://doi.org/10.1111/j.1468-2419.2011.00391.x

Chuang, S., & Wang, G. G. (2018). Confucian philosophy and influence on perceived values and behavioural orientations by Taiwan's millennials. *Human Resource Development International, 21*(4), 362–381. https://doi.org/10.1080/13678868.2018.1433393

Gin, K. J. (2019). Racialized aggressions and sense of belonging among Asian American college students. *Institute for Asian American Studies Publications, 44,* 1–26. https://scholarworks.umb.edu/iaas_pubs/44

Goodenow, C. (1993). The psychological sense of school membership among adolescents: Scale development and educational correlates. *Psychology in the Schools, 30*(1), 70–90. https://doi.org/10.1002/1520-6807(199301)30:1<79::AID-PITS2310300113>3.0.CO;2-X

Harper, S. R., & Quaya, S. J. (2009). *Student engagement in higher education.* Routledge.

Hausmann. L. R. M., Schofield, J. W., & Woods, R. L. (2007). Sense of belonging as a predictor of intentions to persist among African American and White first-year college students. *Research in Higher Education, 48,* 803–839. https://dx.doi.org/10.1007/s11162-007-9052-9

Hom, D. C. (2015). *Understanding Asian American female college students and their sense of belonging* [Unpublished doctoral dissertation]. Northeastern University. https://repository.library.northeastern.edu/files/neu:rx915054v/fulltext.pdf

Hui, K., & Lent, R. W. (2018). The roles of family, culture, and social cognitive variables in the career interests and goals of Asian American college students. *Journaling of Counseling Psychology, 65*(1), 98–109. https://doi.org/10.1037/cou0000235

Hurtado, S., & Carter, D. F. (1997). Effects of college transition and perceptions of the campus racial climate on Latino college students' sense of belonging. *Sociology of Education, 70*(4), 324–345. https://www.jstor.org/stable/2673270

Johnson, D., Soldner, M., Leonard, J., Alvarez, P., Inkelas, K., Rowan-Kenyon, H., & Longerbeam, S. (2007). Examining sense of belonging among first-year undergraduates from different racial/ethnic groups. *Journal of College Student Development, 48*(5), 525–542. https://doi.org/10.1353/csd.2007.0054

Kao, C. I. (2018a). *Asian American student engagement on college campuses* (Publication No. 10976095) [Doctoral dissertation, New England College]. ProQuest. https://www.proquest.com/docview/2135381014

Kao, C. I. (2018b). *Resource guide: How to better support Asian American students.* https://issuu.com/cassiekao/docs/final_comp_project

Kim, B. S. K., Atkinson, D. R., & Yang, P. H. (1999). The Asian Values Scale: Development, factor analysis, validation, and reliability. *Journal of Counseling Psychology, 46*(3), 342–352. https://doi.org/10.1037/0022-0167.46.3.342

Kim, B. S. K., & Park, Y. S. (2015). Communication styles, cultural values, and counseling effectiveness with Asian Americans. *Journal of Counseling & Development, 93,* 269–271. https://doi.org/10.1002/jcad.12025

Kim, B. S. K., Yang, P. H., Atkinson, D. R., Wolfe, M. M., & Hong, S. (2001). Cultural value similarities and differences among Asian American ethnic groups. *Cultural Diversity and Ethnic Minority Psychology, 7*(4), 343–361. https://doi .org/10.1037//1099-9809.7.4.343

Kuh, G. D. (2001). Assessing what really matters in student learning: Inside the National Survey of Student Engagement. *Change: The Magazine of Higher Learning, 33*(3), 10–17. https://doi.org/10.1080/00091380109601795

Lee, R. M., & Davis, C., III. (2000). Cultural orientation, past multicultural experi-ence, and a sense of belonging on campus for Asian American college students. *Journal of College Student Development, 41*(1), 110–115. https://psycnet.apa.org/ record/2000-13605-009

Lee, S. J., & Kumashiro, K. (2005). *A report on the status of Asian Americans and Pacific Islanders in education: Beyond the "model minority" stereotype.* National Edu-cation Association. http://friendsofpubliced.org/wp-content/uploads/2014/02/ Status-Asian-American.pdf

Li, Y. (2018). *Do all Asian Americans feel alike? Exploring Asian American college stu-dents' sense of belonging on campuses* [Unpublished doctoral dissertation]. Bowling Green State University.

Lim, D. Y. (2015). *Exploring and identifying predictors that affect Asian American col-lege students' sense of belonging: "How do I fit in?"* [Unpublished doctoral disserta-tion]. University of Maryland College Park. https://drum.lib.umd.edu/bitstream/ handle/1903/16578/Lim_umd_0117E_15987.pdf?sequence=1&isAllowed=y

Lundberg, C., & Schreiner, L. (2004). Quality and frequency of faculty-student interactions as predictors of learning. *Journal of College Student Development, 45*(5), 549–565. https://doi.org/10.1353/csd.2004.0061

Maramba, D. C., & Palmer, R. T. (2014). The impact of cultural validation on the college experiences of Southeast Asian American students. *Journal of Col-lege Student Development, 55*(6), 515–530. https://doi.org/10.1353/csd.2014.0054

Museus, S. D. (2008). The role of ethnic student organizations in fostering African American and Asian American students' cultural adjustment and membership at predominantly White institutions. *Journal of College Student Development, 49*(6), 568–586. https://doi.org/10.1353/csd.0.0039

Museus, S. D., & Chang, M. J. (2009). Rising to the challenge of conducting research on Asian Americans in higher education. In S. D. Museus (Ed.), *Conducting Research on Asian Americans in Higher Education* [Special Issue] (New Directions for Institutional Research, No. 142, pp. 95–105). https://doi.org/10.1002/ir.299

Museus, S. D., & Maramba, D. C. (2011). The impact of culture on Filipino American students' sense of belonging. *The Review of Higher Education, 34*(2), 231–258. https://doi.org/10.1353/rhe.2010.0022

Museus, S. D., Nichols, A. H., & Lambert, A. (2008). Racial differences in the effects of campus racial climate on degree completion: A structural model. *Review of Higher Education, 32*(1), 107–134. https://doi.org/10.1353/rhe.0.0030

Museus, S. D., & Quaye, S. J. (2009). Toward an intercultural perspective of racial and ethnic minority college students persistence. *Review of Higher Education, 33*(1), 67–94. https://doi.org/10.1353/rhe.0.0107

Museus, S. D., Yi, V., & Saelua, N. (2017). How culturally engaging campus environments influence sense of belonging in college: An examination of differences between White students and students of color. *Journal of Diversity in Higher Education, 11*(4), 467–483. http://dx.doi.org/10.1037/dhe0000069

Pak, Y. K., Maramba, D. C., & Hernandez, X. J. (2014). Asian Americans in higher education: Charting new realities. *ASHE Higher Education Report, 40*(1) 1–136. https://doi.org/10.1002/aehe.20013

Palmer, R. T., & Maramba, D. C. (2015). The impact of social capital on the access, adjustment, and success of Southeast Asian American college students. *Journal of College Student Development, 56*(1), 45–60. https://doi.org/10.1353/csd.2015.0007

Quaye, S. J., & Harper, S. R. (2015). *Student engagement in higher education* (rev. ed.). Routledge.

Reeves, T., & Bennet, C. (2004). *We the people: Asians in the United States. The Asian American and Pacific Islander population in the United States.* https://www.census.gov/prod/2004pubs/censr-17.pdf

Samura, M. (2016). Remaking selves, repositioning selves, or remaking space: An examination of Asian American college students' processes of "belonging." *Journal of College Student Development, 57*(2), 135–150. https://doi.org/10.1353/csd.2016.0016

Slaten, C. D., Elison, Z. M., Lee, J. Y., Yough, M., & Scalise, D. (2016). Belonging on campus: A qualitative inquiry of Asian international students. *The Counseling Psychologist, 44*(3), 383–410. https://doi.org/10.1177/0011000016633506

Strayhorn, T. L. (2012). *College students' sense of belonging: A key to educational success for all students.* Routledge.

Wells, A. V., & Horn, C. (2015). The Asian American college experience at a diverse institution: Campus climate as a predictor of sense of belonging. *Journal of Student Affairs Research and Practice, 52*(2), 149–163. https://doi.org/10.1080/19496591.2015.1041867

Yeh, C. J., & Huang, K. (1996). The collective nature of ethnic identity development among Asian-American college students. *Adolescence, 31*(123), 645–661. https://www.researchgate.net/profile/Christine_Yeh3/publication/14331501_The_Collectivistic_Nature_of_Ethnic_Identity_Development_Among_Asian_American_College_Students/links/0a85e5399399072eca000000.pdf

Yoshikawa, H., Mistry, R., & Wang, Y. (2016). Advancing methods in research on Asian American children and youth. *Child Development, 87*(4), 1033–1050. https://doi.org/10.1111/cdev.12576

Zhou, M. & Lee, J. (2017). Hyper-selectivity and the remaking of culture: Understanding the Asian American achievement paradox. *Asian American Journal of Psychology, 8*(1), 7–15. https://doi.org/10.1037/aap0000069

9

LATINX COLLEGE STUDENTS' SENSE OF BELONGING

Comunidades de Apoyo: (Supportive Communities)

Holly Holloway-Friesen

Latinx college enrollment has increased steadily for the past 2 decades, with growth most pronounced in the past 10 years (Bauman, 2017). The number of Latinx students enrolled in higher education increased by 1.7 million students from 2006 to 2016, and Latinx undergraduates are now the second-largest student population behind Whites (Postsecondary National Policy Institute [PNPI], 2020). With increased enrollments, graduation rates have risen as well. Between 2000 and 2019, Latinx individuals aged 25–29 with at least an associate degree jumped from 15% to 31%, and those earning a bachelor's degree from 10% to 21% (PNPI, 2020).

Despite these gains, college completion rates for Latinx individuals trail other ethnicities, with only 59% of Latinx students completing a bachelor's degree after 8 years compared to 80% of Asian and 73% of White students (National Student Clearinghouse, 2020). Latinx workers tend to be concentrated in low-skilled positions and earn the lowest wages for full-time and salary positions among all major race and ethnic groups (U.S. Bureau of Labor Statistics [BLS], 2021). As education level and occupational attainment are related, it is essential to understand institutional climate features that foster retention and degree completion among Latinx to address these persistent trends (BLS, 2021).

A critical component to promoting a warm college climate is the concept of a sense of belonging. A sense of belonging influences increased retention rates (Gonzales et al., 2015) and bachelor's degree attainment among Latinx students (Gil, 2016). Researchers have characterized a sense of belonging as an awareness of mattering and fitting into one's community that addresses students' need to be connected through formal and informal interactions (Hurtado et al., 2015; Tovar & Simon, 2010). In addition, researchers conceptualized a sense of belonging as cognitive and psychosocial factors where students evaluate their perceived role within a group or institution (Chun et al., 2016).

Sense of belonging may differ by social identity, as some researchers have argued that traditional definitions of sense of belonging neglect Latinx and other students of color and their social integration processes (Holloway-Friesen, 2018b; Nuñez, 2009). Traditional understandings of belonging emphasize connections to the university itself without fully addressing cultural adjustment and external communities relevant to the Latinx college integration process (Chun et al., 2016; Hernández & Bámaca-Colbert, 2016; Rendón et al., 2014).

Cultural Features of Latinx Students' Sense of Belonging

Castellanos and Gloria (2007) introduced the psychosociocultural framework, an approach that explores psychological, social, and environmental contexts to more comprehensively understand the educational experiences of Latinx students. They asserted that understanding Latinx students holistically in their educational context is the first step to fostering a sense of belonging and overall college success (Castellanos & Gloria, 2007). A holistic approach assesses the interplay of the person, relationships, and contextual conditions in which Latinx students learn (Gloria et al., 2019).

Due to Latinx's historical, societal position, and patterns of marginalization on college campuses, Latinx undergraduates are vulnerable to experiencing dissonance between their home culture and that of their institutions of higher education (Hurtado et al., 2015; Rendón et al., 2014). Eurocentric values; including competition, individualism, and personal fulfillment, dominate the typical university context. In contrast, many Latinx students emphasize collaborative approaches that prioritize family needs and obligations and perceive success as a collective process (Gloria et al., 2019; Hernández & Bámaca-Colbert, 2016).

In addition to the dissonance associated with navigating two cultural contexts, many Latinx students experience overt or subtle forms of exclusion that diminish their sense of belonging on campus (Gloria et al., 2016; Holloway-Friesen, 2021). A blatant example is the underrepresentation of

Latinx students at top public universities (Baylor, 2016). Latinx students are significantly concentrated at less-selective public 4-year colleges and community colleges in nearly every state compared to Asian and White students (Baylor, 2016; PNRI, 2020). More subtle forms of exclusion include avoidance from other students, experiences of microaggressions, differential treatment from faculty, and few professors of color with whom Latinx students can identify (Hernández & Villodas, 2019; Yosso et al., 2009). As a result, unwelcoming campus environments contribute to impaired cognitive, emotional, and social adjustment (Herrera et al., 2018; Holloway-Friesen, 2021), isolation from the institution (Cerezo & Chang, 2013; Dueñas & Gloria, 2017), and lower college persistence attitudes among Latinx students (Hernández & Villodas, 2019).

One remedy for cultural dissonance involves fostering Latinx students' cultural congruity (Chun et al., 2016; Holloway-Friesen, 2018a, 2021). Gloria and Kurpius (1996) defined cultural congruity as an overlap of one's cultural and personal values with those of higher education institutions. Research links cultural congruity with several college success outcomes, including a stronger sense of belonging and academic self-beliefs (Holloway-Friesen, 2021), enhanced resiliency to overcome adversity (Chun et al., 2016; Gloria et al., 2016), life satisfaction (Castellanos et al., 2016), and fewer perceptions of career barriers among Latinx undergraduates (Holloway-Friesen, 2018a).

Factors That Promote Sense of Belonging Among Latinx Students

Cultural congruity addresses elements relevant to integration for Latinx students. Tierney (1992) introduced integration theory that assumed students must separate from their families and communities to establish a sense of belonging at higher education institutions. However, evidence has emerged that indicates a simultaneous attachment to communities of origin and institutional connections contribute to Latinx students' sense of belonging (Castellanos et al., 2016; Gloria et al., 2019). Relationships with parents, grandparents, siblings, and community role models provide students examples of overcoming adversity to better integrate into their new academic communities. *Consejos* (advice shared), primarily through mothers and other forms of familial capital, assist Latinx students in forging pathways into higher education communities (Gloria et al., 2019; Hernández & Bámaca-Colbert, 2016; Rendón et al., 2014).

Peer Interactions and Comunidad (Community)

Latinx students' ability to leverage relational connections supports their social integration processes (Castellanos & Gloria, 2016; Gloria et al., 2019; Rendón et al., 2014). To that end, many implement relational strategies of *familia* (family) and *comunidad* (community) to build academic families on their college campuses (Castellanos & Gloria, 2016). Researchers defined an academic family as members of the educational community with whom Latinx students experience emotional ties, connections, and obligations (Gloria et al., 2019). A common phrase, *"Siempre hay lugar para uno mas"* (There is always room for one more), exhibits Latinx value to continuously welcome new relations into their families (Gloria et al., 2019, p. 127). In the same way, Latinx students perceive their academic families as ever open to expand. Latinx students seek out like-minded peers, *madrinas* (godmothers), and *padrinos* (godfathers)—older members of the campus community to become members of their academic families and to serve as mentors and guides in their integration process. These campus community members provide emotional and even spiritual support and serve as safe spaces, fostering a sense of belonging for Latinx students (Dueñas & Gloria, 2017; Nuñez, 2011; Triana et al., 2020).

Faculty Interactions and Mentoring Relationships

The concept of academic families can include Latinx and non-Latinx staff and faculty who intentionally contribute to the social integration process of Latinx students (Gloria et al., 2019). These institutional agents often serve as mentors and guides in students' lives (Castellanos et al., 2016; Gloria et al., 2019; Holloway-Friesen, 2021) and further Latinx academic and social integration (Castellanos et al., 2016; Diaz Solodukhin & Orphan, 2022). According to Johnson (2007), mentoring involves engaging students in emotionally reciprocal relationships that guide students' personal, academic, and career paths. Quality mentoring results in the transfer of knowledge and skills that empowers students to grow personally and academically.

Castellanos et al. (2016) found Latinx undergraduate students with mentors reported greater cultural congruity and compatibility with the university environment than those without mentors. Likewise, a longitudinal study across three institutions found mentored Latinx undergraduates exhibited higher levels of sense of belonging than unmentored peers (Torres & Hernandez, 2009). Moschetti et al. (2017) linked mentoring with academic and emotional support and more profound social integration levels among Latinx undergraduates. Validating faculty interactions increased academic self-efficacy (Holloway-Friesen, 2021), promoted greater college satisfaction

(Diaz Solodukhin & Orphan, 2022), and enhanced retention (Rendón et al., 2014) among Latinx college students.

Furthermore, there is a small but growing body of literature on Latinx graduate students that indicates ties among mentoring, a sense of belonging, and academic success outcomes (Holloway-Friesen, 2021; Rudolph et al., 2015). In a study by Holloway-Friesen (2021), mentoring alone failed to enhance academic self-efficacy. However, the interaction between mentoring and a sense of belonging promoted gains in academic self-efficacy, with mentored students more likely to engage with faculty on academic tasks, participate in classroom discussions, and build peer relationships.

Conclusion

As college campuses continue to diversify, achieving Latinx students' numerical representation is just the initial step to establishing culturally hospitable environments (Hurtado et al., 2015). Higher education institutions are responsible for fostering welcoming environments for ethnically and racially diverse communities (Gloria et al., 2019; Kiyama et al., 2015; Strayhorn, 2019), and colleges and universities that promote academic families will likely lay the groundwork for Latinx relationship building among faculty, peers, and other institutional agents (Castellanos & Gloria, 2016; Gloria et al., 2019; Rendón et al., 2014). The recruiting, hiring, and retaining of culturally competent Latinx faculty, administrators, and staff will increase the number of potential *familia* to serve as mentors and guides to the growing number of Latinx students enrolling in colleges and universities (Gloria et al., 2019; Hurtado et al., 2015). In addition, non-Latinx faculty and staff trained in cultural awareness and person-centered interactions will be equipped to serve as academic *madrinas* and *padrinos* and facilitate academic family building (Castellanos & Gloria, 2016; Diaz Solodukhin & Orphan, 2022). Latinx students who experience validation of their unique cultural backgrounds and receive emotional and relational support will likely perceive themselves as belonging to and mattering within their college or university setting, an essential element in college retention and degree completion.

References

Bauman, K. (2017, August 28). *School enrollment of the Hispanic population: Two decades of growth*. U.S. Census Bureau. https://www.census.gov/newsroom/blogs/random-samplings/2017/08/school_enrollmentof.html

Baylor, E. (2016). *Closed doors: Black and Latino students are excluded from top public universities*. Center for American Progress. https://www.americanprogress.org/issues/education-postsecondary/reports/2016/10/13/145098/closed-doors-black-and-latino-students-are-excluded-from-top-public-universities/

Castellanos, J., & Gloria, A. M. (2007). Research considerations and theoretical application for best practices in higher education. *Journal of Hispanic Higher Education, 6*(4), 378–398. https://doi.org/10.1177/1538192707305347

Castellanos, J., & Gloria, A. M. (2016). Latina/os—Drive, community and spirituality: The strength within *(SOMOS Latina/os—Ganas, comunidad, y el espíritu: La fuerza que llevamos por dentro)*. In E. C. Chang, C. A. Downey, J. K. Hirsch, & N. J. Lin (Eds.), *Positive psychology in racial and ethnic groups: Theory, research, and practice* (pp. 61–82). American Psychological Association. https://doi.org/10.1037/14799-004

Castellanos, J., Gloria, A. M., Besson, D., & Harvey, L. C. (2016). Mentoring matters: Racial ethnic minority undergraduates' cultural fit, mentorship, and college and life satisfaction. *Journal of College Reading and Learning, 46*(2), 81–98. https://doi.org/10.1080/10790195.2015.1121792

Cerezo, A., & Chang, T. (2013). Latina/o achievement at predominantly White universities: The importance of culture and ethnic community. *Journal of Hispanic Higher Education, 12*(1), 72–85. https://doi.org/10.1177/1538192712465626

Chun, H., Marin, M. R., Schwartz, J. P., Pham, A., & Castro-Olivo, S. M. (2016). Psychosociocultural structural model of college success among Latina/o students in Hispanic-serving institutions. *Journal of Diversity in Higher Education, 9*(4), 385–400. https://doi.org/10.1037/a0039881

Diaz Solodukhin, L., & Orphan, C. M. (2022). Operationalizing funds of knowledge: Examining a reciprocal research relationship between a White faculty member and a Latino student. *Journal of Diversity in Higher Education , 15*(2), 207–217. https://doi.org/10.1037/dhe0000286

Dueñas, M., & Gloria, A. M. (2017). ¿*Pertenezco a esta universidad?* The mediating role of belonging for collective self-esteem and mattering for Latin@ undergraduates. *Journal of College Student Development, 58*(6), 891–906. https://doi.org/10.1177/0739986319899734

Gil, E. (2016). First generation Latino college students support four-year college degree completion. *Urban Education Research and Policy Annuals, 4*(2), 34–41. https://journals.charlotte.edu/urbaned/issue/view/70

Gloria, A. M., Castellanos, J., Dueñas, M., & Franco, V. (2019). Academic family and educational *compadrazgo*: Implementing cultural values to create educational relationships for informal learning and persistence for Latinx undergraduates. J. Calvo de Mora & K. J. Kennedy (Eds.), *Schools and informal learning in a knowledge-based world* (pp. 119–135). Routledge. https://doi.org/10.4324/9780429022616

Gloria, A. M., & Kurpius, S. E. R. (1996). The validation of the cultural congruity scale and the university environment scale with Chicano/a students. *Journal of Behavioral Science, 18*(4), 533–549. https://doi.org/10.1177/07399863960184007

Gonzales, S. M., Brammer, E. C., Sawilowsky, S. (2015). Belonging in the academy: Building a "casa away from casa" for Latino/a undergraduate students. *Journal of Hispanic Higher Education*, *14*(3), 223–239. https://doi.org/10.1177/1538192714556892

Hernández, M. M., & Bámaca-Colbert, M. Y. (2016). A behavioral process model of familism. *Journal of Family Theory & Review*, *8*(4), 463–483. https://doi.org/10.1111/jftr.12166

Hernández, R. J., & Villodas, M. (2019). Collectivistic coping responses to racial microaggressions associated with Latina/o college persistence attitudes. *Journal of Latinx Psychology*, *7*(1), 76–90. https://doi.org/10.1037/lat0000107

Herrera, N., Gloria, A. M., & Castellanos, J. (2018). The role of perceived educational environment and high school generation on Mexican American female community college students' emic well-being. *Journal of Diversity in Higher Education*, *11*(3), 254–267. https://doi.org/10.1037/dhe0000056

Holloway-Friesen, H. (2018a). Acculturation, enculturation, gender, and college environment on perceived career barriers among Latino/a college students. *Journal of Career Development*, *45*(2), 117–131. https://doi.org/10.1177/0894845316668641

Holloway-Friesen, H. (2018b). Culture and religiosity: Contributors to Asian American graduate students' belonging. *Journal of Student Affairs Research and Practice*, *55*(4), 426–439. https://doi.org/10.1080/19496591.2018.1474760

Holloway-Friesen, H. (2021). The role of mentoring on Hispanic graduate students' sense of belonging and academic self-efficacy. *Journal of Hispanic Higher Education*, *20*(1), 46–58. https://doi.org/10.1177/1538192718823716

Hurtado, S., Ruiz Alvarado, A., & Guillermo-Wann, C. (2015). Creating inclusive environments: The mediating effect of faculty and staff validation on the relationship of discrimination/bias to students' sense of belonging. *Journal Committed to Social Change on Race and Ethnicity*, *1*(1), 60–80. https://doi.org/10.15763/issn.2642-2387.2015.1.1.59-81

Johnson, W. B. (2007). *On being a mentor: A guide for higher education faculty*. Erlbaum.

Kiyama, J. M., Museus, S. D., & Vega, B. E. (2015). Cultivating campus environments to maximize success among Latino and Latina college students. In M. L. Freeman & M. Martinez (Eds.), *College Completion for Latino/a Students: Institutional and System Approaches* (New Directions for Higher Education, no. 172, pp. 29–38). Jossey-Bass. https://doi.org/10.1002/he.20150

Moschetti, R. V., Plunkett, S. W., Efrat, R., & Yomtov, D. (2017). Peer mentoring as social capital for Latina/o college students at a Hispanic-serving institution. *Journal of Hispanic Higher Education*, *17*(4), 375–392. https://doi.org/10.1177/1538192717702949

National Student Clearinghouse Research Center. (2020). *Completing college national and state reports* [Signature report no. 19]. https://nscresearchcenter.org/wp-content/uploads/Completions_Report_2020.pdf

Nuñez, A. (2009). Latino students' transitions to college: A social and intercultural capital perspective. *Harvard Educational Review, 79*(1), 22–48. https://doi.org/10.17763/haer.79.1.wh7164658k33w477

Nuñez, A. M. (2011). Counterspaces and connections in college transitions: First-generation Latino students' perspectives on Chicano studies. *Journal of College Student Development, 52,* 639–655. http://dx.doi.org/10.1353/csd.2011.0077

Postsecondary National Policy Institute. (2020). *Latino students in higher education.* https://pnpi.org/latino-students/#:~:text=Sixty%2Dseven%20percent%20of%20all,enrolled%20at%20HSIs%20are%20Latino

Rendón, L. I., Nora, A. & Kanagala, V. (2014). *Ventajas/assets y conocimientos/knowledge: Leveraging Latin@ strengths to foster student success.* The University of Texas at San Antonio, College of Education and Human Development, Center for Research and Policy in Education. https://www.utsa.edu/strategicplan/documents/2017_12%20Student%20Success%20_Ventajas_Assets_2014.pdf

Rudolph, B. A., Castillo, C. P., Garcia, V. G., Martinez, A., & Navarro, F. (2015). Hispanic graduate students' mentoring themes: Gender roles in a bicultural context. *Journal of Hispanic Higher Education, 14*(3), 191–206. https://doi.org/10.1177/1538192714551368

Strayhorn, T. L. (2019). *College students' sense of belonging: A key to educational success for all students* (2nd ed.). Routledge.

Tierney, W. G. (1992). An anthropological analysis of student participation in college. *Journal of Higher Education, 63*(6), 603–618. https://doi.org/10.2307/1982046

Torres, V., & Hernandez, E. (2009). Influence of an identified advisor/mentor on urban Latino students' college experience. *Journal of College Student Retention: Research, Theory, & Practice, 11*(1), 141–160. https://doi.org/10.2190/CS.11.1.h

Tovar, E., & Simon, M. A. (2010). Factorial structure and invariance analysis of the Sense of Belonging Scales. *Measurement and Evaluation in Counseling and Development, 43*(3), 199–217. https://doi.org/10.1177/0748175610384811

Triana, C., Gloria, A. M., & Castellanos, J. (2020). Cultivating success for Latinx undergraduates: Integrating cultural spirituality within higher education. *About Campus, 24*(6), 4–9. https://doi.org/10.1177/1086482219896793

U.S. Bureau of Labor Statistics. (2020). *Labor force statistics from the current population survey: Employed persons by detailed occupation, sex, race, and Hispanic or Latino ethnicity.* https://www.bls.gov/cps/cpsaat11.htm

Yosso, T. J., Smith, W. A., Ceja, M., & Solórzano, D. G. (2009). Critical race theory, racial microaggressions, and campus racial climate for Latina/o undergraduates. *Harvard Educational Review, 79*(4), 659–690. https://doi.org/10.17763/haer.79.4.m6867014157m7071

10

SENSE OF BELONGING AMONG BLACK COLLEGE STUDENTS

A Socioecological Perspective

Royel M. Johnson and Alex Kenney

College student sense of belonging—feeling cared about, accepted, respected, valued by, and important to the campus community—is a basic human need (Strayhorn, 2012). Scholars have theorized that satisfying one's basic needs is critical for optimal learning, development, and student success (Maslow, 1943; Strayhorn, 2019). Yet, feelings of belongingness are not equitably experienced across student groups, especially at predominantly White institutions (PWIs), given their historical and contemporary commitments to anti-Blackness (Dancy et al., 2018). Decades of research coalesce around a single point: Campus climates at PWIs largely foster feelings of alienation and marginalization among Black students due to blatant and covert experiences with racism (Harper & Hurtado, 2007; Johnson, 2013).

It is not the responsibility of Black and other minoritized students to "find" a sense of belonging on campus—especially at places that are normed on White, Christian, heterosexual, cisgender men (Johnson, in press). College and university leaders have an *institutional responsibility* to root out inequitable policies, practices, and logics that thwart students' belonging. Yet, many peddle diversity and inclusion discourse (Iverson, 2007)—what Stewart (2017) referred to as a "language of appeasement" (para. 4)—to mollify concerns about racist campus climates without attempting to radically transform oppressive systems and structures.

In this chapter, we propose a socioecological framework to aid college/university faculty and administrators in fostering a sense of belonging among Black college students. While individual- and relational-level programming and interventions (Walton & Cohen, 2011) that promote college student belonging are important, they are insufficient for transforming campuses (Johnson, in press; Kezar, 2014) in service of racial equity and justice. A socioecological perspective is useful for identifying factors across the ecology of a campus community that require change. Drawing from Bronfenbrenner's (1993) ecological theory of human development, we synthesize empirical insights related to factors that influence Black college students' sense of belonging. We also identify and present promising strategies and interventions that campus stakeholders should consider using to facilitate student belonging.

Before presenting our framework, a few caveats deserve mention. An exhaustive, systematic review is beyond the scope of this chapter, although an undertaking of that kind is overdue. Furthermore, empirical research on college student belonging has focused disproportionately on individual and micro-level factors; considerably less is known about the exo and macro system levels. In the absence of research, we speculate based on insights from a broad swath of empirical and theoretical scholarship. In the following section, we present our proposed model, using Bronfenbrenner's (1993) ecology of human development framework to synthesize these insights.

Toward a Socioecological Framework of Black College Students' Belonging

Like *retention, engagement,* and *student success,* the term *sense of belonging* has infiltrated the higher educational lexicon over the past 20 years. While the concept has long enjoyed scholarly attention and popularity in psychology, Hurtado and Carter (1997) prompted the field of higher education to take it up. Drawing on their work, Strayhorn's (2012, 2019) book, *College Students' Sense of Belonging: A Key to Educational Success,* advanced the field by synthesizing insights from his research to illustrate how sense of belonging is experienced among underserved and institutionally marginalized student populations. Strayhorn also proposed a theoretical model of college student sense of belonging that has been instrumental in catalyzing new research. Scholars frequently draw on Strayhorn's work to define, conceptualize, and measure belonging in the postsecondary education context, or as a theoretical framework to examine how underserved and institutionally marginalized students experience belonging and related factors. Still, frameworks are needed that offer insight into *how* to facilitate belonging. Our proposed framework is designed to complement Strayhorn's (2012, 2019) theoretical model, supporting higher education educational professionals in undertaking reforms and interventions that facilitate belonging among Black college students.

We contend that Black college students' sense of belonging is a socio-ecological phenomenon influenced by individual, social, and organizational factors within the campus community, which is nested within broader social, cultural, political, and historical contexts (Johnson, in press). Thus, isolated individual-level interventions are insufficient for sustaining feelings of belonging, especially within racially hostile and exclusive campus environments, which frequently characterize PWIs. Bronfenbrenner's (1993) ecological systems model of human development offers a useful heuristic for identifying individual- and contextual-level factors that impact sense of belonging among Black students. Within this framework, Black college students are at the center of four nested systems (micro, meso, exo, and macro) that affect their sense of belonging. Before describing each context, we focus on individual students and their attributes.

Individual

Fostering sense of belonging among Black college students at PWIs requires attention to a number of individual-level factors and characteristics. For instance, noncognitive factors such as confidence in transition to college was found to be positively associated with sense of belonging among a small sample of Black undergraduate men (Strayhorn et al., 2015). Lack of confidence in transition may be attributed to concern about academic preparation or anticipation of social adversity. Walton and Cohen (2011) found that a brief intervention that normalizes adversity in college among Black students can significantly increase their academic performance and self-reported health and well-being. In other words, affirming and consistent messages that attribute adversity to the college transition process rather than fixed deficits unique to a student or their ethnic group can promote Black student belonging and academic success. Black students' experiences with racism, sexism, xenophobia, and ableism, among other forms of discrimination and oppression, although commonplace, should not be normalized. Thus, intra-level belonging interventions must be matched with institutional-level transformations. An intersectional framework that accounts for the social locations of Black students within a broader matrix of privilege and oppression is necessary.

Micro System

The innermost level, the micro system, is the immediate environmental context (Bronfenbrenner, 1993) where one experiences direct person-to-person interactions. For college students, this may include friendship groups, classrooms, roommates/residence halls, and student clubs or organizations (Renn & Arnold, 2003). Research has found that Black students' sense of belonging is positively associated with frequent interactions with peers from different racial/ethnic backgrounds (Strayhorn, 2008; Strayhorn & Johnson, 2014). That Black students must interact with White students—who are often the perpetrators of various forms of racial abuse—to feel a sense of belonging at PWIs is an inequity that makes efforts to engage White students in learning about race, racism, and their complicity in White supremacy important. Black student interactions with same-race peers can act as a protective factor in facilitating their sense of belonging (Strayhorn et al., 2015). So too can participation in identity-based student clubs/organizations (Harper & Quaye, 2007) and Black cultural centers (Patton, 2006).

Positive, supportive, and humanizing interactions with faculty and staff can also facilitate Black students' sense of belonging (e.g., Johnson et al., 2019; Newman et al., 2015; Strayhorn, 2008). Brooms's (2020) study of 65 Black males at PWIs identified three characteristics of faculty–student interactions that were instrumental in facilitating students' sense of belonging: (a) creating a positive classroom environment, (b) student-centered caring, and (c) mentoring. Similarly, Stebleton and Aleixo (2016) found that Black African immigrant students reported a greater sense of belonging when they developed personal connections with faculty and staff. When asked what constitutes student-centered faculty, Black students described "mother-like" figures (Black women faculty) who provided material, emotional, and psychological support (Guiffrida, 2005). While such relationships can be instrumental in establishing a sense of community and belonging for Black students at PWIs, they can also be burdensome for Black women faculty/staff (Griffin, 2013). Institutional leaders must not only increase the representation of Black faculty and staff at PWIs, but also engage White and other non-Black faculty/staff in professional development training related to intersectional, belonging-centered instruction and advising. All faculty and staff must accept personal responsibility for Black students' inequitable academic and social experiences and work to remediate their practices and pedagogies to promote their belonging, well-being, and academic success.

Meso System

The meso system, the second innermost environmental context, refers to the interconnections within a student's micro systems that directly influence them (Bronfenbrenner, 1993). Interactions (e.g., relationships, symbols, objects, messages) among micro systems (e.g., family, work, peers, classroom) can facilitate or thwart feelings of belonging. For instance, students from low-income families often have to work to cover college costs, which can limit their engagement with campus peers and negatively impact their academic performance in class. In this way, a student's family, peer, and classroom micro systems interact. One study of 30 low-income college students (which included a subsample of Black students) found that financial background negatively influenced students' sense of belonging by limiting their opportunities to socialize with peers, who often made assumptions about their financial capabilities (Nguyen & Heron, 2020). Moreover, participants discussed how their sense of belonging was reduced due to their inability to afford academic materials such as textbooks and software like their peers (Nguyen & Heron, 2020). Black college students are overrepresented among those from low-income family backgrounds (Espinosa et al., 2019); many must work to cover their educational costs, limiting their opportunities to experience belongingness.

Another meso system factor that impacts Black college students' sense of belonging is the cultural dissonance some experience at PWIs due to conflicting messages and values between their family and the campus culture communicated via faculty and staff. Scholars have critiqued Tinto's (1993) notion of academic and social integration, the dominant student success paradigm guiding institutional policy and practice for 3 decades. Academic and social integration, Tinto argued, increases a student's likelihood of retention and degree completion. For Black students whose cultures/communities qualitatively differ from those that characterize PWIs, academic and social integration can represent a form of cultural suicide, whereby they disconnect from their communities of origin and assimilate into the dominant campus culture (Tierney, 1999). Numerous scholars have advocated for new perspectives that celebrate the cultural backgrounds of Black, Indigenous, Latinx, and Asian students while acknowledging the ways in which institutional environments are implicated in student failure (e.g., Museus, 2014; Tierney, 1992). For instance, Strayhorn (2015) urged academic advisors to operate as cultural navigators, helping Black, Indigenous, and people of color (BIPOC) students to hone their cultural knowledge and resources to successfully traverse PWI institutional environments. Numerous other meso system–level factors impact Black students' sense of belonging, such as social capital (Museus & Neville, 2012), living-learning communities (Johnson, 2011), and family support and kinship networks (Barnett, 2004).

Exo System

The exo system refers to "other specific social structures, both formal and informal, that . . . impinge upon or encompass the immediate settings in which [a] person is found" (Bronfenbrenner, 1977, p. 515). For college students, this may include federal, state, and institutional policies and practices, among other factors (Renn & Arnold, 2003). Maslow's (1943) hierarchy of needs, which undergirds Strayhorn's (2012, 2019) framework, posits that one's basic physiological (e.g., shelter, food) and safety needs must be satisfied before higher-order needs such as love and belonging needs emerge. Basic needs insecurity has become a pressing student success issue, especially for Black students, who are most disparately impacted, according to Goldrick-Rab et al. (2019). Thus, addressing basic needs insecurities among Black students is a precursor to fostering their sense of belonging. Developing emergency aid policies and programs that provide students with "just-in-time" cash assistance is one recommended strategy.

Policies and practices related to campus safety and security constitute another exo system–level factor that impacts Black students' sense of belonging. Findings from the National Survey of Student Engagement (NSSE, 2016) suggest that in 2016, roughly one in seven Black students reported feeling physically unsafe on 4-year college campuses. Physical and psychological safety are consistently correlated with sense of belonging and academic success (Strayhorn, 2019). Experiences with bias, discrimination, and anti-Black racism can contribute to concerns regarding safety. Race- and power-conscious campus safety policies are needed that hold individuals accountable for discriminatory acts. Additional exo system factors that can foster Black college students' sense of belonging include centering race and culture in course curriculums, providing federal resources and Pell grants, recruiting and retaining Black faculty and staff, creating comprehensive antiracist policies that permeate campus academic and social spheres, and debt-forgiveness initiatives.

Macro System

The final environmental context, the macro system; encompasses broader social, cultural, economic, historical, and political forces and systems that shape the micro, meso, and exo systems (Bronfenbrenner, 1993). For instance, anti-Black racism permeates U.S. higher education (Dancy et al.,

2018), shaping expectations for Black students to assimilate in White-normed campus cultures. Similarly, U.S. heterogenderism perpetuates the gender binary on college and university campuses, fostering exclusion and alienation of Black trans and gender nonconfirming students in both discourse and practice (e.g., housing, classrooms, involvement opportunities; Lee et al., 2020). Acknowledging these larger forces is useful for understanding how exclusionary policies, practices, and logics are concertized across the other environmental contexts.

Conclusion

Taken together, a socioecological perspective helps account for the multitude of factors within Black college students' ecosystems that impact their sense of belonging. Indeed, holistic and comprehensive frameworks are needed to help institutional stakeholders reform campus policies, practices, and processes to create conditions that foster Black students' sense of belonging. This chapter's proposed framework is one step toward that direction.

References

Barnett, M. (2004). A qualitative analysis of family support and interaction among Black college students at an Ivy League university. *Journal of Negro Education*, *73*(1), 53–68. https://doi.org/10.2307/3211259

Bronfenbrenner, U. (1993). The ecology of cognitive development: Research models and fugitive findings. In R. H. Wozniak & K. W. Fischer (Eds.), *Development in context: Acting and thinking in specific environments* (pp. 3–44). Erlbaum.

Brooms, D. R. (2020). Helping us think about ourselves: Black males' sense of belonging through connections and relationships with faculty in college. *International Journal of Qualitative Studies in Education*, *33*(9), 921–938. https://doi.org/10.1080/09518398.2019.1687956

Dancy, T. E., Edwards, K. T., & Earl Davis, J. (2018). Historically White universities and plantation politics: Anti-Blackness and higher education in the Black Lives Matter era. *Urban Education*, *53*(2), 176–195. https://doi.org/10.1177/0042085918754328

Espinosa, L. L., Turk, J. M., Taylor, M., & Chessman, H. (2019). *Race and ethnicity in higher education: A status report*. American Council on Education. https://1xfsu31b52d33idlp13twtos-wpengine.netdna-ssl.com/wp-content/uploads/2019/02/Race-and-Ethnicity-in-Higher-Education.pdf

Goldrick-Rab, S., Baker-Smith, C., Coca, V., Looker, E., & Williams, T. (2019). *College and university basic needs insecurity: A national #RealCollege Survey report*. https://hope4college.com/wp-content/uploads/2019/04/HOPE_realcollege_National_report_digital.pdf

Griffin, K. A. (2013). Voices of the "othermothers": Reconsidering Black professors' relationships with Black students as a form of social exchange. *The Journal of Negro Education, 82*(2), 169–183. https://doi.org/10.7709/jnegroeducation.82.2.0169

Guiffrida, D. (2005). Othermothering as a framework for understanding African American students' definitions of student-centered faculty. *The Journal of Higher Education, 76*(6), 701–723. https://doi.org/10.1080/00221546.2005.11772305

Harper, S. R., & Hurtado, S. (2007). Nine themes in campus racial climates and implications for institutional transformation. In S. R. Harper & L. D. Patton (Eds.), *Responding to the Realities of Race on Campus* [Special Issue] (New Directions for Student Services, no. 120, pp. 7–24). Wiley. https://doi.org/10.1002/ss.254

Harper, S. R., & Quaye, S. J. (2007). Student organizations as venues for Black identity expression and development among African American male student leaders. *Journal of College Student Development, 48*(2), 127–144. http://doi.org/10.1353/csd.2007.0012

Hurtado, S., & Carter, D. F. (1997). Effects of college transition and perceptions of the campus racial climate on Latino college students' sense of belonging. *Sociology of Education, 70*(4), 324–345.

Iverson, S. V. (2007). Camouflaging power and privilege: A critical race analysis of university diversity policies. *Educational Administration Quarterly, 43*(5), 586–611. https://doi.org/10.1177/0013161X07307794

Johnson, D. R. (2011). Examining sense of belonging and campus racial diversity experiences among women of color in STEM living-learning programs. *Journal of Women and Minorities in Science and Engineering, 17*(3). https://doi.org/10.1615/JWomenMinorScienEng.2011002843

Johnson, R. M. (2013). Black and male on campus: An autoethnographic account. *Journal of African American Males in Education, 4*(2), 103-123. https://jaamejournal.scholasticahq.com/article/18441.pdf

Johnson, R. M. (in press). A socio-ecological perspective on sense of belonging among racially/ethnically minoritized college students: Implications for equity-minded practice and policy. In L. D. Taylor & R. M. Johnson (Eds.), *Enacting Student Success: Critical and alternative perspectives for practice* (New Directions for Higher Education).

Johnson, R. M., Strayhorn, T. L., & Travers, C. S. (2019, December 24). Examining the academic advising experiences of Black males at an urban university: An exploratory case study. *Urban Education*. https://doi.org/10.1177/0042085919894048

Kezar, A. (2014). *How colleges change: Understanding, leading, and enacting change*. Routledge.

Lee, D. H., Sérráno, B., Stewart, D-L, & Dockendorff, K. (2020, July 14). *Improving trans lives on campus. Race and intersectional studies in educational equity*. Race and Intersection Studies in Educational Equity. https://www.chhs.colostate.edu/rise/wp-content/uploads/sites/23/2020/07/RISEreport_Trans-Policy-Brief.pdf

Maslow, A. H. (1943). A theory of human motivation. *Psychological Review, 50*(4), 370–396. https://doi.org/10.1037/h0054346

Museus, S. D. (2014). The culturally engaging campus environments (CECE) model: A new theory of success among racially diverse college student populations. In M. B. Paulsen (Ed.), *Higher education: Handbook of theory and research* (pp. 189–227). Springer.

Museus, S. D., & Neville, K. M. (2012). Delineating the ways that key institutional agents provide racial minority students with access to social capital in college. *Journal of College Student Development, 53*(3), 436–452. https://doi.org/10.1353/csd.2012.0042

National Survey of Student Engagement. (2016). *Engagement insights: Survey findings on the quality of undergraduate education—Annual results 2016.* Indiana University Center for Postsecondary Research.

Newman, C. B., Wood, J. L., & Harris, F., III. (2015). Black men's perceptions of sense of belonging with faculty members in community colleges. *The Journal of Negro Education, 84*(4), 564–577. https://doi.org/10.7709/jnegroeducation.84.4.0564

Nguyen, D. J., & Herron, A. (2020). Keeping up with the Joneses or feeling priced out?: Exploring how low-income students' financial position shapes sense of belonging. *Journal of Diversity in Higher Education, 14*(3), 429–440. https://doi.org/10.1037/dhe0000191

Patton, L. D. (2006). The voice of reason: A qualitative examination of Black student perceptions of Black culture centers. *Journal of College Student Development, 47*(6), 628–646. https://doi.org/10.1353/csd.2006.0068

Renn, K. A., & Arnold, K. D. (2003). Reconceptualizing research on college student peer culture. *The Journal of Higher Education, 74*(3), 261–291. https://doi.org/10.1080/00221546.2003.11780847

Stebleton, M. J., & Aleixo, M. B. (2016). Black African immigrant college students' perceptions of belonging at a predominately White institution. *Journal of the First-Year Experience & Students in Transition, 28*(1), 89–107. https://www.ingentaconnect.com/content/fyesit/fyesit/2016/00000028/00000001/art00005#

Stewart, D-L (2017, March 29). Language of appeasement. *Inside Higher Ed.* https://www.insidehighered.com/views/2017/03/30/colleges-need-language-shift-not-one-you-think-essay

Strayhorn, T., Lo, M., Travers, C., & Tillman-Kelly, D. (2015). Assessing the relationship between well-being, sense of belonging, and confidence in the transition to college for Black male collegians. *Spectrum: A Journal on Black Men, 4*(1), 127–138. https://doi.org/10.2979/spectrum.4.1.07

Strayhorn, T. L. (2008). The role of supportive relationships in facilitating African American males' success in college. *NASPA Journal, 45*(1), 26–48. 10.2202/1949-6605.1906

Strayhorn, T. L. (2012). *College students' sense of belonging: A key to educational success for all students.* Routledge.

Strayhorn, T. L. (2015). Reframing academic advising for student success: From advisor to cultural navigator. *The Journal of the National Academic Advising Association, 35*(1), 56–63. https://doi.org/10.12930/NACADA-14-199

Strayhorn, T. L. (2019). *College students' sense of belonging: A key to educational success for all students* (2nd ed). Routledge.

Strayhorn, T. L., & Johnson, R. M. (2014). Why are all the White students sitting together in college? Impact of *Brown v. Board of Education* on cross-racial interactions among Blacks and Whites. *The Journal of Negro Education, 83*(3), 385–399. http://doi.org/10.7709/jnegroeducation.83.3.0385

Tierney, W. G. (1992). An anthropological analysis of student participation in college. *Journal of Higher Education, 63*(6), 603–618. https://doi.org/10.2307/1982046

Tierney, W. G. (1999). Models of minority college-going and retention: Cultural integrity versus cultural suicide. *Journal of Negro education, 68*(1), 80–91. https://doi.org/10.2307/2668211

Tinto, V. (1993). *Leaving college: Rethinking the causes and cures of student attrition.* The University of Chicago Press.

Walton, G. M., & Cohen, G. L. (2011). A brief social-belonging intervention improves academic and health outcomes of minority students. *Science, 331*(6023), 1447–1451. https://doi.org/10.1126/science.1198364

ECONOMIC STRATIFICATION IN HIGHER EDUCATION

An Asset-Based Approach to Low-SES Students' Sense of Belonging

Amy E. French and Shelley R. Price-Williams

Higher education administrators, faculty, and staff must work to support students, promote a sense of belonging, and implement an intersectional approach that examines various aspects of a student's identity. Over the past 2 decades, the number of undergraduate students from low socioeconomic (SES) status increased (Cahalan et al., 2020). SES represents the social standing or class of a group or individual and is often measured using a combination of education, income, and employment. Understanding how low-SES students establish a sense of belonging in college is critical to support these students in their development, academic endeavors, and social interactions.

This chapter highlights the valuable skills low-SES students bring to college and explores how low-SES students establish a sense of belonging (or fail to do so). We provide a rich discussion surrounding SES and cultural capital, and academic success. Lastly, we introduce asset-based approaches intended to support low-SES students.

SES Among U.S. College Students

College participation for students with less than $43,063 in family income increased from 32% in 1990 to 51% in 2018 (Cahalan et al., 2020). Data revealed that independent students are impoverished at higher rates than dependent students. Twenty percent of dependent undergraduate students in 2016 were in poverty, with an additional 19% near poverty (Frye & Cilluffo, 2019). In addition, 42% of independent undergraduate students were in poverty, with another 25% near poverty as of 2016 (Frye & Cilluffo, 2019).

Further, the gap between the most and least wealthy continues to widen. In 2016, the top 5% of the population held over two thirds of the nation's wealth, the top 1% held 40%, and the bottom 90% held just 21% (Cahalan et al., 2020). Two decades ago, Pell Grant recipients comprised 32% of undergraduate students and peaked in 2011 at 48% (Cahalan et al., 2020). In 2016, 39% of dependent college students and 59% of independent college students with dependents received a Pell Grant (Cahalan et al., 2020).

Student parents are more likely to be low SES. The latest numbers from 2015–2016 revealed more than one in five undergraduate students were raising children (estimated 22% of undergraduate students; U.S. Government Accountability Office [GAO], 2019). Many of these students were Black, American Indian/Alaskan Native, and Hispanic, with women the most likely to be raising children while in college. Intersecting identities of this student population are dynamic and complex and must be recognized when extending support.

Data regarding low-SES students indicate a growing need for colleges and universities to respond to the increasing numbers of low-SES students. The need for these students to feel welcomed on the campus, challenged and supported in the classroom, engaged in social activities, and included in campus programming is paramount to establishing a sense of belonging. The features of how a sense of belonging manifests (or does not) for low-SES students is discussed next.

Sense of Belonging

Establishing a sense of belonging includes the overall campus environment and specific academic and social components. To begin to understand a sense of belonging for low-SES students, Means and Pyne (2017) recommended close attention to collegiate and precollegiate years because students question their sense of belonging prior to arriving on a college campus due to messages they receive and anxieties associated with academic preparedness. Recognition of deficit-focused beliefs prior to arrival on campus is important and offers opportunities for campuses to blend high school experiences into college for low-SES students. Within the college environment, low-SES students frequently encounter classism, racism, and other forms of oppression, both overtly and covertly (Means & Pyne, 2017; Vaccaro & Newman, 2016). Discrimination and other means of upholding oppressive systems are endemic within higher education and emphasize the need to value intersectionality authentically to understand, respect, value, and serve students.

Ostrove and Long (2007) assessed sense of belonging among 324 college students and found class background strongly related to participants' sense of belonging. The authors determined sense of belonging has "critical implications for college experience and performance" (p. 381) that may impact participation, help-seeking behavior, and overall college success. Additionally, Ostrove and Long (2007) found that low-SES and working-class students struggle more with belonging in higher education compared to middle- and upper-class peers.

Further, Vaccaro and Newman (2016) conducted a constructionist grounded theory study with 51 first-year college students from privileged and minoritized backgrounds to examine student definitions and development of a sense of belonging and identified two primary themes: being comfortable and fitting in. In relation to involvement, environment, and relationships, privileged and minoritized students described their meaning-making processes differently. Vaccaro and Newman (2016) found privileged students prioritize fun, friendliness, and familiarity, while minoritized students value authenticity, and this authenticity can be a challenge because they do not see themselves fitting into the normative campus environment.

Moreover, Means and Pyne (2017) recognized that institutional support structures such as need-based scholarship programs, social identity–based student organizations, faculty support, and community building within residence halls contribute to students' sense of belonging; however, these institutional apparatuses can also present challenges within the low-SES student population. For example, low-SES students hesitate to interrupt faculty members who signaled to students their busyness or stress (Means & Pyne, 2017).

Challenges for Low-SES Students

Low-SES students face challenges within the higher education landscape that have historically been steeped in class privilege. These challenges present themselves in multiple contexts such as financial, psychological, academic, and social. Each is discussed in the following sections.

Financial

College affordability remains a hurdle in addition to hidden costs such as time, procurement of technology, transportation, textbooks, clothing, food, and housing. Conversely, college costs covered by the Pell Grant decreased from 67% in 1975 to 25% in 2018 (Cahalan et al., 2020). Nguyen and Herron (2020) identified that students without adequate and current technology and the ability to use money to build relationships (attend costly social gatherings, eat at restaurants, go to the movies, etc.), and who lack ownership of the right academic materials, struggle to establish a sense of belonging. Ultimately, the student's lack of money contributed to their inability to connect with peers and participate in social activities. Furthermore, there is an equity gap in time among student parents versus nonparents. Wladis et al. (2018) examined the connection between time, poverty, and college outcomes and found student parents had less discretionary time due to parenthood, which led to attrition (despite academic abilities) and poorer quality study time.

Psychological

Before arriving on campus, Means and Pyne (2017) found low-SES students formulated negative conceptions about belonging in college. Some reported a sense of invisibility and disconnectedness. The system is built on rules exemplary of the middle and upper classes that are unknown to students from low SES. This minority population is more likely to report feeling like imposters. A sense of belonging can be a critical barrier to success. Jury et al. (2017) differentiated identity management as the greatest challenge for this population as they struggle with confidence and self-perceptions of intelligence. Low-SES students also wrangle with regulation of motivation in goal attainment because of fear of failure (Jury et al., 2017). Cultural norms can also create psychological barriers for low-SES students, especially first-eneration students (Jury et al., 2017). Thus, the university context can reproduce social inequality and psychological barriers.

Academic

Academic success in U.S. higher education often prioritizes high test scores, grade point average, extracurricular activity, and learning opportunities inside and outside the classroom. Low-SES students grapple with ways to navigate the seemingly exclusive academic environment and are assumed to enter college with the same level of academic knowledge. This assumption undervalues assets low-SES students bring to college. Compared to their more affluent peers, low-SES students experience a disconnection with faculty and academia. Faculty play a pivotal role in low-SES students' sense of belonging through use of multiple teaching modalities, accessibility, outreach, and the scaffolding of assignments (Means & Pyne, 2017).

Social

Engagement with peers and in the college environment is limited due to work demands among low-SES students who hold multiple jobs or work full-time. An estimated 44% of low-SES students worked full-time, and 64% attended school part-time (GAO, 2019). Yet, social capital is acquired by building networks of peers, staff, and faculty for support and to establish a sense of belonging (Johnstonbaugh, 2017). In relation, McClure and Ryder (2017) examined the relationship between access to spending money and students' social relationships with peers and found that money had a significant influence on students' ability to establish social relationships. Additionally, access to spending money positively contributed to establishing a sense of belonging. Without available funds, students' ability to belong is stagnated.

Asset-Based Approaches and Implications for Support

Facilitation of an asset-based approach to student support should begin by valuing intersectionality and acknowledging all identities a student may possess. This section will address the skills low-SES students bring to college using Yosso's community cultural wealth model and provide practical strategies for supporting this student population.

Skills Low-SES Students Bring to College

Low-SES students accumulate skills through strategic practices that depend on available capital, and they must be more resourceful in acquiring support through use of social capital, unlike high-SES students who acquire financial capital and experiences from parents (Johnstonbaugh, 2017). With reliance on relationships to succeed, low-SES students possess agency and resiliency (Johnstonbaugh, 2017). Low-SES students must prioritize time in a different way than higher-SES students because they often juggle a job, family, and coursework expectations. This means faculty and staff must prioritize relationship building with students, seek out learning styles and preferences, identify strengths and weaknesses, recognize needs, and establish comfort level with asking for assistance.

Yosso's (2005) community cultural wealth model provides multiple ways educators can consider assets possessed by low-SES students. The community cultural wealth model includes aspirational capital, cultural capital, familial capital, linguistic capital, navigational capital, resistant capital, and social capital. Ardoin (2018) summarized the types of capital:

> Aspirational capital is about future-focus and resiliency. Familial capital focuses on connections to one's family and community through kinship and culture. Linguistic capital is the ability to communicate in more than one language or dialect. Navigational capital "acknowledges individual agency within institutional constraints." Resistant capital is the recognition of inequity and the drive to challenge it. Social capital is an individual's network of resources and the use of those resources to assist others. (p. 78, internal citations omitted)

Yosso's (2005) model provides student affairs professionals a framework by which to develop an asset-based approach to supporting low-SES students. For example, resistant capital provides students with the skills to challenge academic systems that were not designed for them. Navigational capital can be combined with resistant capital to challenge the systems and achieve success despite barriers that exist. This framework invites student affairs professionals to uproot damaging stereotypes, policies, and practices. This begins with mindfulness surrounding the language we use, inclusivity within our programs, acceptance and valuation of difference, and genuine exploration for ways to maximize students' community cultural wealth. Next, we present practical steps professionals can take to build belongingness on campus for low-SES students.

Practical Strategies

First, higher education institutions must work to deconstruct academic classism, center relationship building with students, and provide low-SES students with knowledgeable mentors (Johnstonbaugh, 2017). Professional development for faculty and staff focused on intersectionality, cultural competence, and challenges faced by low-SES students is one way to begin. Given that faculty and staff are personnel who foster a sense of belonging, their professional development must provide applicable strategies focused on relationship building and a student success-centered ethic of care. One suggestion is to include prompts for experiential reflection within general education courses to provide space for students to share their narratives and allow opportunity for faculty to support students based on the individuality brought forth within those experiences. Considerations regarding equity and social justice should remain at the forefront of this asset-based approach with a campus-wide curricular plan (Means & Pyne, 2017). Additionally, a focus on familial capital could allow space for faculty and staff to share their lived experiences, which could foster comradery and a sense of belonging for low-SES students to share and perhaps increase the likelihood that they build rapport with professionals.

Furthermore, Jury et al. (2017) position self-affirmation, difference education, and goal reframing as low-cost interventions universities can employ to facilitate student success. Each of these components reflect Yosso's model. Establishing programs in the residence halls, for example, that capitalize on aspirational wealth to provide an opportunity for students to conceptualize goals and identify strengths to create achievable goals that motivate and encourage students to succeed are suggested. Collectively, these strategies reduce stereotype threat, increase comfort with different backgrounds, and reduce the achievement gap. Social identity-based organizations can be instrumental in fostering a sense of belonging among low-SES students, especially students of color (Means & Pyne, 2017). These authors also found need-based scholarship programs that offer emotional and social support to be impactful.

Higher education institutions should continue developing programs for low-SES students. There are many programs facilitated by academic affairs and student affairs across the United States. Prior studies yielded evidence of effectiveness in development of the affective domain beyond grade point average and persistence, such as increase in efficacy, validation, sense of belonging, and engagement (Quiroz & Garza, 2018). For example, summer bridge programs (that take a variety of forms depending on institution type) have been proven successful in academically acclimating students to the collegiate environment. Additionally, programs should consider student parents, given the high percentage of low-SES students who are parents. Ensuring access to affordable and accessible childcare on or near campus and revising the federal financial aid calculations with consideration of dependent care in the cost of attendance (Wladis et al., 2018) are some of the necessary steps to support this student population.

There are multiple approaches professionals can use to facilitate increased belonging. Creating authentic environments (Vaccaro & Newman, 2016) remains paramount to the success of low-SES students. One current example is a pilot program called Mastering Success at Indiana State University (French & Fjeldal, 2020). This academic coaching-based program started in fall 2020 and comprised graduate student coaches, academic advisors, two general education course faculty, first-year transition staff, and student affairs professionals with a group of low-SES students. The academic coaches met regularly with students to casually discuss collegiate life. Topics of discussion ranged from institutional topics such as "How do I schedule time with a tutor?" to time management questions such as "How do I talk to my work supervisor about my class schedule?" Coaches also provided support in areas such as connecting students to services such as the campus counseling center, student recreation center, and food pantry. While the results are forthcoming, anecdotal data suggest positive outcomes related to building greater campus connections for low-SES students, which in effect could contribute to students' sense of belonging.

Conclusion

This chapter featured low-SES students and their quest to establish (or in some cases not) a sense of belonging in university settings. Through examination of recent data and literature, this chapter has presented practitioners, scholars, and administrators with strategies to champion -low-SES students that center on building relationships, establishing authentic spaces, and creating meaningful involvement opportunities. Given the recent COVID-19 pandemic, all students have experienced additional hurdles to establishing a sense of belonging. For low-SES students, preexisting challenges have been compounded and present opportunities for professionals to creatively respond.

References

Ardoin, S. (2018). Helping poor- and working-class students create their own sense of belonging. In G. L. Martin & B. Elkins (Eds.), *Social Class Identity in Student Affairs* (New Directions for Student Services, no. 162, 75–86). Jossey-Bass. https://doi.org/10.1002/ss.20263

Cahalan, M. W., Perna, L. W., Addison, M., Murray, C., Patel, P. R., & Jiang, N. (2020). *Indicators of higher education equity in the United States: 2020 historical trend report.* The Pell Institute for the Study of Opportunity in Higher Education, Council for Opportunity in Education, & Alliance for Higher Education and Democracy of the University of Pennsylvania.

French, A., & Fjeldal, N. (2020). *Mastering success: Academic coaching pilot program at Indiana State University* [Unpublished manuscript]. Department of Educational Leadership, Indiana State University.

Frye, R., & Cilluffo, A. (2019). *A rising share of undergraduates are from poor families, especially at less selective colleges.* Pew Research Center. https://www.pewresearch.org/social-trends/2019/05/22/a-rising-share-of-undergraduates-are-from-poor-families-especially-at-less-selective-colleges/

Johnstonbaugh, M. (2017). Conquering with capital: Social, cultural, and economic capital's role in combating socioeconomic disadvantage and contributing to educational attainment. *Journal of Youth Studies, 21*(5), 590–606. https://doi.org/10.1080/13676261.2017.1406069

Jury, M., Smeding, A., Stephens, N. M., Nelson, J. E., Aelenei, C., & Darnon, C. (2017). The experience of low-SES students in higher education: Psychological barriers to success and interventions to reduce social-class inequality. *Journal of Social Issues, 73*, 23–41. http://dx.doi.org/10.1111/josi.12202

McClure, K. R., & Ryder, A. J. (2017). The costs of belonging: How spending money influences social relationships in college. *Journal of Student Affairs Research and Practice, 55*(2), 196–209. http://dx.doi.org/10.1080/19496591.2017.1360190

Means, D. R., & Pyne, K. B. (2017). Finding my way: Perceptions of institutional support and belonging in low-income, first-generation, first-year college students. *Journal of College Student Development, 58*(6), 907–924. https://doi.org/10.1353/csd.2017.0071

Nguyen, D. J., & Herron, A. (2020). Keeping up with the Joneses or feeling priced out?: Exploring how low-income students' financial position shapes sense of belonging. *Journal of Diversity in Higher Education, 14*(3), 429–440. http://dx.doi.org/10.1037/dhe0000191

Ostrove, J. M., & Long, S. M. (2007). Social class and belonging: Implications for college adjustment. *The Review of Higher Education, 30*(4), 363–389. https://doi.org/10.1353/rhe.2007.0028

Quiroz, A. G., & Garza, N. R. (2018). Focus on student success: Components for effective summer bridge programs. *Journal of Hispanic Higher Education, 17*(2), 101–111. https://doi.org/10.1177/1538192717753988

U.S. Government Accountability Office. (2019). *More information could help student parents access additional federal student aid.* https://www.gao.gov/assets/710/701002.pdf

Vaccaro, A., & Newman, B. M. (2016). Development of sense of belonging for privileged and minoritized students: An emergent model. *Journal of College Student Development, 57*(8), 925–942. https://doi.org/10.1353/csd.2016.0091

Wladis, C., Hachey, A. C., & Conway, K. (2018). No time for college? An investigation of time poverty and parenthood. *The Journal of Higher Education, 89*(6), 807–831. https://doi.org/10.1080/00221546.2018.1442983

Yosso, T. J. (2005). Whose culture has capital? A critical race theory discussion of community cultural wealth. *Race, Ethnicity, and Education, 8*(1), 69–91. https://doi.org/10.1080/1361332052000341006

12

LANGUAGE UNHEARD, VOICES SILENCED

The Role of Language Minoritization in Sense of Belonging

Kevin J. Bazner and Juan Lopez

English learners (ELs) represent the fastest growing student population in public schools, currently representing 10% of total enrollment (National Center for Educational Statistics [NCES], 2018). *English learners* is a term widely used in K–12 research to refer to students with growing proficiency in English, but it is not as widely used in higher education research and often focuses attention on proficiency (Nuñez et al., 2016). Those numbers are only expected to grow over the next few decades (Field, 2018; Nuñez et al., 2016; Yao, 2016). International students also represent a growing population of students, where language identity is salient yet overlooked in sense of belonging explorations (Yao, 2016). Further still, increased access and more aggressive recruitment has resulted in increased enrollment from areas of the United States where dominant forms of English, or "academic English," may not be as widely spoken and thus cause stigmatization even among native English speakers (Dunstan & Jaeger, 2016). While enrollment among ELs and students with stigmatized dialects of English has increased, research and practice that center the role of language to student sense of belonging is relatively scarce (Dobinson & Mercieca, 2020; Nuñez et al., 2016; Strayhorn, 2019). Global dominance of the English language as the controlling language of academia has resulted in connections of language to sense of belonging being largely ignored (Lillis & Curry, 2010; Salinas, 2017).

This chapter reviews the impact language has on students' overall perception of support and connectedness on campus and calls for expanded considerations of language and language minoritization in the evolving concept of sense of belonging (Strayhorn, 2019). We begin by painting a brief overview of current demographics and reasons for limited scholarship on linguistically minoritized (LM) students. We use the term *linguistically minoritized* to account for both students who are classified by scholarship and legislative documents as ELs (Nuñez et al., 2016) as well as the process of minoritizing English dialects in opposition of dominant forms, or "academic English" (Dunstan & Jaeger, 2016; Salinas, 2017). We follow with an examination of current literature accounting for experiences of LM students and their sense of belonging. Finally, we offer considerations to guide research and implications for practice.

Who Is Coming to College?

In the coming decade, public school enrollment is forecasted to see sharp increases in EL populations, currently accounting for over 10% of the student population in 10 states and the District of Columbia. California (19.2%), Texas (18.0%), and Nevada (17.1%) have the highest EL population, where upward of 78% of ELs identify as Spanish native speakers (NCES, 2018). Aside from domestic EL students, increases in EL populations also caused increased enrollment of students from non-English dominant countries (Rivas et al., 2019; Yao, 2016).

LM students do not always hail from international locations or speak a native language other than English. In fact, LM students can also be native English speakers who have speech patterns that are *othered* within academia or dialects excluded from campus recognition. For instance, Dunstan and Jaeger (2016) called attention to stigmatized dialects of rural Appalachian students, emphasizing how students with speech patterns outside of "standardized" or dominant speech varieties are subject to stereotyping, similar to those who speak other stigmatized varieties of English (e.g., African American vernacular English, Chicano English, Rez accent, Pittsburghese) (Dunstan & Jaeger, 2016; Flores & Rosa, 2015; Johnstone, 2009; Newmark et al., 2016). Unfortunately, when LM students arrive to college campuses, they are often forced to assimilate to the standardized English used in academia or hide their home language/dialect to avoid further discrimination (Dunstan & Jaeger, 2016; Salinas, 2017; Yao, 2016).

Limited Understanding of ELs in Higher Education

Specific EL demographic numbers are hard to establish. A major contributing factor is how EL students are classified by legislation and associations with the legal rights afforded to PK–12 students but not to postsecondary students (Nuñez et al., 2016). The lack of a "legal right" to postsecondary education often absolves postsecondary institutions from having to serve EL students and track this demographic. The fluid nature of who is considered EL and the multiple terms used to describe EL students also limits identification. For example, postsecondary labels may include "linguistic minority," "English as a second language," or "limited English proficient" (Nuñez et al., 2016).

EL status in postsecondary environments is often designated by self-disclosure (Nuñez et al., 2016). Stigma attached to LM students may limit those who self-identify as EL or avoid the term altogether to limit further discrimination based on their linguistic identity. Similarly, students who speak nondominant English dialects may encounter negative stereotyping that further compounds across identities such as race, ethnicity, social class, or geographic location and never claim LM as an identity. Likewise, scholar-practitioners often fail to acknowledge linguistic identity as a contributing factor in sense of belonging. Thus, postsecondary research on LM students will likely encounter incomplete or nonexistent data sets, or student populations less eager to self-disclose or recognize their LM identity.

Relationship of Language Minoritization to Sense of Belonging

Sense of belonging largely deals with a "subjective evaluation" of the environment in which a student exists (Strayhorn, 2019, p. 10). As such, students' sense of belonging can easily shift depending on the identities of a student, the environment itself, or social meaning that can shift based on policy over time or location (Nuñez, 2014; Strayhorn, 2019). For example, a Spanish-speaking Latinx student at a Texas institution with a commitment to dual language immersion and a sizable Spanish-speaking population will likely have a widely different experience than a student who attends an institution in the Midwest with a smaller Spanish-speaking population. In another instance, a student with a rural Southern accent attending a nearby institution is more likely to be surrounded by other students with similar accents than if a student were attending a Northeast institution with fewer students speaking similar dialects.

Among higher education students, language has arisen as a source of frustration in developing an overall sense of belonging (Cuellar &

Johnson-Ahorlu, 2016; Cuellar & Johnson-Ahorlu, 2020; Dunstan & Jaeger, 2016; Garcia et al., 2019; Ryan & Carranza, 1976; Sebanc et al., 2009; Yao, 2016). Edwards et al. (2007), for instance, found Chinese students who doubted their English language skills had difficulty understanding and communicating with faculty and their peers in academic settings. They illuminated the difficulty students had identifying concepts or terms that were used regularly in academic disciplines yet taken for granted by native speakers. Students feared seeking clarification so as not to be viewed as dumb. The recurrent theme of English being the dominant language within academic discourse has presented severe barriers for LM students developing campus connections if confidence in students' language skills is reduced or stigmatized (Flores & Rosa, 2015). LM international students also found language issues were a source of frustration when attempting to build relationships with native English speakers (Li et al., 2010). Frustration then affects students' ability to develop their sense of belonging in the classroom, within student organizations, or in campus residences (Yao, 2016).

Enforcement of implicit language rules within academia can also force students who do not speak dominant varieties of English, or "academic English," to be excluded or othered through racial stigmatization that is historically attached to language (Rosa, 2019). Lippi-Green (2012) referred to this concept as *standard language ideology* (SLI) in which preferred varieties of academic English are expected. Rosa and Flores (2017) referred to *raciolinguistic ideologies*, positioning languages in hierarchical positions to others. This social hierarchy of language is further legitimized within academic spaces historically controlled by White upper-class discourse determining the preferred language at the exclusion of others (Dunstan & Jaeger, 2016). This version of English is understood as "correct," requiring those who do not conform to hold less power, influence students' relationships, or limit LM students from accessing educational resources on campus (Dunstan & Jaeger, 2016).

Salinas (2017) provided a powerful account as a faculty member when giving a lecture and an audience member mocked him for being "stupid." After confronting the audience member, they claimed "Because you have an [Latino] accent" (p. 748). This is an example of a larger pattern in higher education that positions certain use of English as the correct or intelligent way of speaking. For students, this raises fear of asking for help (Dunstan & Jaeger, 2016; Nuñez et al., 2016), seeking out friendships (Yao, 2016), or engaging with the local community (Cuellar & Johnson-Ahorlu, 2020) out of a fear of being judged or discriminated against.

Raciolinguistic ideologies are rooted in colonization and anti-immigrant narratives further legitimized in racialization processes attached to

LM individuals (Hill, 2009; Rosa & Flores, 2017). Elitist and White supremacist discourse has preserved the mentality that exists in the United States today, equating proper English speaking without an accent to Americanization and intelligence (Lippi-Green, 2012). Consequently, college students who experience this stigmatization are less likely to persist or seek out and use available campus resources, which have strong ties to sense of belonging (Strayhorn, 2019). Yet, the lack of research and practice about LM students limits the ability to properly name and recognize language as a contributing factor in students' sense of belonging (Dobinson & Mercieca, 2020; Nuñez et al., 2016; Strayhorn, 2019). Thus, language minoritization is excluded from educational conversations and reifies students' invisibility on campus.

Linguistic Invisibility and Sense of Belonging on Campus

Dobinson and Mercieca (2020) offered the term *linguistic invisibility* to refer to marginalized or unacknowledged language practices that are linked to students' feelings of disconnectedness or lack of belonging while other languages remain more dominant. For instance, LM students whose languages or linguistic patterns are not represented experience invisibility and feel a lost sense of identity, connection, or feeling noticed on campus. As Rivas et al. (2019) noted, international students' feelings of campus belonging are strongly tied to having their full range of identities, including their home language being seen. Similarly, international students whose English development is supported, not stigmatized, report lower levels of stress and more positive academic experiences than their peers with lower levels of confidence who experience bouts of depression and anxiety (Araujo, 2011).

A lack of language inclusion further contributes to the inclusion of campus social spaces and can create *policed* spatial boundaries signaling where language, and thus identities, are welcome. For example, Sebanc et al. (2009) noted Latinx students were met with resistance when speaking Spanish or have accented English in largely White spaces. This stigmatization can further lead to a lack of visibility or cause students to avoid speaking their native languages in public or with friends out of fear of being othered. In turn, students "feel disconnected from other students because they cannot always communicate in a nuanced and personal way through the dominant language" (Dobinson & Mercieca, 2020, p. 793).

Dunstan and Jaeger (2016) asserted "the significant role that language plays in their [students] experiences in terms of finding a place to fit in, feeling a sense of belonging, and becoming accepted and respected members of the campus community" (p. 60). Amit and Bar-Lev (2015) drew connections of sense of belonging to feelings of being "at home," which can be both a physical space and an emotional state of feeling "familiar." However, most definitions and theoretical approaches of sense of belonging are absent of explicit considerations of language. Yosso (2005) stressed that for "Students of Color, culture is frequently represented symbolically through language" (p. 76). Tachine et al. (2017) utilized the peoplehood model, a framework for Indigenous experiences, stating that "language defines place and vice versa" (p. 790). For instance, language is more than simple words of communication but informs knowing and social interactions and is critically important to developing a sense of self. This means sense of belonging cannot be fully separated from identity development.

Implications for Professional Practice

Student affairs practitioners and university administrators should consider ways to promote language inclusion and visibility on their campuses. For instance, Latinx students involved in culturally related organizations had a higher sense of belonging than nonmembers (Hurtado & Carter, 1997). Membership in identity-based organizations may further meditate experiences of discrimination and increase overall sense of belonging. Developing and hosting educational and social programming in other languages is critical to challenging linguistic invisibility. Institutions may consider taking inventory of the languages spoken on their campuses and local communities and hosting language circles or meetups for students to share experiences and stories in their native languages or building connections (Dobinson & Mercieca, 2020; Guardia & Evans, 2008; Sebanc et al., 2009).

Faculty members and instructional designers should consider being more attentive to the representation of languages, dialects, and accents in their curriculum. Incorporating instructional media or inviting guest speakers with a variety of linguistic diversity is crucial for representational diversity. Additionally, faculty should consider including educational resources produced or published in languages other than English. English subtitles and improvements in translation technology mean wider access to educational materials. Students could also be encouraged to speak and write in different languages (Salinas, 2017).

Most importantly, higher education administrators must pay closer attention to sociopolitical developments and how they affect perception of different languages and social identities (Nuñez, 2014). Perceptions of language and the internalization of one's identity are heavily wrapped in developments of economic, social, and political arenas. While many higher education administrators have little control over these arenas, they do have a responsibility to respond and address issues within environments they do influence.

Conclusion

Among rapidly diversifying student demographic student populations and the increasing globalization of higher education institutions, LM students represent one of the fastest growing underserved demographics. Most research and practice centering language exist outside of education literature in sociology or applied linguistics (Dobinson & Mercieca, 2020; Dunstan & Jaeger, 2016; Rosa & Flores, 2017). Scholar–practitioners must do a better job of accounting for language identity among other socially constructed identities and its role in students' sense of belonging. Not only will this result in a better understanding of this underserved identity in postsecondary environments, but practical and impactful implications for practice can also be developed.

References

Amit, K., & Bar-Lev, S. (2015). Immigrants' sense of belonging to the host country: The role of life satisfaction, language proficiency, and religious motives. *Social Indicators Research*, *124*(3), 947–961. https://doi.org/10.1007/s11205-014-0823-3

Araujo, A. D. (2011). Adjustment issues of international students enrolled in American colleges and universities: A review of the literature. *Higher Education Studies*, *1*(1), 2–8. https://doi.org/10.5539/hes.v1n1p2

Cuellar, M., & Johnson-Ahorlu, R. N. (2016). Examining the complexity of the campus racial climate at a Hispanic serving community college. *Community College Review*, *44*(2), 135–152. https://doi.org/10.1177/0091552116632584

Cuellar, M. G., & Johnson-Ahorlu, R. N. (2020, June). Racialized experiences off and on campus: Contextualizing Latina/o students' perceptions of climate at an emerging Hispanic-serving institution (HSI). *Urban Education*. https://doi.org/10.1177/0042085920927772

Dobinson, T., & Mercieca, P. (2020). Seeing things as they are, not just as we are: Investigating linguistic racism on an Australian university campus. *International Journal of Bilingual Education and Bilingualism*, *23*(7), 789–803. https://doi.org/10.1080/13670050.2020.1724074

Dunstan, S. B., & Jaeger, A. J. (2016). The role of language in interactions with others on campus for rural Appalachian college students. *Journal of College Student Development*, *57*(1), 47–64. https://doi.org/10.1080/13670050.2020.1724074

Edwards, V., Ran, A., & Li, D. (2007). Uneven playing field or falling standards? Chinese students' competence in English. *Race Ethnicity and Education, 10*(4), 387–400. https://doi.org/10.1080/13613320701658431

Field, K. (2018, May 14). *More Hispanics are going to college and graduating, but disparity persists.* PBS. https://www.pbs.org/newshour/education/more-hispanics-are-going-to-college-and-graduating-but-disparity-persists

Flores, N., & Rosa, J. (2015). Undoing appropriateness: Raciolinguistic ideologies and language diversity in education. *Harvard Educational Review, 85*(2), 149–171. https://doi.org/10.17763/0017-8055.85.2.149

Garcia, G. A., Núñez, A. M., & Sansone, V. A. (2019). Toward a multidimensional conceptual framework for understanding "servingness" in Hispanic-serving institutions: A synthesis of the research. *Review of Educational Research, 89*(5), 745–784. https://doi.org/10.3102/0034654319864591

Guardia, J. R., & Evans, N. J. (2008). Factors influencing the ethnic identity development of Latino fraternity members at a Hispanic serving institution. *Journal of College Student Development, 49*(3), 163–181. https://doi.org/10.1353/csd.0.0011

Hill, J. H. (2009). *The everyday language of White racism.* Wiley.

Hurtado, S., & Carter, D. F. (1997). Effects of college transition and perceptions of the campus racial climate on Latino college students' sense of belonging. *Sociology of Education, 70*(4), 324–345. https://doi.org/10.2307/2673270

Johnstone, B. (2009). Pittsburghese shirts: Commodification and the enregisterment of an urban dialect. *American Speech, 84*(2), 157–175. https://doi.org/10.1215/00031283-2009-013

Li, G., Chen, W., & Duanmu, J. L. (2010). Determinants of international students' academic performance: A comparison between Chinese and other international students. *Journal of Studies in International Education, 14*(4), 389–405. https://doi.org/10.1177/1028315309331490

Lillis, T. M., & Curry, M. J. (2010). *Academic writing in global context.* Routledge.

Lippi-Green, R. (2012). *English with an accent: Language, ideology and discrimination in the United States.* Routledge.

National Center for Educational Statistics. (2018). *The condition of education 2018.* https://nces.ed.gov/programs/coe/indicator_cpb.asp

Newmark, K., Walker, N., & Stanford, J. (2016). "The rez accent knows no borders": Native American ethnic identity expressed through English prosody. *Language in Society, 45*(5), 633–664. http://10.1017/S0047404516000592

Nuñez, A. M. (2014). Employing multilevel intersectionality in educational research: Latino identities, contexts, and college access. *Educational Researcher, 43*(2), 85–92. https://doi.org/10.3102/0013189X14522320

Nuñez, A. M., Rios-Aguilar, C., Kanno, Y., & Flores, S. M. (2016). English learners and their transition to postsecondary education. In M. Paulsen (Ed.), *Higher education: Handbook of theory and research* (pp. 41–90). Springer. https://doi.org/10.1007/978-3-319-26829-3_2

Rivas, J., Hale, K., & Burke, M. G. (2019). Seeking a sense of belonging: Social and cultural integration of international students with American college students. *Journal of International Students, 9*(2), 682–704. 10.32674/jis.v9i2.943

Rosa, J. (2019). *Looking like a language, sounding like a race.* Oxford University Press.

Rosa, J., & Flores, N. (2017). Unsettling race and language: Toward a raciolinguistic perspective. *Language in Society, 46*(5), 621–647. http://doi.org/10.1017/S0047404517000562

Ryan, E. B., & Carranza, M. A. (1976, January). *Attitudes toward accented English* [Paper presentation]. Conference on College English and the Mexican American, Edinburgh, TX, United States.

Salinas, C. (2017). Transforming academia and theorizing spaces for Latinx in higher education: *Voces perdidas and voces de poder. International Journal of Qualitative Studies in Education, 30*(8), 746–758. https://doi.org/10.1080/09518398.2017.1350295

Sebanc, A. M., Hernandez, M. D., & Alvarado, M. (2009). Understanding, connection, and identification: Friendship features of bilingual Spanish-English speaking undergraduates. *Journal of Adolescent Research, 24*(2), 194–217. https://doi.org/10.1177%2F0743558408329953

Strayhorn, T. L. (2019). *College students' sense of belonging: A key to educational success for all students* (2nd ed.). Routledge.

Tachine, A. R., Cabrera, N. L., & Yellow Bird, E. (2017). Home away from home: Native American students' sense of belonging during their first year in college. *The Journal of Higher Education, 88*(5), 785–807. https://doi.org/10.1080/00221546.2016.1257322

Yao, C. W. (2016). "Better English is the better mind": Influence of language skills on sense of belonging in Chinese international students. *Journal of College & University Student Housing, 43*(1), 74–89. https://www.nxtbook.com/nxtbooks/acuho/journal_vol43no1/index.php#/p/74

Yosso, T. J. (2005). Whose culture has capital? A critical race theory discussion of community cultural wealth. *Race Ethnicity and Education, 8*(1), 69–91. https://doi.org/10.1080/1361332052000341006

13

ANALYZING PSYCHOLOGICAL WELL-BEING ASPECTS OF SENSE OF BELONGING FOR FIRST-GENERATION, PELL-ELIGIBLE, UNDERREPRESENTED MINORITY STUDENTS

Marilee Bresciani Ludvik, Shiming Zhang, Sandra Kahn, Nina Potter, Lisa Gates, Robyn Saiki, Rogelio Beccero Songolo, Stephen Schellenberg, Randall Timm, and Mitch Strahlman

As previous chapters have indicated, sense of belonging (belonging) has been associated with a number of positive student success outcomes, such as increases in cumulative grade point average (GPA; Folger et al., 2004; Stephens et al., 2014; Walton & Cohen, 2007; Walton et al., 2015; Yeager et al., 2016), persistence (Hausmann et al., 2009; Heisserer & Parette, 2002), and full-time enrollment (Yeager et al., 2016). However, those associated outcomes vary among students' identities and their intersections. In addition, the way in which belonging is defined, measured, and cultivated, and for which students, influences the relationship of belonging to these institutional outcomes. As such, in this chapter, we briefly describe how focusing on psychological well-being (PWB) as components of belonging may be useful. We also share a particular useful way to analyze belonging. Our intent is to inform further exploration and analysis of belonging that will promote specific improvements in belonging, particularly the PSW aspects of it, and thus improve student success.

To accomplish this, we describe the findings from our analysis of a one-unit, one-credit university seminar course (USEM) at San Diego State University (SDSU), a Hispanic-serving institution committed to repairing institutional inequities. The course intended to cultivate intrapersonal competencies such as PWB, metacognitive awareness (MAI), prosocial values, positive future self, and belonging, which have been broadly demonstrated to significantly correlate with or predict degree completion and are desirable career-related skills (Bresciani Ludvik, 2018, 2019, 2020; National Academies of Sciences, Engineering, and Medicine [NAS], 2017, 2018).

Formative and summative assessment data were collected throughout the 14-week course, including engagement in out-of-class experiences. Using a quasi-experimental design, cross-culturally valid and reliable intrapersonal competency questionnaires measuring PWB, MAI, mindful self-compassion (MSC), and sense of belonging (SB) were administered pre and post course and compared across five varying intervention designs. These five interventions consisted of (a) the one unit, credit/no-credit Commuter Life Learning Community (CLLC) USEM class; (b) a CLLC USEM class with peer mentoring; (c) a CLLC USEM class within a leadership learning community; (d) residence life learning community students enrolled in a USEM class; and (e) a mixed group of USEM enrollees who were in various other learning communities (engineering, residence life, commuter life, life sciences). The Hoffman et al. (2002) SB pre- and postquestionnaire scale and subscale scores, as well as the other intrapersonal competency inventories (PWB, MSC, and MAI), were analyzed and disaggregated by first-generation, Pell-eligible, underrepresented minority (URM), gender, and their intersections to identify which intervention design had greater gains in belonging and for whom. In addition, intrapersonal competency scores and SB scale and subscale scores were disaggregated and correlated with term-to-term persistence, cumulative GPA, and academic probation to ascertain whether belonging was relevant to these indicators and for whom. Finally, since we did not have a comparison group of students who did not participate in the course, random forest, cluster analysis, and regression analysis provided insights into understanding what SB is for these students and how it could be enhanced for specific populations within the course and accompanying variety of experiences.

Measurements of Belonging

SB is a neurocognitive skill or intrapersonal competency that is known to be malleable and associated with student success (NAS, 2017). The idea of measuring a student's sense of intrapersonal competency has been and is still debated among many higher education institutional researchers. Many quantitative methods exist for measuring belonging (Hagerty & Patusky, 1995; Hoffman et al., 2002; Malone et al., 2011) or its PWB components, such as perceived isolation (Hagerty & Patusky, 1995; Hoffman et al., 2002; Neff, 2003) or general PWB (Ryff & Keyes, 1995). Thus, there are many ways to evaluate belonging and its relationship with academic institutional performance indicators. While belonging can include aspects of PWB, it is unknown whether belonging influences PWB or vice versa. What is well documented is that understanding how to improve educational outcomes cannot be fully understood without also understanding PWB (Keyes et al., 2002; Ryff et al., 2003), of which belonging may be a component.

The way in which belonging is measured must align with the way in which an institution intends to cultivate it, or the institution will not be able to assess how well their students are developing their SB or how to improve institutional efforts and for whom (Bresciani Ludvik, 2018; Montenegro & Jankowski, 2017). In addition, excluding student perceptions of their experiences also excludes crucial contextual and cultural aspects of learning and development (Bresciani Ludvik, 2018, 2019, 2020; NAS, 2018).

Understanding Belonging Within Cluster Analysis

Several years of institutional research informed the collaborative refinement of the previously mentioned USEM course, with outcomes focused on decreasing student stress, enhancing belonging, MAI, and overall PWB, and cultivating MSC. In fall 2018, the course was offered in its refined form and tested using pre and post inventories (Hoffman et al., 2002; Ryff & Keyes, 1995; Schraw & Dennison, 1994), as well as other forms of qualitative narrative data (journal entries, focus groups, instructor feedback on course experience and course design, student feedback on course experience and course design). The intervention closed equity gaps for persistence, but GPA for commuter students still lagged behind residential students. Using regression analysis and the Hoffman et al. (2002) instrument, overall scores and subscale scores for belonging did not emerge as predictive of cumulative end-of-first-term GPA or first-to-second-term persistence even when disaggregated by various identity groups (underrepresented minority, Pell eligible, first generation, gender, and their intersections). However, aspects of PWB and overall sense of well-being did emerge as predictors of GPA for Pell-eligible students—an institutional performance indicator in need of equity repair.

Informed by this data, many revisions of the course ensued for fall 2019, which included the addition of cultivating MSC (i.e., practices designed to emotionally connect with others when experiencing challenges or pain and suffering as a means to reduce isolation and self-pity) and the incorporation of the associated Neff (2003) Self-Compassion Scale in the course's pre and post surveys. The analysis of the fall 2019 data revealed varying statistically significant correlations of assorted scales and subscales among many identities and their intersections, although none of the inventories were predictive of GPA or persistence. While we were closing the GPA equity gap for some students (Latinas, Pell eligible, and first generation), the GPA equity gap was widening for other students (African American males and Latinos). Since belonging was a strategic initiative for SDSU and a focused outcome for USEM, we focused our analysis on whether the intentional cultivation of belonging was influencing GPA.

Figure 13.1 illustrates this analysis process on the matched set of pre- and postassessment inventories. To better understand seemingly insignificant data that were leading to significant differences in cumulative GPA for some of our students, we conducted a random forest analysis (Liaw & Weiner, 2002) on preassessment data exclusively to see how we could institutionally influence SB for students. Random forest analysis uses decision trees to produce and explain predictions concerning given data. The random forest analysis explained which intrapersonal competency inventory variables and incoming academic attribute variables were most important. Next, these variables were used in a clustering analysis to illustrate how identities and other intrapersonal competencies clustered around belonging. Two linear regressions were run. In the first linear regression, we did not enter subscales. This second linear regression analysis included subscales and revealed significant coefficients within some subscales. Such an analysis made sure we not only explored additional potential explanatory demographic variables but also allowed the effects of all variables to be maintained. We argue this process may be crucial for the inclusion of context and culture in understanding belonging that informs how it can be cultivated.

Figure 13.1. Equity-driven cluster analysis with regression process.

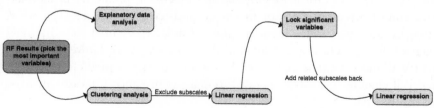

Preassessment Findings

The random forest analysis on the preassessment inventory data revealed key variables that included students' self-assessed mastery of their USEM course learning outcomes, PWB, college of entrance, MSC, MAI, incoming GPA, incoming SAT composite score, and incoming number of college credit units. The two-cluster preassessment inventory analysis of 350 matched pre and post student data sets indicated that there was a significant difference for overall SB between these two clusters, with Figure 13.2 denoting cluster 1 had a significantly higher overall belonging than cluster 2 ($p < .05$).

However, no significant differences existed between the two clusters with respect to their incoming GPA or college-level transfer units. In order to improve experiences for specific students, we needed to discover who these students are within each cluster and whether significant differences existed for any identities and their intersections. Our hope was that we could institutionally repair significant differences that may be harmful to student success.

We discovered there were significant differences in incoming college choice, ethnicity, and gender ($p < .05$). Table 13.1 indicates the overall identities for the group of students under study and how they were clustered. Table 13.2 identifies the identities that were significantly higher between each cluster grouping.

This information informed where USEM could be refined and for whom but not *how*. As such, we conducted a stepwise linear regression to discover which preassessment intrapersonal competencies significantly predicted overall SB. For cluster 1, those with the highest overall SB, overall

Figure 13.2. Two-cluster preassessment identity significance differences.

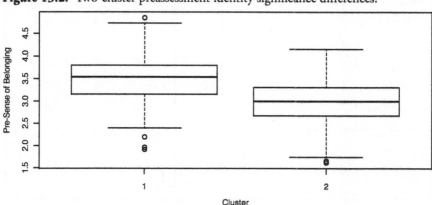

TABLE 13.1

Demographics for Fall 2019 Preassessment Sense of Belonging

Demographic Category	Cluster 1 (N = 176)		Cluster 2 (N = 174)	
	n	*%*	*n*	*%*
Race/ethnicity (NCES)				
Black/African American	2	1.1%	0	0.0%
American Indian/Alaskan Native	0	0.0%	0	0.0%
Asian	30	17.0%	57	32.8%
Hispanic or Latino	66	37.5%	70	40.2%
Two or more races/ethnicities	15	8.5%	12	6.9%
White	57	32.4%	32	18.4%
International student	5	2.8%	2	1.1%
Unknown	1	0.6%	1	0.6%
Gender				
Female	124	70.5%	102	58.6%
Male	52	29.5%	72	41.4%
Pell Grant recipient				
Yes	55	31.3%	58	33.3%
No	121	68.8%	116	66.7%
First-generation student				
Yes	76	43.2%	81	46.6%
No	100	56.8%	93	53.4%
Intervention group				
Leadership	5	2.8%	10	5.7%
Campus resident	60	34.1%	47	27.0%
GEN S 100A	31	17.6%	43	24.7%
GEN S 100B	16	9.1%	16	9.2%
Commuter	22	12.5%	15	8.6%
Other student success program	42	23.9%	43	24.7%
Housing				
Campus resident	60	34.1%	47	27.0%
Not campus resident	116	65.9%	127	73.0%

Demographic Category	Cluster 1 (N = 176)		Cluster 2 (N = 174)	
	n	%	n	%
College				
Business	18	10.2%	8	4.6%
Arts and Letters	20	11.4%	17	9.8%
Education	3	1.7%	9	5.2%
Engineering	19	10.8%	29	16.7%
Health and Human Services	24	13.6%	21	12.1%
Professional Studies/Fine Arts	36	20.5%	22	12.6%
Sciences	43	24.4%	44	25.3%
Undergraduate Studies	13	7.4%	24	13.8%
Underrepresented minority				
Yes	99	56.3%	123	70.4%
No	77	43.8%	51	29.3%
STEM major				
Yes	56	31.8%	67	38.5%
No	120	68.2%	107	61.5%

TABLE 13.2
Two-Cluster Preassessment Identity Significant Differences

Cluster 1: High incoming SOB	Cluster 2: Low incoming SOB	χ^2 (Cohen's d)
College of Business	College of Engineering	4.803 (.523)
College of Professional Studies and Fine Arts	College of Undergraduate Studies	5.527 (.497)
White	Asian	14.221 (.593)
Females	Males	4.851 (.237)
Nonunderrepresented minority	Underrepresented minority	7.255 (.291)

PWB was predictive of belonging ($t = 2.04$, $p = .04$), as was student self-assessed mastery of related USEM course learning outcomes ($t = 3.61$, $p < .001$). In addition, students' MAI planning skill set (i.e., their planning, goal setting, and allocating resources prior to learning) was also significant ($t = 2.20$, $p = .03$).

For cluster 2, student self-assessed mastery of related USEM course learning outcomes was also significant ($t = 2.23$, $p = .03$). What was interesting was the new content item we had added for fall 2019—that of MSC—was also significant ($t = 4.47$, $p < .001$). When we ran the second regression analysis to see what about MSC was predictive, we were surprised to discover that it was not the degree of isolation (which is a subscale of self-compassion and also associated with SB in prior research), but the opposite of isolation: students' ability to identify with others who are also struggling. The opposite of isolation in this context is students knowing that struggles are a part of every human's journey and that they are not alone in their struggles; others experience them as well. This was predictive ($t = 3.70$, $p < .001$).

Postassessment Findings

We then applied this same analysis process to the matched data set using Postassessment data only. Table 13.3 showcases the demographic variables of how students clustered.

In the nonsignificant postassessment cluster analysis around belonging, cluster 1 showed relatively lower overall belonging (Figure 13.3). Those

TABLE 13.3
Demographics for Fall 2019 Postassessment Sense of Belonging:
Two-Cluster Analysis

Demographic Category	Cluster 1 (N = 227)		Cluster 2 (N = 123)	
	n	*%*	*n*	*%*
Race/ethnicity (NCES)				
Black/African American	1	0.4%	1	0.8%
American Indian/Alaskan Native	0	0.0%	0	0.0%
Asian	70	30.8%	17	13.8%
Hispanic or Latino	78	34.4%	58	47.2%
Two or more races/ethnicities	19	8.4%	8	6.5%
White	54	23.8%	35	28.5%
International student	3	1.3%	4	3.3%
Unknown	2	0.9%	0	0.0%
Gender				
Female	147	64.8%	79	64.2%
Male	80	35.2%	44	35.8%

Demographic Category	Cluster 1 (N = 227)		Cluster 2 (N = 123)	
	n	%	n	%
Pell Grant recipient				
Yes	69	30.4%	44	35.8%
No	158	69.6%	79	64.2%
First-generation student				
Yes	100	44.1%	57	46.3%
No	127	55.9%	66	53.7%
Intervention group				
Leadership	10	4.4%	5	4.1%
Campus resident	75	33.0%	32	26.0%
GEN S 100A	47	20.7%	27	22.0%
GEN S 100B	19	8.4%	13	10.6%
Commuter	24	10.6%	13	10.6%
Other student success program	52	22.9%	33	26.8%
Housing				
Campus resident	75	33.0%	32	26.0%
Not campus resident	152	67.0%	91	74.0%
College				
Business	16	7.0%	10	8.1%
Arts and Letters	22	9.7%	15	12.2%
Education	9	4.0%	3	2.4%
Engineering	35	15.4%	13	10.6%
Health and Human Services	35	15.4%	10	8.1%
Professional Studies/Fine Arts	32	14.1%	26	21.1%
Sciences	55	24.2%	32	26.0%
Undergraduate Studies	23	10.1%	14	11.4%
Underrepresented minority				
Yes	145	63.9%	77	62.6%
No	82	36.1%	46	37.4%
STEM major				
Yes	84	37.0%	39	31.7%
No	143	63.0%	84	68.3%

Figure 13.3. Box plot of two-cluster post-sense of belonging differences.

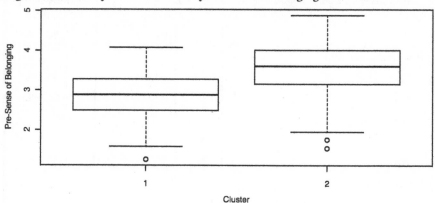

students participating in USEM exhibited no significant differences in the cluster analysis across gender. However, there were significant differences with ethnic ratios (p = .05). In cluster 1, the cluster with lower belonging, there was a significantly higher ratio proportion of Asians. While Hispanics and Whites are significantly higher in ratio in cluster 2, where belonging is higher. The additional significant difference that separated the two postanalysis clusters were those of intrapersonal competencies.

For postcourse cluster 1, post PWB was a significant predictor of post SB (t = 3.75, p < .001). In addition, their post-self-assessed mastery of their USEM course learning outcomes was significant (t = 3.00, p = .003). Their post perceived sense of stress negatively predicted their post SB (t = -2.63, p = .009).

For postcourse cluster 2, post PWB was also a significant predictor of post SB (t = 4.98, p < .001). In addition, their post self-assessed mastery of their USEM course learning outcomes was significant (t = 4.23, p < .001). Post perceived stress was notably absent as a significant predictor (t = -1.78, p = .08) for this group, while their SAT composite score had a significant positive prediction of post SB (t = 2.54, p = .01) and number of incoming college credit transfer units was a significant negative predictor of post SB (t = -2.14, p = .03).

Conclusion

Our quasi-experimental design and analytical approach revealed a number of findings for reflection and action. While incoming GPA, transfer college credit units, and SAT scores appear to have little to do with diverse students' incoming (i.e., pre-course) belonging, the reinforcement of the skills that contributed to these preassessment, or lack thereof, seems to be predicting the postcourse SB scores. In addition, there is no denying—as previous belonging research confirms—that PWB, aspects of MSC, and students' perceptions of their classroom outcome learning mastery are significant predictors of post SB.

While this SB analysis did not reveal explicitly how we could close equity gaps for first-semester GPA among diverse students, the absence of significant differences in postcourse belonging across gender and other identities supports the cultivation of MSC skills as potentially useful in connecting students with each other's challenges and thereby decreasing their sense of isolation and feeling alone within their struggles. This does not exclude the reality that we have increasing opportunities to make significant gains for some ethnic identities, in particular for Asians who began the semester with significantly lower belonging and concluded the semester with lower SB. In addition, we need further investment in all of our students' PWB.

Adding engagement data (the way in which students participate in in- and out-of-class activities), along with reflective journal coding analysis to cluster analysis, may reveal additional opportunities to improve SB. In addition, previous research has shown that the use of multiple measures that directly align with course/programmatic outcomes and delivery design can inform improvement in course design, including adding students' perceptions of how well they have learned. This cluster analysis shows that students who were aware of the course outcomes and could self-assess accordingly were significantly predictive of the course outcome itself—in this case, belonging.

In identifying which identities entered college with significantly high and low belonging, machine learning was used to create high belonging and low belonging clusters. While we considered running a logistic regression model that outlined identities (college, gender, ethnicity, etc.) as predictors of clusters, we discourage this practice as using the results of machine learning (e.g., clusters) as an outcome variable is not in alignment with the integrity of cluster analysis.

If we can better understand how varying groups of students perceive themselves in relation to course and program outcomes (albeit belonging or other employer-desired career readiness outcomes) as they arrive at our colleges and universities, then perhaps we can prevent inequities from occurring, as opposed to needing to repair them in subsequent terms. For these students, the inclusion of MSC practices that promote connection to each other, particularly in relation to shared challenges and struggles, may be our first step in preventing inequities for URM students as they pertain to improving overall PWB and belonging.

References

Bresciani Ludvik, M. J. (2018). *Outcomes-based program review: Closing achievement gaps in and outside the classroom with alignment to predictive analytics and performance metrics* (2nd ed.). Stylus. https://styluspub.presswarehouse.com/browse/book/9781620362303/Outcomes-Based-Program-Review

Bresciani Ludvik, M. J. (2019). Looking below the surface to close achievement gaps and improve career readiness skills. *Change: The Magazine of Higher Learning, 51*(6), 34–44. https://doi.org/10.1080/00091383.2019.1674106

Bresciani Ludvik, M. J. (2020). A new era of accountability: Resolving the clash of public good and economic stimulation performance indicators with evidence. In J. P. Freeman, C. Keller, & R. Cambiano (Eds.), *Higher education's response to exponential societal shifts* (pp. 251–275). IGI Global. https://doi.org/10.4018/978-1-7998-2410-7.ch012

Folger, W. A., Carter, J. A., & Chase, P. B. (2004). Supporting first generation college freshmen with small group intervention. *College Student Journal, 38,* 472–476. https://web.s.ebscohost.com/ehost/detail/detail?vid=1&sid=2c3c6e2d-59c3-48d3-bfc9-6b4254da8f77%40redis&bdata=JnNpdGU9ZWhvc3QtbGl2ZQ%3d%3d#AN=14669499&db=a9h

Hagerty, B. M. K., & Patusky, K. L. (1995). Developing a measure of sense of belonging. *Nursing Research, 44,* 9–13. https://qubeshub.org/community/groups/jan2020/File:/uploads/Sense_of_Belonging.pdf

Hausmann, L. R., Ye, F., Schofield, J. W., & Woods, R. L. (2009). Sense of belonging and persistence in White and African American first-year students. *Research in Higher Education, 50*(7), 649–669. https://doi.org/10.1007/s11162-009-9137-8

Heisserer, D. L., & Parette, P. (2002). Advising at risk students in college and university settings. *College Student Journal, 36,* 69–83. https://advising.sdes.ucf.edu/wp-content/uploads/sites/63/2019/06/Article20-20Advising20At-risk20Students20in20College1.pdf

Hoffman, M., Richmond, J., Morrow, J., & Salomone, K. (2002). Investigating "sense of belonging" in first-year college students. *Journal of College Student Retention: Research, Theory & Practice, 4*(3), 227–256. https://doi.org/10.2190/DRYC-CXQ9-JQ8V-HT4V

Keyes, C. L. M., Shmotkin, D., & Ryff, C. D. (2002). Optimizing well-being: The empirical encounter of two traditions. *Journal of Personality and Social Psychology, 82,* 1007–1022. https://doi.org/10.1037/0022-3514.82.6.1007

Liaw, A., & Wiener, M. (2002) Classification and regression by random forest. *R News, 2,* 18–22. https://cogns.northwestern.edu/cbmg/LiawAndWiener2002.pdf

Malone, G. P., Pillow, D. R., & Osman, A. (2011). The general belonging scale (GBS): Assessing achieved belongingness. *Personality and Individual Differences, 52*(3), 311–316. https://doi.org/10.1016/j.paid.2011.10.027

Montenegro, E., & Jankowski, N. A. (2017, January). *Equity and assessment: Moving towards culturally responsive assessment* [Occasional paper no. 29]. University of Illinois and Indiana University, National Institute for Learning Outcomes Assessment. https://www.learningoutcomesassessment.org/wp-content/uploads/2019/02/OccasionalPaper29.pdf

National Academies of Sciences, Engineering, and Medicine. (2017). *Supporting students' college success: The role of assessment of intrapersonal and interpersonal competencies.* The National Academies Press. https://doi.org/10.17226/24697

National Academies of Sciences, Engineering, and Medicine. (2018). *How people learn II: Learners, contexts, and cultures.* The National Academies Press. https://doi.org/10.17226/24783

Neff, K. D. (2003). The development and validation of a scale to measure self-compassion. *Self and Identity, 2*(3), 223–250. https://doi.org/10.1080/15298860309027

Ryff, C., & Keyes, C. (1995). The structure of psychological well-being revisited. *Journal of Personality and Social Psychology, 69,* 719–727. https://doi.org/10.1037/0022-3514.69.4.719

Ryff, C. D., Keyes, C. L. M., & Hughes, D. L. (2003). Status inequalities, perceived discrimination, and eudaimonic well-being: Do the challenges of minority life hone purpose and growth? *Journal of Health and Social Behavior, 44*(3), 275–291. https://www.jstor.org/stable/1519779

Schraw, G., & Dennison, R. S. (1994). Assessing metacognitive awareness. *Contemporary Educational Psychology, 19*(4), 460–475. https://doi.org/10.1006/ceps.1994.1033

Stephens, N., Hamedani, M., & Destin, M. (2014). Closing the social-class achievement gap: A difference-education intervention improves first-generation students' academic performance and all students' college transition. *Psychological Science, 25,* 943–953. https://doi.org/10.1177%2F0956797613518349

Walton, G. M., & Cohen, G. (2007). A question of belonging: Race, social fit, and achievement. *Journal of Personality and Social Psychology, 92,* 82–96. https://www.goshen.edu/wp-content/uploads/sites/2/2016/08/WaltonCohen2007.pdf

Walton, G. M., Logel, C., Peach, J. M., Spencer, S. J., & Zanna, M. P. (2015). Two brief interventions to mitigate a "chilly climate" transform women's experience, relationships, and achievement in engineering. *Journal of Educational Psychology, 107*(2), 468–485. https://psycnet.apa.org/doi/10.1037/a0037461

Yeager, D., Walton, G., Brady, S., Akcinar, E., Paunesku, D., Keane, D., Ritter, G., Duckworth, A. L., Urstein, R., Gomez E., Markus, H. R., Cohen, G. L., & Dweck, C. S. (2016). Teaching a lay theory before college narrows achievement gaps at scale. *Proceedings of the National Academy of Sciences of the United States of America, 113,* E3341–E3348. https://doi.org/10.1073/pnas.1524360113

14

SENSE OF BELONGING AS PROCESS AND PRODUCT IN THE FIRST-YEAR EXPERIENCE

Jennifer R. Keup and Chelsea Fountain

This chapter introduces a theoretically grounded approach for understanding the first-year experience (FYE) as a holistic and inclusive system that has the potential to facilitate or hinder students' belonging as they transition into and through their undergraduate journey. This approach combines elements of two models for scholarship and practice in higher education that address issues of belonging and connection for first-year students. The first is legitimate peripheral participation, which was first introduced by Lave and Wenger (1991) and adapted to higher education and FYE by Young and Bunting (2019). The second is the campus racial climate model that was first developed and championed by Hurtado et al. (1998, 1999) and expanded by several researchers. The combination of these two theoretical approaches creates an accessible, inclusive, efficient, and effective means of conceptualizing FYE that is easily illustrated in a model for research and practice. Further, this new model acknowledges the diverse pathways of first-year college students through their introduction, transition, integration, and sense of belonging during the first year of college and identifies forces that facilitate or hinder that process.

There is no single approach or process for student adjustment, integration, and success in the first year of college. A broad, flexible, and inclusive approach to FYE is appropriate to the diversity that is characteristic of American higher education. For instance, entering cohorts of college students hold a wide range of individual and intersectional student identities. Data from demographers and higher education scholars indicate increases in entering college students who are from historically underrepresented racial and ethnic backgrounds and are first-generation, low-income, working, adult learners, identify as LGBTQ+, as well as veterans and active duty service members, those who are neurodiverse, and those who are managing emotional and mental health-care issues, have housing and/or food insecurity, and possess physical and learning disabilities (e.g., Bransberger & Michelau, 2016; Eagan et al., 2016; Frey, 2018). Furthermore, FYE must be adaptable and inclusive of the wide range of colleges and universities in the United States, including 4-year institutions and community colleges; public institutions and private campuses; comprehensive institutions, technical colleges, and liberal arts colleges; minority and special-serving institutions; secular and religiously affiliated institutions; online and brick-and-mortar campuses; urban and rural settings; and institutions representing a wide array of sizes, both physically and in terms of student enrollment. One last factor of a multifaceted approach to the FYE is the institutional objectives that represent the goals of FYE. These include academic adjustment and success; major and career exploration and planning; personal and employability skill development; introduction to the campus culture and the expectations of higher education; facilitating interaction with faculty, staff, and fellow students; persistence and retention; and forging a connection with the institution (Association of American Colleges and Universities [AAC&U], 2009; Keup & Petschauer, 2011; Young, 2019).

The nexus among FYE, belonging, and student success overall has been featured in decades of higher education research (e.g., Foote et al., 2013; Skipper, 2005) and validated in recent work. Current FYE literature describes social belonging as "a sense that one has positive relationships with others" (Baldwin et al., 2020, p. 14). Further, Schreiner et al. (2020) identified social connectedness as a key component to the theoretical construct of thriving, which "redefines student success as being fully engaged intellectually, socially, and emotionally; experiencing a sense of psychological well-being that leads not only to persistence and graduation but also to being able to contribute meaningfully to society" (p. 20). Schreiner et al. continued by identifying college transitions as critical junctures for fostering students' thriving, and the first year in particular as what Nelson et al. (2020) described as a "window of opportunity [*that*] should draw institutions' focused efforts because it is the point at which supportive initiatives may have the most powerful long-term effects" (p. 53). Indeed, the first year is a critical period with transformative potential because of the inherent opportunities for students to establish a sense of belonging as well as foster correlated skills such as deconstructing unproductive learning mindsets, seeing challenges as a normal part of college, and developing resilience for the future (Baldwin et al., 2020). Therefore, belonging is a theoretical and practical construct that is critical to a comprehensive and inclusive approach to FYE, empowering it to be a tool for student success and equity.

Legitimate Peripheral Participation

Legitimate peripheral participation (LPP) situates learning within a larger context that is conceptualized as a community of practice, thereby highlighting the importance of belonging. The community of practice may have physical parameters, such as a campus, but it is much more meaningful when conceptualized as a social system comprised of coparticipants with various levels of proficiency, including masters, experienced participants, advanced peers, and new members, which is representative of the undergraduate student experience (Lave & Wenger, 1991). Instead of learning being understood as the acquisition of information and knowledge, LPP frames it as a dynamic, interactive, iterative system of experiences that engages members across all levels and validates attachment and belonging within the community. New participants (e.g., first-year students) begin on the periphery of the community as consumers of information who, ideally, will move to a more central position by engaging with and contributing to the community (Lave & Wenger, 1991; Young & Bunting, 2019). These opportunities for engagement and contributions often occur for students during the first year of college in classrooms; through cocurricular involvement; by interacting with more experienced members of the community such as faculty, staff, and fellow students; via the use of student services and support structures; and by establishing affiliations with different segments of the community, including academic programs and majors, clubs and organizations, housing and residential life, and campus employers. Further, first-year initiatives such as orientation, advising, first-year seminars, residential programs, and learning communities are often developed and delivered with the express purpose of helping new students launch and navigate their journey from the periphery toward a more engaged and central position in the undergraduate community of practice. Sense of belonging increases as students become more active contributors in the campus community, often through participation in FYE opportunities.

A hallmark of a student's path from periphery to full participation within the community of practice is represented by a sense of belonging. A sense of belonging creates the conditions for participants in a community of practice to provide meaningful contributions and maintain the dynamic nature of the learning environment (Lave & Wenger, 1991; Young & Bunting, 2019). When framed as a temporary position within the community of practice, peripherality is a reasonable developmental position for new members and one that new students will likely occupy for a significant portion of their first year of college as they transition to more fully engaged, contributing members of the undergraduate community. However, "any conversation about [movement within the community] is inherently a conversation about access and equity" (Young & Bunting, 2019, p. 2). Thus, it is important to acknowledge that when there are systemic forces within the community of practice that impede the development of a sense of belonging and under-mine new members' ability to contribute, the community of practice does not operate at an optimal level. These conditions result in the obstruction of learning and development and organizations that "perpetuate inequities and maintain the status quo" (Young & Bunting, 2019, p. 2). In other words, when access to the community and positive development toward full par-ticipation within it are structurally or systemically inhibited, peripherality is no longer developmentally appropriate and is recast as marginalization, thereby undermining the potential for FYE as a tool for inclusion and equity (Young & Bunting, 2019).

Campus Racial Climate Model

When combined with LPP theory, the campus racial climate model (CRCM) offers a way of understanding and organizing the various forces that facili-tate or hinder students' sense of belonging in the first year of college, affect momentum toward full participation within FYE as a community of practice, and create marginalization. CRCM identifies campus climate as a multidimensional phenomenon that is shaped by the interaction of internal and external forces: (a) historical (legacy of inclusion/exclusion), (b) organizational and structural, (c) compositional, (d) behavioral, and (e) psychological. It is important to note that these dimensions are not discrete but rather connected constructs due to the interrelated nature of climate. As such, they are used within this chapter to illustrate a holis-tic, systemic, and inclusive approach to understanding the role of sense of belonging in the first college year. These five forces individually or in some combination may further or hinder contributions to the community and sense of belonging.

Historical forces are shaped by the legacy of inclusion and exclusion and vestiges of segregated schools and colleges, which continue to inform government policy and campus programs and initiatives. Examples include outreach and recruitment strategies, admission practices, and financial aid policies that address issues of historic inequities as well as institutional marketing and communication campaigns that feature (or do not feature) issues and images of diversity and inclusion. This dimension of CRCM shapes campus climate and impacts students' sense of belonging by indicating who is "allowed" into the community of practice, thereby maintaining barriers that replicate and reify historic exclusion and facilitating marginalization (Hurtado et al., 1998, 1999; Young & Bunting, 2019). In effect, an institution's historical legacy of inclusion and exclusion serves as the backdrop for campus climate and shapes students' understanding of FYE and their position within the community of practice.

Next, organizational and structural forces illustrate how college benefits some groups over others, which is manifested through the policies, processes, and pedagogical practices of institutions (Milem et al., 2004). This dimension of CRCM is reflected in campus decisions related to curriculum, budget allocations, reward structures, hiring, admissions, tenure, and processes that guide the day-to-day "business" of campuses (Milem et al., 2004). In addition to visible practices, a hidden curriculum (i.e., the norms, values, beliefs, and processes of socialization that students learn but are not overtly taught) is pervasive within higher education, especially during the first year when students are adjusting to their new environment, establishing a sense of belonging, and charting a pathway from the periphery of a community of practice toward full participation (Soria, 2015; Takaki, 1993). As a vehicle of the organizational and structural dimension of campus climate, the ability to understand and navigate the hidden curriculum during the first year of college and beyond can be a critical tool for integration, connection, and contributions for new students. Conversely, this navigational capital can represent a point of disengagement and discouragement for students who are not able to access it, a critical example of the effect of organizational and structural elements on the way new students operate within the FYE community of practice.

The compositional component of CRCM refers to "numerical diversity" and the proportional representation of various student identity areas on campus. It is represented in demographics that comprise the student body, faculty, and campus administrators and in the visual imagery and branding of an institution. While compositional diversity is a prevalent means of evaluating campus community climate and diversity, it provides an incomplete picture. As noted by LPP, a FYE community of practice is characterized by an interactive social system of learning where individuals must communicate, connect, collaborate, and contribute. Therefore, just knowing the characteristics and representation of different student subpopulations in the FYE community of practice without knowing how they interact is insufficient.

Next, behavioral forces in CRCM represent the status of social interactions on the campus, the nature of interactions between and among individuals from different racial and ethnic backgrounds, and the quality of intergroup relations (Hurtado et al., 1998, 1999). This dimension is fundamental to understanding student belonging within FYE. The common understanding of this dimension is typified by a view that race relations are poor and that segregation is on the rise on college campuses. Upon further inspection, when groups are compared, students of color are much more likely to interact across racial/ethnic groups than White students. Milem et al. (2005) argued that the quality of interactions between groups is the most important aspect of the behavioral dimension and the opportunity to engage other students from different backgrounds in regular and structured ways yields growth in important educational outcomes. High-quality interactions among all students afford greater opportunities for engagement, connection, and belonging.

Finally, Hurtado et al. (1998, 1999) described the psychological forces of campus climate as including views held by individuals about intergroup relations as well as institutional responses to diversity, perceptions of discrimination or racial conflict, and attitudes held toward individuals from different backgrounds. It is critical for first-year students to see their "fit" within the cultural tapestry of their newfound environments. Nora and Cabrera (1996) add that new students who feel that they are singled out or treated differently in the classroom report a higher sense of alienation at the end of their first year. Inevitably, the psychological dimension of CRCM illustrates the importance of the belief that the community of practice is accessible and accepting to a wide array of students.

Conclusion

As students become members of the campus community, they are met with myriad internal and external forces that comprise the campus climate. As such, these forces play a dynamic role in how first-year students perceive and develop a sense of belonging and find ways to engage with and contribute to the community of practice represented by the undergraduate experience. Campus faculty, administrators, fellow students, and support personnel are representatives of the institution and thereby agents within the ecosystem who can either promote or discourage engagement behaviors of first-year (and all) students. Thus, FYE educators and advocates need to be continually aware of what is being done, how individuals are interacting within the FYE community, and how the agents, actors, and forces are perceived within the system.

Figure 14.1. A systemic model of institutional influence on belonging in FYE.

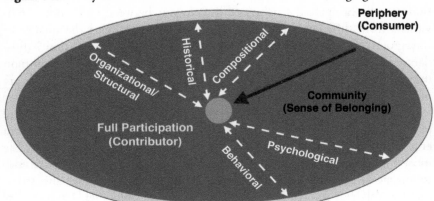

In conclusion, LPP is an effective way to understand the interactive and deeply systemic nature of the first-year experience and, when combined with the CRCM, provides a theoretical and practical frame to situate not only students but ourselves in the campus climate. When integrated into one model, LPP and CRCM represent a comprehensive, flexible, and inclusive model for understanding new students' sense of belonging within FYE (Figure 14.1). The combination of these theoretical perspectives allows both scholars and practitioners to better understand and examine influences on engagement and belonging for first-year students and chart a pathway of success for students in the first year and beyond.

References

Association of American Colleges and Universities. (2009). *Inquiry and analysis VALUE rubric.* https://www.aau.org/initiatives/value-initiative/value-rubrics

Baldwin, A., Bunting, B. D., Daugherty, D., Lewis, L., & Steenbergh, T. A. (2020). *Promoting belonging, growth mindset, and resilience to foster student success.* University of South Carolina, National Resource Center for The First-Year Experience and Students in Transition. https://nrcfye.presswarehouse.com/browse/book/9781942072379/Promoting-Belonging-Growth-Mindset-and-Resilience-to-Foster-Student-Success

Bransberger, P., & Michelau, D. K. (2016). *Knocking at the college door: Projections of high school graduates* (9th ed.). Western Interstate Commission for Higher Education.

Eagan, M. K., Stolzenberg, E. B., Ramirez, J. J., Aragon, M. C., Suchard, M. R., & Rios-Aguilar, C. (2016). *The American freshman: Fifty-year trends, 1966–2015.* Higher Education Research Institute, UCLA. https://www.heri.ucla.edu/monographs/50YearTrendsMonograph2016.pdf

Foote, S. M., Hinkle, S. E., Kranzow, J., Pistilli, M., Miles, L. R., & Simmons, J. G. (2013). *College students in transition: An annotated bibliography*. University of South Carolina, National Resource Center for The First-Year Experience and Students in Transition. https://Supporting-the-Transition-of-Sophomores-Transfers-and-Seniors-Opportunities-for-Residence-Life-Professionals.pdf

Frey, W. H. (2018). *Diversity explosion: How new racial demographics are remaking America*. Brookings Institute Press.

Hurtado, S., Milem, J. F., Clayton-Pedersen, A. R., & Allen, W. R. (1998). Enhancing campus Climates for racial/ethnic diversity through educational policy and practice. *Review of Higher Education, 21*(3), 279–302. https://doi.org/10.1353/rhe.1998.0003.

Hurtado, S., Milem, J. F., Clayton-Pedersen, A. R., & Allen, W. R. (1999). Enacting diverse learning environments: Improving the campus climate for racial/ethnic diversity in higher education. *ASHE-ERIC Higher Education Reports Series, 26*(8), 279–302. https://doi.org/10.1353/rhe.1998.0003

Keup, J. R., & Petschauer, J. W. (2011). *The first-year seminar signing, implementing, and assessing courses to support student learning and success: Vol. 1. Designing and administering the course*. University of South Carolina, National Resource Center for The First-Year Experience and Students in Transition. https://styluspub.presswarehouse.com/browse/book/9781942072027/The-First-Year-Seminar

Lave, J., & Wenger, E. (1991). *Situated learning: Legitimate peripheral participation*. Cambridge University Press. https://doi.org/10.1017/CBO9780511815355

Milem, J. F., Chang, M. J., & Antonio, A. L. (2005). *Making diversity work on campus: A research based perspective*. AAC&U. https://web.stanford.edu/group/siher/AntonioMilemChang_makingdiversitywork.pdf

Milem, J. F., Dey, E. L., & White, C. B. (2004). *Diversity considerations in health professions education*. In B. D. Smedley, A. S. Butler, & L. R. Bristow (Eds.), *The nation's compelling interest: Ensuring diversity in the health care workforce* (pp. 345–390). The National Academies Press.

Nelson, D. D., Vetter, D., & Vetter, M. K. (2020). In L. A. Schreiner, M. C. Louis, & D. D. Nelson (Eds.), *Thriving in transitions: A research-based approach to college student success* (2nd ed.; pp. 53–77). University of South Carolina, National Resource Center for The First-Year Experience & Students in Transition. https://nrcfye.presswarehouse.com/browse/book/9781942072461/Thriving-in-Transitions

Nora, A., & Cabrera, A. F. (1996). The role of perceptions of prejudice and discrimination on the adjustment of minority students to college. *Journal of Higher Education, 67*(2), 119–148. https://doi.org/10.1080/00221546.1996.11780253

Schreiner, L. A., Louis, M. C., & Nelson, D. D. (Eds.). (2020). *Thriving in transition: A research-based approach to college student success* (2nd ed.). University of South Carolina, National Resource Center for The First-Year Experience & Students in Transition. https://nrcfye.presswarehouse.com/browse/book/9781942072461/Thriving-in-Transitions

Skipper, T. L. (2005). *Student development in the first college year: A primer for college educators.* University of South Carolina, National Resource Center for The First-Year Experience & Students in Transition. https://sc.edu/about/offices_and_divisions/national_resource_center/documents/cv/skipper_tracy_lynn_cv_2020.pdf

Soria, K. M. (2015). *Welcoming blue-collar scholars into the ivory tower: Developing class conscious strategies for student success.* University of South Carolina, National Resource Center for The First-Year Experience & Students in Transition. https://sc.edu/nrc/system/pub_files/Peer_Assessment.pdf

Takaki, R. T. (1993). *A different mirror: A history of multicultural America.* Little, Brown & Co.

Young, D. G. (Ed.). (2019). *2017 national survey on the first-year experience: Creating and coordinating structures to support student success.* University of South Carolina, National Resource Center for The First-Year Experience & Students in Transition. https://nrcfye.presswarehouse.com/browse/book/9781942072324/2017-National-Survey-on-The-First-Year-Experience

Young, D. G., & Bunting, B.D. (2019). *Rethinking college transitions: Legitimate peripheral participation as a pathway to becoming* [Unpublished manuscript].

15

DECONSTRUCTING BELONGING

Toward a Redefinition for Transfer Students

Vasti Torres and Claire A. Boeck[1]

Transfer is an integral component of the postsecondary system in the United States. Of the students who first started college in 2011, 38% transferred to another institution (Shapiro et al., 2018). The transfer pathway from a community college to a 4-year institution has the potential to increase access and equity in baccalaureate attainment, although 80% of community college students aspire to a 4-year degree, only one quarter transfer to a 4-year institution (Jenkins & Fink, 2015). In addition, 4-year colleges and universities want transfer students because they can supplement enrollment numbers (Dowd et al., 2008; Jenkins & Fink, 2015).

Similar to first-time students, transfer students are tasked with learning a new institution and building connections. However, transfer students' experiences are distinct from first-year students in that they typically do not enter the university part of a large cohort with shared experiences around being new to college. Transfer students also face additional barriers, such as credit equivalency between institutions. Thus, how transfer students experience sense of belonging in their initial year at the transfer-receiving institution may be different from those of first-year students.

Because the transfer student experience is different from that of a first-year student, it is important to understand how this group of students defines belonging in order to provide better services and transfer programs.

This chapter will present a multimethod study on the transfer student transition to a public 4-year institution. First, we present survey data results around issues of belonging. Then, we will present data from interviews conducted the following fall with transfer students. The concluding discussion will focus on how the transfer student experience creates different concerns that influence how they interpret belonging and how traditional events may not meet their needs.

Definitions of Belonging

There are many ways to define belonging, and as a result measuring the construct becomes ambiguous. We focused on three primary theoretical approaches used in considering aspects of belonging. The first is socialization or integration, which assumes that the individual should shed their values, behaviors, and norms and assume those of the new environment (Tinto, 1993). An institution can exert normative pressures by transmitting its values through social relationships (Weidman, 1989). This approach is no longer seen as desirable and is critiqued for attempting to oppress those who are not from majority white culture (Rendón, 1994; Tierney, 1992).

The second approach used to define belonging is connected to concepts of person–environment fit between a student and the campus community (Johnson et al., 2007). This approach assumes that students will benefit from environments that correspond to their own characteristics (Denson & Bowman, 2015). Environmental fit implies that students will feel "they are an important part of a larger community that is valuable, supportive, and affirming" (Johnson et al., 2007, p. 527).

The third approach frames belonging as a fundamental human need and posits that students will seek opportunities to satisfy it (Strayhorn, 2019). Strayhorn defined *belonging* as students' evaluations of the degree to which they are supported, are a member of a group, and are valued by that group. This approach combines the concepts of community, support, and mattering.

While all these definitions provide insight into the elements that influence belonging, there has been little work considering the experiences of transfer students. We used a sequential mixed-method approach to incorporate elements of the literature and the voices of transfer students. We surveyed transfer students and then interviewed them to see how they viewed aspects of belonging to their transfer institution. Both study components were conducted at a highly selective public university.

Measuring Belonging

The items Bollen and Hoyle (1990) designed to assess perceived cohesion are frequently used for studies measuring college students' sense of belonging (see Hausmann et al., 2007; Hurtado & Carter, 1997; Museus et al., 2017):

- "I feel a sense of belonging to [Institution]."
- "I am happy to see myself at [Institution]."
- "I see myself as part of [Institution]'s community."

In this study we considered these items as core pieces of measuring belonging, but also considered other items that contribute to students feeling supported.

We tested a total of 13 items that reflect aspects of adjustment, belonging, and support. The items were generated by practitioners and not analyzed for their psychometric properties. All items used a *strongly disagree* to *strongly agree* 5-point Likert scale. The survey was administered to all new transfer students at a highly selective university in fall 2017. Four-hundred thirty-nine students responded for a 48% response rate. Almost two thirds of the sample transferred from other 4-year institutions. Only 15% were first generation in college, and the majority were white (48%), with Asian being the next largest group (32%). Black and Latinx students each composed 5% of the sample.

We conducted an exploratory factor analysis to assess the validity and reliability of a potential scale for transfer students' belonging. The principal component analysis showed that that two components had eigenvalues greater than 1, thus we used an extraction method asking for two factors and conducted oblique (oblimin) rotation, allowing for items' standard errors to correlate with one another.

The factor analysis results yielded two factors with loadings above 0.5, explaining 67% of the overall variance. Two items were problematic and were therefore removed. The analysis resulted in the Belonging and Personal Support Scale for Transfer Students (BPST), with two subscales: belonging and personal support (see Table 15.1). The 11 items have high reliability (0.91 Cronbach's alpha) and the two factors, belonging and personal support, were correlated at 0.535.

These results address two important elements in the current scholarship on belonging and support. First, these results illustrate that support influences are highly correlated with belonging. Second, our findings indicate that personal support is a distinct aspect of belonging. This may be due to the relationships implied in each subscale. The items on the belonging subscale

TABLE 15.1

Factor Loadings for the Belonging and Personal Support Scale for Transfer

Item	Belonging Subscale	Personal Support Subscale
I feel valued as an individual at [Institution].	.765	
I feel a sense of belonging to [Institution].	.882	
I see myself as a member of the [Institution] community.	.832	
I feel enthusiastic about being a student at [Institution].	.806	
Other students at [Institution] take my opinions seriously.	.779	
Instructors at [Institution] take my opinions seriously.	.803	
I have friends on campus whose advice I can trust.		.888
I know people at this university who share academic interest.		.825
If I have a sudden problem, I know where to go on campus for help.		.663
I have friends on campus who I feel like I could count on if needed.		.878
I know people at this university who are similar to me in terms of experiences and background.		.771

n = 417

focus on students' relationships with the larger university community or groups of people (faculty, students). In comparison, the items on the personal support subscale ask about personal relationships. Thus, belonging is captured here in terms of two levels: on the macro level, how the student feels accepted and part of the community (institutional environment) as a whole, and on the micro level, the personal relationships students sustain. Treating belonging as having multiple levels allows for distinction between students' relationships with individuals and their perceptions of being a member of the institution overall.

Although having relationships with and being supported by faculty has positive implications for students' sense of belonging (Brooms, 2020; Nuñez,

2009; Strayhorn, 2019), it is possible students feel supported by individuals but do not feel they belong. This may be particularly true for transfer students who already know people from their previous relationships and institution, yet not see themselves as part of the university community due to stigmatizations of transfer students not being academically qualified (Reyes, 2011; Thompson, 2019; Tobolowsky & Cox, 2012), particularly if they started at a less selective institution. The reverse could also be true, with transfer students feeling competent in class and excited about their new institutional affiliation but having difficulty making connections with individual students in their courses, as students who entered the university as first-year students have solidified their friendship groups. The standard deviations for the personal support items were larger than those of the belonging items, suggesting participants had a wider range of experiences around receiving personal support than belonging.

Student Voices

We also explored how transfer students experience belonging or personal support (or not) through interviews with 42 students at the institution in fall 2018. We identified three themes regarding sources of and obstacles to transfer students' belonging. First, institutional barriers were signals to participants that transfer students do not belong or were a low priority:

> When I was wait-listed, I blamed it on the fact that I was a transfer student. . . . When you're wait-listed, you have a lot of thoughts. It's like, "Okay, I know I'm good enough to get in here, but they're waiting to see what other schools accept me 'cause they don't want to mess up their numbers." (Kalee)

Similarly, Malcolm shared that "transfer students, you kind of get bottom-of-the-barrel classes when you first register. Whatever is left, you kind of get the scraps." Institutional barriers also had implications for transfer students' opportunities to build relationships with other students.

> A lot of my credits didn't transfer. They did as elective credit, but not as the [required] class so I have to retake a lot of classes. I have to take summer class[es] if I want to graduate on time. . . . Everyone in my class is a freshman, but then you tell them you're a sophomore and then they're less inclined to be friends with you 'cause you're not a freshman like them. (Jenny)

Second, the traditional support systems in the literature were seen differently by transfer students. Participants described university events and organizations as insufficient support measures:

> I was kind of disappointed with transfer orientation, because the peers that I met there, I didn't really connect with. It might be because I'm a nontraditional, so I'm a little older and stuff like that. The mentor person that I matched up with—I really like talking to her. We don't meet up that much. . . . That's through a setup thing, so it's a little formal. (Rosa)

Other students noted those events were helpful for obtaining information, but not for building a sense of community. In addition, transfer students were aware of how different they were in terms of socioeconomic status, age, and race/ethnicity from the students who started at the university:

> In general I do find that coming from a low SES and being a first-genera-tion student on top of being a transfer student, it's been difficult—also with mental health issues and stuff—to reach out and find a friend base. That's been one major issue I've found. Trying to connect with transfer students through transfer orientation and stuff always seemed—I wasn't very inter-ested in doing it through that way. That felt inorganic in some kind of way. Adjusting to that culture, I came from [the] Southwest [rural part of state], which is more conservative and more low income on a wider basis. . . . The majority of students here probably aren't first generation, probably from higher income. It seems like [the] majority of students who come here have a script to go by, compar[ed] to me . . . I have to teach my parents things about the college process rather than the other way around. I think that dif-ference between my identity and the community around me and majority was intimidating. (Bradley)

Third, while some transfer students formed new friendships at the uni-versity, they frequently relied on existing or familiar support networks. Students turned to family members, friends at other institutions, roman-tic partners, or people at the university they knew prior to transferring for support, encouragement, and affirmation. Participants also sought out religious groups and organizations, rather than traditional new student organizations, for sense of belonging and support. Pat explained, "Then the wrestling and soccer teams, in some ways I'm similar to them, but some ways I'm not. . . . The church group is similar to me." This latter strategy allowed students to find belonging in a new place but within the familiar context of their religion.

Conclusion

The main contributions of this study are adding nuance to measuring belonging for transfer students and complicating how institutional efforts influence students' sense of belonging. This nuanced view reflects and extends Strayhorn's (2019) argument that the importance of belonging is influenced by the context and individual identity. The identity of being a transfer student has implications for considering sense of belonging *to what* and *how* a student knows. Students may perceive they belong to the university but do not receive personal support from individuals on campus, and vice versa. The factor analysis indicates that support and belonging are related but separate aspects of overall feeling of belonging.

Regarding how transfer students construct a sense of belonging, transfer events and interaction with peers were not powerful indicators of belonging. Instead, these students focused more on institutional barriers, peers' demographics, and external support. Welcoming events and organizations, mechanisms frequently used to integrate new students and create a sense of belonging, were not effective means for transfer students to build relationships. This may be because students may have learned from previous experience that formal events do not result in meaningful connections. Furthermore, putting students together for an event cannot overcome transfer students' awareness of how their SES, age, transfer status, or racial/ethnic identity made them stand out from the university's first-year student population.

In addition, this study challenges ideas about integration and socialization as the main aspects of belonging. Both Tinto's (1993) and Weidman's (1989) ideas about socialization regarding interpersonal interactions within the academic and social contexts are what encourages institutions to create traditional events at orientation that focus solely on transfer students.

On the other hand, our findings support other research that transfer and community college students primarily rely on off-campus relationships for personal support and on-campus relationships for information (Rucks-Ahidiana & Bork, 2020; Shaw & Chin-Newman, 2017). In addition, the person– institution fit perspective seemed to be more important for the interview participants' experiences with belonging than feeling like a valued member of the community, thus lending additional support to the possibility that belonging is a multidimensional, complex construct.

Implications for practice should include making transfer orientation more practical and focusing on academic issues rather than socialization activities. Institutions will need to shift their thinking about transfer students to validating past academic experiences and talents and assuring that those experiences are welcomed at the institution. Creating second-class citizens through academic barriers is oppressive to the transfer students' sense of self and further reinforces negative images that they were not as good as those who began at the institution.

Note

1. The authors want to acknowledge the assistance from Nicholas Paulson and Caitlin Corker at the University of Michigan.

References

Bollen, K. A., & Hoyle, R. H. (1990). Perceived cohesion: A conceptual and empirical examination. *Social Forces, 69*(2), 479–504. https://doi.org/10.1093/sf/69.2.479

Brooms, D. R. (2020). Helping us think about ourselves: Black males' sense of belonging through connections and relationships with faculty in college. *International Journal of Qualitative Studies in Education, 33*(9), 921–938. https://doi.org/10.1080/09518398.2019.1687956

Denson, N., & Bowman, N. (2015). The development and validation of an instrument assessing student-institution fit. *Assessment & Evaluation in Higher Education, 40*(8), 1104–1122. https://doi.org/10.1080/02602938.2014.970513

Dowd, A. C., Cheslock, J. T., & Melguizo, T. (2008). Transfer access from community colleges and the distribution of elite higher education. *The Journal of Higher Education, 79*(4), 442–472. https://doi.org/10.1353/jhe.0.0010

Hausmann, L. R., Schofield, J. W., & Woods, R. L. (2007). Sense of belonging as a predictor of intentions to persist among African American and White first-year college students. *Research in Higher Education, 48*(7), 803–839. https://doi.org/10.1007/s11162-007-9052-9

Hurtado, S., & Carter, D. F. (1997). Effects of college transition and perceptions of the campus racial climate on Latino college students' sense of belonging. *Sociology of Education, 70*(4), 324–345. https://doi.org/2673270

Jenkins, D., & Fink, J. (2015). *What we know about transfer*. Community College Research Center, Teacher's College, Columbia University, Teachers College. https://ccrc.tc.columbia.edu/media/k2/attachments/what-we-know-about-transfer.pdf

Johnson, D. R., Soldner, M., Leonard, J. B., Alvarez, P., Inkelas, K. K., Rowan Kenyon, H. T., & Longerbeam, S. D. (2007). Examining sense of belonging among first-year undergraduates from different racial/ethnic groups. *Journal of College Student Development, 48*(5), 525–542. https://doi.org/10.1353/csd.2007.0054

Museus, S. D., Yi, V., & Saelua, N. (2017). The impact of culturally engaging campus environments on sense of belonging. *Review of Higher Education, 40*(2), 187–215. https://doi.org/10.1353/rhe.2017.0001

Nuñez, A. M. (2009). A critical paradox? Predictors of Latino students' sense of belonging in college. *Journal of Diversity in Higher Education, 2*(1), 46–61. https://doi.org/10.1037/a0014099

Rendón, L. I. (1994). Validating culturally diverse students: Toward a new model of learning and student development. *Innovative Higher Education, 19*(1), 33–51. https://doi.org/10.1007/BF01191156

Reyes, M. (2011). Unique challenges for women of color in STEM transferring from community colleges to universities. *Harvard Educational Review, 81*(2), 241–262. https://doi.org/10.17763/haer.81.2.324m5t1535026g76

Rucks-Ahidiana, Z., & Bork, R. H. (2020). How relationships support and inform the transition to community college. *Research in Higher Education, 61*(5), 588–602. https://doi.org/10.1007/s11162-020-09601-z

Shapiro, D., Dundar, A., Huie, F., Wakhungu, P. K., Bhimdiwali, A., Nathan, A., & Youngsik, H. (2018). *Transfer and mobility: A national view of student movement in postsecondary institutions, fall 2011 cohort* [Signature report no. 15]. National Student Clearinghouse Research Center. https://nscresearchcenter.org/wp-content/uploads/Signature-Report-15.pdf

Shaw, S. T., & Chin-Newman, C. S. (2017). "You can do it!": Social support for transfer students during the transition from community college to a four-year university. *Journal of The First-Year Experience & Students in Transition, 29*(2), 65–78.

Strayhorn, T. L. (2019). *College students' sense of belonging* (2nd ed.). Routledge.

Tierney, W. G. (1992). An anthropological analysis of student participation in college. *Journal of Higher Education, 63*(6), 603–618. https://doi.org/10.1080/00221546.1992.11778391

Tinto, V. (1993). *Leaving college rethinking the causes and cures of student attrition* (2nd ed). The University of Chicago Press.

Thompson, M. L. (2019). *Community college stigmatization: Perceptions of vertical transfer students at the university level* [Unpublished doctoral dissertation]. The University of Texas at Arlington.

Tobolowsky, B. F., & Cox, B. E. (2012). Rationalizing neglect: An institutional response to transfer students. *The Journal of Higher Education, 83*(3), 389–410. https://doi.org/10.1080/00221546.2012.11777249

Weidman, J. C. (1989). Undergraduate socialization: A conceptual approach. In J. C. Smart (Ed.), *Higher education: Handbook of theory and research* (Vol. 5, pp. 289–322). Agathon.

16

REFRAMING THE COMMUTER STUDENT EXPERIENCE TO PROMOTE BELONGING

Michael D. Giacalone and Kristina M. Perrelli

Higher education, especially 4-year institutions, generally focuses its design and resources around full-time residential students (Attewell & Lavin, 2012). The assumption through this lens is that college is an immersive experience in which students separate from their homes and families to engage in an academic and cocurricular environment that fundamentally changes their lives. This pristine image of the "college experience," however, is not reality for most students. While living on campus might be thought of as the normative student experience, 76% of students live elsewhere while attending college (National Center for Education Statistics [NCES], 2018). Such a strong emphasis on residential students has led to inaccurate assumptions about commuters as being academically underperforming students with no interest in engaging in campus life and resulted in policies and practices that inhibit their full academic and cocurricular involvement (Jacoby, 2000). Commuter students, however, are as academically engaged as their residential peers (Kuh et al., 2001) and participate in cocurricular activities (Holloway-Friesan, 2018).

We posit that commuters, like the broader population of students, enter college with a need to belong (Strayhorn, 2019), all while they balance outside responsibilities and the demands of pursuing a college education. Given that most students do not live on campus (NCES, 2018), caring about commuter students' sense of belonging needs to be a priority for higher education. In this chapter, we present an approach that utilizes an intersectional perspective by valuing commuters as members of the campus community and prioritizing their experiences and needs when designing efforts to support their sense of belonging.

Characteristics of Commuter Students

Any student who does not live in institutionally owned or operated housing is typically defined as a "commuter" (Jacoby, 2000). Commuter students can be classified according to with whom they reside and the proximity of their home to campus. Independent commuter students live on their own and are responsible for their own needs, while dependent commuter students live with parents or guardians (Clark, 2006). Similarly, commuter students can either live within walking distance from campus or farther than walking distance and be considered walking or driving commuters, respectively (Kuh et al., 2001). These definitions, however, are overly simplistic, as a commuter student's residence, mode of transportation, and responsibilities can fluctuate throughout college (Weiss, 2014).

Demographic analyses of commuter students suggest a wide range of experiences, yet there are some trends among challenges faced by commuter students based on their unique life circumstances. In a review of the literature on commuter students, Burlison (2015) found that commuter students need to work, tend to family commitments, and, therefore, have a limited amount of time to be on campus. Two large national studies using data from the National Study of Student Engagement found that commuter students are more likely to be older, first-generation, students of color (Kuh et al., 2001), transfer students, and likely work more hours than residential students (Graham et al., 2018).

Minimal scholarship has centered marginalized student groups when exploring the commuter experience. For example, a critical race case analysis found that Black students at a commuter campus often missed classes due to an arduous commute (Harper et al., 2018). Similarly, transportation and parking challenges impacted campus accessibility for students of color who were pregnant and also commuters (Perrelli, 2019). Another study described the ways that students of color who are commuters may benefit from specific institutional practices, including identity-based centers, peer support, faculty interactions, and validation and understanding of family and home communities (Kodama, 2015). Waterman (2012) found that Haudenosaunee (Iroquois) students preferred to live in their home communities and commute to college. While these studies provide some insights into the experiences of marginalized students who commute, future research on sense of belonging for commuters should include a diversity of social identities.

Commuter Students and Sense of Belonging

The research on commuter students' sense of belonging is limited. One large national study found that student involvement contributed to sense of belonging for commuter students. Most significantly, leading, actively participating in, and meeting with advisors about student organizations contributed to their sense of belonging. Similarly, the relationships they had with college faculty and staff were associated with belonging. Relationships with their peers were also associated with their sense of belonging, although to a lesser degree (Manley Lima, 2014). Other smaller studies have found that positive and encouraging interactions with faculty members, the ability to be authentic, and involvement in student organizations (Holloway-Friesan, 2018) and fraternity and sorority life (Giacalone, 2020) contribute to belonging. Kirk and Lewis (2015), however, found that commuter students' ability to connect with their peers and the institution, both of which are contributors to belonging (Strayhorn, 2019), was dependent on how well the institution created structures and opportunities that met their students' needs. When institutions are not designed for commuter students, they might only come to campus when necessary and view their institution as "another location in which they received a service, comparable with the grocery store or beauty salon" (Kirk & Lewis, p. 56). With these designs in place, it then follows that commuter students can feel a lower sense of belonging (Jacoby, 2000) and feel less connected to their institutions than residential students (Newbold et al., 2011).

Findings from the broader literature on sense of belonging are useful when considering commuter students. For example, the messages and images used in college marketing efforts send messages about who does and does not belong (Harper et al., 2018). Therefore, an institution that touts a residential experience as synonymous with the college experience also communicates that commuter students do not belong. Sense of belonging scholarship also identifies the importance of commuter students connecting with each other (Pokorny et al., 2017) and with other students who share similar experiences and identities (Strayhorn, 2019). Finally, belonging by way of cocurricular involvement is not just dependent on time, but also whether a student has the discretionary money to pay fees associated with participation, such as ticket fees or membership dues (McClure & Ryder, 2018).

Reframing the Experiences of Commuter Students

Higher education tends to view the challenges that commuters face as deficits attributable to their commuter status (Jacoby, 2000). For instance, a significant amount of scholarship about commuter students has focused only on the challenges that can result from commuting, including a lack of involvement in cocurricular activities (Mayhew et al., 2016), feeling disconnected from the experience of college due to nonacademic life commitments (Burlison, 2015), and a limited connection to the institution (Newbold et al., 2011). Scholarship has also described the negative compounding impacts that result from commuter students holding marginalized identities, such as first-generation status and holding a minoritized racial or ethnic identity (Harper et al., 2018).

Given that commuter students tend to hold multiple marginalized social identities and are unlikely to experience belonging in the same ways (Strayhorn, 2019), we argue that commuter students and their sense of belonging should be reframed using an intersectional approach. Jones and Wijeyesinghe (2011) outlined the tenets of an intersectional approach as centering the experiences of marginalized students, complicating identity by considering the multiple identities often held by students, examining inequities of power in systems (e.g., messages and images, policies, and expectations for peer interactions), and transforming systems in ways that promote equity and social justice. As a starting point to using this approach, we recommend that institutions explicitly value commuters by changing systems and structures in ways that center their multiple identities and diverse lived experiences.

Opportunities for Belonging and Recommendations for Practice

With the scant research on sense of belonging for commuters, we draw from the broader body of work on sense of belonging and other bodies of scholarship to identify potential opportunities for fostering sense of belonging among commuters. These recommendations prioritize the notions that institutions should value the diverse identities and experiences of commuters and use an intersectional approach when designing efforts to foster their sense of belonging and mitigate their challenges. The three areas considered include facilitating authentic connections with peers, reimagining student involvement from a contemporary lens, and centering commuter students through strategic decision-making about resources.

Facilitating Authentic Connections With Peers

Commuter students attempt to develop a sense of belonging while they interact with their college environment, an environment that presents a myriad of barriers that require their navigation (Jacoby, 2000). They do this from the lenses of their multiple social identities and the complex realities of their lives (Kodama, 2015). The scholarship clearly states that connecting with other students who share similar experiences is an important factor to the development of sense of belonging (Pokorney et al., 2017; Strayhorn, 2019). The ability to engage authentically with the campus environment also helps students feel like they belong (Holloway-Friesan, 2018).

We recommend that institutions rethink typical strategies for connecting commuters with their peers to include opportunities beyond commuter-designated spaces. These strategies should explicitly value the complex needs and identities of commuter students by creating opportunities for commuters to connect with each other and with peers with similar life experiences and who hold similar social identities. For example, identity-based centers should be sure their programs consider the needs of the campus commuter population. These opportunities should be designed using contemporary scholarship on how marginalized students build community (see work on resilience by Nicolazzo & Carter, 2019). An effort to make all spaces welcoming to commuter students might increase the likelihood that commuters can interact with their campus environment in authentic ways, access opportunities to build community in a diversity of spaces, and successfully navigate the challenges presented by the college environment.

A Contemporary Approach to Student Involvement

Involvement has been found to increase students' sense of belonging (Strayhorn, 2019). In order for commuter students to participate in extracurricular activities, however, activities must be scheduled and designed in ways that allow for commuter students to participate. Holding all events at night and on campus might work for residential students, but, as Kirk and Lewis (2015) described, those parameters inhibit involvement for commuters given their competing responsibilities.

We recommend a movement away from that status quo of offering involvement opportunities during specific hours and only on campus. Efforts to help commuter students develop a sense of belonging should be multimodal and provide various options for involvement, both in person and virtually. Other options could include scheduling multiple "involvement hours" throughout the week during the day when no classes are scheduled (Kuh et al., 2005), holding events in the communities where commuter students reside, or—similar to adaptations made during COVID-19-affected semesters—implementing synchronous and asynchronous virtual programming. Offering involvement opportunities in this inclusive and equitable way has the potential to communicate to commuters that their lived experiences are valued and their sense of belonging matters.

Centering Commuters in Strategic Ways

Institutions make daily decisions, of every caliber, about where to allocate funding and resources. The commuter experience is not typically at the center of those decisions (Attewell & Lavin, 2012). Given that commuting is the reality of the majority of college students and these students are diverse in their identities and the challenges they face, colleges must do a better job of representing the importance of commuters to the overall health of the institution. This can be done by communicating to the campus community that commuters are an important part of the community by highlighting them in admissions materials, considering them in policies so they do not have to seek exceptions, and allocating resources strategically.

Student employment opportunities for commuter students has been cited as a benefit for commuter students' belonging (Manley Lima, 2014). If an assumption of laziness and lack of ability on the part of commuters persists among employees (Jacoby, 2000), they may interact with commuter students in ways that diminish their experiences, and, in turn, their belonging. Institutions should develop and implement educational opportunities for all faculty and staff that include accurate information about the campus commuter population. This effort should include updated descriptive data about commuter students, including their contribution to the institutional budget. Information should also include data about the other identities they hold, the many attributes they bring to the campus environment, and suggestions for how to effectively support their belonging within the specific campus context. Career centers can also prioritize helping commuters find jobs on campus.

Students are typically assessed fees in addition to tuition for specific services, and institutions rely on these fees for those services to operate. Designing financial systems that rely on fees can cause undue financial burdens on commuter students who may not have the financial resources, time, or need to use the services covered by fees. For example, a student who is on campus for class 2 days a week would likely find it more convenient and cost-effective to join a gym closer to their home rather than use the campus facilities. Understandably, there is a delicate balance, not only for institutional financial planning purposes, but also for belonging. If a student does not have discretionary funds to utilize services or attend campus events, they may miss opportunities to build sense of belonging from connecting with the campus community (McClure & Ryder, 2018). Institutions, therefore, must be thoughtful about the fees they assess commuter students, the allocation of fees, how to offer programs and services at little to no additional cost to students, and the strategies used for engaging commuters in the campus community. While these changes may result in short-term budget decreases, the institution will likely benefit financially in the long term due to the positive influence of belonging on persistence and the subsequent collection of tuition and fees.

Conclusion

It is imperative that efforts to support commuter students' development of sense of belonging acknowledge institutional responsibility as the driver of change rather than place responsibility on individual students whose complex needs and social identities have not historically been centered in higher education scholarship or practice. One strategy for this is using an intersectional approach (Jones & Wijeyesinghe, 2011) to dismantle systems and practices that are exclusionary for more inclusive ones, which may have a positive impact on commuter students' sense of belonging (Museus et al., 2017). This chapter provides some suggestions for using an intersectional approach, but these ideas are not exhaustive. Efforts to foster sense of belonging for today's commuter students must include continual reflection by higher education institutions that is grounded in the most recent scholarship on sense of belonging, commuters, and strategies that aim to transform campus environments to better support students who hold marginalized identities. This includes challenging the status quo of how things are typically done. We encourage institutions to invite commuter students to the table when making decisions about the student experience. Continual assessment of commuter participation, needs, perceptions, and outcomes is an essential part of continually refining and enhancing offerings that aim to foster commuter students' a sense of belonging.

References

Attewell, P., & Lavin, D. E. (2012). The other 75%: College education beyond the elite. In E. C. Lagemann & H. Lewis (Eds.), *What is college for? The public purpose of higher education* (pp. 86–103). Teachers College Press.

Burlison, M. B. (2015). Nonacademic commitments affecting commuter student involvement and engagement. In J. P. Biddix (Ed.), *Understanding and Addressing Commuter Student Needs* (New Directions for Student Services, no. 150, pp. 27–34). Jossey-Bass. https://doi.org/10.1002/ss.20124

Clark, M. R. (2006). Succeeding in the city: Challenges and best practices on urban commuter campuses. *About Campus, 11*(3), 2–8. https://doi.org/10.1002/abc.166

Giacalone, M. D. (2020). *Exploring the Greek-letter organization experience at primarily commuter colleges and universities: A phenomenological study* (Publication No. 27739295) [Doctoral dissertation, University of Rhode Island/Rhode Island College]. ProQuest.

Graham, P. A., Socorro Hurtado, S., & Gonyea, R. M. (2018). The benefits of living on campus: Do residence halls provide distinctive environments of engagement? *Journal of Student Affairs Research and Practice, 55*(3), 255–269. https://doi.org/10.1080/19496591.2018.1474752

Harper, S. R., Smith, E. J., & Davis, C. H. F., III. (2018). A critical race case analysis of Black undergraduate student success at an urban university. *Urban Education, 53*(1), 3–25. https://doi.org/10.1177/0042085916668956

Holloway-Friesan, H. (2018). On the road home: A content analysis of commuter sense of belonging. *College Student Affairs Journal, 36*(2), 81–96. https://doi.org/10.1353/csj.2018.0017

Jacoby, B. (Ed.). (2000). Why involve commuter students in learning? In *Involving Commuter Students in Learning* (New Directions for Higher Education, no. 109, pp. 3–12). Jossey-Bass. https://doi.org/10.1002/he.10901

Jones, S. R., & Wijeyesinghe, C. L. (2011). The promises and challenges of teaching from an intersectional perspective: Core components and applied strategies. In M. L. Ouellett (Ed.), *An Integrative Analysis Approach to Diversity in the College Classroom.* (New Directions for Teaching and Learning, no. 125, 11–20). Jossey-Bass. https://doi.org/10.1002/tl.429

Kirk, C. M., & Lewis, R. K. (2015). Sense of community on an urban, commuter campus. *International Journal of Adolescence and Youth, 20*(1), 48–60. https://doi.org/10.1080/02673843.2013.763833

Kodama, C. M. (2015). Supporting commuter students of color. In J. P. Biddix (Ed.), *Understanding and Addressing Commuter Student Needs* (New Directions for Student Services, no. 150, pp. 45–55). Jossey-Bass. https://doi.org/10.1002/ss.20126

Kuh, G. D., Gonyea, R. M., & Palmer, M. (2001). The disengaged commuter student: Fact or fiction. *Commuter Perspectives, 27*(1), 2–5. https://hdl.handle.net/2022/24256

Kuh, G. D., Kinzie, J., Schuh, J. H., & Whitt, E. J. (2005). *Student success in college: Creating conditions that matter.* Jossey-Bass.

Manley Lima, M. C. (2014). *Commuter students' social integration: The relationship between involvement in extracurricular activities and sense of belonging* (Publication No. 3617177) [Doctoral dissertation, George Washington University]. ProQuest.

Mayhew, M. J., Rockenbach, A. N., Bowman, N. A., Seifert, T. A., Wolniak, G. C., Pascarella E. T., & Terenzini, P. T. (2016). *How college affects students: 21st-century evidence that higher education works.* Jossey-Bass.

McClure, K., & Ryder, A. J. (2018). The costs of belonging: How spending money influences social relationships in college. *Journal of Student Affairs Research and Practice, 55*(2), 196–209. https://doi.org/10.1080/19496591.2017.1360190

Museus, S. D., Yi, V., & Saelua, N. (2017). The impact of culturally engaging campus environments on sense of belonging. *The Review of Higher Education, 40*(2), 187–215. https://doi.org/10.1353/rhe.2017.0001

National Center for Education Statistics. (2018). *National Postsecondary Student Aid Study: 2016 undergraduates* [Data set and code book]. https://nces.ed.gov/datalab/powerstats/codebook.aspx?dataset=121&type=subject

Newbold, J. J., Mehta, S. S., & Forbus, P. (2011). Commuter students: Involvement and identification with an institution of higher education. *Academy of Educational Leadership Journal, 15*(1), 141–153. http:// https://www.abacademies.org/journals/month-march-year-2011-vol-15-issue-1-journal-aelj-past-issue.html

Nicolazzo, Z., & Carter, R. (2019). Resilience. In E. S. Abes, S. R. Jones, & D-L Stewart (Eds.), *Rethinking college student development theory using critical frameworks* (pp. 77–93). Stylus.

Perrelli, K. M. (2019). *Exploring the lived experience of being pregnant while a college student.* (Publication No. 13886140) [Doctoral dissertation, University of Rhode Island/Rhode Island College]. ProQuest.

Pokorny, H., Holley, D., & Kane, S. (2017). Commuting, transitions, and belonging: The experiences of students living at home in their first year at university. *Higher Education, 74*(3), 543–558. https://doi.org/10.1007/s10734-016-0063-3

Strayhorn, T. L. (2019). *College students' sense of belonging: A key to educational success for all students* (2nd ed.). Routledge.

Waterman, S. J. (2012). Home-going as a strategy for success among Haudenosaunee college and university students. *Journal of Student Affairs Research and Practice, 49*(2), 193–209. https://doi.org/10.1515/jsarp-2012-6378

Weiss, M. (2014). *The college experience of commuter students and the concepts of space and place* (Publication No. 3619489) [Doctoral dissertation, University of Rhode Island/Rhode Island College]. ProQuest.

17

STUDENT-VETERAN BELONGING, INCLUSION, AND SUCCESS

Phillip Morris

The isolating nature of transitioning from service member to student can hinder student-veterans' development of a sense of belonging and associated academic outcomes. Military service creates a sense of unity and belongingness that often becomes the primary reason for serving, surpassing an individual's political or ideological reasons (Hoge, 2010; Junger, 2016). Ethnographic investigations into the transition experiences for those leaving the military highlight that the loss of unity and belongingness when service members leave the military can be as damaging as the physical and psychological wounds of war (Junger, 2016). While experiences of combat and trauma are not universal to all service members, the connections that Junger describes as "tribal" among military veterans are common, regardless of service experience.

Student-veterans are more likely than nonmilitary college students to be older, work full- or part-time, be married and/or have children, and be first-generation students (Griffin & Gilbert, 2015; Syracuse University Institute for Veterans and Military Families [IVMF], 2019). Utilizing best-practice recommendations from policymakers and researchers, campuses across the country have expanded services to meet the needs of post-9/11 veterans (American Council on Education [ACE], 2018). Although many service initiatives indirectly impact belongingness, few initiatives directly target sense of belonging, and studies suggest that inclusion and belonging issues for veterans persist (Barry et al., 2019; Hunter-Johnson et al., 2020). Barry et al. (2019) found that after controlling for demographics, 42% of student-veterans reported low sense of belonging on campus compared to their reservist (33%) and civilian (28%) counterparts. McAndrew et al. (2019) examined belongingness for student-veterans through the lens of cultural (in)congruity and found a significant link between feelings of not belonging and maladjustment to college. When combined with qualitative accounts of student-veteran experiences (see, e.g., Hunter-Johnson et al., 2020), these studies highlight the important and persistent need to address belonging for student-veterans.

With an increasing number of veterans transitioning into higher education (Cate et al., 2017; IVMF, 2019), understanding how sense of belonging fits into individual success for student-veterans is increasingly important. This is particularly relevant given evidence that veterans feel as though they do not belong on college campuses (Barry et al., 2014; Lim et al., 2018). Yet, belonging is central to success for all students, and student-veterans may be even more impacted by the loss of purpose and connection experienced during the transition out of the military.

The need-to-belong theory (Baumeister & Leary, 1995) and cultural congruity framework (Gloria & Kurpius, 1996) provide applicable framing for strategies and efforts to promote belongingness for veterans on campus. The need-to-belong theory identifies the value and importance of interpersonal connections, purpose, and identity (Baumeister & Leary, 1995), while the cultural congruity framework focuses on values, beliefs, and expectations.

This chapter provides a foundation for conceptualizing and promoting a sense of belonging for student-veterans through translating theory to practice via presentation of effective strategies. As depicted in Figure 17.1, sense of belonging and cultural congruity theories can help practitioners understand sense of belonging for veterans, and there are four strategy areas that can increase sense of belonging: (a) physical and cultural campus environments, (b) student interactions on campus, (c) veteran identities, and (d) student-veterans with disabilities. The discussion of these four elements link theory to evidence-informed exemplar campus initiatives.

Cultural and Physical Campus Environments

Differences in military and higher education cultures can present challenges to student-veterans as they transition from one culture to the other. Ambiguity and exposure to complexity is a necessary component of the cognitive development process for all college students (King & Kitchener, 2004). However, exposure to ambiguity often manifests in university

Figure 17.1. Veteran student belonging theory to practice.

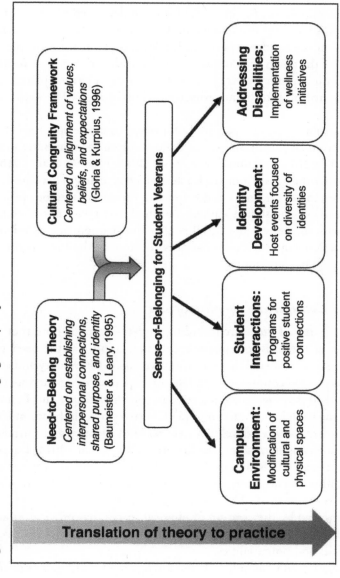

settings in ways that have limited structure. For example, student-veterans may have difficulty adjusting to extended blocks of unstructured time and a lack of clear protocols (DiRamio et al., 2011). Other cultural differences relate to group identity, uniformity, and respect for authority engendered in the military versus the individualism and perceived disrespect for authority veterans have reported about traditional students (Morris et al., 2019). If a goal of the college experience is taking students from simple to complex ways of thinking, it is important to consider the ways of thinking instilled in our military veterans and the new expectations placed on them as they transition into higher education (Lim et al., 2018; Vacchi & Berger, 2014).

First-year seminar courses specifically for veterans create space for dialogue and reflection on transition and have shown promise for acculturation to higher education (McMenamin & Kurzynski, 2016; Mendez et al., 2018). These courses offer the opportunity to teach student-veterans to become better self-advocates, to ask for clarity and help when they need it, to be open to ambiguity, and to develop skilled ways of communication with nonveterans. For campuses with smaller veteran enrollment, actively supporting a student-veteran organization can provide similar opportunities for building connection and belonging to the campus.

Intersection of Cultural and Physical Spaces

In an extensive review of literature regarding student-veterans, Borsari et al. (2017) found that the most consistent recommendation was the need for veteran-specific services, including administrative offices for military and veteran benefits, dedicated counselors with relevant expertise, designated social/study space, and student-veteran organizations. Further, Yeager and Rennie (2020), found the student veteran center (SVC) was a particularly prominent resource for students as they develop a new sense of identity and purpose. These findings are consistent across the literature (Barry et al., 2014; Borsari et al., 2017; Lim et al., 2018) and underscore the intersection of cultural and physical environments and interpersonal relationships—which directly link to the need-to-belong theory. The development of student veteran–specific services is augmented by the creation of physical spaces that provide opportunity for student-veterans to connect with the familiar while also discovering new identities and potentialities.

At the University of Colorado at Colorado Springs (UCCS), we opened a comprehensive student-veteran center in 2016. Through attendance tracking, we know a significant proportion of student-veterans are using the space. When faced with a divergent cultural experience, providing a physical space and associated support services for student-veterans serves as a critical link in the transition experience. This is evidenced in a written comment from a student-veteran recorded in a survey in 2018:

> It's underestimated how powerful and impactful it is just to know there is a place I can go to relax and people understand my PTSD and disabilities. . . . No one looks at me weird there. Kind of like the USO at the airport.

Student Interactions on Campus

Communication and cultural gaps between student-veterans and nonveterans stem from ideological differences on war and the military and a lack of knowledge about challenges facing student-veterans (DiRamio et al., 2008; Elliott et al., 2011). Albright and Bryan (2018) found 44% of faculty to be lacking knowledge about challenges facing student-veterans, and 70% of faculty and staff members did not feel adequately prepared to recognize signs of psychological distress among student-veterans, including PTSD. These difficulties are troubling considering recent findings of high proportions of mental health issues among student-veterans (e.g., 40% of veterans screen positive for PTSD, 24% screen positive for depression, and 8% reported recent suicide ideation; Albright & Bryan, 2018; Currier et al., 2018).

To bridge communication and cultural gaps between student-veterans and nonveterans, ACE (2018) has called for campuses to develop training programs for faculty and staff. The implementation of such training programs can be particularly useful when coupled with program assessment plans purposefully designed to measure the impact of the training. Using 4 years of program data, we examined outcomes for the Veteran Educators Training program at UCCS. These outcomes included retention of content knowledge, application of lessons on campus, and comparison of outcomes for in-person and online training (Morris et al., 2021). Results suggested that participants developed significantly higher confidence and greater capacity to support student-veterans. Our qualitative findings demonstrated that faculty and staff who directly interacted with student-veterans post training incorporated lessons from the training and effectively supported students (Morris et al., 2021). With relationship to belongingness theory, people are more likely to be prejudiced against members of groups with which they perceive little or no opportunity to belong (Baumeister & Leary, 1995). Training events help create positive interpersonal connections between student-veterans and faculty/staff, and thus foster an element of belongingness, which in turn has positive psychological, physical health, and academic impacts.

Identity and Diversity

The U.S. military has consistently increased diversity in the ranks (Barraso, 2019), and any discussion on belongingness and inclusion must consider the intersectional identities of student-veterans. Further, the ways veterans perceive their service and identity is shaped by factors such as age, gender, race, family legacy, time and period of service, rank and branch of service, combat exposure, and military occupation (Doe, 2020). These diverse factors can moderate how veterans assimilate into different settings. For example, for women, the patriarchy and male-dominated culture of the military presents a set of challenges, which may significantly impact their experience as student-veterans (Albright et al., 2019).

Diversity of identities should be considered with any efforts to build a sense of belonging and community for student-veterans. College and community programs often valorize and reify military veterans, while neglecting deeper philosophical discussions on militarization and war policy and the wide variety of perspectives of veterans on these issues (Moore, 2017). Efforts by faculty and staff to support deep discussions on war and the military while promoting justice, equity, diversity, and inclusion (JEDI) is a way to foster a sense of belonging that is attuned to student-veteran diversity.

On the UCCS campus, diverse military perspectives are promoted through hosting events—panels, roundtable discussions, film screenings—related to women in service, diversity in the ranks, geopolitics, military policy, and issues such as the ethics of drone technology in modern warfare. These events create space for dialogue about diversity, including diversity within the military, diversity of military experiences, and diversity of perspectives on militarization. Faculty and staff have put forth a concerted effort to integrate veterans into these events and helped students express a range of viewpoints shaped by their military service and intersecting identities. Further, interactions at these events with nonveterans serve to reduce the divide between student-veterans and nonveterans. The dialogue and facilitated conversations serve to reduce simplification of veterans' experiences to those that are homogeneous and valorized (further discussed in Moore, 2017). Consequently, these events serve to create relationships and acknowledge that diversity of values and beliefs is central to the university environment. These opportunities for veterans to engage the diverse vectors of their identities directly relates to the cultural congruity framework through welcoming and accepting diverse values and beliefs.

Service-Connected Injuries and Belonging

A particularly impactful diversity intersection for many student-veterans is disability status. Reports indicate student-veterans are twice as likely as nonveteran students to have a documented disability (National Survey of Student Engagement [NSSE], 2010). Although veterans carry all conceivable nature of injuries, the "signature" injuries of the global war on terror include posttraumatic stress disorder (PTSD) and traumatic brain injuries (TBI) (Hoge, 2010). For veterans who have experienced trauma, hesitance to seek help can exacerbate feelings of isolation, which in turn hinders one's ability to develop a sense of belonging within the campus community (Gloria & Kurpius, 1996; Hoge, 2010). Given the high rate of exposure to trauma among post-9/11 veterans, campuses should emphasize the importance of fostering social support systems and mechanisms for seeking help for student-veterans. Knowing the expectations of when, how, and where to seek help is particularly important for student-veterans, as they report significantly lower levels of social support than their nonveteran counterparts (Whiteman et al., 2013).

In 2016, UCCS began the Military Veteran Pathways to Success (MVPS) project. The project focused on increasing help-seeking behaviors (further discussed in Morris et al., 2020). Over the course of the 3-year project, retention improved by 3% for new military-connected students, and approximately 90% of veterans continuously enrolled over the duration of the project. Further, 94% of respondents who utilized the student veteran center rated their overall experience as good or excellent (Morris et al., 2020). Although a direct measure of belongingness was not included in the evaluation of the initiative, assessment results indicated higher levels of connection to the campus and connection to each other, key components of both the need-to-belong theory and the cultural congruity framework.

Conclusion

The combined use of the need-to-belong theory and cultural congruity framework provide a structure for enhancing belongingness on campus for student-veterans. Belongingness is tightly coupled with connection to others and a sense of purpose, both fundamental components of military service. The tribal connections veterans developed during their service and the sense of belonging this engenders is often lost in the transition from military to university; therefore, the first year of transition is particularly important for student-veterans (Borsari et al., 2017). For these individuals, building a sense of belonging and connection to a new purpose as a student is critical to their continued success.

Physical and cultural campus environments directly impact student belonging, as the campus conditions and settings are essential for promoting connections to one another, engagement with supportive offices/initiatives, and identifying their individual academic purpose. Multiple studies and accounts of the transition indicate the importance of faculty and staff communications for generating genuine and caring interactions, which can lead to cultural congruity and belonging for student-veterans.

Understanding the nuances and salience of multiple veteran identities is a key component of connecting with student-veterans, and it is imperative for educators to consider how these characteristics shape an individual's relationship with military service and with their institution. These efforts are best implemented through bridging cultural gaps, addressing differences in expectations between the military and higher education, expressions of genuine interest in the diversity of service-member experiences, and the creation of spaces for student-veterans to develop a new sense of belonging.

This chapter does not present an exhaustive overview of support mechanisms linked to student-veteran belonging and success. Instead, the chapter links theory to practice by introducing elements of belongingness salient for veterans and illustrations of select campus initiatives designed to address these elements. Additionally, the supporting examples and references provide sources for further investigation into the promotion of student-veteran belongingness. Lastly, this chapter can serve as a catalyst for further dialogue and future inquiry into belongingness as a central tenet of student-veteran success.

References

Albright, D. L., Thomas, K. H., McDaniel, J., Fletcher, K. L., Godfrey, K., Bertram, J., & Angel, C. (2019). When women veterans return: The role of postsecondary education in transition in their civilian lives. *Journal of American College Health*, *67*(5), 479–485. https://doi.org/10.1080/07448481.2018.1494599

Albright, G., & Bryan, C. (2018). *Are faculty and staff ready to support student veterans?* National Center for Veterans Studies. https://go.kognito.com/Student_Veterans_Whitepaper.html

American Council on Education. (2018). *Toolkit for veteran friendly institutions.* https://www.acenet.edu/Documents/Veterans-Toolkit-2018.pdf

Barraso, A. (2019, September 10). *The changing profile of the U.S. military: Smaller in size, more diverse, more women in leadership.* Pew Research Center. https://www.pewresearch.org/fact-tank/2019/09/10/the-changing-profile-of-the-u-s-military/

Barry, A. E., Jackson, Z. A., & Fullerton, A. B. (2019). An assessment of sense of belonging in higher education among student service members/veterans. *Journal of American College Health*, *69*(3), 335–339. https://doi.org/10.1080/07448481.2019.1676249

Barry, A. E., Whiteman, S. D., & Wadsworth, S. M. (2014). Student service members/veterans in education: A systematic review. *Journal of Student Affairs Research and Practice*, *51*(1), 30–42. https://doi.org/10.1515/jsarp-2014-0003

Baumeister, R. F., & Leary, M. R. (1995). The need to belong: Desire for interpersonal attachments as a fundamental human motivation. *Psychological Bulletin*, *117*(3), 497–529. https://psycnet.apa.org/doi/10.1037/0033-2909.117.3.497

Borsari, B., Yurasek A., Miller M. B., Murphy, J. G., McDevitt-Murphy, M. E., Martens, M. P., Darcy, M. G., & Carey, K. B. (2017). Student service members/veterans on campus: Challenges for reintegration. *American Journal of Orthopsychiatric Health*, *87*(2), 166–175. https://doi.org/10.1037/ort0000199

Cate, C. A., Lyon, J. S., Schmeling, J., & Bogue, B. Y. (2017). *National veteran education success tracker: A report on the academic success of student veterans using the post-9/11 GI Bill.* Student Veterans of America. https://www.luminafoundation.org/files/resources/veteran-success-tracker.pdf

Currier, J. M., McDermott, R. C., & Sims, B. (2018). Do student service members/veterans experience worse mental health stigma than their peers? A comparative study in a national sample. *Journal of American College Health*, *66*(2), 821–825. https://doi.org/10.1080/07448481.2018.1440569

DiRamio, D., Ackerman, R., & Garza Mitchell, R. L. (2008). From combat to campus: Voices of student-veterans. *NASPA Journal*, *45*(1), 73–102. https://doi.org/10.2202/1949-6605.1908

DiRamio, D., & Jarvis, K. (2011). Veterans in higher education—When Johnny and Jane come marching to campus. *ASHE Higher Education Report*, *37*(3), 1–144. http://dx.doi.org/10.1002/aehe.3703

Doe, W. (2020). A personal reckoning with veteran identity. *Journal of Veterans Studies*, *6*(3), 54–60. http://doi.org/10.21061/jvs.v6i3.217

Elliott, M., Gonzalez, C., & Larsen, B. (2011). U.S. military veterans' transition to college: Combat, PTSD, and alienation on campus. *Journal of Student Affairs Research and Practice*, *48*(3), 279–296. https://doi.org/10.2202/1949-6605.6293

Gloria A. M., & Kurpius, S. (1996). The validation of the cultural congruity scale and the university environment scale with Chicano/a students. *Hispanic Journal of Behavioral Sciences*, *18*(4), 533–549. https://doi.org/10.1177%2F07399863960184007

Griffin, K. A., & Gilbert, C. K. (2015). Better transitions for troops: An application of Schlossberg's transition framework to analyses of barriers and institutional support structures for student veterans. *The Journal of Higher Education*, *86*(1), 71–97. https://doi.org/10.1080/00221546.2015.11777357

Hoge, C. W. (2010). *Once a warrior—Always a warrior: Navigating the transition from combat to home—including combat stress, PTSD, and mTBI.* Lyons.

Hunter-Johnson, Y., Liu, T., Murray, K., Niu, Y., & Suprise, M. (2020). Higher education as a tool for veterans in transition: Battling the challenges. *Journal of Continuing Higher Education*, *69*(1), 1–18. https://doi.org/10.1080/07377363.2020.1743621

Junger, S. (2016). *Tribe: On homecoming and belonging.* Twelve Publishing.

King, P., & Kitchener, K. (2004). Reflective judgment: Theory and research on the Development of epistemic assumptions through adulthood. *Educational Psychologist, 39*(1), 5–18. https://doi.org/10.1207/s15326985ep3901_2

Lim, J. H., Interiano, C. G., Nowell, C. E., Tkacik, P. T., & Dahlberg, J. L. (2018). Invisible cultural barriers: Contrasting perspectives on student veterans' transition. *Journal of College Student Development, 59*(3), 291–308. https://doi .org/10.1353/csd.2018.0028

McAndrew, L. M., Slotkin, S., Kimber, J., Maestro, K., Phillips, L. A., Martin, J. L., Credé, M., & Eklund, A. (2019). Cultural incongruity predicts adjustment to college for student veterans. *Journal of Counseling Psychology, 66*(6), 678–689. https://psycnet.apa.org/doi/10.1037/cou0000363

McMenamin, R., & Kurzynski, K. (2016). How are institutions of higher education implementing first-year transition courses for veterans? *Journal of Veterans Studies, 1*(1). https://www.researchgate.net/publication/326360035_How_are_Institutions_ of_Higher_Education_Implementing_First-Year_Transition_Courses_for_Veterans

Mendez, S., Witkowsky, P., Morris, P., Brosseau, J., & Nicholson, H. (2018). Student veteran experiences in a transition seminar course: Exploring the thriving transition cycle. *Journal of Veterans Studies, 3*(2), 33–62. http://doi.org/10.21061/jvs.v3i2.52

Moore, E., (2017). *Grateful nation: Student veterans and the rise of the military-friendly campus.* Duke University Press.

Morris, P., Albanesi, H. P., & Cassidy, S. (2019). Student-veterans' perceptions of barriers, support, and environment at a high-density veteran enrollment campus. *Journal of Veterans Studies, 4*(2), 180–202. http://doi.org/10.21061/jvs.v4i2.102

Morris, P., Barker, L., & Monar, A. (2020). Applying the social ecological framework to enhance wellness for student veterans. *Journal of American College Health.* https://doi.org/10.1080/07448481.2020.1844716

Morris, P., McNamee, M., & St. Louis, K. (2021). Assessing the impact of military cultural competence training: Lessons for creating an inclusive campus environment. *Journal of Continuing Higher Education.* https://doi.org/10.1080/073773 63.2021.1938804

National Survey of Student Engagement. (2010). *Major differences: Examining student engagement by field of study—annual results 2010.* Indiana University Center for Postsecondary Research. https://files.eric.ed.gov/fulltext/ED512590.pdf

Syracuse University Institute for Veterans and Military Families. (2019). *Student veterans: A valuable asset to higher education.* https://ivmf.syracuse.edu/student-veterans-a-valuable-asset-to-higher-education/

Vacchi, D. T., & Berger, J. B. (2014). Student veterans in higher education. In M. Paulson (Ed.), *Higher education: Handbook of theory and research* (pp. 93–151). Springer.

Whiteman, S. D., Barry, A. E., Mroczek, D. K., & MacDermid Wadsworth, S. (2013). The development and implications of peer emotional support for student service members/veterans and civilian college students. *Journal of Counseling Psychology, 60*(2), 265–278. https://doi.org/10.1037/a0031650

Yeager, J., & Rennie, M. (2020). Student veterans' experiences of a campus veterans center revealed through photovoice. *The Journal of Continuing Higher Education, 69*(1), 46–60. https://doi.org/10.1080/07377363.2020.1813483

18

STUDENT-EMPLOYEE
SENSE OF BELONGING

Cynthia Cogswell, Tim Epley, and Brittany Barten

Divisions of student affairs cannot perform their mission without student-employees. During any given year, these divisions host hundreds of events, house and feed thousands of students, provide support services, and champion a strong sense of belonging. Division programs and initiatives allow students to discover their identity and potential, but none of this would be possible without student-employees.

Ohio University (OHIO) is a large, public university with 11 campuses in the United States. OHIO's main campus enrolls approximately 30,000 students, and the student-to-faculty ratio is 17:1. The division of student affairs (the division) is made up of 13 units and employs 300 staff and over 3,500 students. In 2017, the division began a strategic planning effort via listening tours, stakeholder feedback, and collective iteration of drafted strategic plans. The strategic plan launched in 2018 with three priorities: assessment, equity and social justice, and retention and graduation. One key objective for the division's strategic planning committee tasked with increasing student retention and graduation rates was to better understand student-employee experiences and sense of belonging.

This chapter adds to past research on student employment and sense of belonging. First, we review the literature, followed by the process of creating a survey and understanding its results. Lastly, the findings and recommendations are discussed.

Background

Current research regarding student employment during college is complex, in part because all student jobs are not created equally. Certain positions

197

demand more time, some more explicitly connect to in-class learning, others allow time to do homework, and most vary widely in compensation—both form and amount. While student employment can vary in many ways, research (Burnside et al., 2019; McClellan et al., 2018) suggests that student employment can be a vehicle for applying classroom learning in experiential contexts and has been recognized as a critical means for student development.

Student sense of belonging is a construct that encompasses a welcoming and safe environment (Graham-Smith & Lafayette, 2004; Strayhorn, 2012). It is also where a student is connected and integrated into a community (Chickering & Gamson, 1987; Glennen et al., 1996; Heisserer & Parette, 2002) and cared for and supported by its members (Graham-Smith & Lafayette, 2004; Heisserer & Parette, 2002; Tinto, 1993), and where they can express their identities and attributes. The literature articulates numerous variables that influence an individuals' sense of belonging.

Before students can develop a sense of belonging, their basic needs must be met. Maslow's (1943) hierarchy of needs provides a foundation for student development in which individuals must acquire the most basic level needs (food, water, shelter, security, and safety) before moderate and higher-level needs can be attained (belongingness, esteem, and self-actualization). On-campus employment satisfies financial support for basic needs, as well as other elements of Maslow's model, such as belongingness. Student-employees have a structured opportunity to build connections with their coworkers on the job to enhance their belongingness. Supervisors can create environments of belonging to something, whether it is at the department, divisional, or institutional level, by spending one-on-one time with employees, tying classroom learning to workplace responsibilities, or helping a student articulate the connection between their academics and employment when interviewing for professional positions (McCellan et al., 2018). McCellan et al. (2018) argue that campus employment is a vehicle for enhancing a students' sense of belonging and subsequently their retention and persistence, as outlined in several well-known persistence and retention theories.

Schlossberg's (1981) transition theory outlines four S's that influence an individual's transition: situation, self, support, and strategies. Most related to sense of belonging, *support* refers to family, friends, community, and institutional systems. On-campus employment offers additional support structures (supervisor and coworkers) and referrals to campus connections designed to support students in transition (counseling services, career development, advising). Sanford's (1967) theory of challenge and support was designed with academic advisors in mind but can be translated to student affairs professionals. The goal in Sanford's theory is not to eliminate the challenge but to provide the support that buffers the negative effects of the challenge. Sanford believed there is a balance between challenging a student to grow while supporting their efforts through growth. In this application, supervisors can recognize challenges their student-employees are experiencing and tailor support to meet the demands of the students or even create challenging opportunities for students to practice resiliency and development with the support of the supervisor in the workplace. Students are the authors of their experiences, but opting into high-impact practices enhances their persistence (Koproske et al., 2015; Kuh, 2008; Tannous & Moore, 2013). On-campus jobs can take on some of the beneficial aspects of high-impact practices, such as diversity learning, active learning, and shared intellectual experiences, further cultivating students' cumulative learning.

On-campus employment is well positioned to support student-employees' sense of belonging through financial means, peer engagement, recognition of attributes, and guidance through difficult transitions.

Measuring Student-Employee Sense of Belonging at OHIO

The OHIO retention and graduation committee sought to understand how the division could positively impact the retention and graduation rates of undergraduate students. The division does not house tutoring or academic advising services, nor does it have a purview over student success efforts. After completing a literature review, the sense of belonging subcommittee crafted a six-item sense of belonging survey that was shared with the division while the student employment subcommittee crafted a survey to better understand student-employee experiences.

Grounded in the literature and survey best practices, a digital survey was created to collect information about student-employee sense of belonging. Staff reviewed literature on the factors influencing student retention and noted conflicting scholarship regarding employment on campus. The subcommittee sought to learn what current efforts were resonating with student-employees in order to identify areas of improvement.

The 16-item sense of belonging survey focused on themes developed from the sense of belonging question bank (OHIO, n.d.). The survey was reviewed by the division's director of assessment and colleagues in the diversity and equity department for face validity and inclusive language. A pilot survey was conducted with student leaders in the conference and event services department. Once initial results were reviewed and the committee followed up with a small sample of the students as an assurance for response process evidence (American Educational Research Association et al., 2014), an expanded distribution was released to all other division departments that employed students. The survey was open for 3 weeks and then closed.

In total, 470 students responded, with 56% reporting working in their current role for over 1 year. Forty-seven percent reported working over 16 hours per week. Respondents included a range of experienced undergraduate and some graduate staff (93% undergraduate and 7% graduate responses), from student leaders and managers (40%) to entry-level part-time student-employees (60%). Close to 30% identified as first-generation college students. Respondents also reported being involved in Greek life (10%), student organizations (37%), student government (2%), and service organizations (18%). The following sections highlight the results.

Sense of Belonging

Table 18.1 highlights some of the sense of belonging results. Two themes emerged from the results. First, students desired more social opportunities to connect with others from work outside of the work environment. The second theme related to financial concerns. Only 35% of respondents felt that if they were struggling financially they would be comfortable discussing the issue with their supervisor. However, 51% of all respondents felt they could comfortably discuss academic issues with that same supervisor.

TABLE 18.1
Sense of Belonging Data

Question	Yes	No	
I have received a promotion in my department(s).	39.57%; 186	60.43%; 284	
If yes:	Better	About the Same	Worse
Did your promotion impact your sense of belonging in the department?	67.03%; 124	29.73%; 55	3.24%; 6
Question	Agree	Neutral	Disagree
My department welcomed me into my position.	86.87%; 377	9.68%; 42	3.46%; 15
I feel connected to my position because of the facility or location.	73.96%; 321	19.35%; 84	6.68%; 29
I have made a connection with at least one other student at work.	94.47%; 410	3.69%; 16	1.84%; 8

Response Themes

Over 300 open-ended responses to the question "What departmental efforts had the most impact on your sense of belonging?" were coded for themes. Identified themes included community building and recognition. For example, students said "sense of community among employees, managers, student leaders" and "community building and having interactions with coworkers" contributed to their sense of belonging. Others noted that "getting recognized for good work" or being thanked made them feel welcomed by their department. One respondent tied both themes together when they wrote,

> I truly do enjoy working with a variety of coworkers because we all have different skills to bring to the table. The department has biweekly meetings that help solidify news and training in a concise way. During the meetings, we usually do a shout-out for another coworker, so their efforts are recognized, which helps people have a greater sense of belonging.

These same themes emerged when student-employees were asked what their departments could improve. One student wrote that their department could "schedule more meetings or events where [they] could meet, hangout, and/ or work with other people in the department outside of [their] scheduled shifts." Another remarked,

> Acknowledging your students for their successes, in and out of the offices. Having open discussions about issues and solving a problem that way. Talk with students about where they fit in best. Think about their skills and why they come into work every day, and if it's agreed that they're good where they're at, let them stay. If there is a better position, discuss that with them and gauge their interest. If you have different functional parts of your office/department, encourage students to speak to one another so that those functional parts don't become clique-like. Nobody wants that.

Over 67% of respondents stated that a promotion increased their sense of belonging. One student reflected,

> I think the trust that the staff gives me, makes me feel like I belong. They know my abilities and give me tasks based on that. I was encouraged to seek a promotion because they knew I could do it. It made me feel as if I was actually good at this job and it's where I should be.

Support From Work

Survey results revealed that student compensation, along with rewards and recognition, contributed to an employee's sense of belonging by showing

TABLE 18.2
Support From Work

Question	Agree	Neutral	Disagree
My coworkers support me at work.	82.03%; 356	15.21% 66	2.76% 12
My managers support me at work.	77.42%; 336	17.51% 76	5.07% 22
If I am struggling academically, I am comfortable discussing the issue with my supervisor.	50.92%; 221	26.96% 117	22.12% 96
If I am struggling socially, I am comfortable discussing the issue with my supervisor.	40.55%; 176	30.41%; 132	29.03%; 126
I can be myself at work.	77.42%; 336	17.28%; 75	5.30%; 23
I have gained valuable insight about myself through my job.	66.13%; 287	25.58%; 111	8.29%; 36
My employment has increased my ability to succeed at Ohio University.	59.91%; 260	28.80%; 125	11.29%; 49
My employment has an impact on the success of the university.	62.90%; 273	27.42%; 119	9.68%; 42
My efforts are recognized.	64.52%; 280	22.35%; 97	13.13%; 57

value for the role they serve. Rewards and recognition can take many forms, ranging from performance bonuses, award ceremonies, or simply personalized notes acknowledging a job well done. Survey results on employee support and recognition can be found in Table 18.2. Questions centered on support and student perception of fit. Students felt strong support from coworkers (82% agreed) and from managers (77% agreed). Notably, student responses to their comfort discussing social struggles with their supervisor differed: 40% agreed, 30% were neutral, and 29% disagreed.

Discussion

Survey results reinforced what was found in the literature and added more practical insights to better support sense of belonging in the workplace. The majority of student-employees shared that they felt welcomed to their workplace, connected to their colleagues, and recognized for their efforts. While students shared that they felt supported by their peers and managers, results indicated that students wanted more structured opportunities to build connections—be it spending time one-on-one or in a group context. Related to Maslow's (1943) model discussed earlier, on-campus employment satisfies financial support for basic needs, and the results revealed that student-employees were ready to acquire higher-level needs, such as belongingness and connection. Results revealed differences between roles and departments and inconsistent practices. Some units had regularly scheduled all-staff meetings, which included student-employees; some did not. Some units provided official offer letters with all relevant information; some did not. Some students shared that jargon was confusing and hard to make sense of. While the literature reviewed did not specifically call out this level of detail, it was easy for professional staff to discuss how these and other issues could be barriers to a sense of belonging for a student-employee.

Recommendations

After reviewing the results, the subcommittee developed a series of seven guidelines to improve support for student-employees. These guidelines were designed to help boost student engagement efforts and include the following:

- onboarding checklist
- offer letter template
- recommendations on student-employee compensation, rewards, and recognition
- peer mentoring suggestions
- offboarding checklist
- exit interview questions
- recommendations for student-employee performance evaluation

Together, the list aims to provide some level of consistency across the division. The tips for transitioning to college included in the guidelines can serve as a conversational tool, and the standardized offer letter is formatted to be readily adapted for varied departments and positions. Also included in the onboarding checklist is a glossary of common terms and acronyms to be shared with students, as they can feel disoriented, disconnected, and discouraged if they feel they do not speak the "right" language. The many acronyms and jargon that litter higher education can be a barrier to a student-employee's sense of belonging.

An offboarding checklist and exit interview guide, when used, offer student-employees a chance to reflect on employment while ensuring essential final tasks are completed. Student-employees can benefit from the professional and personal development gained through structured interactions and will be able to better articulate their role and growth in resumes and job interviews (OHIO, n.d.).

We recommend that practitioners consider adopting some or all the best practices identified. This list can be readily applied to practice at institutions that employ students in order to better foster student-employee sense of belonging. They can be implemented systematically, across a division, or by one unit, or even by one supervisor. Further, if there is resistance to adopting these exact practices, institutions can use a similar research process, collecting information from student-employees about what makes them feel a sense of belonging, checking findings against the literature, and deriving a generalizable plan to move forward.

Conclusion

The best-practice guidelines assist supervisors in creating an environment where student-employees feel welcomed, safe, connected, integrated into a community, cared for, supported by its members, and valued for their personal identities and attributes. This chapter studied what student-employees view as contributing to their sense of belonging. The findings revealed differences across the division that fostered sense of belonging in the student work environment. These led to recommendations to create consistent practice across the division.

We encourage readers to consider how they onboard, coach, and support student-employees. Understanding student employment beyond its direct impact on divisional success helps further the educational mission of higher education. By infusing sense of belonging into the student-employee experience, supervisors support their retention and persistence (McClellan et al., 2018). As student affairs practitioners, our best work is for and with students. By strengthening student-employee sense of belonging on campus, we can enhance not only a student's financial resources, but also ensure a stronger support system en route to graduation.

References

American Educational Research Association, American Psychology Association, & National Council of Measurement in Education. (2014). *Standards for educational and psychological testing*. American Educational Research Association.

Burnside, O., Wesley, A., Wesaw, A., & Parnell, K. (2019). *Employing student success: A comprehensive examination of on-campus student employment.* NASPA: Student Affairs Professionals in Higher Education. https://www.naspa.org/report/employing-student-success-a-comprehensive-examination-of-on-campus-student-employment

Chickering, A., & Gamson, Z. (1989). Seven principles for good practice in undergraduate education. *Biochemical Education, 17*(3), 140–141. https://doi:10.1016/0307-4412(89)90094-0

Glennen, R. E., Farren, P. J., & Vowell, F. N. (1996). How advising and retention of students improves fiscal stability. *NACADA Journal, 16*(1), 38–41. https://doi.org/10.12930/0271-9517-16.1.38

Graham-Smith, S., & Lafayette, S. (2004). Quality disability support for promoting belonging and academic success within the college community. *College Student Journal, 38*(1), 90–100.

Heisserer, D. L., & Parette, P. (2002). Advising at risk students in college and university settings. *College Student Journal, 36*, 69–83.

Koproske, C., Gfeller, H., & Silverman, A. (2015). *Defining the faculty role in student success: Building ownership for student progression among individual faculty and distributed academic units.* Education Advisory Board. https://eab.com/research/academic-affairs/study/defining-the-faculty-role-in-student-success-2/

Kuh, G. D. (2008). *High-impact educational practices: What they are, who has access to them, and why they matter.* Association of American Colleges and Universities.

Maslow, A. H. (1943). A theory of human motivation. *Psychological Review, 50*(4), 370–396. https://doi.org/10.1037/h0054346

McClellen, G. S., Creager, K., & Savoca, M. (2018). *A good job: Campus employment as a high impact practice.* Stylus.

Ohio University. (n.d.). *Staff onboarding—Undergraduate employees.* https://www.ohio.edu/student-affairs/onboarding/undergrads

Sanford, N. (1967). The development of social responsibility. *American Journal of Orthopsychiatry, 37*(1), 22–29. https://doi.apa.org/doi/10.1111/j.1939-0025.1967.tb01063.x

Schlossberg, N. C. (1981). A model for analyzing human adaptation to transition. *The Counseling Psychologist, 9*(2). 2–18.

Strayhorn, T. L. (2012). *College students' sense of belonging: A key to educational success for all students.* Routledge.

Tannous, J., & Moore, S. (2013). *Improving upper-class engagement and retention: Academic and co-curricular strategies* [White paper]. Education Advisory Board. https://www.csueastbay.edu/oaa/files/docs/acinfo/upperclassengemnt.pdf

Tinto, V. (1975). Dropout from higher education: A theoretical synthesis of recent research. *Review of Educational Research, 75*(1), 89–125. https://doi.org/10.2307/1170024

PART THREE

IMPLICATIONS AND
APPLICATIONS

EXAMPLES IN PRACTICE
NDSUBELONG

A Cross-Collaborative Approach to Student Sense of Belonging

Derisa Collymore, Laura Dahl, and Alyssa Teubner

North Dakota State University (NDSU) is a public, land-grant, primarily White, research institution. The office of new student programs provides on-campus summer orientation days, followed by 2 weeks of welcome week transition programming starting on move-in day. Prior to 2018, welcome week was simply slotted events designated to specific departments. This approach was siloed, did not focus on the developmental needs of students, and did not allow for cross-departmental collaboration. During the initial stages of planning for welcome week 2019, the three-person welcome week planning committee (WWPC) did not feel purposeful in their approach to designing this aspect of the student transition experience. The members recognized that in order to be educators and facilitate effective student transition experiences, they needed to utilize theory and research to intentionally design an effective welcome week experience. In discussions about how welcome week could be more effective in supporting students' transition to NDSU, the WWPC decided to complete a literature review as a key component of the planning process. The WWPC learned that belonging is an integral aspect of a successful first-year student transition. Thus, sense of belonging became the primary learning outcome for welcome week. Recognizing that they did not have the capacity or expertise to design quality "sense-of-belonging" initiatives, the WWPC devised an additional committee.

The WWPC chair, dean of students, and director of orientation met to identify staff from student affairs departments and faculty who should be members of this new committee, and each received individual invitations.

The group of 10, aptly named the committee NDSUbelong, brainstormed and then narrowed down an extensive list of potential learning outcomes to a small set that were developmentally appropriate for first-year students during welcome week.

Maslow's (1943) hierarchy of needs grounded the group's conversation regarding students' basic needs during their transition and theorized that students could not move to the belonging tier until their safety and physiological needs were met during this transition to a new and unfamiliar environment (Maslow, 1943). Schlossberg's transition theory was used to inform the group's understanding of students' "anticipated transition . . . new routines . . . and new role" as college students (Schlossberg et al., 1995, p. 35). The theory provided evidence that students need targeted support via strong relationships within the institutional community to successfully transition into their new role as college students. Schlossberg's theory also indicated that strategies for supporting students amidst transition include "controlling the meaning" or reframing a difficult situation to help students cope (Schlossberg et al., 1995, p. 75). To reframe the transitional experience into NDSU, the committee decided that they would determine what it means to belong at NDSU:

> Students with a sense of belonging at NDSU feel secure, respected, and connected to peers, faculty, and staff. They are embraced as a person of value and empowered to be their genuine selves. We recognize our shared commitment to the cultivation and stewardship of an inclusive community. This is in an email and not accessible online (NDSUbelong Committee, personal communication, July 8, 2019).

The committee knew that students would need the space to engage with belonging as a core campus value; thus, two initiatives materialized—a large group presentation led by faculty and staff, and a small group meeting led by peer mentors to be implemented in the fall of 2019.

"Fitting in" versus Belonging: The Large Group Session

The large group session was NDSU's first ever mandatory presentation included in welcome week. The purpose of the large group session was to demonstrate NDSU's commitment to creating a culture of belonging, have students identify the difference between fitting in and belonging, and help students understand their responsibility in stewarding that culture. Faculty and staff presented the 45-minute NDSUbelong interactive presentation and allowed students to participate by using their phones to anonymously respond to prompts. Students were asked, "How confident are you in being your authentic self around all of these new people?" Real-time displays of student responses were projected for the audience so that students could make connections between their own thoughts and that of their peers.

To provide institutional context, presenters shared a portion of NDSU's brand manifesto, which is an intentionally designed statement published by university relations to publicly articulate the culture of belonging that the campus is striving toward:

> Just beyond our main gates lies a space where you belong. As an NDSU Bison, you'll become immersed in experiences, friendships and moments you'll carry into your future. . . . You have the freedom and support to mature into the person you were meant to be, while remaining true to you. (Olive & Company , 2018, p. 24)

Following the brand manifesto, presenters provided students with Brene Brown's (2010) philosophy on belonging: "Fitting in is about assessing a situation and becoming who you need to be, to be accepted. Belonging, on the other hand, doesn't require us to change who we are; it requires us to be who we are" (p. 145). This philosophy was chosen by the NDSUbelong committee because they believed the concept would resonate with students' prior experiences. Student experiences can range from being deeply rooted in communities of belonging to finding ways to fit in.

Students engaged in introspective activities to help them make sense of the concept of belonging versus fitting in:

- sharing traits they see in others who are great at helping people feel like they belong
- developing metaphors for what it feels like to belong versus fit in
- submitting tangible ideas for how they will steward a culture of belonging on campus

The presentation allowed multiple avenues of engagement and for students to think critically about their personal responsibility in fostering a sense of belonging on campus.

Connections That Support Sense of Belonging: The Small Group Sessions

The welcome week schedule was reformatted so that students spent signifi-cant amounts of time with their residence hall communities. Each floor par-ticipated in three floor meetings led by returning student volunteers with the overarching goal of helping students create connections to campus and one another. The second meeting was devised specifically for students to focus on creating a sense of belonging within their new community. The lesson plan for this session was created by the NDSUbelong committee and a faculty member who is a certified Brene Brown Dare to Lead facilitator. Based on her recommendation that facilitating trust building, practicing courage, and demonstrating vulnerability are central to developing a sense of belonging, these became the strategies for engaging students during the group meeting.

Rather than having mixed groups of students from across campus for the small group meetings, students were assigned by residence hall floor. The committee hoped that vulnerability, courage, and trust building during small group activities would develop a foundation for stewarding cultures of belonging within the residence halls throughout the academic year. The meeting included a variety of activities that integrated Brown's foundational concepts for developing a sense of belonging:

- *Facilitating trust building*—To facilitate trust and peer sharing, each peer leader shared a story of a struggle to connect or belong during their transition.
- *Practicing vulnerability*—Students were asked to practice vulnerability through writing and reflecting on provided prompts. One of the prompts was "What does support look like for you as you start making connections?" Students were then asked to place their requests in the center of the circle and read the requests of their peers.
- *Demonstrating courage*—Peer mentors were asked to share, "It's going to take many small acts and moments of courage for you to make connections and start feeling like you belong here." Students were then asked to think, pair, and share with one another about people in their lives who have role-modeled courage.

At the conclusion of each session, students reflected and developed personal action to have a positive impact on their sense of belonging and that of others. For example, in the NDSUbelong session students were asked, "One way that I am going to help others feel like they belong on campus is . . ." Answers ranged from "saying hi" to "being inclusive in my conversations." Ultimately, the intention was that students would understand that their actions contribute to building cultures of belonging on campus.

Unfortunately, due to time and space constraints, the large group NDSUbelong presentations and the small group meetings were not able to include scaffolded learning. The sessions were intentionally designed with this in mind, and although the concepts within each are connected, they do not build on each other. One session gives the students space to interact and create connections, and the other is a chance to critically explore the idea of belonging at NDSU.

Expanding on That Sense of Belonging

The campus-wide focus on sense of belonging during welcome week prompted the development of additional programming. The NDSUbelong committee recognized deficiencies in the current welcome week structure with regard to specialized programming for students with diverse racial backgrounds. NDSU has an 11% Black, Indigenous, and people of color (BIPOC) student population (NDSU, 2020) and the transition to a university that is 89% White could be difficult. There were not enough BIPOC welcome week leads or resident assistants to ensure that all students in each residence hall would have the opportunity to connect with someone who shares their identity. The committee also recognized that other historically marginalized groups may face the same difficulties.

As such, affinity dinners were implemented during the first weekend of the academic year as a chance for students with similar backgrounds and identities to connect with each other, staff, faculty, and student groups. At the dinners, there were tables for Asian/Pacific Islanders, Black/African Americans, first-generation college students, LGBTQA+, Native Americans, Somalis, women in STEM, and commuter and transfer students. Meals took place in designated dining areas that allowed for additional privacy, and the hosts of these tables received complimentary meal tickets. This initiative provided intentional connection-making space, rather than hoping connections would happen on their own.

NDSU also hosted the first welcome week for students of color social to create opportunities for incoming BIPOC students to begin building community. At the event, students were given information on campus resources and time to connect with BIPOC student organizations. There were two BIPOC entertainers—a professional comedian and an NDSU alumnus who is a professional yoyo performer. The night ended with a raffle of giveaways from local BIPOC-owned businesses.

Implementing Sense of Belonging on Your Campus

Focusing on a sense of belonging during students' transition to college is feasible for any institution, as long as there is consideration for your campus' specific needs and context. NDSU welcome week's focus on sense of belonging was a low-cost, cross-collaborative way to expose students to a campus culture of belonging during their first week. Establishing these cultural expectations as part of the welcome experience is important, regardless of what that process looks like on your campus. There are three points to consider as you navigate implementing this type of initiative:

- *Think cross-collaboratively*—How can staff, faculty, and students from various areas across campus be intentionally brought together to develop these initiatives, rather than operating within a bifurcated or siloed approach? Who are the experts on your campus, and how can their knowledge inform these grassroots initiatives?
- *Emphasize stewardship*—NDSU continuously reiterated the role students have in creating environments where their peers belong. What small group opportunities, peer mentorship positions, or activities would reinforce the belonging messaging that your campus has deemed most important?
- *Commit long-term to fostering a sense of belonging for all students*— Consider the populations of traditionally underrepresented students at your institution and determine what programming you can implement to ensure that they are adequately represented in activities or events.

Examining these points will help higher education professionals consider the context of their institution, provide a lens for them to engage with student sense of belonging, and thoughtfully consider where there are deficiencies in serving marginalized student populations. NDSU's welcome week T-shirts proudly declare "You Belong Here," and through intentionally designed initiatives we have begun the process of ensuring that this statement resonates with all students. Prioritizing students' sense of belonging on your campus is the first step in strategically moving forward in implementing a culture of belonging.

References

Brown, B. (2010). *The gifts of imperfection: Let go of who you think you're supposed to be and embrace who you are.* Hazelden.

Maslow, A. H. (1943). A theory of human motivation. *Psychological Review, 50(4),* 370–396. https://doi.org/10.1037/h0054346

North Dakota State University. (2020). *Total student enrollment history by ethnicity percentages.* Data Reporting and Student Statistics. https://www.ndsu.edu/oira/dashboards/race_ethnicity/

Olive & Company. (2018). *Brand messaging manifesto* [Marketing brief].

Schlossberg, N. K., Waters, E. B., & Goodman, J. (1995). *Counseling adults in transition: Linking practice with theory.* Springer.

19B

REDUCING BARRIERS TO INCREASE SENSE OF BELONGING

Laura Bayless and Hank Parkinson

As seen throughout this book, a sense of belonging is critical to student success. Fitchburg State University's belonging work is grounded in a growth mindset, becoming a student-ready campus, supporting first-generation students in navigating institutions of higher education and belonging. After briefly describing these concepts, the chapter highlights two recent initiatives we implemented using this foundation: (a) new sessions at orientation focused on growth mindset, a sense of belonging, and navigating the Fitchburg State environment, and (b) a mentoring program that targets a particular population of students.

Growth Mindset

Belief systems about one's abilities and potential have a significant influence over behavior and levels of success (Dweck, 2016). A fixed mindset assumes that talent, intelligence, and character are static and cannot be changed in any way. Therefore, any success or failure is a foregone conclusion. A growth mindset views discomfort, challenges, and failure as a springboard for growth and development. A growth mindset can support a sense of belonging through fostering the belief that any condition is temporary and changeable, and our own actions can influence that change. Thus, a student who does not immediately feel they belong at an institution of higher education can take actions that increase their sense of belonging, and the institution can change approaches and opportunities that increase a sense of belonging in students. Fitchburg State has adopted the concept of a growth mindset both inside and outside the classroom to foster this belief that one can improve and feel connected. The university will continue to adapt the curriculum, services, and opportunities to meet the needs of individual students and changing student populations.

Becoming a Student-Ready Campus

Fitchburg State University is shifting more intentionally to a student-ready mindset in an attempt to reduce barriers to success and improve services and opportunities for students (Brown McNair et al., 2016). This emphasis on being student-ready reverses deficit-minded thinking and assumes that all students can succeed when institutions reframe the focus to what they can and must do to better support student learning and development rather than on whether students are ready for college. Faculty and staff on a student-ready campus understand that all those who interact with students are educators (Brown McNair et al., 2016.) Finally, the importance of students' intersectional cultural and social identities and peer relationships are central to being student ready (Brown McNair et al., 2016; Whitley et al., 2018).

Belonging

Strayhorn (2012) conceived of belonging as both a sense of being a valued part of the educational community and of feeling oneself to be an important part of the life and activity of the campus. There are numerous ways that students develop a sense of belonging. Students who engage with peers about course content; connect with faculty, staff, or advisors; or become engaged with cocurricular activities generally have a stronger sense of belonging (Milem & Berger, 1997; Parkinson, 2020). Parkinson (2020) conducted a pilot study to explore and compare the sense of belonging of students who are engaged with any kind of cocurricular experiences, such as student organizations, athletics or recreation, campus employment, and so on, with those who come to campus for classes only and do not engage in other ways. Eighty-eight percent of engaged students believed that their values aligned with the Fitchburg State community, and 94% reported a deep sense of belonging that was tied to their involvement on campus. Conversely, 60% of the unengaged students believed their values aligned with the community, and 67% reported a sense of belonging that was tied to their connection with their faculty and their academic advisor (Parkinson, 2020). This study reinforces the importance of connecting students with faculty and staff and providing opportunities to engage, and highlights the importance of the role of faculty in fostering a sense of belonging in students who are unengaged.

Using the Sociopsychological Intervention Approach

Small, one time sociopsychological interventions have been shown to have lasting effects on students. Yeager and Walton (2011) found that that even brief exercises that target students' thoughts, feelings, and beliefs in and about school can lead to large gains in student achievement and sharply reduce achievement gaps months or years later. For example, a 60-minute session designed to promote African American college students' sense of belonging in school increased the GPA of these students over the next 3 years (Yeager & Walton, 2011). These interventions "allow students to take better advantage of learning opportunities that are present in schools and tap into existing recursive processes to generate long-lasting effects" (p. 293). Internal barriers, such as stereotype threat, a feeling of a lack of belonging, or a fixed mind-set, may prevent students from knowing that skills can be developed and circumstances changed may prevent students from succeeding. Reducing or eliminating these barriers may make students more likely to continue to try despite setbacks in and out of the classroom and to reinforce feelings of belonging by building better relationships with people (Yeager & Walton, 2011).

Fitchburg State University Initiatives

This section details examples of Fitchburg State University initiatives that include an element(s) of belonging.

Orientation

In 2016, a team of staff from student affairs and academic affairs led the rede-velopment of Fitchburg State's summer and fall orientation programs. The goal of this initiative was to create a balanced program focusing on curricular, cocurricular, and personal transition to Fitchburg State, as well as increased sense of belonging and, ultimately, retention.

Several new programs were included in the revised summer and fall orientation programs: The Academic Transitions program was designed and delivered by faculty members; centered on a growth mindset, as pre-viously described; and specifically focused on academic work and making connections with faculty. Decoding College was designed to help students navigate their early days at Fitchburg State by introducing terminology, tips, and information that help all students succeed and by normalizing the many feelings new students may be experiencing. Decoding College explores many of the Fitchburg State–specific acronyms whose meaning may not be obvious to newcomers, using them in case studies with students learning how to engage with faculty, access service, identify engagement opportunities, and solve problems they may encounter. Decoding College also leverages orientation leaders sharing their own experiences with their transition to college while they explore the terminology and case studies, as well as videos featuring employees talking about their experiences as college students. The goal is to help students understand that the range of emotions and experiences they are going through is normal and that everyone who is successful goes through similar experiences and finds their way. Messaging during the orientation sessions centers on struggles, successes, and journeys related to academic planning, wellness and health, events and programs, engagement opportunities, resources, and support.

Each of these short-term interventions were designed to promote a growth mindset, reduce both internal and external barriers that students might experience, and promote a sense of belonging. In the evaluation of summer orientation 2017, prior to implementing Decoding College, 94% of students indicated they felt better prepared for their transition to college. In the summer 2018 evaluation, after we implemented these programs, 97% of students indicated they felt better prepared for the transition. In the evaluation of fall orientation 2017, 81.7% of students agreed or strongly agreed that they understood the importance of belonging and planned to engage in their educational experience. In the fall 2018 evaluation, 90.6% of students reported understanding the importance of belonging and engaging in their educational experience.

Teaching students that they can influence their circumstances; are able to navigate Fitchburg State to access offices, opportunities, and processes; and that they fit at Fitchburg promotes a sense of belonging and is designed to help students find Fitchburg State to be a place where they can thrive.

Latinx Male Mentoring Program

By far, the largest opportunity gap in terms of retention rates at Fitchburg State University is with Latinx males. A 5-year average retention rate from 2012–2016 for all students was 76.9%. For all males it was 74.2%; for all non-White males it was 70.5%; for African American males it was 79.8%; and for Latinx males it was 66.7%. In the fall of 2018, a mentoring program was implemented to increase the retention of first-time, full-time male Latinx students from fall to spring in the 2018–2019 academic year. In the first year of the program, faculty members and peer mentors were assigned to incoming male Latinx students in order to provide guidance and support to this population. Following a prescribed timeline of meetings and proactive outreach focusing on what students would be experiencing at a given point in the semester, faculty members and peer mentors assisted students with navigating the college experience, fostering a sense of belonging with Fitchburg State, and connecting them with appropriate support staff as needed. And the first year was a failure.

Although the research on sociopsychological interventions strongly influenced the development of the program, our approach was too overt. The program was promoted as extra support for Latinx males, which reinforced the stereotype threat of not belonging in the college environment that many students were experiencing, and the effort backfired. The first year of the program corresponded with the worst Latinx male retention rate in years (64% from fall 2018 to spring 2019; 44% from fall 2018 to fall 2019).

In the 2019–2020 academic year, another approach was taken. Rather than framing it for students as the Latinx Male Mentoring Project, the faculty mentors described themselves as "secondary academic advisors." Several populations of students at Fitchburg State have secondary academic advisors, for example TRIO Student Support Services and Athletics, so this approach is seated firmly in the culture of the university. Peers held an even more prominent role in fostering a sense of belonging with Fitchburg State, connecting with students, and guiding them in fostering a growth mindset in and out of the classroom classroom. The 2019–2020 fall to spring retention rate rose to 83% and fall to fall at 58%. An additional tool was added in 2020–2021: These students were put into a specific first-year experience course in addition to working with the "secondary academic advisors." The fall to spring retention rate was 76%, and as of this writing we are still in that spring semester. (Note that this timeframe was affected by COVID-19. Many Fitchburg State students have been less interested in the online learning environment, are experiencing stress in their lives, and are stopping out.)

Fitchburg State Into the Future

Starting in 2021, Fitchburg State is embarking on a new strategic plan that centers on being a student-ready campus (Brown McNair et al., 2016). Our overarching goal is to infuse these concepts throughout our culture in ways both formal and informal. We will continue to develop strategic sociopsychological interventions while educating faculty and staff on how each has an impact on building a sense of belonging. Ultimately, this is the foundation for student success on our campus and others.

References

Brown McNair, T., Albertine, S., Cooper, M. A., McDonald, N., & Major, T., Jr. (2016). *Becoming a student-ready college: A new culture of leadership for student success.* Jossey-Bass.

Dweck, C. (2016). *Mindset: The new psychology of success.* Ballantine.

Milem, J. F., & Berger, J. B. (1997). A modified model of college student persistence: Exploring the relationship between Astin's theory of involvement and Tinto's theory of student departure. *Journal of College Student Development, 38*(4), 387–400. https://scholarworks.umass.edu/cie_faculty_pubs/11/

Parkinson, H. (2020). *Results of the belonging pilot study* [Unpublished manuscript].

Strayhorn, T. L. (2012). *College students' sense of belonging: A key to educational success for all students.* Routledge.

Whitley, S. E., Benson, G., & Wesaw, A. (2018). *First-generation student success: A landscape analysis of programs and services at four-year institutions.* Center for First-Generation Student Success, NASPA–Student Affairs Administrators in Higher Education, & Entangled Solutions. https://www.luminafoundation.org/wp-content/uploads/2019/03/first-gen-student-success.pdf

Yeager, D. S., & Walton, G. M. (2011). Social-psychological interventions in education: They're not magic. *Review of Educational Research, 81*(2), 267–301. https://doi.org/10.3102/0034654311405999

GEMSTONE HONORS PROGRAM

A Living-Learning Community

Jessica Lee, Kristan Cilente Skendall, and Leah Kreimer Tobin

The Gemstone honors program is a living–learning community (LLC), characterized by undergraduate students in a shared academic experience living together in a residence hall in partnership with academic and student affairs, situated in the honors college at the University of Maryland, College Park (UMD) (Inkelas et al., 2018; Inkelas & Soldner, 2011). Started in 1995, Gemstone is one of the only 4-year, team-based, undergraduate research programs in the United States and enrolls about 500 students annually across four cohorts. Grounded in a sequential curriculum, students form teams at the end of their first year and work on those teams through their eighth semester alongside a faculty mentor throughout their entire team research process. Teams are interdisciplinary and focus on a variety of topics, such as transportation innovations, novel cancer treatments, and addressing societal inequities. All teams write and defend a thesis at the conclusion of their research, and many have published papers in professional journals and presented at national and international conferences, and one has even pursued a patent because of their Gemstone team research. Bowers et al. (2020) and Coale et al. (2016) provided additional background on the program as well as more detailed information on the admissions process and curriculum.

The integration of self-directed team research, high levels of faculty–student interaction, and a living-learning environment situated in the honors college provides a unique opportunity for students to apply what they are learning through their collegiate experience to address complex societal problems. The Gemstone honors program is an example of an emergent pedagogical style adopted by honors programs, as noted by Scott and Frana (2008) in their predictive analysis of what honors education might look like by 2025. The Gemstone sequential curriculum is project based and guides students from basic research skills through the team formation and research process by intentionally incorporating collaborative learning, group assignments, journals, discussion, and technology to promote team-work and leadership. Initial courses are offered in lecture and discussion formats, although once students begin their research process the courses are focused on their research experience and vary from team to team. Under the mentorship of UMD's best faculty from across campus, our research teams are addressing complex and ever-evolving societal challenges through innovations related to medical devices and treatments, public health edu-cation, innovative transportation, mental health diagnostic mechanisms, nano materials, and more. These curricular experiences are reinforced through additional leadership opportunities within the program, includ-ing the Gemstone Leadership Council (GLC), the Alumni Mentor Partner program (AMPP), the CONNECT peer mentoring program, teaching assistant opportunities, and coordination and implementation of Gems camp, a 2-night orientation program exclusively for Gemstone students. While each of these experiences on their own is focused on community building, the cohesiveness of Gemstone provides students with a height-ened sense of belonging, defined by Hagerty et al. (1992) "as the experience of personal involvement in a system or environment so that persons feel themselves to be an integral part of that system or environment" (p. 173). Specifically, the Gemstone honors program serves as a practical application of Schlossberg's (1989) framework for marginality and mattering, meaning to feel a sense of belonging. Marginality is described as the "feelings of being peripheral to a group," while mattering is described as "feelings of one's own significance to others, either individually or collectively" (Sriram et al., 2020, p. 1). According to Schlossberg (1989), first-year college students often experience feelings of marginality as they try to fit in academically or socially to the new campus environment. However, Gemstone's context as a living-learning community allows first-year students to transition from feelings of marginality to those of mattering.

Belonging in Gemstone Through Pedagogy and Community

Laufgraben and Tompkins (2004) explained the notion of pedagogy that builds community through shared responsibility for learning, placing an emphasis on learning from one another in the context of careful and intentional thought. Pedagogy that builds community reframes learning as a process, not solely an outcome, a notion that deeply aligns with the mission of the Gemstone honors program and is embedded throughout the course of the 4-year curriculum.

This concept builds on the work of Lave and Wenger (1991), who explained situated learning and communities of practice whereby individuals acquire knowledge through social participation. Essentially, learning is a process of social and personal transformation within the context of communities of practice (Lave & Wenger, 1991). Communities of practice are defined by a process of social learning in which people have a shared domain of interest and collaborate over common ideas or topics to seek solutions and innovate together (Lave & Wenger, 1991). High-impact practices such as team-based undergraduate research undoubtedly can be classified as communities of practice, and as such present a unique experience in which learning takes place in a social and academic context. Living–learning programs are a unique community of practice, and the Gemstone honors program reinforces the conditions of mattering to enhance belonging by exploring intentional ways in which Gemstone enacts this approach and ultimately cultivates what Schlossberg (1989) discussed as belonging within and among our LLC: teamwork, mentorship, and leadership.

Teamwork

The core of the Gemstone experience is collaborative, interdisciplinary, team-based research. Working on the same research team of 10–12 students for just over 3 years allows students to navigate the complexities of interpersonal relationships over a significant period. Team members are responsible for holding one another accountable for their shared goals and navigating conflict as they work on their research endeavor. This team experience reinforces students' sense of belonging as they recognize that each team member is an integral and important part of their collective team research goals. In the team context, this level of dependency can help reaffirm to students that they matter because the team "needs them" (Schlossberg, 1989).

Mentorship

Mentorship is at the core of the Gemstone honors program experience. Students are assigned an upper-class CONNECT (peer) mentor the summer before their first year begins. The CONNECT mentor engages students throughout the first year, offering intentional, personal mentorship as students transition to the program and campus. Beginning with the required first-year course, GEMS 100, and throughout each subsequent

Gemstone course, students are guided by upper-class teaching assistants (TAs) who facilitate discussions, provide feedback, and engage students in every aspect of the research team formation process. Beyond intentional student mentorship experiences, the Gemstone honors program facilitates engagement and mentorship by faculty as each team is paired with a faculty mentor for 3 years. Faculty mentors are compensated with a teaching overload for the duration of their commitment. These formal and informal mentoring experiences cultivate belonging from the very earliest moments of the living–learning experience. Complementing the faculty mentorship, the Gemstone honors program further cultivates belonging through mentorship by program staff through office hours, individual advising, and supportive, caring, and nurturing relationships as part of their job duties. This type of positive affirmation and appreciation from others helps further diminish feelings of marginality that students may experience (Schlossberg, 1989).

Leadership

Whether serving in formal leadership roles on their research teams, pursuing a TA position, becoming a member of GLC, or guiding first-year students as a CONNECT mentor or Gems camp leader, there is no shortage of opportunities to seek formal leadership roles within the Gemstone honors program. Just as learning is a process, so is leadership. These leadership opportunities allow Gemstone students to focus on a common purpose to create community for students in the program, outside of their academic and team research experiences. Through student-driven social events to equity-centered dialogues, the diverse range of leadership opportunities create spaces for students to not only engage with each other, but also self-reflect on their own leadership experiences. These "rituals" within the Gemstone experience—through the events and experiences described, and through hallmark programs, such as Gems camp, a citation ceremony, or a thesis conference—serve as checkpoints for students throughout their 4-year experience in the LLC. These rituals can help mitigate the feelings of marginality and create spaces for mattering (Schlossberg, 1989).

The combination of experiences and focus on self-directed team research allows Gemstone students to understand, apply, and integrate their learning in practical and tangible ways. The scaffolding of the curriculum translates to the connectedness that students experience in the Gemstone honors program through the focus on collaboration and teamwork in and out of the classroom. Gabelnick et al. (1990) highlighted this connectedness as core to the learning community experience, stating, "In learning communities, students and faculty members experience courses and disciplines not as arbitrary or isolated offerings but rather as a complementary and connected whole" (p. 19). The intentionality of the Gemstone honors program approach cannot be overstated. Built on the foundation of a learning community, Gemstone can help students cultivate belonging in carefully crafted ways by creating spaces that help them feel like they matter. Furthermore, Gemstone is an example of how LLCs can enhance the student experience through pedagogical design with teamwork, mentorship, and leadership.

Implications for Practice

Universities, particularly large institutions, are often loosely coupled systems embodied by bureaucracy and decentralization (Weick, 1976). While loosely coupled systems can be more adaptable and allow for innovation, they can also be confusing for students to navigate as they often lack clear mechanisms for support, which ultimately hinders sense of belonging. A significant implication is that LLCs can serve as a hub for students, which ultimately cultivates belonging and a sense of connectedness. In Gemstone's LLC model, the components of teamwork, mentorship, and leadership help foster this connectedness to the larger institution by creating a community home base that simulates a small campus experience. At larger institutions and commuter campuses, creating community can be difficult; however, learning communities "create a unique environment of social and intellectual belonging that is important at any college" (Gabelnick et al., 1990, p. 64). By collaborating with units across campus, such as student affairs departments, academic colleges, student services, and more, practitioners can help provide resources to students through their connections in their LLC. For example, Gemstone's relationships with academic college deans' offices allow for open communication and support for students who may be struggling academically. Similarly, relationships with colleagues in residence life allow for support for students who might be facing social or emotional challenges. These collaborations allow for Gemstone and other LLCs to be a thread for the student experience by mitigating some of the common challenges that students face when navigating large, often decentralized campuses, such as health and wellness concerns, academic probation, and more. As Inkelas (2008) explained, in many ways, Gemstone exemplifies much of what higher education strives to do by creating smaller and more "intimate communities of membership: at their most optimal they unite curricular, co-curricular, residential, and informal peer networks to augment student learning and development" (p. 9). Finally, while Gemstone was not directly based on Schlossberg's (1989) work, practitioners should consider how theories, especially theories of belonging, can be used to create or improve LLCs.

Conclusion

The Gemstone honors program serves as just one of many different LLCs among college campuses. Although Gemstone is unique in nature as a 4-year, team-based, undergraduate research program, all LLCs can utilize intentional pedagogies that build community in the context of mentorship, leadership, and teamwork to cultivate an increased sense of belonging. These components also serve as a reminder for practitioners of the added benefits of LLCs (Bowers et al., 2020). As students continue to navigate their college experiences, LLCs such as Gemstone continue to create spaces for students to feel not only connected to their program, but also the campus community—they help students feel like they matter.

References

Bowers, M. E., Tobin, L. K., Lee, J., Skendall, K. C., & Coale, F. J. (2020). Increasing campus sense of belonging through LLC participation: To Gems camp we go. *Learning Communities Research and Practice, 8*(1). https://files.eric.ed.gov/fulltext/EJ1251797.pdf

Coale, F. J., Skendall, K., Tobin, L. K., & Hill, V. (2016). The Gemstone honors program: Maximizing learning through team-based interdisciplinary research. In M. Peterson & Y. Rubinstein (Eds.), *Directions for mathematics research experiences for undergraduates* (pp. 167–180). World Scientific. https://doi.org/10.1142/9789814630320_0009

Gabelnick, F., MacGregor, J., Matthews, R. S., & Smith, B. L. (1990). Preface. In F. Gabelnick, J. MacGregor, R. S. Matthews, & B. L. Smith (Eds.), *Learning Communities: Creating Connections Among Students, Faculty, and Disciplines* (New Directions for Teaching and Learning, no. 41, pp. 1–4). Jossey-Bass. https://doi.org/10.1002/tl.37219904102

Hagerty, B. M. K., Lynch-Sauer, J., Patusky, K., Bouwsema, M., & Collier, P. (1992). Sense of belonging: A vital mental health concept. *Archives of Psychiatric Nursing, 6*, 172–177. https://doi.org/10.1016/0883-9417(92)90028-H

Inkelas, K. K. (2008). Innovative directions for living-learning program research and practice: Introduction [Special issue]. *Journal of College and University Student Housing, 35*(1), 8–13.

Inkelas, K. K., Jessup-Anger, J. E., Benjamin, M., & Wawrzynski, M. R. (2018). *Living-learning communities that work: A research-based model for design, delivery, assessment.* Stylus.

Inkelas, K. K., & Soldner, M. (2011). Undergraduate living–learning programs and student outcomes. In J. Smart & M. Paulsen (Eds.), *Higher education: Handbook of theory and research* (Vol. 26, pp. 167–180). Springer. https://doi.org/10.1007/978-94-007-0702-3_1

Laufgraben, J. L., & Tompkins, D. (2004). Pedagogy that builds community. In J. L. Laufgraben & N. S. Shapiro (Eds.), *Sustaining and improving learning communities* (pp. 54–75). Wiley.

Lave, J., & Wenger, E. (1991). *Situated learning: Legitimate peripheral participation.* Cambridge University Press.

Schlossberg, N. K. (1989). Marginality and mattering: Key issues in building community. In D. C. Roberts (Ed.), *Designing Campus Activities to Foster a Sense of Community* (New Directions for Student Services, no. 38, pp. 5–15). Jossey-Bass.

Scott, R. I., & Frana, P. (2008). Honors 2025: The future of the honors college. *Honors in Practice, 4.* http://digitalcommons.unl.edu/nchchip/67/

Sriram, R., Haynes, C., Weintraub, S. D., Cheatle, J., Marquart, C. P., Murray, J. L. (2020). Student demographics and experiences of deeper life interactions within residential learning communities. *Learning Communities Research and Practice, 8*(1), 1–17.

Weick, K. E. (1976). Educational organizations as loosely coupled systems. *Administrative Science Quarterly, 21*(1), 1–19. https://doi.org/10.2307/2391875

THE INFLUENCE OF THE TEACHING MODALITY ON BELONGING

Tawnya Means, Jean E. Starobin, and Kasey Uran-Linde

In fall 2018, 35% of students attending a degree-granting postsecondary institution enrolled in at least one online course (National Center for Education Statistics [NCES], 2019). The COVID-19 pandemic spurred an even greater shift to online learning and left institutions of higher education reimagining the future of online education (Jones & Sharma, 2020). As students continue to utilize online learning, it is imperative that higher education professionals understand how nontraditional learning environments intersect with a student's sense of belonging.

Learner experience in relation to delivery mode (e.g., online, blended or hybrid, in-person, etc.) increasingly requires adaptations to be effectively implemented and has been particularly affected by COVID-19 (e.g., Mulrooney & Kelly, 2020). As many higher education institutions in the world have been influenced by the move to remote learning (courses that had been traditionally held face-to-face but temporarily adjusted to online and mixed-mode delivery), there is a strong incentive for institutions to pay attention to the impact of modality on belonging. At the course level, instructors have opportunities to influence students' feelings of belonging through the design of the course, activities within the course structure, and communication with students (Booker, 2008). The delivery modality of the course can shape these practices in significant ways. The pandemic has exacerbated the consequences of a lack of belonging as students are more isolated and many students are not in the learning environment that they initially chose to enter (Arslan, 2020; Tümen Akyıldız, 2020). Students are also likely to pick up on even small cues (e.g., a sense that they do not know anyone in a particular course or field of study) that lead them to believe that they do not belong (Walton & Cohen, 2007), but addressing these cues early may have long-lasting impacts such as encouraging students to persist (Walton & Brady, 2017).

Sense of belonging plays a pivotal role in student success as researchers continue to affirm that when students lack connectedness and personal value within a group (Rosenberg & McCullough, 1981) they often experience lower academic performance (Walton & Brady, 2017; Walton & Cohen, 2007) and greater attrition (Jacoby & Garland, 2004) than their peers. This is especially true for underrepresented student populations (Hurtado & Carter, 1997; Johnson et al., 2007; O'Keeffe, 2013; Strayhorn, 2019).

Background

Through the development of new and revised delivery modalities and the recent transformation of higher education due to the global pandemic, it is valuable to consider and implement pedagogical evidence-based practices. Several theories outline approaches that practitioners can apply in an effort to increase a sense of belonging among students, regardless of the learning environment.

The theory of cooperative learning (CL) is a form of peer learning that focuses on structuring "positive interdependence" (Slavin, 1990, p. 52) to accomplish shared goals using clearly defined roles and responsibilities, individual accountability, and high levels of engagement and participation. In addition to academic achievement, CL has shown to improve intergroup relations when groups exhibit racial or ethnic diversity (Johnson et al., 1983; Slavin, 1985). CL also can positively improve students' self-efficacy, ability to work cooperatively, and attitude toward school (Slavin, 1991). Collaborative learning can be implemented in a variety of delivery modalities to influence student belongingness.

Tinto (1975, 2017) highlighted how academic and social integration, or student integration, influences a student's decision to persist or drop out. Specifically, in online learning environments, academic and social integration plays a vital role in students' academic success (Tinto, 1998). Student integration includes factors such as intellectual development, formal and informal engagement with instructors and peers, and involvement with extracurricular activities. Forming meaningful relationships, in both academic and social environments, increases students' sense of mattering, academic achievement, and persistence (Davidson & Wilson, 2013).

Rovai (2003) proposed a model specifically addressing nontraditional online learners that incorporates aspects of the student integration and student–institution "fit" (Bean & Metzner, 1985) models. Rovai's (2003) model promotes the incorporation of orientation programs to promote meaningful relationships, opportunities for engagement, and awareness of available support services; early intervention efforts to combat potential deficiencies in academic preparedness; and the use of sound instructional design and pedagogy. Additionally, nonschool factors were found to influence student persistence such as family and peer support, course relevance, and learner satisfaction (Park & Choi, 2009; Rovai, 2003).

It is possible to increase a sense of belonging in remote, online, and mixed-modality learning through sound pedagogical practices. Consistent sharing of information, through discussion boards and other computer-mediated communication, has been found to increase a sense of community and belongingness (Rovai, 2001; Thomas et al., 2014). Team-building activities and frequent group interactions promote a strong sense of community within online courses (Geerling et al., 2020; Rovai, 2002), as does incorporating educational technologies that encourage engagement with peers and course materials (Chen et al., 2018). Increasing presence is also shown to impact newly remote, online, and mixed-modality learning students' sense of belonging (Mulrooney & Kelly, 2020) A seemingly simple act such as addressing a student by name in assignment feedback, reminders, or an announcement shows that student that they are noticed in the online environment and could have a lasting impact (Walton & Brady, 2017).

Application

Evidence-based strategies rooted in sound theories can be applied in individual courses across a range of delivery modalities to positively affect sense of belonging. Collaborative activities are one mechanism that can help students feel a sense of belonging while not increasing instructor workload. In a business capstone course taught by one of the coauthors, students participated in a computerized simulation that used an algorithm that generated unique experiences, which required multiple rounds of decisions. Students had course materials, resources, and instructions regarding the elements necessary for success in the simulation and could complete the simulation all on their own. To build a sense of community and belonging, students were encouraged to collaborate with a peer online to reflect on performance, analyze decisions, and determine improvements for a specific round. Students who completed the collaborative activity reported that even though they had unique decisions to make, they could share their simulation screens and review decisions and online reports, and they recognized opportunities in the simulation that they had not previously noted. These students were able to gain new perspectives, realize that others struggled in similar ways, and identify errors to correct moving forward. They also expressed feelings of relief, appreciation for the peer, and a sense of accomplishment as they overcame challenges. These students reported that they felt a stronger connection to the lessons learned by other students through the experience and tended to perform better overall in the simulation.

Online, remote, and mixed-mode learning relies on instructional technologies, such as learning management systems (LMS), to act as the conduit for information sharing, and if they are used well, they can help students feel connected (Shea et al., 2005). Chickering and Ehrmann (1996) highlighted practices for integrating technology in the classroom: (a) employing the features and analytics provided by the LMS to monitor and manage student activity; (b) streamlining information and communication to a single platform (email, LMS chat, announcements, etc.) to give students a consistent and organized location to find pertinent information; and (c) creating a place for students to share about themselves and develop a sense of community (Dolan et al., 2017). Similarly, a consistent design of the LMS course pages can positively influence students' engagement with a course (Sahni, 2019). Whether through the use of modules, pages, or other LMS organizational tools, an organized course that employs a consistent structure week to week provides students with clarity regarding course expectations, available resources, and assessments (Rubin et al., 2010; Shea et al., 2005). Rovai (2003) explained the application of the integration model to nontraditional distance education students. The most important internal factors affecting students' decision to retain after being admitted was "consistency and clarity of online programs, policies, and procedures" (p. 10). This need can be met through the effective use of an LMS.

Personalized and timely communication can influence whether a student feels as though they belong (Martin et al., 2018). By their very nature and regardless of delivery modality, large enrollment courses can make it difficult to effectively communicate with students due to the amount of time it would take to provide personalized feedback in a timely manner. Even if an instructor is able to give detailed feedback on graded assignments, that leaves little time to focus on proactive retention and integration strategies. Incorporating data and tools from the LMS can assist in overcoming many of these hurdles. It is standard for an LMS to allow instructors to send a personalized message to a subgroup of students based on performance criteria without the instructor needing to send a message to each student. For example, instructors could congratulate students who earned a high grade on an exam or extend an invitation to meet during office hours with students who did not score as well. Instructors can utilize the calendar, task list, and appointment scheduling tools that serve as a timely reminder to promote engagement opportunities (e.g., office hours, tutoring, study groups). Additionally, LMS analytics provide valuable data regarding students' time spent in the LMS, participation in discussion boards, and submission status on upcoming assignments.

Students who log in to the course site before the semester begins and students who log in to the LMS at least 5 days within the first 2 weeks are more likely to complete the course (Fain, 2016). The integration of high-touch strategies that include student engagement, personalized communications, and community building have been shown to increase course retention in large online courses (Gay & Betts, 2020). Since students are more likely to persist online if they feel that they matter, that they belong, and that someone cares if they are not there, it is crucial that the learning environment be designed around a sense of belonging (Rovai, 2003). Following up with students if they are not logging in, or if they miss a synchronous session, can help students feel that they are noticed and that they matter.

Instructors can use a variety of tools, technologies, and techniques to help students feel that they belong and can contribute to the course discussions and interactions. Some potential examples could be calling students by name in live sessions, using breakout rooms to encourage smaller discussions, encouraging students to feel comfortable turning on cameras, recognizing student contributions in the discussion board, or highlighting students for exemplary work; these practices can help students feel a sense of belonging even in remote, online, and mixed-delivery learning environments.

Another means to increase a sense of belonging is to build a community for students. Rovai (2002) described the essential elements of a community as "spirit, trust, interactivity, and common expectations and goals" (p. 4). To address the community needs for online students, many institutions have employed virtual communities as a means to intentionally provide space and build a sense of community. Demonstrating that students matter to an institution is one factor that has been shown to impact online students' sense of belonging (Perez, 2020). Another contributing component is providing the means and opportunities for connections to the institution, faculty, staff, and student peers (Perez, 2020). Communities can be built at the individual program level as well as the institutional level. Intended outcomes span from overarching themes of building community, increasing a sense of belonging, providing a platform for social and academic engagement, and improving student success and retention (Angelino et al., 2007; Means et al., 2017; Rovai, 2001; Thomas et al., 2014). Virtual communities can include tactical outcomes such as a connection to needed resources, seamless communications, a place to ask questions, and a consistent space that acts as a repository for necessary forms and documents. The community acts as the virtual campus space for students by specifically addressing the needs of the online student and providing the services and resources in the modality that matches their learning environment (Angelino et al., 2007).

Conclusion

While many of the key components of belonging are similar between on-premise and remote, online, and mixed-mode students, the delivery modality in which students are learning and connecting with institutions must be considered. Delivery modality requires more intentional and thoughtful accommodations in order to provide students high-quality interactions; develop relationships with the institution, instructors, and peers; and receive support that is vital to their academic success.

There is a wealth of additional research and information that further explores this topic. This chapter touches on a few key areas and applications. As online learning has increased during the COVID-19 pandemic, future research and insight on the impact of sense of belonging will be very timely.

References

Angelino, L. M., Williams, F. K., & Natvig, D. (2007). Strategies to engage online students and reduce attrition rates. *Journal of Educators Online, 4*(2), 1–14. http://dx.doi.org/10.9743/JEO.2007.2.1

Arslan, G. (2020). Loneliness, college belongingness, subjective vitality, and psychological adjustment during coronavirus pandemic: Development of the college belongingness. *Journal of Positive School Psychology*, 1–15. https://doi.org/10.31234/osf.io/j7tf2

Bean, J. P., & Metzner, B. S. (1985). A conceptual model of nontraditional undergraduate student attrition. *Review of Educational Research, 55*(4), 485–540. https://doi.org/10.3102/00346543055004485

Booker, K. C. (2008). The role of instructors and peers in establishing classroom community. *Journal of Instructional Psychology, 35*(1), 12–16. https://go.gale.com/ps/i.do?p=AONE&u=googlescholar&id=GALE|A178218782&v=2.1&it=r&sid=AONE&asid=b8e3b329

Chen, J., Wang, M., Kirschner, P. A., & Tsai, C. (2018). The role of collaboration, computer use, learning environments, and supporting strategies in CSCL: A meta-analysis. *Review of Educational Research, 88*(6), 799–843. https://doi.org/10.3102/0034654318791584

Chickering, A., & Ehrmann, S. C. (1996). Implementing the seven principles: Technology as a lever. *AAHE Bulletin*, *49*(2), 3–7. https://sphweb.bumc.bu.edu/otlt/teachingLibrary/Technology/seven_principles.pdf

Davidson, C., & Wilson, K. (2013). Reassessing Tinto's concepts of social and academic integration in student retention. *Journal of College Student Retention: Research, Theory & Practice*, *15*(3), 329–346. https://doi.org/10.2190/cs.15.3.b

Dolan, J., Kain, K., Reilly, J., & Bansal, G. (2017). How do you build community and foster engagement in online courses? In R. A. R. Gurung & D. J. Voelker (Eds.), *Big Picture Pedagogy: Finding Interdisciplinary Solutions to Common Learning Problems* (New Directions for Teaching and Learning, *2017*(151), 45–60). https://doi.org/10.1002/tl.20248

Fain, P. (2016, June 13). Data on student engagement with an LMS is a key to predicting retention. *Inside Higher Ed*. https://www.insidehighered.com/news/2016/06/13/data-student-engagement-lms-key-predicting-retention

Gay, G. H. E., & Betts, K. (2020). From discussion forums to eMeetings: Integrating high touch strategies to increase student engagement, academic performance, and retention in large online courses. *Online Learning*, *24*(1), 92–117. https://doi.org/10.24059/olj.v24i1.1984

Geerling, W., Thomas, N., & Wooten, J. (2020, September 17). Facilitating student connections and study partners during periods of remote and online learning. *SSRN Electronic Journal*. https://doi.org/10.2139/ssrn.3692086

Hurtado, S., & Carter, D. F. (1997). Effects of college transition and perceptions of the campus racial climate on Latino college students' sense of belonging. *Sociology of Education*, *70*(4), 324–345. https://doi.org/10.2307/2673270

Jacoby, B., & Garland, J. (2004). Strategies for enhancing commuter student success. *Journal of College Student Retention: Research, Theory and Practice*, *6*(1), 61–79. http://dx.doi.org/10.2190/567C-5TME-Q8F4-8FRG

Johnson, D. R., Soldner, M., Leonard, J. B., Alvarez, P., Inkelas, K. K., Rowan-Kenyon, H. T., & Longerbeam, S. D. (2007). Examining sense of belonging among first-year undergraduates from different racial/ethnic groups. *Journal of College Student Development*, *48*(5), 525–542. https://doi.org/10.1353/csd.2007.0054

Johnson, D. W., Johnson, R. T., & Maruyama, G. (1983). Interdependence and interpersonal attraction among heterogeneous and homogeneous individuals: A theoretical formulation and a meta-analysis of the research. *Review of Educational Research*, *53*(1), 5–54. https://doi.org/10.3102/00346543053001005

Jones, K., & Sharma, R. S. (2020, January). On reimagining a future for online learning in the post-COVID era. *SSRN Electronic Journal*. https://papers.ssrn.com/sol3/papers.cfm?abstract_id=3578310

Martin, J., Wang, C., & Sadaf, A. (2018). Student perception of helpfulness of facilitation strategies that enhance instructor presence, connectedness, engagement and learning in online courses. *The Internet and Higher Education*, *37*(2018), 52–65. http://dx.doi.org/10.1016/j.iheduc.2018.01.003

Means, T., Phalin, A., & Starobin, J. (2017, October). Building a culture of community in online education settings: Challenges and opportunities. In J. Dron & S. Mishra (Eds.), *Proceedings of E-Learn: World conference on e-learning in corporate, government, healthcare, and higher education* (pp. 203–206). Association for the Advancement of Computing in Education. https://www.learntechlib .org/primary/p/181187/

Mulrooney, H. M., & Kelly, A. F. (2020). Covid 19 and the move to online teaching: Impact on perceptions of belonging in staff and students in a UK widening participation university. *Journal of Applied Learning and Teaching, 3*(2). https:// doi.org/10.37074/jalt.2020.3.2.15

National Center for Education Statistics. (2019, December). *Table 311.15. Number and percentage of students enrolled in degree-granting postsecondary institutions, by distance education participation, location of student, level of enrollment, and control and level of institution: Fall 2017 and fall 2019.* Digest of Education Statistics. https://nces.ed.gov/programs/digest/d19/tables/dt19_311.15.asp

O'Keeffe, P. (2013). A sense of belonging: Improving student retention. *College Student Journal, 47*(1), 605–613.

Park, J.-H., & Choi, H. J. (2009). Factors influencing adult learners' decision to drop out or persist in online learning. *Educational Technology & Society, 12*(4), 207–217.

Perez, M. L. (2020). *Sense of belonging from a distance: How online students describe, perceive, and experience belonging to the institution* (Publication No. 2426216799) [Doctoral dissertation, Portland State University]. ProQuest.

Rosenberg, M., & McCullough, B. C. (1981). Mattering: Inferred significance and mental health among adolescents. *Research in Community & Mental Health, 2,* 163–182.

Rovai, A. P. (2001). Building classroom community at a distance: A case study. *Educational Technology Research and Development, 49*(4), 33–48. https://doi .org/10.1007/bf02504946

Rovai, A. P. (2002). Building sense of community at a distance. *The International Review of Research in Open and Distributed Learning, 3*(1). https://doi .org/10.19173/irrodl.v3i1.79

Rovai, A. P. (2003). In search of higher persistence rates in distance education online programs. *The Internet and Higher Education, 6*(1), 1–16. https://doi .org/10.1016/s1096-7516(02)00158-6

Rubin, B., Fernandes, R., Avgerinou, M. D., & Moore, J. (2010). The effect of learning management systems on student and faculty outcomes. *Internet and Higher Education, 13*(1–2), 82–83. https://doi.org/10.1016/j.iheduc .2009.10.008

Sahni, J. (2019). Does blended learning enhance student engagement? Evidence from higher education. *Journal of e-Learning and Higher Education, 2019,* 1–14. https://doi.org/10.5171/2019.121518

Shea, P., Sau Li, C., Swan, K., & Pickett, A. (2005). Developing learning community in online asynchronous college courses: The role of teaching presence. *Journal of Asynchronous Learning Networks, 90*(4), 59–82. http://dx.doi.org/10.24059/olj .v9i4.1779

Slavin, R. E. (1985). Cooperative learning: Applying contact theory in desegregated schools. *Journal of Social Issues, 41*(3), 45–62. https://doi.org/10.1111/j.1540-4560.1985 .tb01128.x

Slavin, R. E. (1990). Research on cooperative learning: Consensus and controversy. *Educational Leadership: Journal of the Department of Supervision and Curriculum Development, 47*(4), 52–54. https://eric.ed.gov/?id=EJ400501

Slavin, R. E. (1991). Synthesis of research of cooperative learning. *Educational Leadership, 48*(5), 71–82. https://eric.ed.gov/?id=EJ421354

Strayhorn, T. L. (2019). *College students' sense of belonging a key to educational success for all students.* Routledge.

Thomas, L. K., Herbert, J., & Teras, M. (2014). A sense of belonging to enhance participation, success and retention in online programs. *The International Journal of the First Year in Higher Education, 5*(2), 69–80. https://doi.org/10.5204/intjfyhe.v5i2.233

Tinto, V. (1975). Dropout from higher education: A theoretical synthesis of recent research. *Review of Educational Research, 45*(1), 89–125. https://doi.org/10.3102/00346543045001089

Tinto, V. (1998). Colleges as communities: Taking research on student persistence seriously. *The Review of Higher Education, 21*(2), 167–177. https://eric.ed.gov/?id=EJ557144

Tinto, V. (2017). Through the eyes of students. *Journal of College Student Retention: Research, Theory & Practice, 19*(3), 254–269. https://doi.org/10.1177/1521025115621917

Tümen Akyıldız, S. (2020). College students' views on the pandemic distance education: A focus group discussion. *International Journal of Technology in Education and Science, 4*(4), 322–334. https://doi.org/10.46328/ijtes.v4i4.150

Walton, G. M., & Brady, S. T. (2017). The many questions of belonging. In A. J. Elliot, C. S. Dweck, & D. S. Yeager (Eds.), *Handbook of competence and motivation: Theory and application* (pp. 272–293). Guilford.

Walton, G. M., & Cohen, G. L. (2007). A question of belonging: Race, social fit, and achievement. *Journal of Personality and Social Psychology, 92*(1), 82–96. https://doi.org/10.1037/0022-3514.92.1.82

20

WHEN LIKES AREN'T ENOUGH

The Impact of Belongingness on Mental Health in the Age of Social Media

Timothy J. Bono

A few years ago, *The Washington Post* published an article featuring an adolescent named Katherine who spent nearly all her free time scrolling through social media posts (Contrera, 2016). Describing her iPhone as "the place where all of her friends are always hanging out," (para. 4) the author explained the way Katherine "interacts" with those "friends": She earns Likes from them by commenting on their pictures, and un-likes the photos of anyone who upsets her—the ultimate form of revenge. And those Likes mean something! Any photo with less than 100 Likes Katherine will remove altogether. Why keep a memory of something that was not admired by Instagram followers you've never even met in real life?

But even if a young adult has hundreds (or thousands) of followers—with enough Likes, comments, shares, and retweets to stimulate the reward center of their developing brain all day—does that activity actually translate to belongingness? And what implications does online connection have for well-being? This chapter reviews the implications belongingness has for mental health and the extent to which social media plays a role.

Belongingness and Mental Health

Mental health is multifaceted. It can manifest in one's emotional experience, cognitive abilities, and goal pursuit. This section examines research related to each of these aspects.

Emotional Well-Being

In a landmark paper from 2002, Diener and Seligman investigated the well-being of hundreds of college students and found that, without exception, the happiest 10% all had one thing in common: rich and satisfying social relationships. Such findings are consistent with other research identifying social connection as the single most important predictor of well-being (Berscheid, 2003; Reis & Gable, 2003). Strong relationships with others are associated with optimism, life satisfaction, self-esteem (Schwager et al., 2020), a stronger immune system (Kiecolt-Glaser et al., 1984), and more successful recovery from disease (Goodwin et al., 1987).

On the other hand, individuals who do *not* feel a sense of belonging are more likely to experience anxiety and depression, among other forms of psychological distress that have been rising precipitously in recent years among college students (Hoyle & Crawford, 1994; Twenge, 2017). The worry that comes from the loss of relationships is often accompanied by grief and loneliness (Leary & Downs, 1995), and the angst of social isolation is correlated with depression, jealousy, and low self-esteem (Baumeister & Leary, 1995). College students who experience loneliness during their first year have difficulty adjusting to university life and to implementing healthy coping strategies in response to adversity (Quan et al., 2014). Social isolation impairs learning, memory, and attention (Cacioppo & Hawkley, 2009) and has implications for persistence, retention, and academic success (Kilgo et al., 2016). Loneliness during the college years can also have long-term consequences, playing out in later psychological problems and physical ailments, and increasing depressive symptoms and suicidal ideology (Van Dulmen & Goossens, 2013). Further, lack of belongingness is not merely a psychological experience. Neuroimaging studies have shown that the brain regions that process social exclusion are the same as those involved with the experience of physical pain. From the brain's perspective, it seems, a broken heart has a lot in common with a broken arm—at very least, they activate the same emotional alarm system (Eisenberger et al., 2003).

Cognitive Skills

Belongingness and social interaction also have implications for cognitive performance. Consider a study that assessed working memory and speed of processing capacity in a group of college students. Those who spent time discussing a current event with another student beforehand performed significantly better on the cognitive tasks than those who did a more mundane activity like watching TV. Engaging with others, taking their perspective during a discussion, and maintaining a conversation all require cognitive skills that are strengthened with each turn of the exchange. A sense of belongingness with others therefore invites social discourse, a practice that helps keep us mentally sharp (Ybarra et al., 2008).

Goal Pursuit

In addition to performing well on cognitive tasks, belongingness can also increase *motivation* to pursue the task. One study found that college students became more motivated to prepare for an upcoming exam when they first considered reasons a close friend or family member would want to help them succeed on the task (Lee & Ybarra, 2017). This study illuminates another benefit of belongingness for well-being: Close others in our lives become our cheerleaders when we are faced with challenging situations. Knowing we have others supporting us motivates us to work even harder and to remain steadfast in pursuit of our goals and dreams.

Quality Over Quantity

Given the importance of belongingness for mental health, it would make sense that one way to strengthen student mental health would be to increase the number of social interactions a college student has. Although seemingly a step in the right direction, social contact itself does not guarantee belongingness, nor is it necessarily a safeguard against loneliness (Reis, 1990; Wheeler et al., 1983). As Al Capone once stated, "Be careful who you call your friends. I'd rather have four quarters than 100 pennies." Mr. Capone may have been onto something there. His insight has been reinforced by empirical evidence showing that lonely and nonlonely people do not differ drastically in how much time they spend with others or the number of people with whom they spend time. Instead, the key distinction stems from the *quality* of those interactions (Jones, 1981; Williams & Solano, 1983). Although lonely people may have a large number of "friends," their interactions with them tend to be more casual and lead to less inclusion and acceptance (Spivey, 1990). A study conducted at a university in Turkey found that the students with the greatest psychological well-being were not simply *involved* with cocurricular activities. Critically, such involvement was associated with a sense of *belongingness*—the feeling they are part of a group of individuals whose companionship is consistent, stable, and characterized by mutual concern for each other's well-being (Civitci, 2015). As important as group membership is for well-being, needs for connectedness are not satisfied by simply a large number of acquaintances who provide surface-level interactions and whose availability and friendship are infrequent and unreliable. Instead, substantive contact on a regular basis with close others is a crucial element (Hawkley et al., 2005).

Social Media and Well-Being

Recall the story of Katherine, featured at the beginning of this chapter, whose primary socialization comes in the form of social media apps on her iPhone. Like Katherine, nearly 90% of young adults use social media sites daily, and that proportion has increased sharply in recent years (Twenge, 2017). Most people now spend more time interacting on Facebook and Instagram than they spend interacting with other people in person (Verduyn et al., 2017). Many college students find their use of technology addictive, owed largely to a desire to form social connections, seemingly to improve their well-being (Roberts et al., 2014). Ironically, the rise in social media use has occurred in tandem with the rise in the proportion of young adults suffering from psychological distress (Twenge, 2017). Experimental methods have confirmed that it's not just people already experiencing sadness or anxiety who are more likely to turn to social media; rather, it is time spent with the endless scroll of political rants, vague booking, and funny cat videos that *causes* declines in well-being (Kross et al., 2013).

Fortunately, involvement with social media does have some benefits. Under the correct parameters, social media can increase well-being. What determines whether it is helpful or harmful to one's mental health, however, is not *time* on social networking sites, but instead *how* an individual engages with these platforms.

Active versus Passive Use of Social Media

Users of social media may do so either actively or passively. Each is associated with different psychological outcomes.

Active use involves communicating directly with another user or posting content more broadly for others to see. Such activity is associated with increases to well-being, especially when such communication involves self-disclosure and increases perceptions of support from others (Frison & Eggermont, 2015). Even if an individual was motivated to browse through social media due to fear of missing out (FoMo), such activity can be psychologically favorable if the end result is authentic social connection (Roberts & David, 2020). Active use also presents opportunities for close others to offer guidance, concern, and other forms of support. Even for processing negative events, online responsiveness offers psychological benefits when it prompts an individual to reframe an experience from a broader perspective instead of fixating on smaller details of the event. Re-construal that leads one to reflect on the big picture of what happened and what they have learned from the situation also increases feelings of closure (Lee et al., 2020).

On the other hand, *passive use*—such as viewing others' posts and pictures without contributing anything—is associated with worse overall well-being, including feeling less connected to others (Matook et al., 2015). Some have described this phenomenon as *social snacking*, a "temporary but illusory fulfillment of social needs" (Clark et al., 2018, p. 33). Passive engagement is especially detrimental to the extent it activates social comparison and envy—common consequences of the endless scroll of others' accomplishments and accolades (Krasnova et al., 2015). Feelings of inadequacy that stem from passive engagement are especially pronounced for users whose Facebook "friends" are primarily strangers (Chou & Edge, 2012). Unfortunately, although not surprisingly, passive engagement is significantly more common than active (Verduyn et al., 2017).

In sum, social media *can* be a tool for strengthening belongingness—provided it is used correctly, involving substantive, reciprocal exchanges with others that ultimately lead to authentic connection.

Conclusion

In this chapter scientific literature underscoring the importance of belongingness for mental health and well-being has been reviewed. Although social media has fundamentally changed the ways young adults interact with others and establish belongingness, recent scientific discoveries offer insight into how we can encourage our students to optimize their psychological health. Curbing the mental health crisis is not a matter of eliminating social media. Instead, it is about educating young people about the appropriate ways to use this technology:

- Encourage students to make their primary goal on social media to maintain relationships with people they genuinely care about. They might consider unfollowing individuals whose posts routinely leave them feeling worse, especially if they do not know those individuals.
- Instead of aiming to have as many online contacts as possible, remind students that it is better to prioritize quality over quantity. Focus on a smaller number of friends and followers with whom they can meaningfully engage and increase direct communication with those who offer the potential for authentic connection.
- Encourage students to engage actively instead of passively. Rather than scrolling mindlessly, suggest students offer messages of support and encouragement directly to others, and post content that positions

others to do the same. Remember that social networking sites have the *potential* for relational benefits similar to those afforded in person—so long as self-disclosure yields appropriate responsiveness from caring friends.

- Help students understand that social media should supplement, not supplant, in-person interactions. Nothing can replace the experience of belonging to a group with whom we can share the same physical space, allowing all to seek support during the difficult times and to share joy during the good times.

- In addition to engagement on social media, encourage students to become involved with organizations that align with their interests and values. Help them select one or two they will immerse themselves in fully instead of signing up for every group that catches their eye at the activities fair. Importantly, help them identify opportunities that will afford deep and consistent connection with a small number of individuals instead of occupying every minute of the day hanging out with as many different people as the social calendar will allow.

Prioritizing relationships—both in person and online—can strengthen many facets of well-being. Heeding the recommendations outlined in this chapter may help ensure that we spend less time curating Instagram and Facebook posts and more time cultivating authentic connection and belongingness.

References

Baumeister, R. F., & Leary, M. R. (1995). The need to belong: Desire for interpersonal attachments as a fundamental human motivation. *Psychological Bulletin, 117*(3), 497–529. https://doi.org/10.1037/0033-2909.117.3.497

Berscheid, E. (2003). The human's greatest strength: Other humans. In L. G. Aspinwall & U. M. Staudinger (Eds.), *A psychology of human strengths: Fundamental questions and future directions for a positive psychology* (pp. 37–47). American Psychological Association. https://doi.org/10.1037/10566-003

Cacioppo, J. T., & Hawkley, L. C. (2009). Perceived social isolation and cognition. *Trends in Cognitive Science, 13*(10), 447–454. https://doi.org/10.1016/j.tics.2009.06.005

Chou, H.-T. G., & Edge, N. (2012). "They are happier and having better lives than I am": The impact of using Facebook on perceptions of others' lives. *Cyberpsychology, Behavior, and Social Networking, 15*(2), 117–121. https://doi.org/10.1089/cyber.2011.0324

Civitci, A. (2015). Perceived stress and life satisfaction in college students: Belonging and extracurricular participation as moderators. *Procedia: Social and Behavioral Sciences, 205*(9), 271–281. https://doi.org/10.1016/j.sbspro.2015.09.077

Clark, J. L., Algoe, S. B., & Green, M. C. (2018). Social network sites and well-being: The role of social connection. *Current Directions in Psychological Science*, *27*(1), 32–37. https://doi.org/10.1177/0963721417730833

Contrera, J. (2016, May 25). 13, right now. *The Washington Post*. http://www.washingtonpost.com/sf/style/2016/05/25/13-right-now-this-is-what-its-like-to-grow-up-in-the-age-of-likes-lols-and-longing/

Diener, E., & Seligman, M. E. P. (2002). Very happy people. *Psychological Science*, *13*(1), 81–84. https://doi.org/10.1111/1467-9280.00415

Eisenberger, N. I., Lieberman, M. D., & Williams, K. D. (2003). Does rejection hurt? An FMRI study of social exclusion. *Science*, *302*(5643), 290–292. https://doi.org/10.1126/science.1089134

Frison, E., & Eggermont, S. (2015). Toward an integrated and differential approach to the relationships between loneliness, different types of Facebook use, and adolescents' depressed mood. *Communication Research*, *47*(5), 701–728. https://doi.org/10.1177/0093650215617506

Goodwin, J. S., Hunt, W. C, Key, C. R., & Samet, J. M. (1987). The effect of marital status on stage, treatment, and survival of cancer patients. *Journal of the American Medical Association*, *258*, 3125–3130. https://doi.org/10.1001/jama.1987.03400210067027

Hawkley, L. C., Browne, M. W., & Cacioppo, J. T. (2005). How can I connect with thee?: Let me count the ways. *Psychological Science*, *16*(10), 798–804. https://doi.org/10.1111/j.1467-9280.2005.01617.x

Hoyle, R., & Crawford, A. M. (1994). Use of individual-level data to investigate group phenomena issues and strategies. *Small Group Research*, *25*(4), 464–485. https://doi.org/10.1177/1046496494254003

Jones, W. H. (1981). Loneliness and social contact. *Journal of Social Psychology*, *113*(2), 295–296. https://doi.org/10.1080/00224545.1981.9924386

Kiecolt-Glaser, J. K., Garner, W., Speicher, C., Penn, G. M., Holliday, J., & Glaser, R. (1984). Psychosocial modifiers of immunocompetence in medical students. *Psychosomatic Medicine*, *46*, 7–14. https://doi.org/10.1097/00006842-198401000-00003

Kilgo, C. A., Mollet, A. L., & Pascarella, E. T. (2016). The estimated effects of college student involvement on psychological well-being. *Journal of College Student Development*, *57*(8), 1043–1049. https://doi.org/10.1353/csd.2016.0098

Krasnova, H., Widjaja, T., Buxmann, P., Wenninger, H., & Benbasat, I. (2015). Why following friends can hurt you: An exploratory investigation of the effects of envy on social networking sites among college-age users. *Information Systems Research*, *26*(3), 585–605. https://doi.org/10.1287/isre.2015.0588

Kross, E., Verduyn, P., Demiralp, E., Park, J., Lee, D. S., Lin, N., Shablack, H., Jonides, J., Ybarra, O. (2013). Facebook use predicts declines in subjective well-being in young adults. *PLoS One*, *8*, e69841. https://doi.org/10.1371/journal.pone.0069841

Leary M. R., & Downs D. L. (1995). Interpersonal functions of the self-esteem motive. In M. H. Kernis (Ed.), *Efficacy, agency, and self-esteem* (pp. 123–144). Springer. https://doi.org/10.1007/978-1-4899-1280-0_7

Lee, D. S., Orvell, A., Briskin, J., Shrapnell, T., Gelman, S. A., Ayduk, O., Ybarra, O., & Kross, E. (2020). When chatting about negative experiences helps—and when it hurts: Distinguishing adaptive versus maladaptive social support in computer-mediated communication. *Emotion, 20*(3), 368–375. https://doi .org/10.1037/emo0000555

Lee, D. S., & Ybarra, O. (2017). Cultivating effective social support through abstraction: Reframing social support promotes goal-pursuit. *Personality and Social Psychology Bulletin, 43*(4), 453–464. https://doi.org/10.1177/0146167216688205

Matook, S., Cummings, J., & Bala, H. (2015). Are you feeling lonely? The impact of relationship characteristics and online social network features on loneliness. *Journal of Management Information Systems, 31*(4), 278–310. https://doi.org/ 10.1080/07421222.2014.1001282

Quan, L., Zhen, R., Yao, B., & Zhou, X. (2014). The effects of loneliness and coping style on academic adjustment among college freshmen. *Social Behavior and Personality: An International Journal, 42*(6), 969–978. https://doi .org/10.2224/sbp.2014.42.6.969

Reis, H. T. (1990). The role of intimacy in interpersonal relations. *Journal of Social and Clinical Psychology, 9*, 15–30. https://doi.org/10.1521/jscp.1990.9.1.15

Reis, H. T., & Gable, S. L. (2003). Toward a positive psychology of relationships. In C. L. Keyes & J. Haidt (Eds.), *Flourishing: The positive person and the good life* (pp. 129–159). American Psychological Association. https://doi .org/10.1037/10594-006

Roberts, J. A., & David, M. E. (2020). The social media party: Fear of missing out (FoMO), social media intensity, connection, and well-being, *International Journal of Human–Computer Interaction, 36*(4), 386–392. https://doi.org/10.1080/ 10447318.2019.1646517

Roberts, J. A., Yaya, L. H., & Manolis, C. (2014). The invisible addiction: Cellphone activities and addiction among male and female college students. *Journal of Behavioral Addictions, 3*(4), 254–265. https://doi.org/10.1556/JBA.3.2014.015

Schwager, S., Wick, K., Glaeser, A., Schoenherr, D., Strauss, B., & Berger, U. (2020). Self-esteem as a potential mediator of the association between social integration, mental well-being, and physical well-being. *Psychological Reports, 123*(4), 1160–1175. https://doi.org/10.1177/0033294119849015

Spivey, E. (1990). *Social exclusion as a common factor in social anxiety, loneliness, jealousy, and social depression* [Unpublished master's thesis]. Wake Forest University.

Twenge, J. (2017). *iGen: Why today's super-connected kids are growing up less rebellious, more tolerant, less happy—and completely unprepared for adulthood.* Atria.

Van Dulmen, M. H. M., & Goossens, L. (2013). Editorial: Loneliness trajectories. *Journal of Adolescence, 36*(6), 1247–1250. https://doi.org/10.1016/j .adolescence.2013.08.001

Verduyn, P., Ybarra, O., Résibois, M., Jonides, J., & Kross, E. (2017). Do social network sites enhance or undermine subjective well-being? A critical review. *Social Issues and Policy Review, 11*(1), 274–302. https://doi.org/10.1111/sipr.12033

Wheeler, L., Reis, H. T, & Nezlek, J. (1983). Loneliness, social interaction, and sex roles. *Journal of Personality and Social Psychology, 45*(4), 943–953. https://doi.org/10.1037/0022-3514.45.4.943

Williams, J. G., & Solano, C. H. (1983). The social reality of feeling lonely: Friendship and reciprocation. *Personality and Social Psychology Bulletin, 9*(2), 237–242. https://doi.org/10.1177/0146167283092007

Ybarra, O., Burnstein, E., Winkielman, P., Keller, M. C., Manis, M., Chan, E., & Rodriguez, J. (2008). Mental exercising through simple socializing: Social interaction promotes general cognitive functioning. *Personality and Social Psychology Bulletin, 34*(2), 248–259. https://doi.org/10.1177/0146167207310454

21

SENSE OF BELONGING

Findings During the Time of COVID-19

Sherry Woosley and Dianne Timm

COVID-19's impact on higher education in the United States was swift and dramatic. According to a CNBC article, the University of Washington was the first large system to close on March 7, 2020. Less than 3 weeks later, the total closures exceeded 1,100 U.S. institutions (Hess, 2020). Campus closures meant moving courses online, closing buildings, evacuating students, discontinuing in-person delivery of services, canceling in-person events and activities, and more. Institutions also adjusted academic calendars and turned to virtual environments, electronic communications, and masks and socially distanced interactions. In this chapter we explore what can be learned about sense of belonging by examining the words of students who experienced the closures and disruption that occurred with COVID-19.

Skyfactor, a Macmillan Learning company, collaborated with Pharos Resources to develop a complimentary survey for institutions that wanted to check in with students in spring 2020. The questions were focused on helping institutions understand student concerns and experiences while also prompting students to reflect on the actions they might need to take. Thirty-nine institutions administered the survey between late March and June 2020. The results provide a unique look at student experiences during COVID and insights into sense of belonging. The participating institutions were predominantly 4-year institutions varying in size, control (public, private), religious affiliation, U.S. region, urbanicity, and selectivity. Of the 79,969 students emailed, 15,831 responded, for an overall response rate of 20%. More than 14,000 students responded to an open-ended question asking what students missed the most by not being on campus.

On average, responses were 80 characters long. For this study, we examined the 97 responses that exceeded 500 characters.

Arslan (2021), in a study on the impacts of a very strict lockdown, during COVID-19 in the country of Turkey, found that students' high feelings of loneliness led to maladaptive experiences and fewer strategies for adjustment to new modes of functioning. Loneliness is the antithesis of belonging and can prevent individuals from engaging. Arslan also found that positive social relationships led to greater vitality and ability to cope during this time. In research prior to the pandemic, college students' sense of belonging was linked to a variety of outcomes, including academic motivation, performance, and retention (Freeman et al., 2007; McMillan & Chavis, 1986; O'Keeffe, 2013; Strayhorn, 2012). In understanding what sense of belonging is for college students, we need to also look at it in the sense of community. McMillan and Chavis (1986) identified four elements of community: membership, influence, reinforcement, and emotional connection. Because belonging is impacted by the community around an individual and the interactions that occur in those spaces, these four elements of community are powerful in identifying the ways students belong. Therefore, our findings related to COVID-19 and belonging are organized around this framework.

Membership

In understanding membership, McMillan and Chavis (1986) described how boundaries, cultural inclusion, personal investment, common symbols, and emotional safety can influence one's identity within the group. Ostrove (2007) also indicated that group identification was very important to developing belonging. In this study, students described classrooms as places to ask questions, interact with other students, and focus on learning. One student wrote specifically about a study group "where [they] are able to work together and study for exams." Students also wrote about membership in terms of social interactions, such as "seeing my friends every single day, not necessarily to do anything special, but just to study together or grab lunch before we both have to run to class." Students also mentioned membership through phrases like "as a business major" and "my [institutional name] experience." Finding commonality in shared classes served as the boundaries for their intellectual groups, and social memberships were tied to their living arrangements, campus involvement, and academic associations.

One's status also impacts an individual's ability to belong (Arslan, 2021). While Arslan (2021) wrote about statuses such as race, income level, gender, and national origin, students in this study identified that returning home and switching from the status of a student to a family member was a challenge. One student wrote,

> Having friends around me who make an effort at creating structure really helps me understand my own need for structure. . . . Here at home, I have to live based on the desires of my family, and I feel like I'm losing myself.

Another student contrasted the support and physical structures of college versus home:

> On campus, I had resources and strong support systems that I do not have at home. My friends/roommates were my biggest support system, and it is difficult to be motivated to do schoolwork without having that solid support. Also, on campus it is easy to go to the library or another study spot in order to completely focus on studies or homework, but at home, I live in a small space with multiple people, and it is hard trying to focus having to stay in the same room all day or even find a quiet place to do anything.

As another student described,

> It's hard to go from being completely independent (so I miss my independence too), knowing that you have a job postgrad, to living back at home with little to no independence and no job. So basically, I miss my life on campus, who I could be.

When asked to reflect on what they missed about being on campus, students described campus groups, academic settings, spaces, and interactions that reflected their feelings of community membership. They also wrote that losing those experiences created a loss of belonging and identity.

Influence

Influence describes the ability of an individual to be influenced as well as to influence others (McMillan & Chavis, 1986). Freeman et al. (2007) highlighted two main influences on belonging in the academic arena: interactions with faculty and with peers. Although faculty influence students during a normal academic year, that influence shifted during the pandemic. One student described the changes:

> [I miss] person-to-person interaction, attending actual in-person classes, being able to show my teacher what I am confused about instead of having to show her through an email that they can respond to hours later, then again making me take longer to do the paper which causes conflict with other classes work.

Students shared how faculty interaction influenced them related to their academic progress. "I'll miss dropping into my professors' offices during their open hours and talking about projects I'm working on, jobs I'm applying to and receiving invaluable personal feedback." Peers, an influence identified by Freeman et al. (2007), can be one place where there is give and take as membership is developed (McMillan & Chavis, 1986). One student described how COVID was decreasing their ability to engage in the classroom:

> I miss the physical interaction of class; it feels so difficult to interact with classmates and professors in the online meetings, and I am much less likely to speak up and participate in class simply because I do not feel comfortable with the online medium.

The students also wrote about the importance of classroom peer interactions. For instance, one student will miss "starting up a discussion to ask a classmate if they are 'getting' this or that. A chance to express interest level and get excited about what we are learning with someone who is having the same experience." Students highlighted the importance of sharing of different perspectives: "I will miss the interaction of being in a classroom with my peers, which makes discussion on a topic more interesting and hearing other students' feedback on issues or other things I may have not thought about." One student noted that the virtual environment impacted interactions outside the classroom as well:

> I feel like having people around me doing the same thing made me more motivated to keep studying or finish whatever I was working on. Being able to have study groups also helped me a lot, and doing it over the phone or on FaceTime just isn't the same.

Overall, students identified how much the virtual learning environment was reshaping their experience. The themes not only demonstrate the impact of

COVID, but they also underscored that what students say is important to creating influence and environments that engage them.

Reinforcement

Group membership needs to be reinforced through the level of conformity to the group, integration in the group, and the fulfilment of one's needs within that group (McMillan & Chavis, 1986). One student shared,

> What I miss most about being on campus is the sense of community and solidarity. It's comforting to know that after a long, tiring lecture, I can go decompress in the [building]. If I feel overwhelmed or even if I am having a wonderful day, I can stay in the [building] and study. After a test, it's wonderful to be able to meet up with other students and go get lunch. It very much so felt like we were all in it together. All of us were working toward getting a degree and putting in our best effort. While we still are going through the same thing together now, that feeling isn't there. There is comfort in knowing that people who can help me, whether it is professors, staff, or students, are there.

The students also wrote about how much other people reinforced their ability to succeed, grow, and be challenged through community membership. One participant spoke about this in detail:

> The biggest thing that I miss is the people. Isolation makes one realize the effect in which people have on you. Without people, it is harder to make people smile as you can't see them. Without people, ideas suffocate because nobody is there to realize their potential and fish them out of the river of potential. The good ideas may be able to stay afloat for a while, some may even make it to rocks that reside above the waterline, but the rest will be looking for the helping hand that is not there. It is embedded inside of the wall of socially distant isolation. Through video calls, the wall cracks, but it never shatters. So these ideas reach out to the hands, their fingers touch, but the current washes them away before they clasp together. Without people, emotions are bottled inside and the truest feelings repress themselves. This [is the] kind of feeling that should be expressed in person. Isolation reveals those feelings that you did not know that you were hiding. Isolation makes you realize how alone you are. Even with family around you, you feel alone. Dagnabit! Writing this makes me realize just how much I miss people.

McMillan and Chavis (1986) stated that to be a member of a group and feel belonging requires that people have their own needs fulfilled. Goodenow and

Grady (1993) further explained that feelings of respect, acceptance, inclusion, and support are necessary to sense of belonging. One student, who attended a small, private, religiously affiliated institution shared,

> THE COMMUNITY!! [Institution] has the best community I have ever been a part of. I have never been in another space where so many people want to pour into me. Almost everyone I come into contact with wants to get to know me for who I am and what my heart is, not for how I meet their agenda. I know, around every turn, no matter where I go, there will always be someone there to support me and love on me. I have never been in a place where it is so okay to be vulnerable and to fail. I know that no matter what I am going through, there are people who care deeply about me and would love to help me and support me.

Students shared how their experiences at the institution reinforced who they were or who they were becoming. For example, one student stated, "Being at [specific institution], I was consistently my happiest and healthiest self. The people around me pushed me and challenged me to be better always, and I was." Reinforcement was a clear theme.

Emotional Connection

Feeling a part of something as well as finding your own sense of belonging can provide an important emotional response (McMillan & Chavis, 1986). Hoffman et al. (2002) found that relating to members of the group was as important as the social support students receive from the group. One student wrote about connections in the classroom:

> I miss being around my peers in class. . . . It's spontaneous, you're engaged, you make friends. You can't just ask a random stranger how they feel about an exam or something the way you can lean over to the person next to you. There's no small talk, no jokes, no solidarity. . . . But I came to college to be around similar minds—to engage, to be challenged, to collaborate. College is just as much about carving out those interpersonal skills as it is about informational retention and analysis. I miss the connections built and memories made that only the classroom experience provides.

Another wrote specifically about friends: "The community I have formed at school is irreplaceable, and it's hard to have the motivation to do any school work when the environment of campus and your best friends that you do life with everyday [*sic*] is missing." Some students wrote about the campus environment and their connection to it, such as "I miss not being able to see the beautiful campus. [Institution] is such a beautiful campus and I loved just getting to walk around and getting to see everyone. It has such an amazing atmosphere." One student focused on "the sights, sounds, flavor of being 'in college' . . . hallway wisdom from classmates, the 'feel' of being an [institution nickname] member." Other participants wrote more holistically about emotional connections. For example, one student wrote, "I picked [institution initials] because I fell in love with its campus. I truly felt welcomed and comfortable here." Emotional connections and the loss of connection were common themes.

Students who were graduating wrote uniquely about their situation, having long-term connections to the campus and memberships in various subgroups. What they identified was missing out on the closure that comes through the special events the institution had established to help them find a way to exit the institution in a positive manner. One student wrote,

> Being a senior this year has been a hard adjustment because there were so many things I was looking forward to besides graduation itself. Not being able to attend my honors ceremony or pinning has affected me. These are ceremonies that I have worked toward since I first started at [institution] in 2016, and now I won't be able to enjoy these moments with my family and friends.

Similarly, one participant described the loss as "I feel as if I do not get any closure for how hard I have worked for the past 4 years," and another wrote "All those 'lasts' are now gone; that's what I will miss most."

Overall, the students used their pre-pandemic positive emotional connections to describe the losses created by COVID-19. The themes stress the importance of belonging, in all its forms, to the student experience.

Conclusion

The elements of belonging (membership, influence, reinforcement, and emotional connections) should all be considered when developing specific strategies. As higher education professionals, we are really good about orienting students at the beginning of their collegiate experience to create membership. We introduce students to institutional values, traditions, and even vocabulary, using experiences like summer orientation, welcome week activities, and first-year student experiences. All these activities build membership. Some of the student comments emphasize the importance of having a continuous orientation plan that occurs in different ways and in different parts of the institution throughout the entire student experience. Comments even reflect the importance of developing pathways out of the institution to build alumni connections. Throughout these orientations, institutions should continue to emphasize the community identity and students' place in that community.

In considering the influence area, practitioners need to consider how they develop relationships with students where they can positively impact students' lives, in both the in-person and virtual spaces. At the same time, practitioners need to have intentional ways for students to provide feedback regarding their experiences. As seen in the comments, even in unique situations like COVID-19, a lack of influence over the situation and the institution's response to it disrupted students' sense of belonging. Implementing assessments, student advisory panels, and other mechanisms for students to exert influence is critical. But institutions also need to emphasize those activities, so students not only contribute but also are aware of it. Influence must go both directions to support belonging.

The third area of belonging was reinforcement. Students need reinforcement that they are seen and that they are doing a good job. This reinforcement can come in a variety of ways, as seen in the student comments. Everything from informal interactions to end-of-the-year awards is important. Practitioners need to consider ways to reinforce student engagement and accomplishment in different formats.

Emotional connections are the last piece of belonging, and if we, as authors, have given proper attention to the three other parts, this one is often a part of the same activities and interactions as the other three. In general, students need positive connections with key people, places, and even experiences at their institution. Students may also need time and space to engage in, reflect on, and even celebrate those emotional connections. The emotional connections are what sustain students through and long after their membership at the institution.

To get better at addressing sense of belonging, practitioners need not only to focus on what to do to improve belonging, they also need to develop assessment methods that include these four areas. The data and insights are important for practitioners as they engage in good intentional conversations to make impactful improvements to student belonging and experiences now and in the future.

References

Arslan, G. (2021). Loneliness, college belongingness, subjective vitality, and psychological adjustment during coronavirus pandemic: Development of the college belongingness questionnaire. *Journal of Positive School Psychology*, 5(1), 17–31. https://doi.org/10.47602/j929.v5il.240

Freeman, T. M., Anderman, L. H., & Jensen, J. (2007). Sense of belonging in college freshmen at the classroom and campus levels. *The Journal of Experimental Education*, *75*(3), 203–220. https://psycnet.apa.org/doi/10.3200/JEXE.75.3.203-220

Goodenow, C., & Grady, K. E. (1993). The relationship of school belonging and friends' values to academic motivation among urban adolescent students. *The Journal of Experimental Education*, *62*(1), 60–71. https://doi.org/10.108000220 973.1993.9943831

Hess, A. (2020, March 26). *How coronavirus dramatically changed college for over 14 million students*. CNBC. https://www.cnbc.com/2020/03/26/how-coronavirus-changed-college-for-over-14-million-students.html

Hoffman, M., Richmond, J., Morrow, J, & Salamone, K. (2002). Investigating "sense of belonging" in first year college students. *Journal of College Student Retention*, *4*(3), 227–256. https://doi.org/10.2190%2FDRYC-CXQ9-JQ8V-HT4V

McMillan, D. W., & Chavis, D. M. (1986). Sense of community: A definition and theory. *Journal of Community Psychology*, *14*(1), 6–23. https://doi.org/10.1002/1520-6629(198601)14:1<6::AID-JCOP2290140103>3.0.CO;2-I

O'Keeffe, P. (2013). A sense of belonging: Improving student retention. *College Student Journal*, *47*(4), 605–613. https://researchrepository.rmit.edu.au/esploro/outputs/journalArticle/A-sense-of-belonging-Improving-student/9921862552801341

Ostrove, J. (2007). Social class and belonging: Implications for college adjustment. *The Review of Higher Education*, *30*(4), 363–389. https://psycnet.apa.org/doi/10.1353/rhe.2007.0028

Strayhorn, T. L. (2012). *College students' sense of belonging: A key to educational success for all students*. Routledge.

22

MEASURING BELONGING IN HIGHER EDUCATION

Review, Summary, and Guidance for Researchers and Practitioners

John Eric M. Lingat, Michael D. Toland, and Shannon O. Sampson

I nitiatives, interventions, and research regarding sense of belonging at institutions of higher education (IHEs) have led to increased interest in the measurement of this construct. The standards for educational and psychological testing (American Educational Research Association [AERA] et al., 2014) serve as a crucial resource to navigate construct measurement. In this chapter, we draw on these standards and review self-report instruments used to measure postsecondary students' sense of belonging to provide a summary of considerations and guidance for researchers and practitioners.

Sense of belonging, in general, has been studied through evolving frames and different contexts, resulting in a variety of definitions. Extending the classification of this construct beyond a basic human need (Maslow, 1943), Baumeister and Leary (1995) proposed the belonging hypothesis, or the "pervasive drive to form and maintain . . . lasting, positive, and significant interpersonal relationships" (p. 496). Applying the belonging hypothesis to education, Goodenow (1993) initially framed sense of belonging as middle school students' psychological process of "being accepted, valued, included, and encouraged by others . . . feeling oneself to be an important part of the life and activity of the class" (p. 25). Among higher education researchers, Strayhorn (2018) most comprehensively described postsecondary students' sense of belonging as "feeling cared about, accepted, respected, valued by, and important to the campus community or others on campus such as faculty, staff, and peers" (p. 4). Varying definitions and intended uses have led to unclear measurement approaches, resulting in instruments that diverge in characteristics (i.e., item types, length) and psychometric quality. These different instruments directly impact substantive claims and lead to sample-dependent conclusions. Although initiatives designed to foster postsecondary students' sense of belonging have become more sophisticated (e.g., Student Experience Project, 2019), consensus on the conceptualization of this construct in higher education and its measurement using modern techniques remain in progress (Allen et al., 2021; Sharkness & DeAngelo, 2011; Slaten et al., 2016).

This chapter is intended as a guiding tool kit for anyone interested in gathering information—whether descriptive, correlational, experimental, or anything in between—involving postsecondary students' sense of belonging. We provide critical reviews of existing instruments, summarize modern expectations for measurement, and present guidance that promotes purposeful research design decisions and responsible consumption of current and future belonging research.

To identify existing instruments, we conducted a systematic search informed by synthesizing guidelines for instrument selection (McClure, 2020) with methodology from similar reviews (e.g., Buros Center for Testing, 2020; Cooke et al., 2016; Fredricks & McColskey, 2012; Kohl et al., 2013). We cross-referenced primary search engine results from the Web of Knowledge with results from APA PsycINFO, EBSCO, ERIC, Health and Psychosocial Instruments, and Mental Measurement Yearbook, delimited within 1980 to October 2020 and capturing the emergence of belonging research (circa 1990s). Specific terms included *belonging, higher education, college, university*, and *postsecondary*. Articles that included elementary, middle, or high school were filtered from the results. Over 970,000 articles were initially returned, so we refined our search to areas of education, psychology, and sociology. After filtering for sense of belonging, 1,802 refereed articles remained. However, only articles pertaining to students in IHEs (n = 287) were reviewed. From these articles, we identified instruments that (a) measured sense of belonging; (b) were developed for use with postsecondary students; (c) included more than one item; and (d) had an English language version available, resulting in 33 instruments reviewed for this chapter. In the following sections, we review a sample of these self-report instruments (see Table 22.1), summarizing strengths and limitations as guidance for future investigations into *belonging*.

TABLE 22.1

Instrument Information

Title	Items	Reliability	Response format	Author(s)
Psychological Sense of School Membership Scale (PSSM)	18	$\alpha_{samples}$ = .77 to .88	1 = *not at all true* to 5 = *completely true*	Goodenow (1993)
University Belonging Questionnaire (UBQ)	24	α = .93	1 = *strongly disagree* to 4 = *strongly agree*	Slaten et al. (2018)
Sense of Belonging Scale (SoBS)	26	α_{scale} = .90 $\alpha_{subscales}$ = .84 to .93	1 = *completely true* to 5 = *completely untrue*	Hoffman et al. (2002)
General Belonging Scale (GBS)	12	$\alpha_{samples}$ = .92 to .95	1 = *strongly disagree* to 7 = *strongly agree*	Malone et al. (2012)
Perceived Cohesion Scale: Belonging subscale (PCS)	3	α = .94	1 = *strongly disagree* to 10 = *strongly agree*	Bollen and Hoyle (1990)
Interpersonal Needs Questionnaire: Thwarted Belongingness subscale (INQ)	9	α = .85	—	Van Orden et al. (2012)
Perceived Belonging in Sport scale (PBS)	11	α = .89	1 = *strongly disagree* to 10 = *strongly agree*	Allen (2006)
Perceived Cohesion Scale: Belonging subscale (adapted)	3	α = .94	1 = *strongly disagree* to 10 = *strongly agree*	Hurtado and Carter (1997) Hausman et al. (2007)
College Student Experiences Questionnaire	3	α = .76		Strayhorn (2008)

(Continued)

Table 22.1 (*Continued*)

Title	Items	Reliability	Response format	Author(s)
Beginning Postsecondary Students Longitudinal Study	1		--	Gopalan and Brady (2019)
Assessment of Collegiate Residential Environments and Outcomes	5	$\alpha = .91$	--	Duran et al. (2020)
Diverse Democracy Project Study—Perceived Cohesion Scale: Belonging subscale (adapted)	5	$\alpha = .88$	--	Nuñez (2009)
Diverse Democracy Project Study—Perceived Cohesion Scale: Belonging subscale (adapted)	3	$\alpha = .90$	--	Maestas et al. (2007)
Community College Survey of Student Engagement (CCSSE)	8	$\alpha_{\text{factors}} = .66$ to $.81$	--	Fong et al. (2019)
Sense of Belonging Scale (SoBS)	3	--	1 = *strongly agree* to 7 = *strongly disagree*	
Combination of original item and item from a large data set	2	$\alpha = .85$	1 = *not at all* to 5 = *a great deal*	Ostrove and Long (2007)

Multiple Paths of Measurement

Similar to the measurement of other constructs, such as engagement (Fredricks & McColskey, 2012) and self-regulation (González-Torres & Torrano, 2008), belonging is commonly measured using self-report instruments (Ribera et al., 2017). Several types have emerged in the belonging literature, including original or adapted instruments and subscales, instruments using items from datasets, and instruments that have been shortened or include less than three items.

Original Instruments and Subscales

Various teams have developed original instruments to measure belonging based on their unique purpose. Goodenow (1993) contributed an original instrument designed for use with adolescents, conceptualizing belonging as student perceptions of feeling "accepted, respected, included, and supported" (p. 80) within the learning environment and among peers. Despite being named a membership scale, the Psychological Sense of School Membership scale (PSSM) was unmistakably designed as a "measure of individual differences in belonging" (p. 81). She developed this instrument with school principals on her research team and field tested it at three different schools: one suburban middle school and two urban junior high schools. Across two administrations of the instrument, the PSSM was refined to 18 items and scored as an average of item responses derived from individual item responses using a 5-point Likert-type format. Goodenow attempted to provide reliability and validity evidence based on classical test theory techniques (i.e., item reliability analysis, group comparisons using ANOVA, and raw score correlations); however, researchers have critiqued Goodenow's claim that the PSSM measures belonging as a single construct (e.g., Freeman et al., 2007; You et al., 2011). Despite these limitations, the PSSM remains a staple across belonging research and is used with a variety of contexts and populations, including IHEs. Freeman et al. (2007) justified using the PSSM at IHEs since their particular sample—first-year undergraduate students—were within the adolescent age group, albeit at the top of the developmental stage compared to middle school students who were part of Goodenow's (1993) field test groups.

Despite the popularity of the PSSM, other instruments have been proposed with belonging conceptualized differently as a multidimensional construct. Most recently, the University Belonging Questionnaire (UBQ) (Slaten et al., 2018) was designed to measure belonging at the institutional level, reflecting interactions with a broader community beyond the classroom. Similar to the PSSM, Maslow's (1943) foundational work was used to generate UBQ items, but the divergence from the PSSM resulted from interviews with undergraduate students (Slaten et al., 2014) and reviews provided by experts. Through an iterative process, the UBQ was refined from 40 items to 24 items. In contrast to the PSSM, the UBQ was extensively field tested. This included exploratory and confirmatory factor analysis (CFA), as well as establishing validity evidence based on correlations with general belonging, social support, connectedness, and loneliness. Participants responded using a 4-point Likert-type format, with higher scores indicating stronger university affiliation, support, acceptance, and connection—the factors proposed by Slaten and his team. The UBQ has received less critical feedback than the PSSM, potentially due to its novelty, but also due to the utilization of modern measurement techniques (e.g., CFA) to more thoroughly report the psychometric properties of the instrument.

Other original instruments proposed between the publication of the PSSM and the UBQ reflect attempts toward advanced psychometric testing. For example, Hoffman et al. (2002) developed the Sense of Belonging Scale (SoBS) to specifically measure the first-year college experience. The 26-item SoBS is a multidimensional self-report instrument with items rated on a 5-point Likert-type format. Limited validity testing was initially conducted, but future studies (Tovar & Simon, 2010) provided evidence around the multidimensionality and reliability of data gathered from the SoBS. Another instrument, the 12-item General Belonging Scale (GBS) by Malone et al. (2012), included postsecondary students during field testing but was not designed for exclusive use at IHEs. The GBS was developed as a brief instrument of general belonging with an equal set of positively and negatively oriented items rated on a 7-point Likert-type format. The instrument development and psychometric investigation of the GBS demonstrate a level of rigor similar to the UBQ process: field tested with multiple samples with validity evidence reported, including correlations to connectedness and life satisfaction.

For researchers and practitioners interested in measuring belonging as a component of a more broad, global construct (i.e., perceived cohesion), belonging subscales within an original instrument are sometimes used as an alternative to full belonging instruments. Researchers (e.g., Hausmann et al., 2007, Hurtado & Carter, 1997; Lewis et al., 2019) have used or adapted Bollen and Hoyle's (1990) three-item Perceived Cohesion Scale: Belonging subscale from an instrument intended to measure cohesion and field tested with both undergraduates and general city residents. Situated in sociology and psychology, this subscale was part of an instrument intended to measure the self-appraisal of an individual's relationship to a group using an 11-point Likert-type format. Bollen and Hoyle (1990) used a CFA approach to examine the two-factor model, measuring cohesion and belonging separately. Other researchers who have used this subscale report strong reliability evidence (i.e., Hurtado & Carter, 1997; Lewis et al., 2019).

The Interpersonal Needs Questionnaire: Thwarted Belongingness subscale (INQ; Van Orden et al., 2012) is another original subscale that has been used with undergraduate students but was not specifically designed for use within IHEs. This nine-item subscale, rated on a 7-point Likert-type format, indicates greater levels of thwarted belonging, or the psychological state when the need to belong is unmet, based on higher total scores. This original subscale is notable because of the psychometric investigation that the researchers conducted during instrument development. Specifically, the researchers ensured measurement invariance (based on CFA techniques) was present across groups (i.e., young adults versus outpatients, young adults versus older adults) before comparing the data and interpreting the results.

Original instruments and subscales allow researchers and practitioners to investigate a targeted context or guiding question that may not have been previously measured using items developed with a specific framework or similar intended purpose in mind. In addition to the instruments we summarized, a number of original belonging instruments have been developed for

- international contexts (e.g., First Year Experience Belonging Scale [Australia]; Social Integration Scale [United Kingdom]);
- specific student groups (e.g., Sense of Campus Belonging Scale [students with psychiatric disabilities]; Sense of Belonging Measure [part-time]); and
- academic disciplines (e.g., Math Sense of Belonging Scale [math]; Sense of Academic Fit Scale [computer science]; Sense of Belonging Instrument [nursing]).

Subscales that measure belonging are similarly varied (e.g., Interpersonal Support Evaluation List; Engagement Evaluation Questionnaire; Survey of Student "Belongingness," Engagement and Self-Confidence), with strengths that may match a specific purpose or context.

Adapted Instruments and Subscales

Individuals have adapted existing instruments to avoid the item development process or capitalize on items that are ideal for their specific purpose. The PSSM (Goodenow, 1993) and PCS: Belonging subscale (Bollen & Hoyle, 1990) have been regularly adapted within IHEs. Explicitly naming the institution—rather than the class or subject—is a common adaptation of the PSSM when used in IHEs (e.g., Freeman et al., 2007; Pittman & Richmond, 2008). However, this instrument has also been adapted to reflect domain-specific revisions. Allen's (2006) study on postsecondary students and sport involvement serves as an example of this option. To develop the Perceived Belonging in Sport Scale (PBS), items from the PSSM were adapted to apply specifically to the sports context. For example, "Other students in this school take my opinions seriously" was adapted to "Other [players on my team] take my opinions seriously" as part of the PBS. All 18 items from the PSSM were adapted, but only 11 items were retained for the final instrument due to a negative phrasing effect—an established issue with the unidimensional model originally proposed by Goodenow (1993). Allen (2006) conducted factor analytic-based comparisons of different models to identify the items to be removed. Additionally, the factor analytic investigation was extended by conducting measurement invariance testing across genders, in which equivalence for factor loadings was established.

Subscales were similarly adapted. Hurtado and Carter (1997) were the first to adapt the PCS subscale by simply identifying "the campus community" as the object of the three original items, using the same 11-point Likert-type format. Hausman et al. (2007) followed but adapted the belonging subscale items using the specific name of the IHE where the participants were recruited as the object. Both studies were part of a larger data collection process in collaboration with institutional research partners to answer specific questions regarding students' experience at IHEs, such as campus climate and retention. Of note, researchers and practitioners should expect adaptations of instruments to lead to additional generations of adaptation. For example, Hurtado and Carter's (1997) adaptation of the PCS was adapted and used with a larger data set (e.g., Johnson et al., 2007; Nuñez, 2009), discussed in the next section.

Items From Data Sets

In certain situations, a number of items from large data sets have been used to collect responses from multiple IHEs. Gopalan and Brady (2019) used a single item from the Beginning Postsecondary Students Longitudinal Study to descriptively report on belonging at IHEs across the nation. Duran et al. (2020) used five items from the Assessment of Collegiate Residential Environments and Outcomes. Both studies were able to descriptively report on longitudinal trends across multiple IHEs. In addition to Strayhorn (2008), who used three items from the College Student Experiences Questionnaire, other large data sets with items that have been used to descriptively report on belonging include the National Study of Living-Learning Programs,

National Longitudinal Study of Adolescent to Adult Health, and Student Experience in Research University.

The use of specific belonging-related items from large data sets extends beyond descriptive reporting. For example, Maestas et al. (2007) and Nuñez (2009) both used three items (adapted from the PCS: Belonging subscale) drawn from the Diverse Democracy Project Study, but Nuñez included two additional items and analyzed the data using structural equation modeling (SEM) techniques. Maestas et al. (2017) maintained the three items and conducted correlational analyses. Some studies not only collected data across multiple IHEs, but also partnered within their own institutional research units for internal reporting, intervention design, or program development. As an example, Fong et al. (2019) identified eight items that loaded onto three factors from the Community College Survey of Student Engagement to measure a Native-specific conceptualization of belonging. This team was able to provide evidence in partnership with their institution that the belonging items were interpreted differently by Indigenous students compared to non-Indigenous students and link different factors of belonging to various student outcomes.

Shortened Instruments

Some researchers and practitioners may truncate an existing instrument to three or fewer items to measure belonging. Several reasons may account for the prevalence of this practice. For some, administering an extremely brief survey may simply be more convenient. For others, it may be an intentional decision to use a limited number of items—either as part of a longer questionnaire or as an independent poll—to take a pulse on belonging, rather than deeply investigate a construct to develop interventions for specific groups or widespread programming. The justification for adopting this approach was rarely stated in the articles we reviewed. For researchers considering shortened instruments (as with the selection of any instrument type), we greatly emphasize the importance of explicitly stating the intended use of the selected option and providing reliability and validity evidence for their approach.

Dorum et al. (2013) used three statements for the Sense of Belonging Scale (SoBS). Like the PCS: Belonging subscale (Bollen & Hoyle, 1990), these three statements were administered with six additional items to measure other aspects of student life but were treated as an independent subscale. However, the three SoBS statements were analyzed separately, whereas the belonging subscale on the PCS was intended to be analyzed with its counterpart subscale that measured cohesion. Items on the SoBS were rated on a 7-point Likert-type format. The psychometric investigation was limited, but the authors did state that because "the measure of sense of belonging used in this study is of a general nature . . . it is difficult to draw causal conclusions about the relationship between sense of belonging and attitudes" (p. 77), acknowledging the limitations of their approach. Ostrove and Long (2007) used two items—one from a large data set and the other an original statement—rated on a 5-point Likert-type format. Despite the limited information gathered from two items, the authors achieved their purpose of measuring belonging in two ways: objectively and subjectively. Based on the goal of their investigation, they suggested that the data provided sufficient information on the implications of social class and belonging on student adjustment to IHEs.

The assumed simplicity of the development, administration, and analysis of self-report instruments persistently attract both researchers and practitioners. However, purposeful design and refinement should drive the instrumentation process (Bandalos, 2018) to effectively capture cognitive or affective perceptions. Regardless of the type of instrument, by prioritizing these practices and not sacrificing them for expediency, useful data can be collected and used to make valid interpretations.

Considerations

First, we reinforce that purpose and use statements, as well as psychometric investigations, should guide measurement (AERA et al., 2014). Doing so will provide insight on whether the latent construct is measured (a) as conceptualized for the intended sample, and (b) with evidence to support reliability and validity—in this case, for postsecondary students' sense of belonging. Additionally, data collected should be tested for different characteristics, such as precision, dimensionality, and measurement invariance. This information supports the validity of any interpretation, especially comparisons between groups. Some instruments that emerged from the search, such as the UBQ and the INQ, approached these standards more closely than other instruments.

We offer observations from the instruments that we summarized, reflecting modern practices. With the exception of a few original instruments, the utilization of focus groups, expert review, cognitive pretesting, and measurement invariance testing were rarely documented. Additionally, criticisms were persistent within the literature regarding the dimensionality of belonging, as well as the treatment of items as continuous, rather than polytomous, indicators. Furthermore, current belonging instruments may not accurately measure the full continuum of the construct, specifically missing the experience of students who may feel alienated or thwarted belonging. Last, conceptualizations reflecting underrepresented cultures, highlighted further by qualitative studies (e.g., Alejandro et al., 2020), did not appear to be a priority when these instruments were developed.

The prevalent use of shortened instruments or a brief set of items (e.g., three or fewer) perpetuates construct underrepresentation and contributes to misleading results. By using a limited number of items, less information can be derived had there been sufficient data to model. More items in an instrument allows for analyses using modern measurement techniques. Shortened instruments tend to be created in response to specific demands, usually after lengthier instruments have been extensively tested. This is a practice recommended by large testing companies but is applicable to self-report instruments. Thus, belonging researchers and practitioners could learn from other fields that have derived short forms from instruments with originally longer forms that have been subject to psychometric testing (see Chiesi et al., 2018).

The psychometric investigations that were conducted on belonging instruments were mostly from a classical test theory approach, which relies on observed scores instead of more modern techniques, such as SEM, item response theory (IRT), and Rasch modeling. Reliability was consistently reported using Cronbach's alpha coefficient (α) rather than alternative and more advanced measures of reliability (see Zinbarg et al., 2005). Observed scores were most commonly limited to correlations and ANOVAs, which do not provide the type of model fit, item-level/cross-classification information, and measurement error accountability that modern measurement techniques can produce. The use of observed scores has its own assumptions that often researchers are not testing and can have consequences (e.g., equal weight and intervals, unidimensionality; McNeish & Wolf, 2020).

Finally, measurement invariance testing was conducted for only a few instruments, but the number and size of samples were limited. When measurement invariance testing was conducted, authors erroneously treated categorical Likert-type item response data as continuous indicators, which is known to produce biased statistical results (Rhemtulla et al., 2012) that could be mitigated had differential item functioning (DIF) been investigated. Martinková et al. (2017) recommended DIF testing as a measurement practice that should "have a routine role in all our efforts to develop assessments that are more equitable measures of scientific knowledge" (p. 11) to ensure that data can be compared across groups. By ignoring this important psychometric evaluation, any claims about comparative differences are tentatively weak due to the lack of psychometric evidence that items are measuring the construct similarly across different groups (Rutkowski & Svetina, 2014).

A related issue, which was noted specifically for the PSSM and UBQ, is that instruments were not field tested with more diverse students. You et al. (2011) stated in their critique of the PSSM that researchers should "expand the examination of psychological measures to diverse populations within and between countries and cultures" (p. 234). This requires that researchers recognize the diverse experiences of belonging at IHEs and that field testing with a majority identity group of students (e.g., White, female, middle class, undergraduate) is insufficient for generalizability. Without addressing these limitations present in existing belonging instruments, investigation at IHEs will continue to remain elusive, lacking both precision and accuracy, and will likely result in inconsistent findings about belonging.

Guidance

Individuals may hesitate to choose a more difficult path at the onset of their journey to measure belonging at IHEs. As a gentle reminder, the path toward quality measurement is often difficult, but worthwhile. Should individuals decide to "go under the hood" of their chosen instrument, not only would a more purposeful investigation lie ahead, but an opportunity to contribute valid interpretations based on robust data to expand the study of belonging (e.g., Fong et al., 2019). Having questions about these measurement considerations is expected, but these practices can be better navigated in collaboration with psychometricians who may not have expertise in belonging, but have specific training in selecting, developing, refining, and evaluating an instrument. Much like providing medical care, a team of experts who specialize in specific roles can ensure a successful diagnosis and increase the efficacy of the treatment plan.

Although expertise may differ, researchers and practitioners carry the responsibility of intentional design and measurement that adhere to measurement standards (AERA et al., 2014). Both should deliberately organize information and build a strong conceptual framework prior to selecting an instrument (see McClure, 2020). Researchers and practitioners should establish interpretation/use arguments (Kane, 2013) to explicitly state the purpose of the study to narrow instrument options.

For the Applied Researcher

After selecting or developing an instrument (e.g., via focus groups), researchers should gather data on interpretability and understandability of items on the instrument by conducting cognitive pretesting (Peterson et al., 2017), regardless of the source of the items (e.g., author developed, derived from a database). Then, selected instrument(s) or adaptations should be field tested for reliability and aligned to appropriate analyses to produce data results that can be interpreted with validity (Bandalos, 2018). Finally, instruments should be tested for measurement invariance and/or DIF, particularly when the data is treated as categorical (Wu & Estabrook, 2016), and specifically for lengthier instruments. Instruments with 10 or more items are ideal for a thorough investigation of DIF, which can be accomplished through several methods (see Martinková et al., 2017). In addition to the listed guidance for instrumentation, researchers should consider guidance for reporting quantitative research by Appelbaum et al. (2018). As a note, a corresponding reporting guide for qualitative data is available (Levitt et al., 2018).

For the Evidence-Based Practitioner

In addition to the examination of existing instruments and collaboration with researchers, practitioners should engage in evidence-based strategies to gather information about belonging. For example, we recommend practitioners consult research on related constructs that have also tackled similar measurement issues. Specifically, the literature on engagement in schools reflects challenges with conceptualization and instrumentation (Fredricks & McColskey, 2012; Sinatra et al., 2015). Another example is from the Buros Center for Testing (2020) team, who have produced guidance on the measurement of social and emotional learning based on contributions from leading substantive and psychometric experts. Last, Bandura (2006) has provided guidance on the instrumentation of self-efficacy that can be extended to the construct of belonging.

Conclusion

The measurement of belonging at IHEs requires meticulous planning and intentional design to gather information in a way that supports academic environments to promote authentic community building and facilitate student success. Instruments need to be selected and utilized with caution. Whether developing original instruments or adapting instruments for use in a novel context, a process guided by purposeful objectives and that incorporates sound measurement practices, such as expert review, cognitive interviewing, and psychometric testing using modern techniques such as SEM and IRT (see Bond & Fox, 2015; De Ayala, 2009; Kline, 2016) should be employed. Researchers and practitioners should consider supplemental or complimentary methods from qualitative (e.g., focus groups; Mallinckrodt et al., 2016) and critical (e.g., QuantCrit; Garcia et al., 2018) frameworks to mitigate limitations of quantitative methods and achieve more rigorous and inclusive measurement of belonging.

References

American Educational Research Association, American Psychological Association, National Council on Measurement in Education, & Joint Committee on Standards for Educational and Psychological Testing. (2014). *Standards for educational and psychological testing.* AERA.

Alejandro, A. J., Fong, C. J., & De La Rosa, Y. M. (2020). Indigenous graduate and professional students decolonizing, reconciling, and indigenizing belongingness in higher education. *Journal of College Student Development, 61*(6), 679–696. https://doi.org/10.1353/csd.2020.0069

Allen, J. B. (2006). The perceived belonging in sport scale: Examining validity. *Psychology of Sport and Exercise, 7*(4), 387–405. https://doi.org/10.1016/j.psychsport.2005.09.004

Allen, K.-A., Kern, M. L., Rozek, C. S., McInerney, D. M., & Slavich, G. M. (2021). Belonging: A review of conceptual issues, an integrative framework, and directions for future research. *Australian Journal of Psychology, 73*(1), 87–102. https://doi.org/10.1080/00049530.2021.1883409

Appelbaum, M., Cooper, H., Kline, R. B., Mayo-Wilson, E., Nezu, A. M., & Rao, S. M. (2018). Journal article reporting standards for quantitative research in psychology: The APA Publications and Communications Board Task Force report. *American Psychologist, 73*(1), 3–25. http://dx.doi.org/10.1037/amp0000191

Bandalos, D. L. (2018). *Methodology in the social sciences: Measurement theory and applications for the social sciences.* Guilford.

Bandura, A. (2006). Guide for constructing self-efficacy scales. In F. Pajares & T. Urdan (Eds.), *Self-efficacy beliefs of adolescents* (Vol. 5, pp. 307–337). Information Age.

Baumeister, R. F., & Leary, M. R. (1995). The need to belong: Desire for interpersonal attachments as a fundamental human motivation. *Psychological Bulletin, 117*(3), 497–529. https://doi.org/10.1037/0033-2909.117.3.497

Bollen, K. A., & Hoyle, R. H. (1990). Perceived cohesion: A conceptual and empirical examination. *Social Forces, 69*(2), 479–504. https://doi.org/10.2307/2579670

Bond, T. G., & Fox, C. M. (2015). *Applying the Rasch model: Fundamental measurement in the human sciences* (3rd ed.). Erlbaum.

Buros Center for Testing. (2020). *Social-emotional learning assessment technical guidebook.* https://buros.org/sel-assessment-technical-guidebook

Chiesi, F., Morsanyi, K., Donati, M. A., & Primi, C. (2018). Applying item response theory to develop a shortened version of the Need for Cognition Scale. *Advances in Cognitive Psychology, 14,* 75–86. https://doi.org/10.5709/acp-0240-z

Cooke, P. J., Melchert, T. P., & Connor, K. (2016). Measuring well-being: A review of instruments. *The Counseling Psychologist, 44*(5), 730–757. https://doi .org/10.1177/0011000016633507

De Ayala, R. J. (2009). *Methodology in the social sciences: The theory and practice of item response theory.* Guilford.

Dorum, K., Bartle, C., & Pennington, M. (2013). Social media encourages sense of belonging among off-campus university students. In H. H. Yang & S. Wang (Eds.), *Cases on formal and informal e-learning environments: Opportunities and practices* (pp. 68–80). IGI Global. https://doi.org/10.4018/978-1-4666-1930-2 .ch004

Duran, A., Dahl, L., Stipeck, C., & Mayhew, M. (2020). A critical quantitative analysis of students' sense of belonging: Perspectives on race, generation status, and collegiate environments. *Journal of College Student Development, 61*(2), 133–153. https://doi.org/10.1353/csd.2020.0014

Fong, C. J., Alejandro, A. J., Krou, M. R., Segovia, J., & Johnston-Ashton, K. (2019). Ya'at'eeh: Race-reimaged belongingness factors, academic outcomes, and goal pursuits among Indigenous community college students. *Contemporary Educational Psychology, 59,* 1–15. https://doi.org/10.1016/ j.cedpsych.2019.101805

Fredricks, J. A., & McColskey, W. (2012). The measurement of student engagement: A comparative analysis of various methods and student self-report instruments. In S. L. Christenson, A. L. Reschly, & C. Wylie (Eds.), *Handbook of research on student engagement* (pp. 763–782). Springer. https://doi.org/10.1007/978-1- 4614-2018-7_37

Freeman, T. M., Anderman, L. H., & Jensen, J. M. (2007). Sense of belonging in college freshmen at the classroom and campus levels. *Journal of Experimental Education, 75*(3), 203–220. https://doi.org/10.3200/JEXE.75.3.203-220

Garcia, N. M., López, N., & Vélez, V. N. (2018) QuantCrit: Rectifying quantitative methods through critical race theory. *Race Ethnicity and Education, 21*(2), 149–157. https://doi.org/10.1080/13613324.2017.1377675

González-Torres, M. C., & Torrano, F. (2008). Methods and instruments for measuring self-regulated learning. In A. Vally & J. C. Nunez (Eds.), *Handbook of instructional resources and applications* (pp. 201–219). Nova Science. https://www .researchgate.net/publication/295103631_Methods_and_instruments_for_ measuring_self-regulated_learning

Goodenow, C. (1993). Classroom belonging among early adolescent students: Relationships to motivation and achievement. *The Journal of Early Adolescence, 13*(1), 21–43. https://doi.org/10.1177/0272431693013001002

Gopalan, M., & Brady, S. T. (2020). College students' sense of belonging: A national perspective. *Educational Researcher, 49*(2), 134–137. https://doi .org/10.3102/0013189X19897622

Hausmann, L., Schofield, J., & Woods, R. L. (2007). Sense of belonging as a predictor of intentions to persist among African American and White first-year college students. *Research in Higher Education, 48*, 803–839. https://doi.org/10.1007/ s11162-007-9052-9

Hoffman, M., Richmond, J., Morrow, J., & Salomone, K. (2002). Investigating "sense of belonging" in first-year college students. *Journal of College Student Retention: Research, Theory & Practice, 4*(3), 227–256. https://doi.org/10.2190/ DRYC-CXQ9-JQ8V-HT4V

Hurtado, S., & Carter, D. F. (1997). Effects of college transition and perceptions of the campus racial climate on Latino college students' sense of belonging. *Sociology of Education, 70*(4), 324–345. https://doi.org/10.2307/2673270

Johnson, D. R., Soldner, M., Leonard, J. B., Alvarez, P., Inkelas, K. K., Rowan-Kenyon, H., & Longerbeam, S. (2007). Examining sense of belonging among first-year undergraduates from different racial/ethnic groups. *Journal of College Student Development, 48*(5), 525–542. https://doi.org/10.1353/csd.2007.0054

Kane, M. T. (2013). Validating the interpretations and uses of test scores. *Journal of Educational Measurement, 50*(1), 1–73. https://doi.org/10.1111/jedm.12000

Kline, R. B. (2016). *Methodology in the social sciences. Principles and practice of structural equation modeling* (4th ed.). Guilford.

Kohl, D., Recchia, S., & Steffgen, G. (2013). Measuring school climate: An overview of measurement scales, *Educational Research, 55*(4), 411–426. https:// doi.org/10.1080/00131881.2013.844944

Levitt, H. M., Bamberg, M., Creswell, J. W., Frost, D. M., Josselson, R., & Suárez-Orozco, C. (2018). Journal article reporting standards for qualitative primary, qualitative meta-analytic, and mixed methods research in psychology: The APA Publications and Communications Board Task Force report. *American Psychologist, 73*(1), 26–46. http://dx.doi.org/10.1037/amp0000151

Lewis, J., Mendenhall, R., Ojiemwen, A., Thomas, M., Riopelle, C., Harwood, S., & Huntt, M. (2019). Racial microaggressions and sense of belonging at a historically White university. *American Behavioral Scientist, 65*(8), 1049–1071. https:// doi.org/10.1177/0002764219859613

Maestas, R., Vaquera, G. S., & Zehr, L. M. (2007). Factors impacting sense of belonging at a Hispanic-serving institution. *Journal of Hispanic Higher Education, 6*(3), 237–256. https://doi.org/10.1177%2F1538192707302801

Mallinckrodt, B., Miles, J. R., & Recabarren, D. A. (2016). Using focus groups and Rasch item response theory to improve instrument development. *The Counseling Psychologist, 44*(2), 146–194. https://doi.org/10.1177/0011000015596437

Malone, G. P., Pillow, D. R., & Osman, A. (2012). The General Belongingness Scale (GBS): Assessing achieved belongingness. *Personality and Individual Differences, 52*(3), 311–316. https://doi.org/10.1016/j.paid.2011.10.027

Martinková, P., Drabinová, A., Liaw, Y.-L., Sanders, E. A., McFarland, J. L., & Price, R. M. (2017). Checking equity: Why differential item functioning analysis should be a routine part of developing conceptual assessments. *CBE—Life Sciences Education, 16*(2), 1–13. https://doi.org/10.1187/cbe.16-10-0307

Maslow, A. H. (1943). A theory of human motivation. *Psychological Review, 50*(4), 370–396. https://doi.org/10.1037/h0054346

McClure, K. S. (2020). *Concise guides to conducting behavioral, health, and social science research. Selecting and describing your research instruments.* American Psychological Association. https://doi.org/10.1037/0000192-000

McNeish, D., & Wolf, M. G. (2020). Thinking twice about sum scores. *Behavior Research Methods, 52*, 2287–2305. https://doi.org/10.3758/s13428-020-01398-0

Nuñez, A.-M. (2009). A critical paradox? Predictors of Latino students' sense of belonging in college. *Journal of Diversity in Higher Education, 2*(1), 46–61. https://doi.org/10.1037/a0014099

Ostrove, J. M., & Long, S. M. (2007). Social class and belonging: Implications for college adjustment. *Review of Higher Education, 30*(4), 363–389. https://doi.org/10.1353/rhe.2007.0028

Peterson, C. H., Peterson, N. A., & Powell, K. G. (2017). Cognitive interviewing for item development: Validity evidence based on content and response processes. *Measurement and Evaluation in Counseling and Development, 50*(4), 217–223. https://doi.org/10.1080/07481756.2017.1339564

Pittman, L. D., & Richmond, A. (2008). University belonging, friendship quality, and psychological adjustment during the transition to college. *Journal of Experimental Education, 76*(4), 343–361. https://doi.org/10.3200/JEXE.76.4.343-362

Rhemtulla, M., Brosseau-Liard, P. É., & Savalei, V. (2012). When can categorical variables be treated as continuous? A comparison of robust continuous and categorical SEM estimation methods under suboptimal conditions. *Psychological Methods, 17*(3), 354–373. https://doi.org/10.1037/a0029315

Ribera, A., Miller, A. L., & Dumford, A. D. (2017). Sense of peer belonging and institutional acceptance in the first year: The role of high-impact practices. *Journal of College Student Development, 58*(4), 545–563. https://doi.org/10.1353/csd.2017.0042

Rutkowski, L., & Svetina, D. (2014). Assessing the hypothesis of measurement invariance in the context of large-scale international surveys. *Educational and Psychological Measurement, 74*(1), 31–57. https://doi.org/10.1177/0013164413498257

Sharkness, J., & DeAngelo, L. (2011). Measuring student involvement: A comparison of classical test theory and item response theory in the construction of scales from student surveys. *Research in Higher Education, 52*, 480–507. https://doi.org/10.1007/s11162-010-9202-3

Sinatra, G. M., Heddy, B. C., & Lombardi, D. (2015). The challenges of defining and measuring student engagement in science. *Educational Psychologist, 50*(1), 1–13. https://doi.org/10.1080/00461520.2014.1002924

Slaten, C. D., Elison, Z. M., Deemer, E. D., Hughes, H. A., & Shemwell, D. A. (2018). The development and validation of the University Belonging Questionnaire. *The Journal of Experimental Education, 86*(4), 633–651. https://doi.org/10.1080/00220973.2017.1339009

Slaten, C. D., Ferguson, J. K., Allen, K.-A., Brodrick, D.-V., & Waters, L. (2016). School belonging: A review of the history, current trends, and future directions. *The Educational and Developmental Psychologist*, *33*(1), 1–15. https://doi .org/10.1017/edp.2016.6

Slaten, C. D., Yough, M. S., Shemwell, D. A., Scalise, D. A., Elison, Z. M., & Hughes, H. A. (2014). Eat, sleep, breathe, study: Understanding what it means to belong at a university from the student perspective. *Excellence in Higher Education*, *5*(1), 1–5. https://doi.org/10.5195/ehe.2014.117

Strayhorn, T. L. (2008). Fittin' in: Do diverse interactions with peers affect sense of belonging for Black men at predominantly White institutions? *NASPA Journal*, *45*(4), 501–527. https://doi.org/10.2202/1949-6605.2009

Strayhorn, T. L. (2018). *College students' sense of belonging*. Routledge. https://doi .org/10.4324/9781315297293

Student Experience Project. (2019). *About: SEP 101*. https://studentexperiencepro-ject.org/about

Tovar, E., & Simon, M. A. (2010). Factorial structure and invariance analysis of the Sense of Belonging Scales. *Measurement and Evaluation in Counseling and Development*, *43*(3), 199–217. https://doi.org/10.1177/0748175610384811

Van Orden, K. A., Cukrowicz, K. C., Witte, T. K., & Joiner, T. E., Jr. (2012). Thwarted belongingness and perceived burdensomeness: Construct validity and psychometric properties of the Interpersonal Needs Questionnaire. *Psychological Assessment*, *24*(1), 197–215. https://doi.org/10.1037/a0025358

Wu, H., & Estabrook, R. (2016). Identification of confirmatory factor analysis models of different levels of invariance for ordered categorical outcomes. *Psychometrika*, *81*, 1014–1045. https://doi.org/10.1007/s11336-016-9506-0

You, S., Ritchey, K. M., Furlong, M. J., Shochet, I., & Boman, P. (2011). Examination of the latent structure of the Psychological Sense of School Membership Scale. *Journal of Psychoeducational Assessment*, *29*(3), 225–237. https://doi.org/10.1177/0734282910379968

Zinbarg, R. E., Revelle, W., Yovel, I., and Li, W. (2005). Cronbach's α, Revelle's β, and McDonald's ωh: Their relations with each other and two alternative conceptualizations of reliability. *Psychometrika*, *70*, 123–133. https://doi.org/10.1007/s11336-003-0974-7

23

CONCLUSION

Erin M. Bentrim and Gavin W. Henning

All humans have the fundamental need to form connections. Baumeister and Leary (1995) defined belonging as a "pervasive drive to form and maintain at least a minimum quantity of lasting, positive, and significant personal relationships" (p. 497). Maslow (1943) included belonging as a portion of his five-part classification on human needs. In the context of higher education, Tinto's (1975) foundational piece theorized that college students' integration into academic and social environments had a positive impact on retention, persistence, and graduation rates. Vaccaro and Newman (chapter 1) provide a more in-depth analysis of the theoretical history of belonging in their chapter and provide evidence that studies and conversations on the significance of sense of belonging are not novel concepts.

As is demonstrated throughout this book, developing and maintaining a sense of belonging is inherent to the academic and cocurricular success of college and university students. There is a continuity of research by scholars who contend that institutions of education should play an active role in supporting their students. Viewing the student from a deficit model is no longer an acceptable approach. In his chapter, Strayhorn (chapter 2) calls this institutional responsibility an equity imperative, while Johnson and Kenney (chapter 10) challenge institutions to root out inequitable practices, policies, and procedures that provide roadblocks to the growth of sense of belonging. Strayhorn also focuses on the characteristics that make a college an engaging college and discusses the impact an engaging college can have on student retention and graduation.

Vaccaro and Newman (chapter 1) argue that campus environments, campus relationships, and campus involvement lead to academic success. Similarly, Braxton and Ellison share research stressing the importance of students having an institutionally anchored sense of belonging. This means institutions must tailor belongingness efforts to match their particular student characteristics. Keup and Fountain (chapter 14) call for a more granular institutional approach in their chapter about first-year students. An institutional investment in the first year of college infrastructure (learning communities, residential curriculum, advising) promotes "fit" and sense of belonging in new students, which leads to positive academic and social outcomes.

Several practical applications of theories are presented in this text. Collymore, Dahl, and Teubner (chapter 19a) share how their campus reimagined new student orientation so that sense of belonging became the primary learning outcome for students transitioning to campus. On their campus, Bayless and Parkinson (chapter 19b) used a growth mindset to overhaul new student orientation and to develop a student mentor program. Lee, Skendall, and Tobin (chapter 19c) share the creation of an honors program living–learning community, while Means, Starobin, and Uran-Linde (chapter 19d) consider types of instructional technologies to support student connections.

Connection Between Belonging and Social Identities

As was readily apparent upon opening this book, identity is at the heart of belonging. How college students experience belonging depends on the identities that they hold. The chapter authors discussed unique influences on belonging for various student identity groups, and some of those points are highlighted next.

Challenge to Latinx students feeling a sense of belonging are cultural dissonance and incongruity. Holloway-Friesen (chapter 9) discusses how traditional understandings of belonging emphasize connection to the institution without addressing cultural adjustment and connection to home communities, which may conflict.

Kao (chapter 8) describes how Asian students experience similar struggles as Latinx students do, as cultural ties can negatively influence a sense of belonging to an institution. Many Asian students seek out cultural ties and cultural validation by joining ethnic student organizations. Another issue is the impact of the model minority myth, with one component being the assumption that all Asian students are high achieving. This myth does not account for the wide diversity of Asian students on college campuses, with Southeast Asians lagging behind East and South Asians in academic achievement.

Native American students also experience cultural dissonance, but the source is different than it is for Latinx or Asian students. As Albanaza (chapter 7) notes, the dissonance that Native students experience is a result of colonization, which included government-sanctioned removal from land and extermination, leading to erasure of Native culture and identity. Forced assimilation, sometimes through Indian boarding schools, thrust Eurocentric ideas such as valuing the individual over community upon Native students.

Sense of belonging for LGBTQ+ students is highly affected by campus climate. However, Gano (chapter 5) argues that traditional senses of belonging do not include issues such as safety, which are a major factor in belonging for LGBTQ+ students. As a result, LGBTQ+ students may search for belonging outside of the campus environment.

Low socioeconomic status students also experience unique challenges to belonging. As French and Price-Williams (chapter 11) discuss in their chapter, low-SES students may feel like imposters on campus. Their involvement in cocurricular activities that foster belonging can be hindered by lack of money to participate, and/or their time to get involved could be limited by the need to work or care for children.

Giacalone and Perrelli (chapter 16) outline the ways in which commuter students share similar challenges with low-SES students as they are often pulled away from campus for work or family responsibilities. This balancing of multiple responsibilities, coupled with reduced time on campus, negatively influences belonging.

Institutional systems may signal to transfer students that they do not belong. Torres and Boeck (chapter 15) describe how poor selection of courses at registration and few credits transferring into an institution send a message to transfer students that the college/university does not care. In their research they learned that because of these signals transfer students relied on existing support networks rather than creating new ones on campus.

Morris (chapter 17) outlines the cultural gaps that exist for student veterans, which are similar to the cultural challenges that non-White students experience. Leaving a highly structured environment in the military and entering a relatively unstructured environment of higher education can make transitions and thus belonging difficult. Student veterans may hesitate to share psychological and physical trauma such as posttraumatic stress disorder (PTSD) and traumatic brain injury (TBI). Not sharing these trauma-related injuries may limit these students' ability to make connections that lead to belonging and/or seek support services.

The intersection of identities can be even more important than the salience of any one identity. Williams and Udoh (chapter 6), when discussing gender, note that Black women have a different experience on campus than Black men or White women. The intersection of race and gender plays a role in belonging. Gano (chapter 5) points out that the intersection of race and sexual identity affect sense of belonging citing Terrell Strayhorn's work (2019) who found that a majority of ethnic gay men became involved in an ethnic organization rather than an LGBTQ+ organization. Giacolone and Perrilli (chapter 16) note that commuter students of color face different challenges to developing a sense of belonging than White commuter students. Morris (chapter 17) discusses the intersection of gender and veteran status positing that women student veterans have a different experience than men student veterans transitioning from the military because of the military's hierarchical, patriarchal structures.

Strategies to Support Belonging on Campus

All students need a sense of belonging. There are several benefits when students have a sense of belonging on campus or feel connected to an institution, and if students cannot experience belonging on campus, they will seek it out elsewhere. As Johnson and Kenney contend in chapter 10, institutions have a responsibility to address a sense of belonging by identifying and changing policies, practices, and logistics that hinder it.

In their chapter regarding intersectionality (chapter 4), Hallett, Kezar, Kitchen, and Perez discuss their research, which provides insights into effective strategies for foster student belonging. First, institutions should create experiences that validate students' multiple identities. Second, faculty and staff should be conscious of students' multiple identities so that they are attuned to the role of identity in students' experiences without privileging some identities and minimizing others. As has been articulated earlier, different subgroups have different needs related to belonging, thus programs and services should be tailored to meet the needs of various identity subgroups. The fourth and final finding is that there is a continuum of belonging, and students may only feel a minimal sense of belonging to any one program or service, and faculty and staff should help students find the places and spaces on campus where they can experience belonging.

Seeing faculty, staff, and other students who look like them furthers a sense of belonging for minoritized students because students do not feel alone. This type of representation may signal an open, welcoming community. Relatedly, knowing people at the institution who hold similar values, observe similar holidays, and uphold similar traditions facilitates belonging. One reason is because students feel there are other people who are similar.

Another reason is that students may have others with whom to share these cultural elements. Given these connections to people who look the same and have comparable cultures, having a space for similar people to convene furthers belonging. Being able to physically connect and socialize is vital. Not only is the space important to offer opportunities for connection, but the space is symbolic as well. The institution is saying, "You are important. We value you. We will provide a place for you to meet and be with others."

Chapter authors shared it is important for faculty and staff to be identity conscious. Regardless of students' identities, faculty and staff should view students as whole people. The issue of validating students and their identities was discussed multiple times as an effective strategy for further belonging as well as developing programs and services that address students' specific identities and needs.

It is also important to know that activities neither need to be intense nor long-term to further identity. Many authors cited the study by Walton and Cohen (2011). In this study, a brief 1-hour intervention was developed to normalize social adversity as common and transient for all students who are not BIPOC (Black, Indigenous, people of color) students. African American students in the study read stories from White students that featured worries regarding belonging and how these improved with time. Then, participants wrote essays regarding how this process was true for them and delivered a brief speech of their essay. This intervention had a positive impact on academic engagement, increased GPA, and increased belonging and happiness. The key is following the four suggestions by Hallett, Kezar, Kitchen, and Perez noted earlier and being intentional with program development.

Impact of Nation, State, and Local Events on Sense of Belonging

Authors noted a number of geographical issues that affect sense of belonging including COVID-19, social justice and activism, and an incident at the University of Missouri.

COVID-19

As already seen in this text, feeling a sense of belonging in college is crucial not only for a student's academic and social success, but also to their mental well-being. But what happens when local, national, or worldwide events disrupt an institution's best efforts to create sense of belonging on campus? Over the last 4 years, there have been unprecedented and unanticipated events for which colleges could not plan. One of the most dramatic was COVID-19, which caused college campuses to close beginning in March 2020.

In their chapter, Woosley and Timm (chapter 21) discuss results of a survey questioning students about their experience and the impact of COVID-19 on their lives and sense of belonging once universities were closed. Students reported loneliness, struggling with their sense of identity (living full-time with family members can exacerbate this), and a genuine feeling of loss of connectedness with peers and faculty. Among other things, students reported struggling with a lack of engagement, both socially and academically.

The consequences of students being moved to a fully virtual environment because of the pandemic resulted in feelings of marginality and isolation due to the lack of opportunities to engage. In essence, students often no longer experience a sense of belonging. Takeaways from COVID-19 include extrapolating what campuses learned and applying them to other student populations. For example, many campuses implemented strategies that intentionally increased engagement opportunities. They added additional virtual counseling sessions and more virtual faculty availability, and used technology to put students in contact with each other. Effective strategies and support systems like these need to remain in place for students after the return to campus. As evidenced through this book, the aforementioned "COVID-19 stressors" are what many students experience on a daily basis, whether or not there is a pandemic. For example, Giacolone and Perrelli (commuter student experience; chapter 16) and Torres and Boeck (transfer student experience; chapter 15) address barriers that these particular student populations face. Not surprisingly, there are many similarities between "normative" students who experienced COVID-19 stressors and the daily experiences of the "nonnormative" students attending a traditional campus.

Social Justice Issues and Student Activism

Campus protests, marches, and sit-ins, and other clashes related to differing ideologies are certainly not unheard of phenomena. The occurrence of systemic racism and the oppression of minoritized students on college campuses is not new either. These are all complex issues that did not suddenly materialize as a byproduct of the 2016 election or the murders of George Floyd, Ahmaud Arbery, Breonna Taylor, and others.

However, as Johnson and Kenney (chapter 10) point out, it is not the responsibility of marginalized students to create or find a sense of belonging on campus. Institutions of higher education have the responsibility to create policies and procedures that are equitable and that do not work from a deficit model where marginalized students are considered "at risk." Williams and Udoh (chapter 6) agree and go one step further by stressing the importance of considering the intersectionality of socioeconomic status and race and ethnicity. Although their chapter focuses primarily on gender identity and Black male initiatives, they discuss the complexities of sense of belonging on all socially defined constructs. Williams and Udoh also point to national political events over the last several years. The nation watched the differential treatment of lawful activism of Black Lives Matter participants versus the unlawful activities of White insurgents who stormed the U.S. Capitol on January 6, 2021.

Mizzou Effect

College and universities do not exist in a bubble; therefore, administrators must examine the realities of institutional ideologies and how they themselves respond to national events. Ignoring the outside world, refusing to take a stand, or being insensitive to the voices of students can do irrevocable harm to an environment of student belonging on campuses.

In 2015, for example, frustrations over what students believed to be weak responses from campus administrators and the University of Missouri system president regarding racist incidents at the University of Missouri (Mizzou) resulted in weeks of protests on campus. To provide additional context, in August 2014, an 18-year-old Black man named Michael Brown was shot by a White police officer in the city of Ferguson. Ferguson is approximately 115 miles from the Mizzou campus, and a large percentage of Black Mizzou students grew up in that area. University officials never made a public statement about the shooting. Once the jury failed to indict the officer responsible for Brown's death, racially motivated occurrences aimed at Black students skyrocketed on campus. Again, university officials failed to respond. By 2017, freshmen enrollment was down by 42% among Black students and 21% among White students. Seven residence halls were closed, and 400 jobs lost. The Evergreen State College, Middlebury College, and University of California, Berkeley have also suffered from what is now termed "The Mizzou Effect."

Future Directions and Implications

One of the purposes of this book was to synthesize into one text the existing research and literature regarding a sense of belonging in college students that would serve as a starting framework around the topic of belonging. The field is rapidly expanding and contains a multitude of diverse perspectives and theoretical approaches. Little agreement exists on how to measure belonging, how to advance belongingness outcomes, or even how to define the construct of belonging. However, there is agreement across a variety of disciplines that belonging is a human need and can be vital to the social and academic success not only of students enrolled in higher education, but also all beings.

To increase consensus among the many disparate perspectives, Strayhorn (chapter 2) posits the first steps must be to clarify terms, definitions, and the specific elements that comprise belonging. He also speaks to the critical aspect of defining and viewing belonging, involvement, and engagement through an equity-minded lens. Continuing the present-day understanding without reevaluating the impact of dominant groups, identity, and power dynamics is objectionable. Albanza (chapter 7) carries this forward with research specific to Native and Indigenous people. Because of European colonialism and systemic policies to assimilate and marginalize Native Americans, many of these individuals were unable to sustain an identity and connection to their culture and land, among other things. Even modern-day curricula continue misrepresenting and "White washing" the true events that occurred during colonization. Albanza makes the connection between these historical experiences and sense of belonging for Native American students and makes several recommendations for future considerations. One of Albanza's recommendations for future practices involves physical space and how it impacts belonging. His research shows this is especially true for Native American students. In addition, a few new studies have shown physical campus spaces (e.g., student unions, pathways across campus, residence halls) can influence a sense of belonging for all students regardless of identity and have called for additional research on the topic.

Bazner and Lopez (chapter 12) consider the impact of language minoritization and linguistic invisibility on sense of belonging in their chapter. They urged higher education administrators to pay attention to their increasingly diverse student populations and to implement new practices that promote language inclusion and remove existing barriers to equity.

In their chapter about measuring sense of belonging in higher education, Lingat, Toland, and Sampson (chapter 22) present guidance and considerations for developing new tools (and using existing ones). Measuring belonging is critical to understanding students' sense of belonging and to developing and evaluating initiatives intended to increase belonging. Lingat, Toland, and Sampson provide a detailed analysis of and suggestions for current tools being used for this purpose. The authors specifically address the use of psychometric testing when adapting and creating instruments as well as purpose and use statements to guide measurement. In other words, validity and reliability of instruments must be investigated. They also contend that instruments need to be field tested with more diverse students. Field testing with primarily majority identity students, among other limitations, is insufficient for generalizability. Gano (chapter 5) agrees, since research has shown that LGBTQ+ students may not feel sense of belonging in the same manner as straight, cisgender students might. By neglecting the voice of the LGBTQ+ community, researchers may be neither measuring appropriate constructs nor implementing inclusive policies.

Braxton and Ellison (chapter 3) elaborate on institutional commitment to student welfare for future research and new directions. When students feel like the institution is emphasizing helping them succeed, research findings show a positive correlation with how committed the students are, in turn, to the institution (they feel like they belong). The greater a student commits academically and socially to an institution, the more likely they are to retain, persist, and graduate from that institution. The authors recommend that institutions formalize the relationship between belonging and persistence during a student's journey from matriculation to graduation.

In order to take advantage of advances in technology and studies of the human brain, Vaccaro and Newman (chapter 1) suggest using social cognitive neuroscience to learn more about the need to belong. Neural functioning can be used to measure and monitor social connections as a biological construct of the brain. The authors make an argument for using empirically based theories to tease out how neural pathways are shaped and the connection to the need for belonging. Of particular interest is Vaccaro and Newman's discussion around the circuitry of the adolescent's brain.

Conclusion

Although the construct of sense of belonging is complex and multilayered, a consistent theme was brought forward throughout the text of this book. The relationship between sense of belonging and intersectionality of identity cannot be ignored and must be integrated into theoretical frameworks and other pedagogical approaches. In addition, factors that make up social location (e.g., religious orientation, age, ability, religious beliefs, and social class) should be regarded. This speaks to the need to use research and findings from other countries along with viewpoints from other cultures.

Norming instruments and conducting research primarily on male students, especially in light of the fact that the majority of undergraduate students (and graduate students) enrolled in higher education are female, erases the significance of sex and gender in belonging research and practice.

Other considerations include having educational psychologists partner with cognitive neuroscientists to identify how a student's self-efficacy, motivational behaviors, and strategies for self-regulated learning influence a strong sense of belonging. Understanding the relationship between metacognition and sense of belonging holds great promise for applied research and applications on college campuses.

On a final note, this text would not be complete without drawing attention to the darker side of sense of belonging. Research on sense of belonging and applications designed to create sense of belonging assume a positive outcome for individuals and groups. In closing, here are several questions for reflection: What happens when individuals find sense of belonging within a group (e.g., White nationalists) that espouses offensive ideologies and whose behaviors are outwardly destructive? Is this type of belonging preventable and/or reversible by intentional interventions and practices? Simply put, is sense of belonging a state or a trait? Finally, how do individuals find belonging in what most would consider highly reprehensible groups? Is it to fill a belonging void? Or, do these groups have an extreme fear that the sense of belonging the "other" feels will threaten and replace their own? Each of these questions and others need to be considered with future research.

References

Baumeister, R. F., & Leary, M. R. (1995). The need to belong: Desire for interpersonal attachments as a fundamental human motivation. *Psychological Bulletin, 117*(3), 497–529. https://doi.org/10.1037/0033-2909.117.3.497

Maslow, A. H. (1968). *Toward a psychology of being* (2nd ed.). Van Nostrand.

Strayhorn, T. L. (2019). *College students' sense of belonging: A key to educational success for all students* (2nd ed.). Routledge.

Tinto, V. (1975). Dropout from higher education: A theoretical synthesis of recent research. *Review of Educational Research, 45*(1), 89–125. http://dx.doi.org/10.2307/1170024

Walton, G. M., & Cohen, G. L. (2011). A brief social-belonging intervention improves academic and health outcomes of minority students. *Science, 331*(6023), 1447–1451. https://doi.org/10.1126/science.1198364

EDITORS AND CONTRIBUTORS

Editors

Erin M. Bentrim is a senior education and training specialist for assessment in education services at Anthology, Inc. Bentrim provides expert training and education through Anthology Academy to ensure clients are getting the most out of their Anthology experience. Prior to joining Anthology, Bentrim's career has spanned over 25 years on college and university campuses. Her higher education portfolio includes management-level positions in institutional research and effectiveness, academic assessment, student affairs assessment, and strategic planning. In addition to her administrative roles, Bentrim has experience teaching graduate- and undergraduate-level courses in diverse subject matters, including psychology, higher education administration, and educational statistics. Bentrim holds a PhD in educational psychology and research and an MEd in student personnel services, both from the University of South Carolina, and is a Phi Beta Kappa graduate of Wofford College where she earned a BA in English.

Gavin Henning is professor of higher education and director of the Master of Science in Higher Education Administration and Doctor of Education programs at New England College in New Hampshire. Henning has served as president of ACPA—College Student Educators International and the Council for the Advancement of Standards in Higher Education. Henning received a PhD in education and policies studies and an MA in sociology from the University of New Hampshire and an MA in college and university administration and BA in psychology and sociology from Michigan State University.

Contributors

Mark Villar Alabanza has worked in higher education for 15 years. He earned his bachelor's degree in music from the University of Virginia, master's degree in management from Notre Dame de Namur University, and doctoral degree in educational leadership with distinction from

California State University, Stanislaus. He is a member of the Honor Society of Phi Kappa Phi and Sigma Beta Delta International Honor Society for Business, Management, and Administration. His research focuses on Native American students' sense of belonging in higher education. He lives in Chico, California, with his husband, Browning. He serves as the tribal administrative officer for the Mechoopda Indian Tribe of Chico Rancheria and as a lecturer of American Indian Studies at California State University, Chico.

Brittany Barten is the assistant director for operations and engagement for university well-being and recreation at Ohio University, where she oversees the Charles J. Ping Recreation Center's operations and departmental member services. She is an engaged member of the national recreation association, NIRSA: Leaders in Collegiate Recreation, and served on the Division of Student Affairs' Committee for Retention and Graduation. Barten led a team of colleagues to review the relationship between well-being and college students' sense of belonging. She also provided student affairs professionals with materials to assess the effectiveness of their programs, events, and services in connection with sense of belonging. Barten holds an MS in exercise science from Eastern Illinois University.

Laura A. Bayless is the vice president for student affairs at Fitchburg State University in Massachusetts. She is passionate about the growth and development of both students and employees, fostering environments in which all contribute to the community we create and make a difference in the world. Bayless currently serves on the Massachusetts NASPA board and has served on the governing board of ACPA-College Student Educators International. Bayless earned her PhD from Virginia Tech, MS from Miami University of Ohio, and BA from Denison University.

Kevin J. Bazner is an assistant professor of educational leadership at Texas A&M University-Corpus Christi. He received his PhD in higher education administration from Texas A&M University-College Station. His research examines issues at the intersections of equity, diversity, and inclusion in higher education organizations, as it pertains to minoritized administrators and students. His work is designed to illuminate institutional practices, policies, and discourses that perpetuate racial inequity and understand how administrators can enact organizational transformation within higher education organizations. Prior to the professoriate, he served as a student affairs practitioner with roles in student activities, new student orientation, and leadership programs.

Claire A. Boeck is a doctoral candidate in the Center for the Study of Higher and Postsecondary Education (CSHPE) at the University of Michigan. Her research interests include discourses defining "Good Students" and first-year students' classroom experiences. She previously worked at a community college.

Tim Bono is a faculty member in the Department of Psychological and Brain Sciences at Washington University in St. Louis where his teaching and research focus on positive psychology and college student development. He summarizes the research from those courses, along with how his students have put that information into practice in their own lives, in his book *Happiness 101: Simple Secrets to Smart Living and Well-Being* (Grand Central Life & Style, 2018; formerly published as *When Likes Aren't Enough;* Seven Dials, 2018). Tim is also assistant dean for assessment and analytics in the Division of Student Affairs at Washington University in St. Louis. He holds a PhD in psychology from Washington University in St. Louis.

John M. Braxton is professor emeritus of higher education leadership and policy program at Peabody College of Vanderbilt University, a resident scholar of the Tennessee Independent College and University Association, and an affiliate scholar with the Center for Enrollment Research and Policy at the University of Southern California. One of Professor Braxton's programs of research focuses on college student persistence; this work entails the assessment of theory on college student persistence, the revision and construction of new theory, the empirical testing of newly formulated theories, and making this work accessible to practitioners. Braxton is a recipient of the Research Achievement Award from the Association for the Study of Higher Education and the Contribution to Knowledge Award from ACPA-College Student Educators International. Both awards are for outstanding contributions to knowledge that advance the understanding of higher education.

Cynthia Cogswell is the director of strategic planning and assessment for the Division of Student Affairs and an adjunct instructor for the College Student Personnel Program at Ohio University. She is also a researcher for the fraternity and sorority experience survey published by Pennsylvania State University. Through her work and research, she aims to enrich the scholarly dialogue about student learning, engagement, and institutional change in higher education. She studies how institutions use the process of assessment to improve student experiences and learning; the relationship between institutions and accreditors; and supporting institutional improvement through regional accreditation. Cogswell holds a PhD in higher education and student affairs from Indiana University.

Derisa V. Collymore is an education doctoral student at North Dakota State University and a hall director in the university's department of residence life. Her current projects center on developing practical solutions for fostering sense of belonging in students of color at predominantly White universities. Her research interests are in that area. She earned her MS in administrative leadership for higher education at the University of Wisconsin-Milwaukee and her BA in English language and literature at Brenau University Women's College.

Laura S. Dahl is an assistant professor in the School of Education at North Dakota State University and the principal investigator for the Assessment of Collegiate Residential Environments and Outcomes (ACREO) project. Her research examines how collegiate environments can influence outcomes such as sense of belonging, self-authored worldview commitment, career outcome expectations, appreciative attitudes toward diverse others, and integrative learning. She earned her PhD in higher education and student affairs from The Ohio State University, MEd in College Student Affairs Administration from the University of Georgia, and BS in applied mathematics from the Georgia Institute of Technology.

Bert Ellison is an academic counselor and STEM advisor in the Office of Academic Advising at Wake Forest University, where he works with students, faculty, and staff to cocreate spaces of belonging. He earned his PhD in sociology in the City, Culture, and Community program at Tulane University, MDiv at Duke University, and BS in psychology from the University of North Carolina at Chapel Hill. He has held a variety of professional positions in higher education, including student affairs, residence life, admissions, academic advising, and career advising. Most recently, he coauthored an article in *Strategic Enrollment Management Quarterly* on leveraging institutional databases to improve college student persistence.

Tim Epley is the associate director for business operations in the office of conference and event services at Ohio University where he oversees department finances, retail, ticket sales, and building operations. He has served on two strategic planning efforts in the Division of Student Affairs, most recently the Student Affairs Retention and Graduation Strategic Planning committee. Epley has presented regionally on space utilization in student centers and strategic planning. He is interested in the role of shared governance in higher education and presently serves as the chair of the university's administrative senate. Epley holds an MPA from Ohio University.

Chelsea Fountain is currently serving as a consultant for the National Resource Center and CAO for Fountain Transport Services alongside her husband and business partner. Prior to maternity leave in fall 2021, she was the program coordinator for the Advising Success Network at the National Resource Center. Fountain's passion is working with marginalized populations, which grew from her experiences abroad in Spain and Nicaragua and through her work as a college advisor at West Bladen High School. As part of the North Carolina State College Advising Corps, Fountain worked primarily with low-income, first-generation college students to advance enrollment and postsecondary success. She holds an MEd in higher education and student affairs from the University of South Carolina.

Amy French is an associate professor in the Student Affairs program at Bowling Green State University. She is also the program coordinator of the Student Affairs and Higher Education master's program. French holds a PhD in higher education leadership from Indiana State University, an MA from Loyola University Chicago, and a BA from Kentucky Wesleyan College. Her research interests include social justice issues related to race, identity, social capital, and disability. French's teaching areas include student development theory, leadership and administration, and program evaluation. She approaches the field of student affairs with a scholar-practitioner lens.

Brian C. Gano is most recently a graduate assistant at the University of North Carolina Wilmington (UNCW). He holds an EdD in higher education leadership (UNCW), an MA in higher education (University of Louisville), an MPA (University of North Carolina Greensboro), and a BA in history and art (Greensboro College). His research interests include sense of belonging and campus climate for LGBTQ+ students. Gano has over 10 years of experience working in student affairs, primarily in residence life, student conduct, and student advocacy at small, private colleges. Gano lives in Raleigh, North Carolina, with his husband. He identifies as a gay/queer, White, cisgender man.

Lisa Gates is an award-winning educator. With extensive experience in the college classroom and executive coaching, she is an equity-minded educator. She teaches graduate and undergraduate students at San Diego State University (SDSU) and serves as director and advisor for the MA in postsecondary educational leadership/student affairs and the SDSU leadership minor.

Michael D. Giacalone is the former interim assistant director of student activities at Rhode Island College, a primarily commuter institution, where he spent eight years overseeing campus programming, fraternity and sorority life, and student organizations. He holds a PhD in education from Rhode Island College and the University of Rhode Island's joint doctoral program, and his dissertation explored sense of belonging for commuter students in Greek-letter organizations. Giacalone currently works as a facilitator for leadership programming at a financial institution in Rhode Island.

Ronald E. Hallett is a professor in the LaFetra College of Education at the University of La Verne and a research associate in the Pullias Center of Higher Education at the University of Southern California. His research focuses on improving college access and retention for underserved students, including those who are low-income, first-generation, racially minoritized, and homeless or housing insecure. Hallett holds a PhD in urban educational policy from the University of Southern California.

Holly Holloway-Friesen is an associate professor of psychology and former director of the Bachelor of Arts in Psychology program at Azusa Pacific University. She also is a former editorial board member of the *Journal of the First-Year Experience & Students in Transition*. She has published her research in several peer-reviewed journals. Her research focuses on historically marginalized college students' sense of belonging, cultural and religious identities, mentoring, and career development. She holds a PhD in education from Claremont Graduate University, a MEd in college student affairs from Azusa Pacific University, and a BA from Claremont McKenna College. She was awarded a graduate student research fellowship from the National Career Development Association for Exemplary Research in Career Development. She is married to Michael, and they have two children.

Royel M. Johnson is an associate professor of higher education and social work at the University of Southern California (USC). He also serves as director of student engagement of the USC Race and Equity Center and is a faculty member in the Pullias Center for Higher Education. His research focuses on issues of educational access, equity, and student success. Johnson has more than 40 academic publications including peer-reviewed articles; and he has been awarded over $5.1 million in grants and contracts. For his early career accomplishments, ACPA—College Educators International honored him with their Emerging Scholar Award in 2020 and Outstanding Contribution to Multicultural Education and Research in 2022.

Sandra Kahn is the data administrator for the College of Education at SDSU. Her work focuses on strategic and enrollment planning, student success analytics, data visualizations, data governance, and software development. Khan holds an MA in education.

Cassie Kao is the owner of Kao Consulting, Inc., which exists to provide excellent educational services to support student success by working intentionally and deliberatively to meet individual and organizational needs. As a first-generation, Christian, Asian American, professional woman, Kao has used her identities to advocate on behalf of students and educate colleagues at local and national levels. She completed her EdD in higher education administration at New England College, her MS in criminal justice at Salem State University, and her BS in business administration at Babson College.

Alex Kenney is a PhD candidate in the higher education program at Pennsylvania State University. His research interests focus on the experiences and perceptions of Black students enrolled at predominantly White institutions. Additionally, Alex serves as a counselor at Penn State's Multicultural Resource Center (MRC), where he helps to foster academic, professional, and social goal achievement among undergraduate students. In his role at the MRC, Alex also facilitates two student support groups, the Black and Latino Male Empowerment group and Blends of Traditional Heritages for biracial and multiracial students. These groups are designed to engender a sense of belonging among minoritized and marginalized students.

Jennifer Keup is the executive director of the National Resource Center for the First-Year Experience and Students in Transition, where she provides leadership for the operational, strategic, and scholarly activities in pursuit of its mission "to support and advance efforts to improve student learning and transitions into and through higher education." In this role, she builds on the center's history of excellence as the founder and leader of the first-year experience movement to develop and pursue the organization's efforts to serve a worldwide network of educators. Keup also serves as an affiliated faculty member in the Department of Educational Leadership and Policies at the University of South Carolina. Keup holds a PhD in higher education and organizational change from UCLA.

Adrianna Kezar is a professor in higher education at the University of Southern California and director of the Pullias Center for Higher Education. Kezar is a national expert of change and leadership in higher education, and her research agenda explores the change process in higher education institutions and the role of leadership in creating change. She also conducts work on diversity/equity/inclusion, nontenure-track faculty, STEM reform, collaboration, governance, leadership development, and change. Kezar holds a PhD in higher education administration from the University of Michigan.

Joseph A. Kitchen is an assistant research professor in the Pullias Center for Higher Education at the University of Southern California. Kitchen conducts quantitative, qualitative, and mixed-methods research, and his research agenda spans several areas, with a central focus on the role of college transition, outreach, and support programs and interventions in promoting equitable outcomes and college success among first-generation, low-income, and underrepresented students. Kitchen has a PhD in educational policy and leadership with a focus in higher education and student affairs from The Ohio State University.

Jessica Lee is the program manager for student engagement at the University of Maryland Alumni Association. She previously served as the coordinator for student engagement in the Gemstone honors program and received both her BS in neurobiology and MEd in student affairs from the University of Maryland, College Park. Her research interests include first-year student experiences and engagement, living–learning programs, and career development.

John Eric M. Lingat completed his dissertation research on the measurement of postsecondary students' sense of belonging in the Department of Educational, School, and Counseling Psychology at the University of Kentucky. Broadly, his research interests include cognitive, affective, and psychomotor measurement, as well as learning outcomes assessment and program evaluation. A graduate of American University, Lingat began his career by serving as a dual-language elementary teacher and school administrator in the District of Columbia Public Schools. Through his research and practice, Lingat advocates for innovative, socially just, equitable education and culturally responsive pedagogy for minoritized and marginalized learners.

Juan Lopez is an academic advisor for the College of Education and Human Development at Texas A&M University and an adjunct professor at Central Michigan University. He received his PhD in educational administration with an emphasis on higher educational administration from Texas A&M University. His research focuses on the attrition and retention rates of Latino males across P–20 education, higher education access, and degree-completion issues of Latinx students; the academic, and educational experiences of Spanish native-speaking English-learning students in higher education; as well as rural Latinx students' higher education access and degree completion issues. His work contributes to research that looks to amplify the visibility of Latinx stories that often go unheard because of systemic oppression, both educationally and socially, and which continue to marginalize Latinx voices.

Marilee Bresciani Ludvik is professor and chair of the Educational Leadership and Policy Studies Department at the University of Texas Arlington. Prior to that, she served as professor of educational leadership at San Diego State University and in a multitude of administrative positions within higher education. Bresciani Ludvik's research focuses on using emotional and social neuroscience to decrease student and staff stress and anxiety while also increasing their attention and emotion regulation, cognitive flexibility, and compassion. The intent of this research is to inform in- and out-of-class learning design that will close equity gaps and improve career readiness. Bresciani Ludvik holds a PhD in administration, curriculum, and instruction from the University of Nebraska Lincoln.

Tawnya Means is assistant dean for educational innovation and chief learning officer in the Gies College of Business at the University of Illinois Urbana-Champaign. Prior to this role, Tawnya served as assistant dean and director of the Teaching and Learning Center for the College of Business at the University of Nebraska-Lincoln. Means received her BS in education, MS in educational technology, and PhD in information science and learning technologies with an emphasis on learning systems design, all from the University of Missouri. Her research interests are in online and blended learning, active learning, student engagement, learning space design, technology for teaching, access to digital learning resources, and faculty preparation to teach.

Phillip Morris is an assistant professor with a primary research focus on veteran and military student success and access to higher education. In addition to his academic role, he has served as program director for Veteran and Military Student Affairs and director of multiple federal, corporate, and private philanthropy grant initiatives. Morris earned his doctorate in higher education administration from the University of Florida and is a U.S. Army veteran. He teaches courses on research methods, measurement, and assessment in higher education.

Barbara M. Newman is professor emerita in human development and family studies at the University of Rhode Island. She is coauthor with Philip Newman of 14 books, including *Development Through Life: A Psychosocial Approach* (13th ed.), *Theories of Human Development* (2nd ed.), and *Theories of Adolescent Development* (Cengage Learning, 2017). Her research focuses on psychosocial development during adolescence with an emphasis on social support, a sense of belonging, and well-being in the transition from high school and college. She currently participates in a team project on the emerging sense of purpose among college students with disabilities. Newman holds a PhD in developmental psychology from the University of Michigan.

Hank Parkinson is currently the at Fitchburg State University; he has 24 years of progressive experience in higher education administration and is a leadership trainer. He earned a BS in business administration from Quinnipiac University, an MEd from Sacred Heart University, and an EdD in higher education and leadership from Nova Southeastern University. He has worked at multiple institutions and is experienced in student activities, operations, orientation, first-year experience, leadership development, volunteerism, Greek life, residence life, multicultural affairs, and recreation services. His research interests include first-year experience, leadership development, and student development. He has recently received a Massachusetts Commonwealth Citation for diversity, equity, and inclusion work and was elected for NASPA Region I Massachusetts State Director.

Rosemary J. Perez is an associate professor in the Center for the Study of Higher and Postsecondary Education at the University of Michigan. Her research uses student development and organizational theories to explore learning and development in collegiate contexts. Perez's scholarship explores three interrelated lines of inquiry: (a) how people make meaning of collegiate experiences; (b) diverse learning environments and intercultural development; and (c) the professional socialization of graduate students. Across her program of research, Perez's work explores the tensions between structure and agency and how power, privilege, and oppression affect individuals and groups within higher education. Perez earned her PhD from the Center for the Study of Higher and Postsecondary Education from the University of Michigan.

Kristina M. Perrelli is a former director of new student programs and part-time faculty in the School of Education at the University of Rhode Island. She has a PhD in education from the joint doctoral program of Rhode Island

College and the University of Rhode Island. Perrelli is committed to the ongoing process of actively engaging in social justice praxis in her administrative and teaching roles. Her research interests include exploring the experiences of pregnant and parenting college students, sense of belonging for college students, intersectional feminism, social justice praxis in student affairs, and qualitative methodologies.

Shelley Price-Williams is an assistant professor of postsecondary education at the University of Northern Iowa. She holds 2 decades of experience in student and academic affairs, spanning program development and management as well as academic advising, career counseling, and assessment. Price-Williams is experienced in the use of mixed methods, with a proclivity for qualitative research. Her research interests center on noncognitive factors of college student development and persistence, inclusion of nondominant groups in the college environment, and multicultural organizational development. She enjoys teaching legal aspects of administration, the American community college, and applied research design. Price-Williams holds a PhD in higher education administration from Saint Louis University.

Nina Potter is currently the director of assessment and accreditation for the College of Education at SDSU. She received both her MEd in early childhood education and PhD in educational psychology with an emphasis in measurement, statistics, and research design from the University of Washington. Her research interests include formative program evaluation and outcomes-based assessment. Previously, Potter worked for the Shoreline School District in Washington State where she was the director of assessment. She has experience evaluating educational programs in pre-K–12 as well as in higher education.

Shannon O. Sampson is director of the University of Kentucky College of Education Evaluation Center and faculty in the Department of Educational Policy Studies and Evaluation. Her background is in educational measurement related to language acquisition, but in her work with program evaluation she now applies educational measurement principles within an array of disciplines, including education, engineering, agricultural safety and health, and medicine. As the Evaluation Center director, Sampson employs an apprenticeship teaching model, giving graduate students the opportunity to apply their research knowledge within diverse evaluation contexts while also creating space for students to belong within an academic community. She holds a PhD in educational policy and evaluation from the University of Kentucky.

Stephen Schellenberg is the associate vice president for curriculum, assessment, and accreditation at SDSU, where he is also a professor in the Department of Geological Sciences. Schellenberg coordinates various campus-wide efforts to demonstrate and improve student learning, success, and achievement through curriculum development, program assessment, academic review, and institutional accreditation. As a faculty member and administrator, he has a strong commitment to student-centered learning through multiple modalities and has developed and implemented core major courses, general education courses, advanced graduate seminars, and seminars for first-year and honor students. Schellenberg holds a PhD in earth sciences from the University of Southern California.

Kristan Cilente Skendall is an affiliate faculty member in the University of Maryland Student Affairs Concentration formerly served as the associate director in the Gemstone Honors Program. She served as coeditor of *The Social Change Model: Facilitating Leadership Development* (Wiley, 2017). Skendall earned a PhD in college student personnel at the University of Maryland.

Rogelio Becerra Songolo is the assistant director for commuter life in the Student Life and Leadership Department at SDSU. Songolo's work revolves around creating and sustaining avenues of growth for students from minoritized communities. Currently, he works closely with academic departments to create course packages designed for first-year students who commute to campus. By collaborating in the development of university seminars, he contributes to the institution's goal of holistically serving students. Songolo received his BA in French from the University of Wisconsin-Madison and his MEd in educational leadership from DePaul University.

Jean Starobin is a consultant for the Gies College of Business at the University of Illinois Urbana-Champaign. She provides leadership and guidance for the Online Undergraduate Initiative to identify opportunities and develop strategies to advance academic achievement and student success and persistence, develop metrics and identify trends, and provide research and benchmarking. Additionally, Starobin is a career coach for online undergraduate students and teaches educational outcomes for online master's students. Starobin received her BS in biology from McGill University, MS in botany from the University of Massachusetts, MS in decision and information science from the University of Florida, and EdD in higher educational administration with an emphasis on student success and retention from the University of Florida.

Terrell Strayhorn is provost and senior vice president of academic affairs at Virginia Union University, where he also serves as professor of urban education in the Evelyn Reid Syphax School of Education and as director of the Center for the Study of Historically Black Colleges and Universities (HBCUs). One of the foremost authorities on college student success and sense of belonging, Strayhorn is author of 11 books and over 200 peer-reviewed journal articles, book chapters, and scientific reports. His research is broadly focused on race and educational equity, especially issues facing underrepresented or underserved populations in STEM, professional fields, PWIs, and HBCUs. He holds a BA in music and religious studies from the University of Virginia (UVA), a MEd in education policy from UVA, and a PhD in educational leadership from Virginia Tech.

Alyssa A. Teubner is an education doctoral student at North Dakota State University and the assistant director of new student programs. Her primary focus is exploring how practitioners can implement research and theory to increase student sense of belonging, especially during the transition to college. She earned her MA in educational policy and leadership studies at the University of Iowa and her BS in management communication at North Dakota State University.

Dianne Timm is an associate professor at Eastern Illinois University in the College Student Affairs graduate program. She has had over 25 years of experience in higher education and student affairs administration, both as an instructor and administrator. Her research interests focus on assessment; student development; and providing support to students in transitioning to, through, and out of college. Timm holds a PhD in college student affairs administration from the University of Georgia.

Leah Kreimer Tobin is the director of student leadership and involvement at West Chester University of Pennsylvania. She recently completed her PhD at the University of Maryland, College Park in student affairs. Her research interests include college student resilience and hope, living–learning programs, and high-achieving students.

Michael D. Toland is the executive director of the Herb Innovation Center and professor of statistics and measurement at The University of Toledo. Toland has expertise in multilevel modeling, psychometrics, longitudinal studies, randomized designs, and general statistical methodologies for use in education and other applied areas. He holds a PhD in educational psychology from the University of Nebraska-Lincoln. His current research focuses on the application of statistical and latent variable modeling techniques (e.g., belonging, self-efficacy) and writing pedagogical "how-to" manuscripts. Toland's collaborative research endeavors have been funded by Institution of Education Sciences (IES), National Institutes of Health (NIH), state departments of education, and private agencies in applied areas (e.g., attention-deficit hyperactivity disorder, autism, leadership, and disabilities broadly).

Vasti Torres is a professor of educational leadership and policy studies at the Indiana University School of Education. Previously, she was a professor in the CSHPE and associate faculty member in Latino studies at the University of Michigan. She has been the principal investigator for several grants, including a multiyear grant investigating the choice for Latinx students to stay in college as well as a multiyear grant looking at the experiences of working-college students. She has worked on several community college initiatives, including Achieving the Dream and Rural Community College Initiative. Torres holds a PhD from the University of Georgia.

Ekaete Udoh is a PhD student in the College of Education and Human Development at the University of Missouri. Udoh's research broadly explores the social and emotional well-being of minoritized student populations. Specifically, Udoh's scholarship examines (a) student (e.g., first-year, transfer, graduate) transitional experiences, (b) identity, and (c) factors that facilitate belonging and success for Black women in college. Udoh's role as a graduate research assistant on the Williams Research Group and her previous experience fosters her development as a multidisciplinary researcher.

Kasey Uran-Linde is an associate director in the College of Business Teaching and Learning Center and instructor at the University of Nebraska-Lincoln. In her role she leads the peer tutoring program, assists in faculty training, and disseminates pedagogical best practices within the college. Uran-Linde holds degrees in higher education administration with a focus on student development theories and the organizational structures within higher education.

Annemarie Vaccaro is an associate dean and professor in the College of Education and Professional Studies at the University of Rhode Island (URI). Vaccaro's research explores educational inclusion and belonging, or lack thereof, for diverse students. Her belonging research, conducted with Barbara Newman and colleagues, can be found in a variety of higher education and human development journals. Vaccaro has received a number of awards for her scholarship, including the 2018 NASPA Pillar of the Profession; 2017

NASPA George D. Kuh Award for Outstanding Contribution to Literature; and 2010 ACHE Alex Charter's Research Award. Vaccaro holds a PhD in higher education from the University of Denver.

Michael Steven Williams is an assistant professor in the College of Education and Human Development at the University of Missouri. His teaching and research broadly focus on inclusion, diversity, equity, students' sociopsychological development, and institutional excellence in American postsecondary education. He centers his inquiry on (a) interpersonal relationships, particularly socialization, mentoring, and belonging for students, administrators, and faculty, and (b) the institution, focusing on organizational improvement and accountability. Williams is committed to translating his research to inform policies and practices that promote social justice and student success in higher education. Williams earned his PhD in educational policy and leadership with a focus on higher education and student affairs from The Ohio State University.

Sherry Woosley is the senior director of analytics and research at Macmillan Learning. She and her team drive content strategy for 50-plus assessments and student retention tools. Prior to Macmillan, she worked in institutional research and assessment, taught, and founded an institutional research graduate program. She has spent more than 20 years researching college student transitions, student success, and higher education assessment. Woosley holds a PhD in educational leadership and organization from the University of California, Santa Barbara.

Shiming Zhang is a biostatistics PhD student at The University of Texas Health Science Center at Houston. He also serves as a researcher for the Texas Coronavirus Antibody Response Survey (TXcares) program. He has solid statistical knowledge and multiple projects experience, which involves medical clinical analysis and educational research.

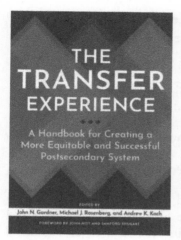

The Transfer Experience

A Handbook for Creating a More Equitable and Successful Postsecondary System

Edited by John N. Gardner, Michael J. Rosenberg, and Andrew K. Koch

Foreword by John Hitt and Sanford Shugart

Copublished with the Gardner Institute

"The achievement and graduation of transfer students in higher education is one of the most important issues confronting colleges and universities. Given that nearly half the undergraduate enrollees are in community colleges, we have to work together across the community college and 4-year sector to find structures, programs, and policies to strengthen their success. The authors provide nuanced perspectives on how transfer student success must be addressed."—**Scott E. Evenbeck**, *Founding President, Stella and Charles Guttman Community College, City University of New York*

"Helping students achieve their educational goals is a win for everyone, and brings the 'American Dream' closer to reality. A key, underutilized strategy in reaching this goal is an effective, holistic transfer system that begins when a student enters an institution of higher education and continues through completion. *The Transfer Experience: A Handbook for Creating a More Equitable and Successful Postsecondary System* is authored by 'transfer warriors' who understand and are passionate about transfer. The book is a comprehensive educational masterpiece that challenges and inspires higher education leaders and policymakers to skillfully and purposefully foster transfer student success, thereby enhancing the quality of life for students." —**Paula K. Compton**, *Associate Vice Chancellor, Articulation and Transfer, Ohio Department of Higher Education*

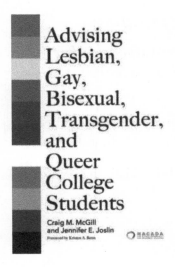

Advising
Lesbian,
Gay,
Bisexual,
Transgender,
and
Queer
College
Students

Craig M. McGill
and Jennifer E. Joslin

Advising Lesbian, Gay, Bisexual, Transgender, and Queer College Students

Edited by Craig M. McGill and Jennifer Joslin

Foreword by Kristen A. Renn

Copublished with NACADA

"McGill and Joslin created this exciting new resource for department advisors and student affairs staff as well as higher ed faculty and graduate students. Advisors in every area of campus must be aware of issues unique to LGBTQ students and how these issues affect students' ability to persist to graduation. This important work offers LGBTQ historical foundations and holistic ways of providing informed services for LGBTQ students. It invites not only thought and emotion but also action to create an enduring connection that furthers student development."—*Ronni Sanlo, Founder, Lavender Graduation*

Changes on college and university campuses have echoed changes in U.S. popular culture, politics, and religion since the 1970s through unprecedented visibility of LGBTQA persons and issues. In the face of hostile campus cultures, LGBTQA students rely on knowledgeable academic advisors for support, nurturance, and the resources needed to support their persistence. This edited collection offers theoretical understanding of the literature of the field, practical strategies that can be implemented at different institutions, and best practices that helps students, staff, and faculty members understand more deeply the challenges and rewards of working constructively with LGBTQA students. In addition, allies in the field of academic advising (both straight/cis-identified and queer) reflect on becoming an ally, describe obstacles and challenges they have experienced, and offer advice to those seeking to deepen their commitment to ally-hood.

Beyond Access

Indigenizing Programs for Native American Student Success

Edited by Stephanie J. Waterman, Shelly C. Lowe, and Heather J. Shotton

Foreword by George S. McClellan

"*Beyond Access: Indigenizing Programs for Native American Student Success* is another important work in the growing body of Indigenous scholarship. Stephanie Waterman, Shelly Lowe, and Heather Shotton have once again assembled an impressive group of contributing authors. Members of tribes and campus communities from across the country, the authors report on model programs designed to support the success of Native American students in undergraduate and graduate majors in a variety of institutional settings. One can clearly see that these programs are framed in Indigenous ways of knowing and being, and the 4 Rs—respect, relevance, reciprocity, responsibility—are in clear evidence throughout all of them."—*From the Foreword,* **George S. McClellan***, Former Vice Chancellor for Student Affairs, Indiana University– Purdue University Fort Wayne*

"Authors in this book engage powerful stories, Indigenous knowledge systems, and pragmatic innovations to inspire culturally strength-based college access and retention programs for Native Peoples into and through colleges and universities. Indigenous epistemologies of identity, relationship, resiliency, respect, interconnection, reciprocity, mentoring, community, spirituality, social capital, success, and well-being are highlighted. Indigenized approaches to matriculate, educate, and graduate Native college students are shared. This book offers essential learning pathways for all who serve in education."—***Alicia Fedelina Chávez****, (Apache, Spanish American) Former Dean of Students, University of Wisconsin—Madison and Coeditor of Indigenous Leadership in Higher Education*

Understanding the Latinx Experience

Developmental and Contextual Influences

Vasti Torres, Ebelia Hernández, and Sylvia Martinez

Foreword by Sarita Brown and Deborah Santiago

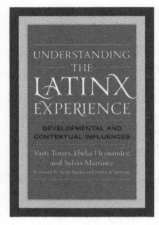

"This book provides an important resource in understanding the Latino/a experience in the United States. Our nation is in desperate need of a diverse highly educated workforce. By 2060 more than 25% of the total US population will be Latino/a and our school systems across the country are already Hispanic Serving Districts. Thus, it is imperative that we understand the students we serve and provide them the tools necessary to succeed. This book is essential if we are to indeed educate the future of our nation." —*Mildred García, President, American Association of State Colleges and Universities*

The Latino presence continues to grow in traditional population enclaves and has tripled in areas that are not traditionally associated with this pan-ethnic group.

The dramatic growth of this population in the United States requires a considerably deeper understanding of individuals that share this multifaceted identity. This timely book synthesizes new research and its implications for practice that is critical for professionals working with Latinos in educational and counseling contexts.

The authors provide insight into identity development, environmental influences, and how these factors influence persistence in higher education. By using a synthesis approach to organize multiple studies around how being Latinx influences the experiences of students in college and beyond, the authors offer a holistic view of the Latino population.

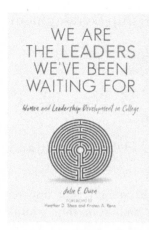

We Are the Leaders We've Been Waiting For

Women and Leadership Development in College

Julie E. Owen

Foreword by Heather D. Shea
and Kristen A. Renn

"*We Are the Leaders We've Been Waiting For* is a compelling and necessary contribution to the scholarship on leadership and gender. Julie Owen integrates foundational and contemporary concepts and frameworks with powerful narrative in thoughtful and critical ways to advance our understanding of women's leadership. The book will undoubtedly transform students, educators, and our world. I can confidently say this is the book I've been waiting for."—***Paige Haber-Curran***, *Associate Professor, Texas State University*

At this time of social flux, of changing demographics on campus and the world beyond, of recognition of intersectional identities, as well as the wide variety of aspirations and career goals of today's women undergraduates, how can colleges and universities best prepare them for the demands of modern leadership?

This text speaks to the changing context of today's women students' experiences, recognizing that their work life goals may go beyond climbing the corporate ladder to include social innovation and entrepreneurial goals, policy and politics, and social activism.

This book is a product of multiple collaborations and intellectual contributions of a diverse group of undergraduate and graduate women who helped shape the course on which it is based. They provided research support, critical readings, as well as the diverse narratives that are included throughout the book, not as an ideal for readers to aspire to but as an authentic expression of how their distinct and sometimes nonconforming lived experiences shaped their understandings of leadership. It goes beyond hero/she-ro person-centered approaches to get at the complex and intrapersonal nature of leadership. It also situates intersectional identities, critical consciousness, and student development theory as important lenses throughout the text.

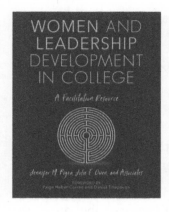

Women and Leadership Development in College

A Facilitation Resource

Edited by Jennifer M. Pigza, Julie E. Owen, and Associates

Foreword by Paige Haber-Curran and Daniel Tillapaugh

This text is a detailed resource for anyone interested in women and leadership education, whether through a full-length course, a weekend workshop, or a one-time topical session. It also serves as a companion to the book *We Are the Leaders We've Been Waiting For: Women and Leadership Development in College* (Owen, 2020).

"This book is a testament to [the editors'] commitment to helping all students—but centering women, in particular—think critically about the ways gender and leadership are intertwined in systems of power, privilege, and oppression. The lessons provided in this text promise to serve as powerful learning experiences for learners to gain critical self-awareness around their own identities and leadership practice. This text is a gift to the field of leadership education and will undoubtedly empower and help prepare the next generation of leaders in our society."—From the Foreword, ***Paige Haber-Curran***, *Associate Professor at Texas State University*; and ***Daniel Tillapaugh***, *Associate Professor at California Lutheran University*

As leadership educators shift from teacher- to learner-centered environments, from hierarchical to shared responsibility for learning, and from absolute to constructed ways of knowing, a desire for new inclusive and creative pedagogies is also emerging. This text includes over 40 easy-to-follow modules related to women and leadership development crafted by experienced leadership educators and practitioners. Each module includes learning objectives, detailed instructions, and ideas for adapting the module to diverse learning spaces and audiences.

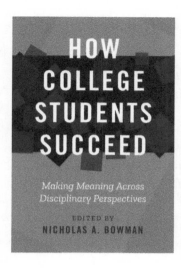

How College Students Succeed

Making Meaning Across Disciplinary Perspectives

Edited by Nicholas A. Bowman

"Essential. Timely. Requisite reading. This interdisciplinary compendium not only provides a theoretical framework to advance our knowledge of college student success, but also serves as an indispensable guide for higher education institutions to anticipate the postpandemic needs of our students and eliminate the institutional barriers that inhibit their success. *How College Students Succeed* will help inform practice for years to come."—***Doneka R. Scott***, *Vice Chancellor and Dean for the Division of Academic and Student Affairs, North Carolina State University*

Receiving a college education has perhaps never been more important than it is today. While its personal, societal, and overall economic benefits are well documented, too many college students fail to complete their postsecondary education. As colleges and universities are investing substantial resources into efforts to counter these attrition rates and increase retention, they are mostly unaware of the robust literature on student success that is often bounded in disciplinary silos.

The purpose of this book is to bring together in a single volume the extensive knowledge on college student success. It includes seven chapters from authors who each synthesize the literature from their own field of study, or perspective. Each describes the theories, models, and concepts they use; summarizes the key findings from their research; and provides implications for practice, policy, and/or research.

The disciplinary chapters offer perspectives from higher education, public policy, behavioral economics, social psychology, STEM, sociology, and critical and poststructural theory.

Multiracial Experiences in Higher Education

Contesting Knowledge, Honoring Voice, and Innovating Practice

Edited by Marc P. Johnston-Guerrero and Charmaine L. Wijeyesinghe

Foreword by G. Reginald Daniel

Recipient of the 2021 Innovation Award of the Multiracial Network (MRN)

"This book offers unique and complex explorations of *diverse* multiracial experiences in higher education. Unlike many volumes, it highlights the lives of multiracial faculty, staff, and graduate and undergraduate students who differ across racial backgrounds, racial identities, and campus locations (including four- and two-year institutions, and HBCUs). Because chapters offer theoretical analyses, narrative storytelling, and practical tools and strategies the material will resonate with readers with diverse interests and learning styles. This book is an essential resource for anyone who leads, teaches, serves, or studies at institutions of higher education and who seeks to understand and empower multiracial people on their campuses."—**Belinda P. Biscoe**, *Interim Senior Associate Vice President for University Outreach/ College of Continuing Education, University of Oklahoma*

"How do multiracial people navigate a society that prioritizes monoracism? *Multiracial Experiences in Higher Education* beautifully addresses this question. The narratives are the heart of this book, and the authors underscore the richness and complexities of multiracial people's experiences. Current doctoral students and recent graduates also contributed chapters, illustrating the importance of having perspectives across various generations. This book restored my faith in story-sharing and vulnerability as vehicles for change, and I applaud the authors for their courage."—**Stephen John Quaye**, *Associate Professor, Department of Educational Studies, The Ohio State University*

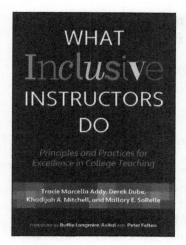

What Inclusive Instructors Do

Principles and Practices for Excellence in College Teaching

Tracie Marcella Addy, Derek Dube, Khadijah A. Mitchell, and Mallory E. SoRelle

Foreword by Buffie Longmire-Avital and Peter Felten

This book uniquely offers the distilled wisdom of scores of instructors across ranks, disciplines, and institution types, whose contributions are organized into a thematic framework that progressively introduces the reader to the key dispositions, principles and practices for creating the inclusive classroom environments (in person and online) that will help their students succeed.

The authors asked the hundreds of instructors whom they surveyed as part of a national study to define what inclusive teaching meant to them and what inclusive teaching approaches they implemented in their courses.

The instructors' voices ring loudly as the authors draw on their responses, building on their experiences and expertise to frame the conversation about what inclusive teachers do. The authors in addition describe their own insights and practices, integrating and discussing current literature relevant to inclusive teaching to ensure a research-supported approach.

Inclusive teaching is no longer an option but a vital teaching competency as our classrooms fill with racially diverse, first-generation, and low-income and working-class students who need a sense of belonging and recognition to thrive and contribute to the construction of knowledge.

The book unfolds as an informal journey that allows the reader to see into other teachers' practices. With questions for reflection embedded throughout the book, the authors provide the reader with an inviting and thoughtful guide to develop their own inclusive teaching practices.

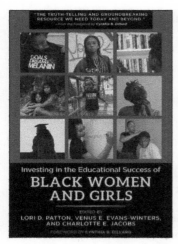

Investing in the Educational Success of Black Women and Girls

Edited by Lori D. Patton, Venus E. Evans-Winters, and Charlotte E. Jacobs

Foreword by Cynthia B. Dillard

"*Investing in the Educational Success of Black Women and Girls* demonstrates, from our own lived experiences, the multifaceted and continued need to look critically at the historically and present-day exclusionary policies, practices, and structure of U.S. education that serve to predetermine our success. This anthology pushes us all to dig deeper into the organizational intent of learning as a transformational and liberatory practice, and to cast aside its role as indoctrination."—*Clarice Bailey, Faculty, Organizational Development and Leadership, Saint Joseph's University*

While figures on Black women and girls' degree attainment suggest that as a group they are achieving in society, the reality is that their experiences are far from monolithic, that the educational system from early on and through college imposes barriers and inequities, pushing many out of school, criminalizing their behavior, and leading to a high rate of incarceration.

The purpose of this book is to illuminate scholarship on Black women and girls throughout the educational pipeline. The contributors—all Black women educators, scholars, and advocates—name the challenges Black women and girls face while pursuing their education as well as offer implications and recommendations for practitioners, policymakers, teachers, and administrators to consider in ensuring the success of Black women and girls.

This book is divided into four sections, each identifying the barriers Black girls and women encounter at the stages of their education and offering strategies to promote their success and agency within and beyond educational contexts.

At the Intersection

Understanding and Supporting First-Generation Students

Edited by Robert Longwell-Grice and Hope Longwell-Grice

"The phrase *first-generation student* has become such a ubiquitous moniker in higher education that the diversity of experiences and needs of the first-in-family enrolled college students it denotes has been obscured and reduced to a hollow catchphrase. In their edited text, *At the Intersection,* Robert Longwell-Grice and Hope Longwell-Grice—along with an assemblage of expert scholar-practitioners—recapture the value and substance of the designation by providing readers with an accessible primer and guidebook. *At the Intersection* offers readers an instrumental resource for understanding and effectively responding to these students' divergent, shared, and intersectional identities in service of their access, retention, learning, well-being, and success."—*Jason A. Laker, Professor of Higher Education, Student Affairs, and Community Development; San José State University*

"This book beautifully and boldly unveils the marriage between the body of research and on-the-ground experiences of first-generation students—from an intersectional approach that is often overlooked. As a first-generation graduate, I urge every staff and faculty member to read *At the Intersection* to understand the complexities of a student's journey beyond academic determinants. If you are passionate about understanding, cultivating, and amplifying first-gen students' success, start here."—*Jocelyn G. Salcedo, Member, Class Action First Gen Summit Planning Committee and Career Engagement Coordinator, Bennington College*

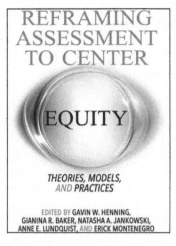

Reframing Assessment to Center Equity

Theories, Models, and Practice

Edited by Gavin W. Henning, Gianina R. Baker, Natasha A. Jankowski, Anne E. Lundquist, and Erick Montenegro

"Assessment practitioners are change agents. The very design of assessing for learning implies that what is learned from the process will create a need for change and improvement. But what if the assessment work is not fair and equitable? What if we unintentionally create or continue a system that works against fairness and inclusivity? *Reframing Assessment to Center Equity* is foundational to how we think about assessment as a tool for positive and responsible change."
—*Catherine M. Wehlburg, Provost and VPAA at Athens State University*

This book makes the case for assessment of student learning as a vehicle for equity in higher education. The book proceeds through a framework of "why, what, how, and now what." The opening chapters present the case for infusing equity into assessment, arguing that assessment professionals can and should be activists in advancing equity, given the historic and systemic use of assessment as an impediment to the educational access and attainment of historically marginalized populations.

22883 Quicksilver Drive
Sterling, VA 20166-2019   Subscribe to our email alerts: www.Styluspub.com